DESIGNING
ENTERPRISE
APPLICATIONS
WITH MICROSOFT®
VISUAL BASIC® .NET

Microsoft®

Robert Ian Oliver

PUBLISHED BY
Microsoft Press
A Division of Microsoft Corporation
One Microsoft Way
Redmond, Washington 98052-6399

Library of Congress Cataloging-in-Publication Data
Oliver, Robert Ian, 1976-
    Designing Enterprise Applications with Microsoft Visual Basic .NET / Robert Ian Oliver.
        p. cm.
    Includes index.
    ISBN 0-7356-1721-X
    1. Microsoft Visual Basic.   2. Basic (Computer program language)   3. Microsoft
.NET Framework.   I. Title.

    QA76.73.B3 O45   2002
    005.2'768--dc21   2002027879

Printed and bound in the United States of America.

1 2 3 4 5 6 7 8 9   QWE   7 6 5 4 3 2

Distributed in Canada by H.B. Fenn and Company Ltd.

A CIP catalogue record for this book is available from the British Library.

Microsoft Press books are available through booksellers and distributors worldwide. For further information about international editions, contact your local Microsoft Corporation office or contact Microsoft Press International directly at fax (425) 936-7329. Visit our Web site at www.microsoft.com/mspress. Send comments to *mspinput@microsoft.com*.

Acquisitions Editor: Danielle Bird
Project Editor: Devon Musgrave
Technical Editors: Marzena Makuta and Bill McCarthy

Body Part No. X08-82201

To Cathy

Contents at a Glance

Part I **Moving to Enterprise Development with Visual Basic .NET**

1	Enterprise Application Development and Visual Basic .NET	3
2	Visual Basic .NET for the Enterprise	19
3	Multithreaded Programming	73
4	Playing Nice with Others: Native Code and COM Interoperability	107

Part II **Building an Enterprise Infrastructure**

5	Distributed Programming in .NET	153
6	Custom Network Communication	185
7	Windows Services	219
8	Integrating Enterprise-Level Services	251
9	Adding Security to Your Applications	297

Part III **Performance and Debugging**

10	Essential Debugging Techniques	323
11	Common Performance Issues	351
12	The Art of Performance Tuning	383
A	Using Visual Basic .NET in a Multideveloper Environment	399
B	Getting Started with Application Center Test	415
C	Common Language Runtime Performance Counters	427
D	Performance Counter Quick Reference	453

Table of Contents

Introduction   xv

Part I   **Moving to Enterprise Development with Visual Basic .NET**

1   **Enterprise Application Development and Visual Basic .NET**   **3**

    Enterprise Application Development   3

      Team Development   4

      Performance, Scalability, and Reliability   4

      Implementation Technologies and Integration   5

      The Distributed Environment   6

    The Development Process   6

      Collecting Requirements   7

      Design and Architecture   8

      Implementation   11

      Testing   11

      Deployment   12

    Visual Basic .NET   12

      Visual Basic Then and Now   12

      Good Coding Practices   15

    Conclusion   18

2   **Visual Basic .NET for the Enterprise**   **19**

    Moving Beyond Visual Basic 6.0   21

    Option Strict Is Not Optional   21

      Short-Circuiting Your Operators   26

      Calling Platform Functions Directly: *Declare* and *DllImport*   29

    Types in Visual Basic .NET   32

      Type Magic: Boxing and Unboxing   33

      Classes and Modules   34

      Structures   35

Interfaces	37
Enumeration Types	38
Delegates and Events	41
Visual Basic and OOP	45
Making the Most of Namespaces	45
Inheritance: The Wily Beast of OOP	49
Singletons	61
Exception Handling Redux	63
Exception Handling Basics	63
Throwing Exceptions	65
Exception Handling No-Nos	66
Custom Exceptions	67
Resource Management and *IDisposable*	69
The Garbage Collector	69
The *IDisposable* Interface	70
Conclusion	72

3	**Multithreaded Programming**	**73**
	An Overview of Basic Threading Concepts	74
	Processes and Threads	74
	Creating Threads	76
	Encapsulating Threads	78
	Wrapping a Thread with a Class	78
	Controlling Thread Execution	81
	The *ThreadState* Property and the Life Cycle of a Thread	81
	Referencing the Current Thread	85
	Thread Control Methods	85
	Tying It All Together	91
	Thread Synchronization	92
	Race Conditions and You	92
	Synchronization Constructs	93
	Thread Pooling	102
	The *ThreadPool* Class	104
	Conclusion	105

4   Playing Nice with Others: Native Code and COM Interoperability   107

The PInvoke Service   109

Calling Native Methods   110

Marshaling Types   118

Implementing Callback Functions   134

Wrapping Things Up   137

COM and Visual Basic .NET   137

What Is COM Interop?   137

COM vs. .NET   138

What COM Interop Does   140

Using COM from Visual Basic .NET   140

Using Visual Basic .NET from COM   144

COM Threading Models   147

Performance Considerations   147

Memory Considerations   148

Conclusion   149

Part II   Building an Enterprise Infrastructure

5   Distributed Programming in .NET   153

Serialization   154

Serialization Formats   154

The *Serializable* Attribute   157

XML Web Services   161

Getting Started   162

SOAP Header Extensions   163

Performance   166

Limitations of Web Services   168

Security   168

Remoting   170

Getting Started   171

Picking the Right Channel   173

Marshaling Data   174

Using a Separate Interface   175

Remoting Singletons   176
Security   177
Tying It All Together   178
Conclusion   183

6   Custom Network Communication   185

An Overview of Network Communication   186
Network Architectures   186
Communications Protocols   188
The *WebRequest* Class: More Than Meets the Eye   192
Supporting Client Authentication   194
Managing Your Connections   194
Creating Custom *WebRequestModules*   196
Advanced *WebRequest* Features   198
The *WebClient* Class   203
Socket Programming   206
Getting Started with Addressing   206
Using the *TcpClient*, *TcpListener*, and *UdpClient* Classes 208
Down to the Wire: Socket-Level Network Programming   212
Conclusion   218

7   Windows Services   219

Introduction to Windows Services   220
The *ServiceController* Class   222
The Service Manager Application   225
The Windows Event Log   228
A Simple Service   230
A Timely Example of a Service   233
Communicating with the Service   234
Updating the Date and Time   238
Installing a Service   244
Debugging a Service   247
Debugging the *OnStart* Method   248
The *Trace* Class   249
Conclusion   250

8   Integrating Enterprise-Level Services   **251**

Understanding COM+ and Enterprise Services   251

COM+ Requirements   253

Creating a Serviced Component   253

Understanding Application Activation   256

Understanding COM+ Contexts   258

COM+ Object Construction   260

Object Pooling   262

Just-in-Time Activation   269

COM+ Transactions   272

Messaging   280

Messages   281

Message Queues   281

Messaging in Visual Basic .NET   283

Creating Your First Queue   284

Working with Your Queue   286

Automating Queue Installation   294

Conclusion   295

9   Adding Security to Your Applications   **297**

Security Features in .NET   298

Role-Based Security   298

Web Application Security   299

Evidence-Based Security   299

Cryptography   301

Buffer Overrun Detection   305

Enterprise Security Scenarios   305

Code Security   305

User Identity   310

Scripting Security   311

Authentication and Authorization   313

Conclusion   320

Part III   Performance and Debugging

10   Essential Debugging Techniques   323

Debuggers   323
The Visual Studio .NET Debugger   324
Other Debuggers   325
Better Debugging with the .NET Diagnostic Tools   330
The *Debugger* Class   330
Event Logs   331
The *Trace* and *Debug* Classes   341
Conclusion   350

11   Common Performance Issues   351

String Concatenation   352
StringBuilder Makes the Grade   353
Format Strings   354
String Performance by the Numbers   356
Late Binding   358
Designing Types   360
Error Handling   364
On Error Goto and *On Error Resume Next* vs. Exceptions   364
Exception Handling Best Practices   366
Database Issues   366
Database Connection Leaks and Connection Pooling   366
Using a *DataReader* with a Stored Proc Whenever Possible   370
Using Ordinals Instead of Column Names   371
Resource Management and *IDisposable*   373
ASP.NET   374
ASP.NET Session State   374
STA COM Interop in ASP.NET   374
Loading the Right Runtime   377
Conclusion   382

12   The Art of Performance Tuning   **383**

  Performance Testing   383
    Tools of the Trade   384
    Performance Test Planning   391
  Performance Tuning   393
    The Sanity Check   394
    Attaching a Debugger   397
    Low-Level Analysis   397
  Conclusion   398

A   Using Visual Basic .NET in a Multideveloper Environment   **399**

  Architecture and Design Issues   399
    Analyzing Business Requirements   400
    Defining the Technical Architecture for a Project   400
    Visual Studio .NET Enterprise Architect   401
  Making the Most of Visual Studio .NET   401
    Modeling Tools   401
    Enterprise Templates   402
    Visual SourceSafe and Source Control   406
    Managing Web Projects   409
    Managing Dependencies   410
    Customizing the Start Page   412

B   Getting Started with Application Center Test   **415**

  An Overview of ACT   416
    Using the Standalone Version of ACT   417
  Useful Techniques for Customizing ACT Tests   421
    Inserting Random Delay into Your Tests   421
    Extracting ASP.NET *ViewState* from the *Response* Object   422
    Appending ASP.NET *ViewState* to a Request   422
  The ACT Test Object Model   423

C   **Common Language Runtime Performance Counters**   **427**

    .NET Performance Counters   429
        .NET CLR Data   429
        .NET CLR Exceptions   429
        .NET CLR Interop   431
        .NET CLR JIT   431
        .NET CLR Loading   432
        .NET CLR LocksAndThreads   434
        .NET CLR Memory   436
        .NET CLR Networking   442
        .NET CLR Remoting   442
        .NET CLR Security   444
    Performance Counters for ASP.NET   445
        ASP.NET Applications   447

D   **Performance Counter Quick Reference**   **453**

    Common Performance Counters   453
    Application-Specific Counters   454
        ASP.NET and Web Services   455
        SQL Database Applications   456
        Applications That Use Interop or Remoting   457

    Index   459

Introduction

Why, you might ask, did I decide to write an entire book about Microsoft Visual Basic .NET and enterprise development? After all, enterprise development usually conjures up pictures of industrial strength computer systems, something Visual Basic has not traditionally been associated with. First of all, Visual Basic .NET is more than just an evolutionary change to the Visual Basic platform. It is now truly an enterprise-class development platform that frees the developer of many of the constraints of previous implementations. For seasoned Visual Basic developers, this platform offers so many new ways of doing things that design decisions are often trial-and-error-based. Even when design decisions are based on the developer's past experience, the fundamental differences of Visual Basic .NET mean that the "old way" is not always going to be the "right way." This is why I have written this book: to provide guidance on a number of issues based on my own past experience (and trial-and-error experience) with Visual Basic .NET. I think this is reason enough to write this book, but there is another reason.

Despite the interest in and popularity of the C# language, Visual Basic has been and remains the most accessible programming language for the Microsoft Windows platform. You do not need to be a hard-core developer to program in Visual Basic .NET. Much of the C# language syntax is nonintuitive (for those lacking a background in C/C++), and the declarative nature of the Visual Basic language (which has often been derided by more classically trained developers as being too wordy) lends itself nicely to the less experienced programmer.

There is a downside to the accessibility of the Visual Basic language: it can allow programmers with insufficient knowledge to create applications that may appear to work just fine but that suffer from severe architectural flaws, flaws that quickly make modifications or improvements to the application unmanageable and usually don't lend themselves to high performance, reliability, or scalability. This is simply because precious few technical books that are accessible to the novice programmer give programmers guidance on how to build these kinds of systems. This is the second reason for writing this book: helping developers to understand why they need to make particular design decisions as well as communicating some best practices.

Most of what I'll cover in this book applies to a broad spectrum of applications. Our discussion will focus on development for the enterprise, but you can use the advanced programming techniques and strategies presented here to write better and more sophisticated applications of all kinds in Visual Basic .NET. In addition, much of the techniques, technologies, and development approaches covered here apply equally well to all .NET languages, including C#.

The Purpose of This Book

Many fundamental programming books introduce technologies to the reader, but they seldom go beyond the surface. This leaves the reader with no real guidance as to how those technologies should be used or even when. It's not always obvious how to use technologies that are available to the developer. In fact, it's quite easy to shoot yourself in the foot by making an incorrect assumption. Sometimes documentation is a part of the problem, but a better understanding of the implications of certain programming practices is vitally important.

On the other hand, most advanced books focus too much on theory and delve little into implementation. In this book we strive for a balance between introducing important technologies and concepts and providing guidance on how the technologies should be applied in your applications.

This is not a design patterns book. This book will instead focus on how to use more advanced features of Visual Basic .NET and the .NET Framework to build into your applications common features that have in the past been too difficult to build in. Also, do not think that the purpose of this book is to make you an "enterprise developer." This book provides a set of fundamental skills and technologies in an accessible fashion for the average developer. Think of this book as a stepping-stone to more advanced development topics.

Who Should Read This Book

There are two core audiences for this book: the novice Visual Basic .NET programmer and the classically trained Visual Basic developer who, already familiar with the Visual Basic .NET language, wants to see how new platform features can be and should be integrated into applications. Most of the material in this book is intended to be an extension of existing technical resources. If you're expecting a ground-up introduction to Visual Basic .NET, you'll be disappointed. I have an expectation that you have a basic familiarity with the language and platform. If you do not, there are plenty of excellent books from Microsoft Press on the subject of Visual Basic .NET and I'd recommend starting there.

The majority of the material in this book is written from the perspective of a Visual Studio .NET developer, and I'll often reference how the Visual Studio IDE can help you develop your applications. This is not to say that I've made the material dependent upon a single release version of Visual Studio or even the .NET Framework. Although it is admittedly impossible to anticipate all future changes to the platform, I believe that much of the subject matter contained in this book will last for quite a while. Even though the topics are more advanced than you might find in your average book about Visual Basic, they are mostly about fundamental concepts and techniques that should not change drastically as time goes on. Fingers crossed.

Note   All the samples and technologies included in this book apply equally well to the original Visual Studio .NET release as well as the Visual Studio .NET 2003 product. What I have attempted to convey are more fundamental concepts that should have longevity, even as future versions of the .NET Framework and Visual Basic .NET are released.

Organization of This Book

This book is loosely organized into three sections that cover, respectively, core technologies, advanced technologies, and performance and debugging. Part I, "Moving to Enterprise Development with Visual Basic .NET," covers fundamental concepts that are critical to enterprise development: an overview of enterprise development, core language features, threading, and interoperability.

Part II, "Building an Enterprise Infrastructure," covers various forms of network communications, Windows services, COM+, Windows Messaging, and security. The purpose of this section is to provide an introduction to many of the application infrastructure technologies, building off of the topics introduced in Part I.

Part III, "Performance and Debugging," covers the remaining major topics for this book: debugging techniques, top Visual Basic .NET performance issues, and performance tuning concepts.

The four appendices contain a wealth of information that serves as either supporting or additional reference material for the preceding chapters. This includes information on leveraging Visual Studio .NET Enterprise for team development, an introduction to Application Center Test (ACT) for performance testing, information on .NET performance counters, and a common performance counter reference for performance analysis.

Updates and Other Information

The topic of enterprise application development is as broad and diverse as the applications that exist in the real world. This book cannot serve as a one-stop reference to enterprise application development—no single book can—but we'll cover the advanced features of Visual Basic .NET that are critical to enterprise applications and we'll explain how you can use these features effectively.

Also, aside from some syntactic issues, the material in this book applies equally well to developers who use any language on the common language runtime. Remember that Microsoft is evangelizing the various .NET languages as a "lifestyle" choice: program in the language that you're most comfortable with. This is why we're seeing languages such as COBOL, Perl, and FORTRAN coming to the .NET platform. As long as these languages are CLR-compliant, they have an equal footing and thus can take advantage of most, if not all, of the same platform features.

Acknowledgements

This book would not have been possible without the efforts of a great many people. From the editorial staff to my contributing authors, all played an integral role in making this book possible. I would like to first thank Danielle Bird, Microsoft Press Acquisitions Editor, who didn't laugh (out loud anyway) when I first proposed this book. On the editorial side of things I'd like to extend my most sincere thanks to both Bill McCarthy and Marzena Makuta for their technical editorial work. The rest of the editorial staff also did yeoman's work on everything, and thus I am extremely grateful to Ina Chang, copy editor, and, most of all, Devon Musgrave, project editor, neither of whom ever threw up their hands in disgust.

I would also like to thank my contributing authors: Sarath Kumar Mallavarapu for his technical contributions to the book; Devin Breshears, a Porting Lab cohort; and Vishnu Patankar, a developer in Windows Security and a friend going back to my Intel days. Thanks to all of you for your technical expertise!

My family and friends are definitely owed gratitude in their own right. My family for being supportive throughout the whole project, even though I didn't see much of them. My friends—well, let's just say I'm thankful that they are returning my calls even after a long period being incommunicado. (I personally think that some were expecting my corpse to wash up on the shores of the Puget Sound any day now.)

Finally, thanks much to Ed Robinson, who got me writing in the first place.

System Requirements

The examples in this book have been built and tested using Windows XP Professional. Most samples will also run using Windows 2000 Server (SP3 recommended). Of course, you'll also need to have Visual Studio .NET installed.

To run some samples, you will also need the following:

- Microsoft Internet Explorer 5.5 or later
- Internet Information Services (IIS)
- .NET Framework SDK, which installs with Microsoft Visual Studio .NET

Installing the Sample Files

The sample files can be downloaded from the Web at *http://www.microsoft.com/mspress/books/5956.asp*. To download the sample files, simply click the "Companion Content" link in the More Information menu on the right side of the Web page. This will load the Companion Content page, which includes links for downloading the sample files.

Support

Every effort has been made to ensure the accuracy of this book and of the contents of the practice files Web site. If you do run into a problem, Microsoft Press provides corrections for its books through the World Wide Web at the following address:

http://www.microsoft.com/mspress/support/

If you have comments, questions, or ideas regarding the presentation or use of this book, please send them to Microsoft Press via postal mail to

Microsoft Press
Attn: Designing Enterprise Applications with Microsoft Visual Basic .NET Editor
One Microsoft Way
Redmond, WA 98052-6399

or via e-mail to

MSPINPUT@MICROSOFT.COM

Please note that product support isn't offered through the preceding mail addresses.

Part I

Moving to Enterprise Development with Visual Basic .NET

1

Enterprise Application Development and Visual Basic .NET

Microsoft Visual Basic has long labored under the misperception that it is a "toy" language that serious developers should avoid at all costs. Certainly, Visual Basic has not been without its problems—it has often been behind the technological curve, and advanced users have really had no choice but to learn the Win32 API in order to really spread their wings. But Visual Basic .NET addresses these concerns.

The focus of this chapter is the enterprise application development process and how Visual Basic .NET can finally facilitate rather than impede that process. I'll begin with a discussion of enterprise applications and the development process and then look at Visual Basic .NET and how it fits into the overall enterprise development picture. The overarching goal is to demystify how Visual Basic .NET fits into the process of developing more sophisticated or complex applications in a way that wasn't previously possible.

Enterprise Application Development

The word *enterprise* has been overused to the point where it has lost a great deal of meaning, if it really had any to begin with. To call oneself an "enterprise developer" is almost to invite ridicule—after all, we are all enterprise developers of some sort. So, what really distinguishes an enterprise developer from a so-called "run-of-the-mill" developer? Not a lot. Enterprise applications typically have higher stakes and thus require more skill and experience on the part of the developers involved, but the project's developer is still just a developer.

For the purposes of this book, I'll define an enterprise application as an application or system that has at least two of the following characteristics:

- It is a large application that requires team development.

- It has specific performance, scalability, and reliability requirements.

- It uses a variety of implementation technologies and/or integrates multiple platforms.

- It is an application or system that is distributed across machines, networks, or companies.

Team Development

A team environment puts unique constraints on the development process. A good organizational structure with well-defined roles and responsibilities can make the difference between a successful team and project implosion. Granted, most projects are developed in circumstances that are less than desirable, but a well-structured team environment is a good goal to strive for.

Infrastructure is also extremely important. Having a good source-control system, accurate specs, and documentation will help ensure that the whole team is on the same page.

More Info   Appendix A discusses team development in Visual Basic .NET and looks at a number of common hurdles that developers encounter.

Performance, Scalability, and Reliability

Performance, scalability, and reliability are often considered the "big three" of e-commerce applications and other large-scale systems that serve critical business functions. Attaining these three goals requires the use of technologies in very specific and purposeful ways to avoid running into problems or system failures. And these goals can often be at odds with one another. For example, an application might need to sacrifice performance in favor of better scalability and or reliability. I used to have a sign posted in my office: "Quality, speed, cost. Pick two."

Or, to state it another way: given an infinite amount of time and money, you can accomplish anything. Everything else is a compromise. This is the quandary that every developer and project manager ultimately faces. Although it is possible to strike a balance, you cannot always find an optimal solution. Reliability in a system implies additional overhead, which adversely affects performance. The trade-offs you make will depend on your application's requirements and available resources.

Performance

Performance is all about making the most efficient use of your hardware resources. In server applications, performance tuning—leading to greater throughput and potentially less overhead—provides a direct cost savings. It requires less server hardware to satisfy the same number of requests.

Performance also implies responsiveness to the end user. Users are not tolerant of slow applications—slow performance can doom an Internet application. Imagine a mapping service that takes five minutes to load a map to a single address. How often would you go back?

Scalability

A scalable application or system is one that can accommodate growth. There are effectively two types of scalability: resource scalability and system scalability. Resource scalability implies that your application performance will scale reasonably well with additional processors, memory, or disk space. System scalability relies on the notion of server farms—increasing system throughput by adding machines. In that scenario, you must ensure that your application can play well with others and make efficient use of its resources.

Reliability

Reliability can have several meanings. First, and most obviously, it can mean that an application doesn't crash (often). But in a corporate environment, data is king, so reliability also means protection against data loss, regardless of the circumstances. You might include security in this category as well. The notion of security is almost implicit in a "reliable" system. After all, think of all of the electronic cash transactions that circulate on the Internet today. You would not think of them as reliable if some sort of security were not implemented. Various security mechanisms make possible the positive identification of both the source and the recipient of the transaction.

Implementation Technologies and Integration

If there's one thing Visual Basic .NET does not lack, it's choice. Take string concatenation, for example. There are many different ways to perform something as intuitively simple as combining two strings, but your choice can have a significant effect, either positive or negative, on your application. Also, a great many other technologies lie at the heart of the Microsoft .NET Framework. Deciding which classes to use can be difficult, especially given the newness of the platform itself and most people's relative unfamiliarity with it.

With enterprise development, you also face the daunting challenge of integration. Nothing causes greater fear than having to integrate a modern Web application with a 20-year-old mainframe that talks only through an AS-400 terminal. Yet many large companies still have mainframes at the heart of their most important business functions. I won't look at integration issues in this book, unless you count COM. Plenty of other resources are dedicated to this topic.

More Info   If you're interested in what Microsoft has to offer, you might check out Microsoft Host Integration Server 2000. The book *Microsoft Host Integration Server 2000 Resource Kit* (Microsoft Press, 2000) is loaded with great information about this product and how to make the most of it.

The Distributed Environment

A distributed environment makes specific demands on an application and its architecture. Poorly architected systems will not yield the desired performance or responsiveness. Throw in the possibility that parts of your system might not always be immediately available, and things really start getting complicated. In those situations, dropping transactions or losing data is simply not an option. This mirrors the reliability issue, but a distributed environment presents unique challenges to system reliability.

The Development Process

As I've mentioned, developing enterprise applications requires a balancing act between many functional and cross-organizational requirements. You must approach the design from four perspectives—business, application, information, and technology—in order to create a cohesive design that can adapt and grow to meet the needs of the business over time.

Figure 1-1 provides an overview of this process. The diagram is an abstraction of what, in practice, should be an organic and fluid process with natural feedback mechanisms that closely interrelate each phase of the process. Communication across all of the development phases will help ensure the success of the project.

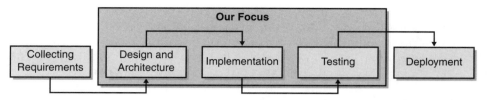

Figure 1-1   An overview of the enterprise application development process.

Let's take a closer look at each stage in the process.

Collecting Requirements

Developing a set of requirements at the outset is crucial to developing a successful product. This list of requirements will help you prioritize and drive the infrastructure development and the application development simultaneously (with the goal that they'll meet somewhere at the end of the process). The requirements fall into four main categories:

- Customer requirements
- Infrastructure and availability requirements
- Performance requirements
- Deployment requirements

I'll deal with each of these points in turn.

Customer Requirements

Ask yourself these questions. How will your customer use your application? What are the common user scenarios that you need to satisfy, at a bare minimum? Spelling these out at the start will not only help you keep better track of the progress of development, but it will also help you ensure that you're spending your time on the important parts of the product rather than on features that have minimal use.

Infrastructure and Availability Requirements

If you're creating a client-server type application, what resources do you have at your disposal? By resources, I mean both workforce and hardware. Certainly, the scope of your application will influence your workforce requirements, but the converse is also true: your available workforce will influence what development is possible to meet your market window. Also, you need to consider what support your application will need once it is deployed.

On the hardware side, you should evaluate your user scenarios. How will customers use your system? Given finite resources, how will you distribute the application load? And given the client requirements, what flexibility do you have to locate execution code elsewhere? Can you implement caching to reduce server loads? All of this and more has to go into your thinking.

Performance Requirements

No one wants an application that is slow, but user expectations can have as much to do with responsiveness as with speed. When you're dealing with a large amount of data, an operation might take a long time to complete, but you should always give the user the impression that, no matter what, your application is doing something. This is, in part, an issue of user interface responsiveness. On the other hand, some operations simply cannot take a long time to complete. Recall the mapping company example. Taking too long to perform a common and frequent operation is clearly unacceptable. You must therefore set your expectations up front so it is clear where you and your team should focus your effort on performance optimizations.

Deployment Requirements

Can you expect the customer to perform installations or maintenance? What system requirements can you rely on? Do you need network or Internet connections? If so, what bandwidth can you expect? From a deployment perspective, you should profile your potential customers. Will they likely be corporate users with an IT support infrastructure and a T1 Internet connection, or will they likely be retirees with machines that have only a 56K modem that was set up by a relative? What support are you prepared to provide? These are all important considerations.

Design and Architecture

Using the requirements you've developed, you can begin architecting a system. A lot of effort will go into this phase (or should, anyway). Skimping on the design and architecture will cause huge problems on larger projects. (Goodness knows, we all can and do get away with it frequently on smaller projects.) Ideally, you should spend the time needed to develop quality system specifications that define how your application will look, behave, and perform. Using this information, you can start modeling the system, looking for design flaws before they can affect the schedule. Of course, there's also the ultimate goal of development: extensibility. Implementing an architecture that will grow with your business requirements is a nontrivial task, but it's better to deal with it at this point so you don't have to scramble to apply a messy set of patchwork fixes at some later stage.

Your architecture should take into account the following three technological considerations:

■   The user interface

■   The component architecture (Of course we're using .NET, but how can you structure your application into components in a logical way?)

■   The network architecture

The User Interface

I've discussed some considerations for for determining a client architecture. What does this usually translate into? Four main options are available for client applications, as described in the following sections.

Option 1: client only   In a client-only application, also known as a *single-tier application*, all of the application resides in one place. The vast majority of applications, even in this day and age, fall into this category. There are no distributed components to the application, unless you count possible Internet-based application updates. Granted, this category is gradually shrinking, but I am fairly sure that it will never go away. Productivity, utility, and graphics applications, as well as games, are typical examples of client-only applications.

Option 2: thin client   The most common example of a thin client is an application that uses a Web browser. Aside from minimal scripting logic, the application's logic and execution are handled on the server side. This involves minimal download time for the client; graphics and page layout constitute the majority of the download time. In this way, you can minimize your client requirements and take advantage of the widely installed base of Web browsers. The advantages here are obvious. Changes need to be made only on the server side, you have far more control over changes to the system, and you can reduce the number of things your users can do to mess things up. In addition, you produce a client that is loosely coupled to the underlying implementation. A Web browser doesn't care whether the server is IIS or even Apache, as long as it talks HTTP and serves up HTML.

Option 3: fat client   The fat client definitely falls on the larger side of the client-server application category. Typically, a fat client application is something like a Windows Forms–based application. All of the user interface and possibly some or all of the business logic is contained in the client application. The client might even do some direct data access. The server has to deal only with some of the business logic and most of the data access. You can typically think of a fat client as being more tightly coupled to the underlying system and more sensitive to changes.

Option 4: mixed client   The mixed client falls somewhere between a thin and a fat client in a client-server application. You can think of it as a Web application that contains user controls. Essentially, the appearance and function of the client is generated by both the client and server. You can use a mixed client application as a way to provide greater user interaction without the overhead of a fat client, but the mixed client application does incur more client-side overhead than a simple thin client.

The Component Architecture

With larger applications, it's important to divide the application into components and subsystems, usually based on functional areas. Visual Basic .NET also has the added ability to build up a hierarchy of classes through the use of namespaces. Namespaces are an integral part of the .NET Framework. Using namespaces in your projects to place your classes into some sort of logical hierarchy can provide more information to developers about the purpose of each and every class you create. Namespaces can also provide some direction on how your components and classes should be used.

More Info   Chapter 2 deals with namespaces and how to organize your application into specific areas that can make larger class libraries much easier to understand.

The Network Architecture

By dividing your application into components along functional-specific lines, you can simplify the task of splitting it into distinct functional tiers. Why? It's all about performance and scalability. A multitier system enables separation of components in a way that enables distribution of processing resources. Imagine a situation in which you have a Web service that is performing poorly. You might determine that the client load is too much for a single machine but that your database is hardly being used. In this scenario, with a multitiered application architecture, you can move the database to another machine and put additional systems in place to handle the incoming client requests.

Leveraging an existing component architecture makes separation of the application into distinct tiers much more feasible. This enables companies to focus financial resources on the parts of the system that would benefit from hardware upgrades. It is often good practice to design your application with a tier structure in mind. Even if all of the "tiers" are resident on the same machine, they can be easily moved elsewhere to improve performance or add capacity at a later date.

More Info   Chapter 9 describes in greater detail the benefits of tiered application architectures and what the technology and infrastructure considerations are.

Implementation

Implementation can be the hardest part of the whole product cycle. As I mentioned earlier, good teamwork is essential. It is also important to have clearly defined roles and responsibilities. These don't always have to be strictly enforced, but you need to know who can make definitive decisions for any given area of the product.

During the implementation phase, you must focus on both security and reliability. These should already be part of your design and architecture, of course. Every team member should be on the lookout for potential issues and be proactive about addressing them. Remember the old saying: "A chain is only as strong as its weakest link." Even a small flaw in an otherwise robust system can bring the whole thing crashing down.Another important part of the implementation phase is working feedback into the specifications. A specification should never be treated as an immutable document. It should adapt as problems are encountered and solutions are formulated. Follow this up with good documentation and peer code reviews, and you should have a fairly robust process in place.

Testing

Testing is an often unappreciated phase of product development. For a large applications or system, you cannot just say, "The devs will test their own code." Developers, like writers, are usually poor judges of their own work. They tend to be great at unit testing, but they don't usually have time to worry about whole-system testing. Experience does help in knowing what to look for, but ultimately you need people who are dedicated to testing the whole product.

When you develop your test plan, you should first build off of functional requirements, but performance requirements should also be a primary consideration. Testing should also take into account your application's planned deployment scenarios. Your customer's perception of your product will be greatly influenced by the effort your team puts into the testing process. Fixing a bug early is far less expensive than fixing it after a product has shipped.

Deployment

Deployment—delivering the product to the customer—is the true test of the entire product development process. It is important to work out your product support strategy ahead of time. You must also ensure that your support team can channel feedback to the spec, development, and test people on your team so that customer experiences can be worked into the design, implementation, and test phases of future revisions.

Visual Basic .NET

I haven't really said much about Visual Basic yet. Everything I've said so far applies to all applications, regardless of what language they're implemented in. But since this book is about enterprise application development in Visual Basic .NET, I should spend a least a little time looking at the language itself.

Visual Basic has traditionally been about lowering the bar for developers and about making development more accessible to more people. Microsoft's vision for Visual Basic .NET has not really changed in this regard, but Microsoft has added a host of important features to the language and thrown out a lot of legacy deadweight. Still, it is important to understand Visual Basic .NET in its historical context.

Visual Basic Then and Now

In the past, I always said that you don't build large applications in Visual Basic, you build them *around* Visual Basic. This was true because the needs of enterprise or large-scale applications were at odds with Visual Basic—mostly because of the lack of important object-oriented programming (OOP) features that would make large-scale development projects manageable. This often led to code bloat and odd designs that were difficult to maintain.

Classic Visual Basic was not without its benefits, however. Thanks to a development environment and COM-based architecture, you could create large, complex applications quickly. Visual Basic has always been known as a rapid application development (RAD) platform. One fairly common approach to developing applications was to implement them quickly in Visual Basic and then isolate the critical performance areas and replace the components with

Visual C++ components. This type of development offered three distinct advantages:

- You could create a fully functional application relatively quickly.

- You had a reference implementation for the admittedly harder-to-build C++ components.

- Your test people could build tests based on the Visual Basic code right away, providing a great functional check against any replacement components.

The Limitations of COM

Visual Basic wasn't the only problem when it came to developing large applications, however. COM didn't always make things easy, either. COM has to be the most successful component architecture in the entire history of computing. It made its first appearance in 1993 and has become the dominant component architecture for the Windows platform. Visual Basic 6.0 is by far the best platform for creating COM components quickly and easily. But COM is not without its own problems:

- You cannot inherit from COM components. The only way to leverage existing components is to encapsulate and tack on the functionality you need. COM offers no inherent ability to extend COM components. This is a significant architectural limitation, although it obviously has not presented too great a limitation—otherwise, COM would not occupy a position of such prominence.

- COM is dependent on the registry. This causes interesting deployment issues. Your applications cannot be copied from one machine to another without going through the registration process and defining key application paths. Most COM applications therefore cannot be deployed without some kind of installation package.

- COM components don't always play nice with each other. Versioning under COM is its own sort of hell. Over time, a new term was coined to describe this situation: *DLL hell*. In addition, bad installation practices that overwrite newer DLLs with older versions (due to a lack of version checking) and DLLs with the same name being installed in a common directory have all contributed to this problem.

Visual Basic: The Next Generation

Visual Basic .NET is a major advancement as a language and development platform. The years of cut-and-paste "inheritance" are finally over now that a real

OOP infrastructure of implementation inheritance is available. Even though Visual Basic .NET offers several improvements over previous versions, it has retained its RAD roots. At the same time, the combination of Visual Basic .NET and the .NET Framework provides a wealth of features unmatched by classic Visual Basic.

More Info   Chapter 2 addresses many of the advanced language and platform features that are critical to large system implementations and maintenance.

Moving Beyond COM

Visual Basic .NET and the .NET common language runtime (CLR) address the limitations of COM in four key areas:

- **Implementation inheritance**   Visual Basic .NET not only provides implementation inheritance, but it goes a step further. The architecture of the .NET Framework allows components to be extended through inheritance mechanisms. This addresses a major failing of classic COM development, and the glorious consequence is visual inheritance. Visual inheritance makes possible a whole new way to build components in your applications—not only by leveraging existing code but by leveraging existing designs and enforcing development standards. Visual inheritance allows you to architect and build user interface elements that can extend existing user interface elements.

- **Type-aware runtime**   COM is built on interfaces, so it has a form of runtime checking. You can query an object to determine whether it supports a particular interface, but you cannot inspect a COM object at run time to determine all of the interfaces it supports. With the .NET CLR, you can take any object and dynamically discover all of its interfaces, inheritance hierarchy, properties, methods, and fields.

- **Reduced registry dependencies**   .NET components do not require the use of the system registry (unless they're registered for COM—see Chapter 4 for more details). The recommended way to manage your Visual Basic .NET application's settings is through an application configuration file (App.Config), not the registry. On occasion you'll need to use the registry—backward compatibility comes to mind—but it's generally not a requirement for .NET applications.

- **Side-by-side deployment**   Supporting two versions of the same application on the same machine used to require a lot of work. You had to ensure that newer versions of the same COM components wouldn't overwrite each other. (This was especially challenging because they were often stored in a common location). You also had to ensure that each component was versioned properly—otherwise, the new registry settings for that component could cause applications that used the previous version to break. In Visual Basic .NET, this all changes. No longer does installing a new version of an application mean that your previous version will be killed—unless you overwrite any of the application's dependencies. But this should not be a problem as long as you store the different versions of the application in different directories.

Good Coding Practices

Nothing can substitute for good coding practices. Despite the features of Visual Basic .NET and the .NET Framework that enable better application design and implementation, nothing can prevent someone from designing a poorly implemented application. Quite the contrary. With the .NET Framework being so new, it will take developers time to train and adjust to a new way of thinking. It is all too easy to fall into the trap of thinking in "the old ways," leading to some pretty poor designs. Unfortunately, this is an inevitability for any new platform and the .NET platform will not be any different.

Implicit vs. Explicit Programming

This is a point that I'll periodically revisit throughout the book and that you should burn into the back of your mind: explicit programming gooood; implicit programming baaad. Implicit programming can take many forms. But it can be summed up as a practice in which the intent of the code is not obvious, nor is it enforced. When I say the intent of the code is not obvious, I mean precisely that. The interfaces supported by a class give you no indication of how they should be properly used. Enforcement, on the other hand, is all about the original developer preventing unsupported use of a class. When you design classes, methods, and interfaces, you should always do so in a way that makes their intended use obvious and makes it difficult or impossible to use them in an unintended way.

From the OOP design perspective, this can mean several things. For example, if a class should not be inherited from, you should declare it *NotInheritable*. If a class should only be derived from, not instantiated, you should declare it with *MustInherit*. Methods should always define their parameters as specifically as possible. Using *Object* as a type provides flexibility but can also lead to errors.

When you declare regular variables, you should also use the most specific type possible. This will reduce the options other developers have when they use your libraries and will minimize the chances for mistakes. Explicit programming also lets you do more design-time validation of your code, which can save you a lot of headaches. Design-time validation is essential to the modern programmer. It essentially allows you to detect certain errors as you type, rather than having to first compile the application and then run it to detect errors. This can be a huge time-saver and reduces the potential for common types of programming errors.

More Info I'll talk more about implicit programming in Chapter 2, where I'll also discuss the use of late binding.

Naming Conventions

Visual Basic .NET is, like all earlier versions of Visual Basic, case-insensitive. This can lead to poor or inconsistent variable and function names, but Microsoft has established a set of style guidelines for the .NET platform that are reasonably easy to follow.

In the past, the recommended form of naming more or less followed the rules of Hungarian notation. If you've ever dealt with variables that look like *pszName* or *lpszClassName*, you know what I'm talking about. Visual Basic was never so strict, but you do see variations on the theme. There were, and continue to be, several reasons for this usage in languages such as C++. First and foremost, you cannot evaluate types at run time. (COM objects do allow this through *QueryInterface* but in a limited way.) If a type is already known, you're in good shape—hence the funny-looking variable names. The .NET Framework frees you from some of these problems. Through the miracle of reflection, you can always evaluate not only the *Type* (note the capital *T*) of a variable but also all the types from which it's derived and all the interfaces it implements. This is intrinsic to the platform itself and alleviates the potential confusion of variable types.

More Info Check out Chapter 6 for more information on runtime type checking and evaluation.

Given this new ability to evaluate types at run time, the designers of the NET Framework decided that they could do away with Hungarian notation—it was never very pretty anyway—and employ a more readable and user-friendly notation. The following sections describe the naming practices that Microsoft recommends for methods and variables. (This material is adapted from a paper entitled "Coding Techniques and Programming Practices" by Rob Caron. You can find the full document at *http://msdn.microsoft.com/library/en-us/dnvsgen/html/cfr.asp.*)

Methods   Follow these guidelines regarding methods:

- Avoid ambiguous names that are open to interpretation, such as *Analyze()* for a routine or *xxK8* for a variable.

- In object-oriented languages, it is redundant to include class names in the name of class properties, as in *Book.BookTitle.* Instead, use *Book.Title.*

- Use the verb-noun method for naming routines that perform some operation on a given object, as in *CalculateInvoiceTotal().*

- In languages that permit function overloading, all overloads should perform a similar function. For languages that do not permit function overloading, establish a naming standard that relates similar functions.

Variables   Follow these guidelines regarding variables:

- Append computation qualifiers (*Avg, Sum, Min, Max,* or *Index*) to the end of a variable name, where appropriate.

- Use customary opposite pairs in variable names, as in *min/max, begin/end,* and *open/close.*

- Most names are constructed by concatenating several words, so you should use mixed-case formatting to make them more readable. In addition, to help distinguish between variables and routines, use Pascal casing (where the first letter of each word is capitalized) for routine names, as in *CalculateInvoiceTotal.* For variable names, use camel casing, where the first letter of each word except the first is capitalized, as in *documentFormatType.*

- Boolean variable names should contain *Is,* which implies *Yes/No* or *True/False* values, as in *fileIsFound.*

- Avoid using terms such as *Flag* when you name status variables, which differ from Boolean variables in that they might have more than two possible values. For example, instead of *documentFlag,* use a more descriptive name such as *documentFormatType.*

■ Use a meaningful name even for a short-lived variable that might appear in only a few lines of code. Use single-letter variable names, such as *i* or *j*, for short-loop indexes only.

■ If you use the Hungarian naming convention or some derivative thereof, develop a list of standard prefixes for the project to help developers name variables consistently.

■ For variable names, it can be useful to include notation that indicates the scope of the variable, such as using the prefix *g_* for global variables and *m_* for module-level variables in Visual Basic.

■ Constants should be all uppercase, with underscores between words, as in *NUM_DAYS_IN_WEEK*. Also, begin groups of enumerated types with a common prefix, as in *FONT_ARIAL* or *FONT_ROMAN*.

> **More Info**   You'll find an excellent document titled "Coding Techniques" at *http://msdn.microsoft.com* that describes the recommended programming practices for .NET development. Some of the information contained in the article I have also covered here, but the document provides a broader overview of the topic.

Conclusion

Visual Basic .NET fits into the enterprise development process in a way that previous versions of Visual Basic never could. I hope this chapter gave you some perspective on how to approach the overall process of developing your applications. Each choice you make along the way—from the choice of the client to the overall system architecture—is crucial to the health of your final product.

On the technology side of things, the foundation laid by the .NET Framework and the CLR provides an extremely powerful starting point for your project. The platform enhancements (over the old COM way of doing things) address some of the real problems that Windows developers have faced for many years. It's quite liberating for seasoned developers.

As you work more and more with Visual Basic .NET and the .NET Framework, I hope you'll discover the sheer joy of using a language and platform that do their best to get out of your way and let you develop the kinds of applications you want. An adjustment period for developers is inevitable, but the benefits and flexibility of Visual Basic .NET make it a truly first-class development platform for the enterprise.

2

Visual Basic .NET for the Enterprise

Microsoft Visual Basic .NET is a language that was designed from the start to specifically address the needs of the next-generation applications for the Microsoft Windows platform. As a result, it has introduced many language and platform enhancements that are of special interest to enterprise developers. These changes have made for a significant departure from prior releases of Visual Basic, but they are intended to simplify the development process as well as significantly increase your development productivity.

This chapter will not address every feature of the Visual Basic .NET language. I will instead focus on the features and language elements that are important to enterprise application development. As any experienced developer knows, the improper use of features within any language or platform can have subtle implications that can cause logical errors or performance problems. It is therefore important to ensure that you use any feature in the most optimal way, especially when performance or resource consumption are critical. Throughout this chapter, I'll point out such issues, when they exist, to give you the information you need to make the right choices.

More Info For our purposes, it is important that you have a basic familiarity with Visual Basic .NET. For an introduction to Visual Basic .NET, you can investigate one of the Visual Basic .NET references available from Microsoft Press.

Although Visual Basic .NET is a common language runtime (CLR) language, many of its features rely on the .NET Framework and all of the utility classes and functionality it provides. (See the upcoming sidebar.) Sometimes Visual Basic .NET language features are so closely tied to the .NET Framework that it's virtually impossible to distinguish the two. Together, Visual Basic .NET and the .NET Framework make possible many things that were impossible or impractical using previous incarnations of Visual Basic. These new features allow Visual Basic .NET to fit into the enterprise application development process in a fundamentally different and more meaningful way. For example, the CLR makes it possible to implement core object-oriented programming (OOP) features and flexible componentization that enables integrated team development and true code reuse across projects, applications, and organizations. The .NET Framework libraries, on the other hand, provide a rich set of features that offer many simpler solutions to common development tasks.

The Common Language Runtime

The CLR is the environment that all managed applications, including those developed in Visual Basic .NET, run in. The CLR provides a language-independent infrastructure for all .NET managed applications. It uses an assembly-like language called Microsoft intermediate language (MSIL). All managed applications are compiled to MSIL before they're executed in the CLR. The advantage of compiling to MSIL is that it enables cross-language development support. Components can be designed in one language and consumed in another. Cross-language inheritance is one interesting and powerful outcome of this design. For more detailed information, see the MSDN documentation provided with Visual Basic .NET or see the .NET Framework SDK.

This chapter will start by looking at special features that take us beyond Visual Basic 6.0. We'll then investigate types in Visual Basic .NET, OOP language features, error handling, and resource management. Other books cover similar material, but here we're interested in how these features facilitate development of larger and more sophisticated applications.

Moving Beyond Visual Basic 6.0

Visual Basic .NET provides a number of new language-specific features. I'll focus here on three of them: the *Option Strict* compilation option, operator short-circuiting, and the *Declare* statement. All of these features are either unique to Visual Basic .NET or are implemented in a very language-specific way.

Option Strict Is Not Optional

Visual Basic developers are all familiar with the *Option Explicit* compilation option and know how important it is as a development practice. Without the *Option Explicit* directive, Visual Basic won't require using the *Dim* statement to declare a variable—it will implicitly create variables for you as they are referenced. This will cause problems if you misspell a variable. If you specify *Option Explicit*, Visual Basic will generate a compiler error. If you don't use *Option Explicit*, Visual Basic will create a new variable each time you misspell an existing one. Worse, Visual Basic will always create a variable of type *Variant* (if you use Visual Basic 6.0) and type *System.Object* (if you use Visual Basic .NET). Not only will your variables be declared for you, but you'll lose control over the variable's type. This makes bugs terribly hard to track down. Making the situation worse, in Visual Basic 6.0 *Option Explicit* is not the default—you have to be diligent to ensure that each of your class and module files has the *Option Explicit* declaration at the top. Thankfully, in Visual Basic .NET *Option Explicit* is on by default.

Visual Basic .NET also goes further and adds a related compilation directive: *Option Strict. Option Strict On* imposes four essential restrictions on your code:

- You must use a cast operator when you cause a narrowing conversion.

- Late binding is forbidden.

- Any operations on type *Object* other than =, <>, *TypeOf...Is*, and *Is* are not permitted.

- You must explicitly specify the variable type in all variable declarations by using the *As* clause.

Of these four requirements, two require a little more investigation: the restrictions on narrowing conversions and the prohibition against late binding.

Narrowing Conversions

Type conversion is the process of converting one type into another. The simplest example of a type conversion is storing a *String* object as a variable of type *Object*. This involves casting to a type further up its inheritance hierarchy and is referred to as a *widening conversion*. (All classes have *System.Object* as a base class.) A narrowing conversion, on the other hand, is a special type of conversion that comprises one or more of the following:

■   A type conversion that cannot be proven to always succeed at compile time

■   A conversion that is known to possibly lose information (for example, converting from a *Double* to an *Integer*)

■   A conversion across types that are sufficiently different from each other to necessitate using explicit narrowing notation

The following conversions are among those classified as narrowing conversions by the MSDN documentation. The list is excerpted from section 11.4 of the Visual Basic Language Specification.

■   Conversions from any type to a more derived type (down the inheritance hierarchy to derived types instead of base types).

■   Numeric type conversions in the following direction: *Double --> Single --> Decimal --> Long --> Integer --> Short --> Byte*. Each conversion results in an implicit loss of data.

■   Conversions from *Boolean* to any numeric type. The literal *True* converts to the literal 255 for *Byte* and to the expression *-1* for *Short, Integer, Long, Decimal, Single*, and *Double*. The literal *False* converts to the literal 0.

■   Conversions from any numeric type to *Boolean*. A 0 value converts to the literal *False*. Any other value converts to the literal *True*.

■   Conversions from any numeric type to any enumerated type.

More Info   Enumerated types are explained in more detail in the section titled "Types in Visual Basic .NET" later in this chapter.

■   Conversions from any enumerated type to any other enumerated type.

■   Conversions from any enumerated type to any type its underlying type has a narrowing conversion to.

- Conversions from any enumerated type to any other enumerated type. A narrowing enumeration conversion between two types is processed by treating any participating enumerated type as the underlying type of that enumerated type, and then performing a widening or narrowing numeric conversion between the resulting types.

- Conversions from any class type to any interface type, provided that the class type does not implement the interface type.

- Conversions from any interface type to any class type.

- Conversions from any interface type to any other interface type, provided that there is no inheritance relationship between the two types.

- Conversions from an array type *S* with an element type *SE* to a covariant-array type *T* with an element type *TE*, provided that all of the following are true: *S* and *T* differ only in element type, both *SE* and *TE* are reference types, and a narrowing reference conversion exists from *SE* to *TE*.

- Conversions from *String* to *Char*.

- Conversions from *String* to *Char()*.

- Conversions from *String* to *Boolean* and from *Boolean* to *String*. The literal *True* converts to and from the string *"True"*; the literal *False* converts to and from the string *"False"*.

- Conversions between *String* and *Byte*, *Short*, *Integer*, *Long*, *Decimal*, *Single*, or *Double*. The numeric types are converted to and from strings at run time using the current runtime culture information.

- Conversions from *String* to *Date* and from *Date* to *String*. Date values are converted to and from strings at run time using the current runtime culture information.

- Conversions from any interface type to any value type that implements the interface type.

Even a brief reading of this list should give you a sense that the conversions are dangerous from the standpoint of logical correctness. It's clearly important to ensure that if the conversion is intended, it is stated explicitly. Otherwise, with *Option Strict* set to *Off*, you might perform a narrowing conversion without realizing it, which can result in unexpected application behavior. These kinds of logic errors are often difficult to track down.

This is not to say that narrowing conversions are never appropriate. *Option Strict* just requires that you explicitly specify the cast (making the code very easy for the casual reviewer to understand). It is a way of forcing developers to explicitly state their intentions rather than assuming that others will know that a narrowing conversion was intended.

Late Binding

As mentioned earlier, *Option Strict* disallows something called late binding. For anyone unfamiliar with the concept of late binding, I'll provide a little background. *Binding* is the process of evaluating an object's type information. *Early binding* means that an object's type information is evaluated and processed at compile time. Early binding typically requires the use of strongly typed variables—variables whose type is defined explicitly. It also requires the use of a method or property that is explicitly defined by an object's type. This gives the compiler the required information to resolve the type's method and property signatures at compile time, resulting in simple method invocations at run time because that object's signature (interfaces, methods, parameters, and properties) are known.

Late binding delays the resolving of the object's type information until run time. Essentially, it provides a way to access objects in a typeless manner using the *System.Object* type. (The real type is uncertain at compile time.) Thus, method invocations are handled on a method-by-method basis and Visual Basic inserts code to dynamically look up an object's methods and properties at run time.

Note   Late binding allows a single variable to contain a variety of unrelated types. This can give you extraordinary design flexibility but often leads to subtle programmatic errors. In Visual Basic 6.0, late binding was implemented using COM Automation (implementing the *IDispatch* interface). Late binding in Visual Basic .NET is accomplished through a mechanism called reflection. Despite the two different implementation mechanisms, the end result is the same: runtime method signature lookups. Visual Basic .NET allows you to design much better solutions by using class and interface inheritance and thereby avoiding late binding altogether.

Even though late binding provides a great deal of flexibility, it has two major drawbacks: bugs and performance issues. Consider the following code example:

```
Sub Main()
   Dim o = New System.Random()
   Console.WriteLine(o.Value)
End Sub
```

This code compiles fine but it will throw a *System.MissingMethodException* at run time because the *Random* class does not contain a public method called *Value*. If *Option Strict* is set to *On*, the compiler will not allow you to specify methods that don't exist, which forces you to fix the problem then and there. The compiler will do this in two ways. First, the background compiler will insert a "squiggly" line underneath the errant method along with a tooltip error message that corresponds to an entry in the Visual Basic .NET task list. Second, if you attempt to build the component, the build operation will fail and the errant method will be listed in the task list.

Option Strict ultimately gives you the choice between generating a compile-time error or a runtime failure. Allowing late binding prevents the detection of possible code failures that might otherwise be caught at compile time. Having to locate and fix the bug at some later point (especially if your product has already shipped) can be significantly more costly than catching it up front at compile time. In addition to these problems, using late binding means you lose many productivity-enhancing features of the Visual Basic IDE. You won't get IntelliSense assistance on your late-bound objects.

More Info   I'll explore performance issues related to late binding in Chapter 11, "Common Performance Issues."

As mentioned earlier, even if the method does exist on the object, the compiler must generate more code to look up the method and execute it. Turning on *Option Strict* will prevent this. For example, in the previous code snippet we set *Option Strict* to *On*, and therefore we must declare all variables explicitly. In this case, the variable o must be declared as type *Random* so that we can access its properties. When we do so, we discover that we want to use the *Next* property, not the *Value* property. If you were to declare o as type *Object* (and set *Option Strict* to *Off*), the Visual Basic .NET compiler would have to insert code to look up the property *Next* at run time.

The following code makes a call to the *Next* property without all of the extra behind-the-scenes method calls and gives you the benefit of additional compile-time validation:

```
Option Strict On
Sub Main()
   Dim o As New System.Random()
   Console.WriteLine(o.Next)
End Sub
```

The important thing to take away from this discussion is that the compiler can generate more optimized (faster and less resource-intensive) code if *Option Strict* is set to *On*. It also enables you to catch simple programming problems at compile time that otherwise might slip through and be discovered by users, resulting in a bad user experience. Nothing says *confidence* like an application that crashes!

I encourage you to play with *Option Strict* in your projects just to get a feel for it. The importance of using this feature cannot be overstated. In small development projects, developers can get away with programming idiosyncrasies. Larger development projects require a higher level of quality and standards for everyone involved, otherwise the process itself will spiral out of control. So use *Option Strict On* and do not consider it optional for any of your projects.

Short-Circuiting Your Operators

We're all familiar with the logical operators *And* and *Or*. They perform simple but necessary logical evaluations. The behavior of these operators is not always obvious and can lead to some confusion, especially if you've used other languages such as C++ or C#. To see what I'm talking about, look at the following code sample:

```
Sub Main()
   ' Case 1:
   If FunctionTrue() Or FunctionFalse() Then
      ' Do Something
   End If

   ' Case 2:
   If FunctionFalse() And FunctionTrue() Then
      ' Do Something else
   End If
End Sub

Function FunctionTrue() As Boolean
   ' Huge computation logic
```

```
     Return True
End Function

Function FunctionFalse() As Boolean
    ' Lots of Database activity
    Return False
End Function
```

In *Sub Main*, both cases result in *FunctionTrue* and *FunctionFalse* being called, regardless of the return values. In this respect, the *And* and *Or* logical operators always evaluate their arguments—without exception. With me so far?

Table 2-1 and Table 2-2 describe how these operators work. But notice that with both operators, the output is highly predictable. In the case of the *And* operator, if the first argument is *False*, the result is always *False*. In the case of the *Or* operator, if the first argument is *True*, the result is always *True*. What does this mean? It means that there's a way to optimize the *And* and *Or* operators: conditional short-circuiting.

Table 2-1
Truth Table for the *And* Operator (Result = A *And* B)

A	B	Result
False	False	False
False	True	False
True	False	False
True	True	True

Table 2-2
Truth Table for the *Or* Operator (Result = A *Or* B)

A	B	Result
False	False	False
False	True	True
True	False	True
True	True	True

Visual Basic .NET introduces the *AndAlso* and *OrElse* operators to allow conditional short-circuiting. Both of these operators determine whether to evaluate the second argument depending on the value of the first argument. (Remember that *And* and *Or* always evaluate both arguments.) Table 2-3 and

Table 2-4 show the result when the second argument is evaluated. The *AndAlso* operator looks at the first argument of the expression *A*. If it is *False*, *AndAlso* doesn't bother to evaluate *B*. (The *X* in the table means "don't care" because the expression cannot be *True*.) On the other hand, if *A* is *True*, *AndAlso* must evaluate *B* to determine the result.

Table 2-3
Truth Table for the *AndAlso* Operator (Result = A *AndAlso* B)

A	B	Result
False	X	False
True	False	False
True	True	True

Table 2-4
Truth Table for the *OrElse* Operator (Result = A *OrElse* B)

A	B	Result
False	False	False
False	True	True
True	X	True

Using the previous code example, replacing *Or* with *OrElse* and *And* with *AndAlso* in the *Sub Main* will eliminate the need to run *FunctionFalse* in the first case and *FunctionTrue* in the second case. This can increase the efficiency of your application's logical expressions, but it can also lead to confusion. If you decide to use the short-circuit conditional operators, be sure that you aren't relying on some of the arguments for critical code (such as initialization routines), especially if the argument might not get evaluated. On the other hand, short-circuited operators allow more compact code. Take a look at the following example and notice how the *AndAlso* operator allows the evaluation logic to be performed with a single *If* block:

```
Dim cust As Customer
...
' Short-circuiting allows a nice compact statement
If (Not cust Is Nothing) AndAlso cust.IsValid Then
   ...
End If

' If we tried this, we would get a
' NullReferenceException if cust = Nothing
```

```
If (Not cust Is Nothing) And cust.IsValid Then
   ...
End If

' The standard operators require a little more
' verbose code to get it right
If Not cust Is Nothing Then
   If cust.IsValid Then
      ...
   End If
End If
```

Blindly converting operators in existing projects can introduce logical errors. When you're converting operators in existing projects, do so carefully and thoughtfully. If you're starting a new project using Visual Basic .NET, there is absolutely no reason why these operators shouldn't be in your repertoire. They can contribute to both execution and coding efficiency as well as code readability. Rock on.

Note   In early beta versions of Visual Basic .NET, the *And* and *Or* operators were short-circuited by default, but this was changed for backward compatibility reasons and the *AndAlso* and *OrElse* operators were introduced. I'm not exactly thrilled by this—I prefer the earlier behavior—but the decision was made for a reason and highlights beautifully the reality that software development (including development languages) is an exercise in balancing competing interests.

Calling Platform Functions Directly: *Declare* and *DllImport*

The .NET Framework class library is quite extensive. It provides a great deal of functionality—for creating Windows Forms and Web applications, data access, data structures, Windows services, and so on. For the most part, the .NET Framework provides for all of your development needs. But in some situations you'll need to call Win32 functions directly. (A custom DLL is a good example.) Visual Basic .NET continues to support and enhance the *Declare* statement for just this purpose. *Declare* statements are valid only in classes and modules. We'll briefly discuss this topic here and cover it in much more depth in Chapter 4.

Warning Be careful when you decide to use a Win32 API call instead of the .NET Framework. Sometimes it can be difficult to find certain features in the .NET Framework (especially when you're first familiarizing yourself with the framework), and it might take a good deal of searching to find them. A lot of work has gone into making the framework classes very robust. If you choose to forgo using the .NET Framework, you'll have to do more coding to achieve the level of error checking and handling that the framework classes provide. If the functionality just isn't exposed, fine. Otherwise, you probably shouldn't bother trying to reproduce what is already available in the .NET Framework. The .NET Framework significantly reduces the need to use Win32 APIs, so you should question their use each and every time.

One possible reason for using *Declare* is to support INI configuration file access. The .NET Framework does not provide direct support for INI files—XML configuration files are the preferred way to store configuration information. However, some businesses still rely on INI files. For example, older applications that use INI files might need to share them with newer versions. In this case, you need to be able to read INI files from your application. This functionality is not provided by the .NET Framework, so you have to call the *GetPrivateProfileString* Win32 API method directly from the Kernel32 library. The following code shows one way to do this:

```
Public Declare Ansi Function GetPrivateProfileString Lib "kernel32" Alias _
    "GetPrivateProfileStringA" (ByVal applicationName As String, _
                    ByVal keyName As String, _
                    ByVal defaultValue As String, _
                    ByVal returnedString As System.Text.StringBuilder, _
                    ByVal size As Integer, _
                    ByVal fileName As String) As Integer

Sub Main()
    Dim sb As New System.Text.StringBuilder(256)
    Dim x As Integer = GetPrivateProfileString("Mail", _
                                    "MAPI", _
                                    "Default", _
                                    sb, _
                                    sb.Capacity, _
                                    "C:\WINDOWS\win.ini")

        Console.WriteLine(sb.ToString)
End Sub
```

Visual Basic .NET provides an alternative way to import native methods without using the *Declare* statement: the *DllImport* attribute. The following code is similar in functionality to the previous example:

```
Imports System.Runtime.InteropServices

Public Module Module1
    Sub Main()
        Dim sb As New System.Text.StringBuilder(256)
        Dim x As Integer = GetPrivateProfileString("Mail", _
                                    "MAPI", _
                                    "Default", _
                                    sb, _
                                    sb.Capacity, _
                                    "C:\WINDOWS\win.ini")
        Console.WriteLine(sb)
    End Sub

    <DllImport("KERNEL32.DLL", EntryPoint:="GetPrivateProfileStringA", _
    SetLastError:=True, CharSet:=CharSet.Ansi, ExactSpelling:=True, _
    CallingConvention:=CallingConvention.WinApi)> _
    Public Function GetPrivateProfileString( _
                        ByVal applicationName As String, _
                        ByVal keyName As String, _
                        ByVal defaultValue As String, _
                        ByVal returnedString As System.Text.StringBuilder, _
                        ByVal size As Integer, _
                        ByVal fileName As String) As Integer
    End Function
End Module
```

The *DllImport* attribute forwards all calls to the *GetPrivateProfileString* method to the *GetPrivateProfileStringA* function in the Kernel32 library. Note that these two native method invocation forms are functionally distinct. The *DllImport* attribute is a syntax that is common across languages; the *Declare* statement is specific to Visual Basic .NET. In addition, the *Declare* statement often injects more parameter attributes to ensure that the *Declare* statement mirrors the Visual Basic 6.0 *Declare* statement behavior as closely as possible. This means that the *Declare* statement is often not the most performance-inducing option. It also lacks the flexibility of *DllImport*—it gives you fewer options and less control over the method importing process.

So when should you use *Declare*? When performance is not an issue and the default *Declare* behavior is suited to your needs, there is no reason to choose *DllImport*. You should absolutely use *DllImport* when performance is a consideration or the target method has requirements that cannot be addressed using the *Declare* statement (such as nonstandard calling conventions or tricky parameter marshaling). Generally speaking, for the enterprise developer I wholeheartedly endorse using *DllImport* consistently. This allows you to ignore any performance considerations and ensures a reliable standard throughout your project regardless of the development language.

Types in Visual Basic .NET

Types are an integral part of the CLR. By extension, this obviously makes types an important part of Visual Basic .NET and, indeed, of any CLR language. Types can be broken down into two distinct categories: value types and reference types. Value types are typically stored directly on the stack, inside an array, or within another type. If a value type is contained by a reference type, it is stored on the heap along with that reference type's other member variables. Value types are accessed directly. Reference types are stored in the runtime heap and can be accessed only indirectly, through a reference to that type. When you assign one reference variable to another, you do not copy the underlying reference type—you merely copy the reference to the object. (Both variables point to the same object.) When you assign a value type to another value type, you in effect copy the value of the object.

Aside from the primitive types (*Boolean, Byte, Short, Integer, Long, Single, Double, Decimal, Date, Char, String,* and *Object*), Visual Basic .NET defines five main types: *Enum, Structure, Module, Interface,* and *Class*. Structures, enumerations, and all the primitive data types except *String* and *Object* are value types. All other types are reference types.

Note   All value types inherit from *System.ValueType.* At run time, you can use the *Microsoft.VisualBasic.IsReference* method to determine whether an object is a value type or a reference type. Alternatively, you can use the object resolution syntax with the *TypeOf* operator, as in *If TypeOf(obj) Is System.ValueType Then.*

Whenever any member of a reference type is accessed, the runtime must first dereference the pointer to the heap in order to perform the desired operation. This is intuitively slower than accessing values directly from the stack without the pointer redirection. What this really means is that you should carefully consider whether a reference or value type is most advantageous when you build your applications. The reality is that developers tend to prefer reference types (classes) over value types (structures) because classes offer more flexibility. In most cases, the additional overhead of a reference type is negligible and becomes significant only when you perform intensive calculations (as in graphics applications and games).

Type Magic: Boxing and Unboxing

Riddle me this: when is a reference type not a reference type? Answer: When it's a value type, of course! Crummy jokes aside, the CLR does allow a value type to be treated as a reference type. What makes this possible is *System.Object* and a process known as *boxing*.

All objects (including *System.ValueType*) inherit from *System.Object*, which is itself a reference type. *System.Object* is the base of all reference and value types and can be a container for both types. The framework is designed this way because in some situations it is advantageous for a value type to behave like a reference type. To help put this in perspective, consider the *Console.WriteLine* method and the *Date* data type. There is no specific overload of *Console.WriteLine* that accepts a *Date* type (which is a value type). There is, however, an overload that accepts an *Object* parameter. If it were possible to coerce the *Date* type into an *Object*, *Console.WriteLine* would work just fine, right? Exactly.

What actually happens is that a wrapper for the value type, in this case a *Date*, makes it look like a reference type. This wrapper is allocated on the heap, and the value type's value is copied into the wrapper (so a copy of the date is stored in the heap). The system marks the wrapper to identify it as a value type masquerading as a reference type. This process of moving a value type onto the heap and providing a reference type wrapper is known as boxing, and the reverse process is known as unboxing. Essentially, the process of boxing and unboxing allows any type to be treated as an object.

The one caveat to all of this wonderful type wizardry is performance. Loading value types onto the heap and generating a wrapper does not come without cost. As you can see, not understanding the impact of boxing and when it occurs can introduce lots of performance bugs. Consider the following code:

```
Sub Main()
   Dim i As Integer = 5
   Console.WriteLine("{0}, {1}", i, i)

   ' Manually box the Integer
   Dim o As Object = i
   Console.WriteLine("{0}, {1}", o, o)
End Sub
```

Console.WriteLine provides a lot of overloads, none of which defines *Date* as the parameter type, so one of the overloads using *System.Object* is used. In the above code, the first *Console.WriteLine* boxes the *Integer* twice: once for each parameter. A more efficient approach would be to box the *Integer* only once and pass it to *Console.WriteLine*. This is exactly what's happening with the second call to *Console.WriteLine*. Storing the value of any value type in a variable of type *System.Object* is an explicit way to perform the boxing operation. When I assign *i* to *o*, the runtime boxes the value of *i*. By passing the *o* variable to *Console.WriteLine*, I avoid an additional boxing call because the boxing was done explicitly. That's boxing in a nutshell.

Note   Manual boxing is not always more efficient. There is a performance difference if you're dealing with an immutable value type (*Date*) versus a mutable type (such as *Integer* or *Double*). If the type to be boxed is immutable, you're better off just passing the variable to a method and allowing the runtime to box it as normal. You'll see a benefit to manually boxing your variables if you need to pass them repeatedly to functions that would otherwise result in a boxing operation each time the variable was marshaled. (To investigate this subject further, you can check out the MSIL and CLR specifications at *http://msdn.microsoft.com*.)

Let's take a closer look at each type that's available through Visual Basic .NET.

Classes and Modules

Classes are the definitive reference type. They are extremely flexible in that they can contain data members (constants, variables, and events), function members (methods, properties, indexers, operators, and constructors), events, and nested types. Class types support implementation inheritance—the heart and soul of all object oriented programming. All Visual Basic .NET classes by definition derive from the *System.Object* class.

Modules are also reference types, but that distinction isn't very helpful. Behaviorally, modules don't work any differently than their Visual Basic 6.0 counterparts, with the exception of namespace resolution. In other words, Visual Basic 6.0 does not support hierarchical modules or resolving members through complete names such as *Module1.MyFunction*. Modules are part of a flat structure. By contrast, you can think of Visual Basic .NET modules as restricted classes. All of their members are *Shared*; cannot be nested inside other classes, structures, or modules; can never be instantiated; do not support inheritance; and cannot implement interfaces.

Structures

The *Structure* type in Visual Basic .NET is an evolution of the user-defined type (UDT) from Visual Basic 6.0. Structures can now have public methods and can even implement interfaces. Structures are similar to classes; the key difference is that structures are value types and classes are reference types. Being a value type offers structures certain performance advantages over classes, but structures lack other OOP functionality that make classes so versatile. Structures work best when you use them to design your own composite data types. Consider, for example, the *Point* structure from the *System.Drawing* namespace, which might look something like this:

```
Public Structure Point
    Public X As Integer
    Public Y As Integer

    Public Sub New(ByVal x As Integer, ByVal y As Integer)
        Me.X = x
        Me.Y = y
    End Sub

    Public Overloads Function Equals(ByVal obj As Object) As Boolean
        Dim pt as Point
        If TypeOf obj Is Point Then
            pt = CType(obj, Point)
            Return (X = pt.X) And (Y = pt.Y)
        End If
    End Function

    Public Overrides Function ToString() As String
        Return String.Format("(X={0}, Y={1})", X, Y)
    End Function
End Structure
```

Notice that I defined not only a constructor, but two overloaded methods (overriding the base *System.ValueType* class methods). In this way, I customized the behavior of the structure and made it more user friendly. But that's not the half of it. Read on.

Structures and Interfaces

It might seem odd that a structure can implement interfaces, but any doubts you have will be quickly swept away when you see what you can do with it. Let's extend the *Point* structure example for our own nefarious purposes. Let's say that we're developing a graphics application. We're using the *MyPoint* structure to store coordinate pairs, but we want to sort these pairs in order of distance from the origin (coordinates *x=0, y=0*). The calculation itself is pretty simple, but we don't want to have to implement a sort algorithm along with all of the logic. It would look ugly and be a pain to maintain. The solution can be found in the *IComparable* interface. Check this out:

```
Public Structure MyPoint
    Implements IComparable
    Public X As Integer
    Public Y As Integer

    Public Function CompareTo( obj As Object ) _
        As Integer Implements IComparable.CompareTo

        Dim pt As MyPoint = CType(obj, MyPoint)
        Dim d1 As Double = (X^2) + (Y^2)
        Dim d2 As Double = (pt.X^2) + (pt.Y^2)

        Return CInt(d1 - d2)

    End Function

End Structure
```

This sample demonstrates that we can now compare two *MyPoint* types using the *IComparable* interface. This is only part of the trick. Let's say we also have an array of *MyPoint* structures like this:

```
Dim pts() As New MyPoint(100)
```

How can we sort these values efficiently? It turns out that this is easy. The *System.Array* class defines a *Sort* method that will do the work for us. All we need to do in advance is implement the *IComparable* interface. (This works for classes, too.) Sorting the array is as simple as the following line:

```
System.Array.Sort(pts)
```

Doesn't get much easier than that, does it?

Remember that structures are very efficient storage objects and that you can extend them to provide very flexible behavior, but they are no substitute for classes. Furthermore, using the *IComparable* interface when implemented on a structure would cause a lot of boxing and unboxing. In fact, with the previous example, the boxing and unboxing overhead could very easily make a reference type a far better solution. In other words, because of the boxing overhead a class-based implementation of the point structure would be more efficient if you expect the *IComparable* interface to be used frequently.

Choosing between structures and classes is not always easy; both types have their own strengths and weaknesses. Consider not only how your objects will be stored but also how they will be used. This will greatly affect your choice of a class versus a structure implementation. Remember that when efficiency of storage and access is required, structures are more likely to fit the bill. When flexibility, inheritance and all of those other object-oriented niceties are needed, a class implementation is probably what you need.

Interfaces

COM developers are no strangers to interfaces, and rightly so. COM wouldn't be much use without interfaces—the entire concept of COM revolves around interface-based programming. In Visual Basic .NET, an *Interface* is a specific reference type and provides some interesting twists on the classic COM idea of an interface:

- Interfaces can define properties, methods, and events.

- Interfaces can derive from other interfaces.

- Interfaces support multiple inheritance.

- Only classes and structures can implement interfaces.

- Classes and structures can implement any number of interfaces.

Note   You might have noticed that interfaces are similar to abstract classes in that the implementation details are left to the child class. The major limitation of classes is that only single inheritance is supported, whereas a class can implement a virtually unlimited number of interfaces.

The fundamental reason for using interfaces over classes is the same in Visual Basic .NET. They allow you to separate definition from implementation, which reduces the risk of breaking existing applications as your objects evolve. Interfaces help group together functionality that can be implemented by many objects, and they provide a useful distribution method. If you design your objects to implement specific interfaces, client objects only need to know about the interface to use those objects. You don't need to distribute the classes themselves.

Naming Conventions

When you create your own interfaces, try to follow the conventions used by the .NET Framework. Start the name with a capital *I*, followed by a capital letter of the first part of the name, and then follow the Pascal casing rules described in Chapter 1. Examples include *IComparable*, *IComboBox*, *IControl*, and *IListBox*.

You'll see more examples of interfaces being used in different contexts throughout this book. This should start you thinking about how they might fit into your applications. Interfaces are an important part of Visual Basic .NET, and you should familiarize yourself with them.

Enumeration Types

Enumerations are a special kind of value type that inherits from the *System.Enum* type. They symbolically represent a set of values of one of the primitive integral types (*Byte*, *Short*, *Integer*, or *Long*). In other words, enumerations are a way of giving nice names to a list of constants. They are also special in that they are strongly typed, which prevents unintentional misuse. The standard syntax for declaring enumerations looks like the following:

```
Enum Identifier [ As IntegralTypeName ]
    EnumMember1 [= Value]
    EnumMember2 [= Value]
    ...
End Enum
```

Let's start with a simple example of declaring enumerations:

```
Enum DayOfWeek
    Sunday
    Monday
    Tuesday
    Wednesday
    Thursday
    Friday
```

```
    Saturday
End Enum
Enum DayOfWeekA
    Sunday = 0
    Monday = 1
    Tuesday = 2
    Wednesday = 3
    Thursday = 4
    Friday = 5
    Saturday = 6
End Enum
```

It is interesting to note in the above code that the two declared enumerations (*DayOfWeek* and *DayOfWeekA*) are functionally equivalent. If you do not assign a value to each member of the enumeration, Visual Basic .NET will implicitly do it for you. When Visual Basic .NET assigns values to enumeration members, it assigns them incrementally. This means that an enum with four members and no explicit value assignments will be numbered 0, 1, 2, and 3. The general rule is that the value assigned to enum members is either 0 (if it is the first member) or the value of the immediately preceding member incremented by one.

Enumerations offer a type-safe way to provide constant values throughout an application. In your implementations of enumerations, it is generally good design practice to group them according to their function and intended use. After all, that is the point behind using them in the first place. Misusing enumerations will lead to general confusion in your projects, and they won't be worth the bother.

The *Enum* declaration also gives you control over how the values are stored. By using the optional *As* argument, you can control the size of the underlying value type. As I already mentioned, you can use enumerations to represent *Byte*, *Short*, *Integer*, or *Long* values. You can make your memory allocations more efficient by selecting an appropriate integral type for the *Enum*.

Enumerations do have other uses, however. If it is important that the underlying value represent a specific number, you must select an appropriate storage type. Consider the following example:

```
Public Enum Test As Integer
    A = &H4000
    B = &HB0000000
    C = 3242938
    D = -213784383
End Enum
```

Here we needed to store values that required at least 4 bytes, so we defined the *Enum* to have an underlying type of *Integer*. If you were to select a storage type that is too small to properly represent the values (for example, a *Short*), you would get a compile error that states "Constant expression not representable in type 'Short'." The default storage type for enumerations is *Integer*. For the most part, I'd recommend sticking to the default underlying type for most of your enums. If size is an issue, going with a smaller type is perfectly reasonable.

Neat *Enum* Tricks

The *System.Enum* class has many useful members that can help you make your code more robust as well as make your life easier. For example, you can use enumerations to perform input validation. *System.Enum* defines the *IsDefined* method to check whether a constant is a legal value for that *Enum*. Using the previous example of the *DayOfWeek Enum*, check out the following example:

```
' This returns False. The integer 10 is not a valid Day of the Week
System.Enum.IsDefined(GetType(DayOfWeek), 10)

' This returns True for any integer between 0 and 6
System.Enum.IsDefined(GetType(DayOfWeek), 5)
```

Using *IsDefined* makes input validation easier, but there's plenty more where that came from. In all, the *System.Enum* type defines the shared methods described in Table 2-5 for common use with all enumerations.

Table 2-5
System.Enum Methods

Method	Description
Format	Converts the specified value of a specified enumerated type to its equivalent string representation based on the specified format.
GetName	Retrieves the name of the constant in the specified enumeration that has the specified value.
GetNames	Retrieves an array of the names of the constants in a specified enumeration.
GetType (inherited from *Object*)	Gets the *Type* of the current instance.
GetUnderlyingType	Returns the underlying type of the specified enumeration.
GetValues	Retrieves an array of the values of the constants in a specified enumeration.

Table 2-5
***System.Enum* Methods**

Method	Description
IsDefined	Indicates whether a constant with a specified value exists in a specified enumeration.
Parse	Overloaded. Converts the string representation of the name or numeric value of one or more enumerated constants to an equivalent enumerated object.
ToObject	Overloaded. Returns an instance of the specified enumeration type that's set to the specified value.

Go ahead and play with the *Enum* type. There's a great deal that you can do with it to make your life easier.

Delegates and Events

Unlike procedural languages, Visual Basic is based on an event-driven programming model. The application responds to user-generated or system-generated events. An event is simply a signal sent by an object that informs all the interested parties that something has occurred. In the nomenclature of events, we talk of publishers and subscribers. Applications become subscribers by signing up for events provided by publishers. Events are implemented in Visual Basic .NET using delegates. Delegates are a way of defining a method signature that a subscriber must adhere to.

Note   You can think of a delegate as a strongly typed function pointer.

Defining Your Delegates

The syntax for defining a delegate is simple. Take the following example from the .NET Framework that defines the *MouseEventHandler* delegate:

```
Public Delegate Sub MouseEventHandler( sender As Object, _
                                 e As MouseEventArgs)
```

This example defines the signature of a method that can receive mouse events. When you publish events using this delegate type, clients must define their event handler methods so that the signatures match. Note that delegates are not limited to publishing events. You can use delegates in many ways. Here's a creative example that uses an external class to provide custom sort methods for another class:

```
' This is a class that implements a sort method. The specific sort
' method used on the internal array m_Array is customizable by
' setting the sort method property to the address of a method that
' has the same signature as the SortHandler delegate.
Public Class MyStuff

    Public Sub New()
        m_Array = New String(5) {"0", "1", "2", "3", "4", "5"}
        SortMethod = AddressOf Me.DefaultSort
    End Sub

    ' Defining the Delegate
    Public Delegate Sub SortHandler(ByVal ary As System.Array)

    ' This is a variable that stores a reference to a delegate
    Private m_SortMethod As SortHandler
    Private m_Array() As Object

    Private Sub DefaultSort(ByVal ary As System.Array)
        Console.WriteLine("Calling DefaultSort")
    End Sub

    Public Sub Sort()
        m_SortMethod(m_Array)
    End Sub

    Public WriteOnly Property SortMethod() As SortHandler
        Set(ByVal method As SortHandler)
            m_SortMethod = method
        End Set
    End Property

End Class


' This is a class that implements custom sort algorithms for an array
' each of the sort methods signatures match the signature of the SortHandler
' delegate. The power to doing this is it allows custom behavior to be
' specified completely outside of the
Public Class CustomSortAlgorithms

    Public Sub QuickSort(ByVal ary As System.Array)
        ' Implement a quicksort algorithm
        Console.WriteLine("Calling QuickSort")
    End Sub
```

```
Public Sub BubbleSort(ByVal ary As System.Array)
    ' Implement a bubblesort algorithm
    Console.WriteLine("Calling BubbleSort")
End Sub

Public Sub SimpleSort(ByVal ary As System.Array)
    ' Implement a simplesort algorithm
    Console.WriteLine("Calling SimpleSort")
End Sub

End Class


Public Module Module1

    Public Sub Main()
        Dim m As New MyStuff()
        Dim s As New CustomSortAlgorithms()

        ' Let's try out each of the sort methods, starting
        ' with the default one. We'll replace the sort method
        ' with our three custom ones.
        m.Sort()
        m.SortMethod = AddressOf s.BubbleSort
        m.Sort()
        m.SortMethod = AddressOf s.SimpleSort
        m.Sort()
        m.SortMethod = AddressOf s.QuickSort
        m.Sort()
        Console.ReadLine()
    End Sub

End Module
```

Notice that you can use delegates to define a variable that represents a method. You can replace the contents of that variable at any time without having to fundamentally modify your code. Because the method signature is guaranteed by the delegate, you can dynamically change the actual method being called, by replacing the contents of the delegate. Pretty darn cool, huh?

Declaring and Publishing Events

Continuing with the example of the *MouseEventHandler* delegate, let's look at how publishing and subscribing to an *Event* is not much more difficult than declaring your delegates. Declaring the events is easy. You can declare events on your interfaces and/or classes. The syntax is the same either way and looks like this:

```
Public Class MouseEventClass
   ...
   Public Event MouseUp As MouseEventHandler
   Public Event MouseDown As MouseEventHandler
End Class
```

Raising the event requires only a little more work and another keyword: *RaiseEvent*. A typical practice is to create a protected class method to actually raise the event (to ensure that only the class and its derived types can actually fire the event). If the base class does not provide any method to raise an event, that event can be raised only by that base class; none of its derived classes will have that capability. Ultimately, this is a design decision you have to make, but providing protected members for raising events is a common design practice that's used extensively throughout the .NET Framework. Here is an example:

```
Protected Sub OnMouseUp( e As MouseEventArgs )
   RaiseEvent MouseUp( Me, e )
End Sub
...
' Fire the Event
OnMouseUp( new MouseEventArgs(MouseButtons.Left, 1, 0, 0, 0) )
```

That pretty much covers the publisher side of the event process. Now we just need to look at how to subscribe to these events.

Note   You can create an event without first declaring a delegate, by using an alternate form of the *Event* declaration. The problem is that this results in the creation of a separate delegate type for each event. Defining your delegates separately, as we just did, allows them to be reused and is better overall design practice. If you're interested in investigating this further, see Section 7.3 of the Visual Basic .NET Language Specification for more information about declaring events.

Subscribing to the event is simple. First, you must declare the variable containing the event using the *WithEvents* keyword. Your class's methods only have to match the signature of the delegate (the types, not the variable names— the variable names are not important) and use the *Handles* keyword on your methods, as in the following example:

```
Public Sub MyMouseHandler( sender As Object, _
                           e As MouseEventArgs ) _
                           Handles SampleClass.MouseUp
   ...
End Sub
```

An alternative method of subscribing to events is available through the use of the *AddHandler* and *RemoveHandler* statements. *AddHandler* allows you to mirror the functionality of the *Handles* clause—hooking up an event handler—and *RemoveHandler* allows you to unsubscribe from an event. These two statements give you much greater flexibility over how you subscribe to events in an application. Instead of the more traditional static compile-time event subscription, you can handle everything at run time and provide much more sophisticated behaviors. For instance, you can subscribe one method to multiple events (as long as the delegate signatures are identical), subscribe multiple methods to the same event, or anything in between. Even better, you do not need to use the *WithEvents* clause on your variable declarations if you use *AddHandler* and *RemoveHandler*.

More Info   I haven't provided a sample showing *AddHandler* and *Remove-Handler*, but the syntax is very easy to understand and the Visual Basic .NET documentation is an excellent reference.

Visual Basic and OOP

Rather than bore you again by extolling the virtues of OOP, we'll be brief. This section is all about how to use OOP features to improve your applications. We'll start by looking at how you can use namespaces to improve your project organization and make your class hierarchy easier to work with. Then we'll look at how to spice up your projects with inheritance and look at singletons—something every advanced developer should know about.

Making the Most of Namespaces

Namespaces are really about taming the unruly set of classes and methods that littered programming projects and libraries of the past. Visual Basic was no stranger to this problem, but other languages and platforms suffered from clutter as well. Namespaces help address this problem by providing a framework for structuring your program elements into logical hierarchical groupings.

Caution   Namespaces can be dangerous. Developers who tend to overdo things might create a massive hierarchy with more namespaces than classes. (Yes, we've seen this, and no, it isn't pretty.) Keep it under control, and keep it logical.

Namespaces are not just a new feature of Visual Basic .NET—they lie at the heart of the CLR. It is through namespaces that most type references are resolved by the CLR. In Visual Basic .NET, namespaces are used both implicitly and explicitly. When you create a new Visual Basic project, a namespace is automatically created that defaults to the name of the project. You can change this default name using the project's property page by entering a different name for the root namespace (as shown in Figure 2-1). You can explicitly create additional child namespaces in your projects using the *Namespace* statement.

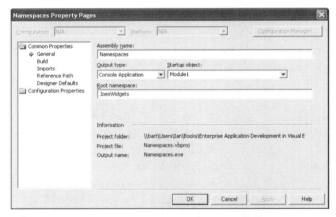

Figure 2-1   The Visual Basic General Project Settings panel.

Organizing Your Applications

Namespaces are all about organization. They're designed to produce a logical hierarchical structure for applications. From an organizational perspective, namespaces should start very general and become more specific as you ascend the hierarchy. In this way, you can create a logical organization that provides guidance to other developers on how to use your objects.

Let's look at an example. Let's say we've created a Visual Basic console application project using the name *JoesWidgets* as the default namespace. In the module1.vb file (which is created by default), we add the following code:

```
Module Module1
    Sub Main()
    End Sub
End Module

Namespace Project
    Namespace UI
        Namespace Widgets
            Public Class MyWidget
                ...
            End Class
        End Namespace
    End Namespace
End Namespace
```

You can see how we've defined a namespace hierarchy for the *MyWidget* class. A fully qualified name for *MyWidget* would look like this:

```
JoesWidgets.Project.UI.Widgets.MyWidget
```

Looks familiar, right? The entire .NET Framework is based on namespaces. Notice how the namespace is designed to become more specific as you move from left to right. You should always follow this design pattern. It will make your namespace hierarchy much easier to comprehend (especially for those who are unfamiliar with it). All types in the .NET Framework are grouped in this way. This allows the creation of classes that have the same name but are contained in different namespaces. An example is the *Control* class inside the *System.Windows.Forms* namespace. *System.Windows.Forms.Control* is a completely different class from the *System.Web.UI.Control* class in the *System.Web.UI* namespace.

Note   The name of the assembly does not have to correspond to any of the contained namespaces. It can be a good practice to establish some relationship, but the CLR really doesn't care what your assemblies are called.

All of your namespaces do not have to be in the same code file, let alone the same project. If we add another file to our project and add the following code, the new code will just add itself to the namespace structure.

```
Namespace Project
    Namespace Data
        Module EmployeeData
            Function GetWidgetData() As DataTable
            End Function
        End Module
    End Namespace
End Namespace
```

You can see the results in Class View (as shown in Figure 2-2). The Class View window displays your project's namespace hierarchy. This view can be very useful for discovering types that have been put into the wrong namespace or for getting a general overview of how your types are organized.

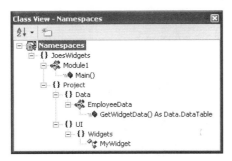

Figure 2-2   The Class View of our sample project.

Namespace Tips

Generally, it's good namespace practice to group functionally related classes inside the same namespace. Microsoft's own base class libraries are good examples of this. For example, many of the classes relevant to Visual Basic programmers are inside the *Microsoft.VisualBasic* namespace, and all of the data access classes are inside the *System.Data* namespace (and get more specific with the *OleDb* and *SqlClient* namepaces).

The nesting of namespaces is allowed to any arbitrary depth (be practical, though) and can be spread across source code files and assemblies. The .NET Framework does this all the time. Many common namespaces exist in different assemblies, yet they all combine to form the *System* namespace hierarchy. For example, the complete *System* namespace is spread across mscorlib.dll and System.dll, but *System.Data* is contained in System.Data.dll. Remember that namespaces help create logical groupings and are not generally affected by physical separation.

> **Note**   If you cause a namespace conflict by creating a class in two projects that share the same namespace, you'll definitely run into problems. The ability to spread namespaces across assemblies can be as much a hindrance as a help unless you keep the design of your namespace hierarchy under strict control.

You can access members of any given namespace in three ways:

- By fully qualifying them
- By using an *Imports* statement to avoid fully qualifying them
- By adding the namespace to the project's settings in the Imports pane (as shown in Figure 2-3)

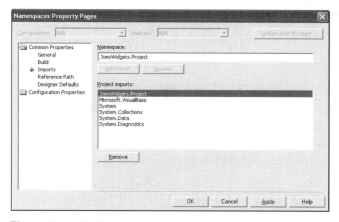

Figure 2-3   Adding Imports at the project level.

As you can see, namespaces are quite powerful, and Visual Basic .NET gives you a number of options for implementing them. Use them well, and use them wisely.

Inheritance: The Wily Beast of OOP

Inheritance is a tricky subject. By all accounts, inheritance is a good thing, but developers don't always use it in the way it was intended. Inheritance just for the sake of inheritance is a really bad idea. The most common reason for using inheritance is code reuse. But other, valid reasons include standardization (pre-defining critical subclass structures), extending behaviors of existing classes, and encapsulation.

Inheritance: The Rules of the Road

There are two forms of inheritance in Visual Basic .NET: interface inheritance and implementation inheritance. Interface inheritance is what interfaces do. Implementation inheritance is supported only by classes. The CLR has very specific rules governing inheritance. It allows multiple interface inheritance but only single implementation inheritance. This means that classes can inherit only from a single base class while interfaces can inherit from many interfaces.

> **Note**   When a class supports an interface, we say that it "implements" that interface. This is quite literally true because adding an interface to a class requires that the class provide an implementation for the interface's members.

The following rules apply specifically to class inheritance:

- A derived class can inherit directly from only one base class.
- All classes ultimately have *System.Object* as the base class.
- A class can implement more than one interface.
- A class can require inheritance (*MustInherit*). This means that a class that is marked *MustInherit* cannot be instantiated directly, but must first be derived from. If the derived class is to be instantiated, it must also implement all methods that have been marked *MustOverride*.
- A class can be declared as not inheritable (*NotInheritable*).

The following rules apply to specifically to interfaces:

- An interface can stand alone but cannot be instantiated.
- Interfaces can be implemented only in structures and classes.
- An interface can inherit from multiple interfaces.

Inheritance: No Substitute for Good Design

A recurring theme throughout this book is design, design, design. Logical errors are the outgrowth of poor design decisions. Don't fool yourself into thinking that inheritance will solve all of your design problems. In fact, preventing inheritance can sometimes be necessary or even desirable. After you write code and build classes, the next developer that comes along will make certain decisions about your code based on what it allows her to do. If your class allows inheritance, it would not be unreasonable to assume that it was designed with that purpose in mind. You should always design with an eye to preventing unintended uses of your code. If you build a class that should never be inherited from, you prevent inheritance. This will prevent confusion and force other developers—and yourself—to use your objects as they were intended. Apply this logic to all aspects of your classes and interfaces. A good design should make the right coding decisions easy (or at least not optional).

Inheritance Nuances

Inheritance is a surprisingly rich topic with many subtle aspects. Here we'll attempt to cover some of the more important issues or features that you need to be aware of in order to make effective use of inheritance within your applications.

Controlling inheritance   When you define a class, you have three ways to control its inheritance properties:

■   Allow inheritance (the default)

■   Prevent inheritance (*NotInheritable*)

■   Require inheritance (*MustInherit*)

Allowing inheritance is the simplest option and requires no further action on your part. All classes support and allow inheritance by default. If you decide that it is safe and advantageous to allow inheritance of your class, by all means allow it.

On the other hand, you might have a class that you do not want others to inherit from. You might have a utility class that should never be used as a base class. Or you might have a class that you aren't sure anyone would want to inherit from. In these situations and others, it's smart to prevent inheritance of your class simply to avoid confusion. Realistically, if a class was not designed with inheritance in mind, you probably shouldn't allow other classes to derive from it. In these cases, you should use the *NotInheritable* class qualifier, as in the following example:

```
' I can't inherit from this class!
Public NotInheritable Class MyFinalClass
    ...
End Class
```

If, on the other hand, you define a class that should be used only as a base class (that is, you should not be able to create an instance of it), you can use the *MustInherit* class qualifier. In this way, a client that wants an object of this type must first create a derived class that inherits from your base class. The following example shows *MustInherit* at work and shows how you can use both *MustInherit* and *NotInheritable* in an inheritance hierarchy:

```
' I can't create an instance of this class!
Public MustInherit Class MyBaseClass
   ...
End Class

' I can create an instance of this class and subclass it!
Public Class MySubClass
   Inherits MyBaseClass
   ...
End Class

' I can create an instance of this class, but I can't subclass it!
Public NotInheritable Class MyOtherClass
   Inherits MyBaseClass
   ...
End Class
```

Polymorphism and inheritance   Polymorphism in implementation inheritance is essentially the ability to redefine the functionality of methods inherited from a base class. When we do this, we typically refer to it as "overriding" the base class method. There are three scenarios for polymorphism:

- When a base method is marked *Overridable*. (Overriding is optional.)

- When a base method is marked *MustOverride*. (Overriding is mandatory.)

- When you use the *Shadows* keyword in the derived class. (The original method was not intended to be overridden.)

The simplest scenario might look like this:

```
Public Class MyBaseClass
   Public Overridable Sub HelloWorld()
      Console.WriteLine("Hello World")
   End Sub
End Class

Public Class MyNewClass
   Inherits MyBaseClass

   Public Overrides Sub HelloWorld()
      Console.WriteLine("Hello new World!")
   End Sub
End Class
```

In this situation, we defined a base class with an *Overridable* member *HelloWorld*. It is up to the derived class to determine whether it is appropriate to override that method, but it is allowed.

MustOverride indicates that a method is not implemented in the base class and must be implemented in a derived class in order for that class to be creatable. If you mark a method or property with *MustOverride*, you must also mark your class as *MustInherit*. This is because you are defining a method without an implementation, and that logically prevents the containing class from being instantiated. After all, you cannot create a class instance if you lack an implementation. The following example illustrates this:

```
Public MustInherit Class MyBaseClass
    Public MustOverride Sub HelloWorld()
End Class

Public Class MyNewClass
    Inherits MyBaseClass

    Public Overrides Sub HelloWorld()
        Console.WriteLine("Hello new World!")
    End Sub
End Class
```

Last but not least, there's the *Shadows* keyword. Shadowing is probably one of the most confusing features of Visual Basic .NET. When you override a method, you typically provide another method with the same name and signature. This substitutes the base class method implementation with one you have defined. There is a caveat. The base class must have marked that method as *MustOverride* or *Overridable*—otherwise, you cannot override that method.

Shadows lets you not only overload a base method but hide it as well, regardless of how that method was originally defined. One side-effect of *Shadows* is that because it is based on the method name, it hides all base-class overloads of that method. This defeats the purposes of polymorphism. One consequence of using *Shadows* is that if you use it on a method in a derived class, you run into strange behavior if you obtain a reference to the base class and call the method. The shadowed method will not be called in this instance, thus preventing you from changing the behavior of the base class—a major feature of polymorphism. Check out the following example:

```
Class ClassBase
    Public Sub MyMethod()
        Console.WriteLine("BaseClass.WillBeShadowed")
    End Sub
    Public Sub MyMethod(ByVal i As Integer)
        Console.WriteLine("BaseClass.WillBeShadowed(Integer)")
```

```
      End Sub
   End Class
   Class ClassDerived
      Inherits ClassBase

      Public Shadows Sub MyMethod(ByVal i As Integer)
         Console.WriteLine("BaseClass.WillBeShadowed(Integer)")
      End Sub
   End Class
```

In the above code, the *ClassDerived* class's *MyMethod* will hide both of the *ClassBase* class's *MyMethod* procedures. If I also cast a reference to the *ClassDerived* object to a *ClassBase* type, the derived type's implementation of *MyMethod* will be completely inaccessible.

In general, you should avoid shadowing unless it is absolutely necessary. Shadowing complicates the inheritance hierarchy and makes code use and maintenance more challenging. The need to use *Shadows* is often due to a failure in the design process, necessitating what is in essence a bandage over a bad design.

Me, MyBase, and MyClass   Visual Basic .NET provides three keywords to help you navigate the reference complexities of OOP. The *MyBase* keyword refers to the base class object of a current instance of a class. It is mainly used to access base class members that are overridden or shadowed in a derived class. Probably the most common use is for calling *MyBase.New* to call a base class constructor from a derived class constructor.

Note   *MyBase* has some limitations. The biggest limitation is that if your base class contains methods defined with *MustOverride*, those methods will not have any implementation and therefore cannot be called.

The *Me* keyword always refers to the current instance of a class. (It is the same thing as the *this* pointer in C#.) Probably the most common use of the *Me* keyword is to pass an instance of a class as a parameter to another function.

The *MyClass* keyword is an object variable that refers to the current instance of a class. *MyClass* is similar in behavior to the *Me* keyword, but all method calls on *MyClass* are treated as if the methods are *NotOverridable*. In other words, *MyClass* allows access to the immediate members of a class, regardless of whether a method has been overridden by a derived class.

The following example clearly illustrates how these keywords work:

```
Class BaseClass

    Public Overridable Sub MyMethod()
        Console.WriteLine("Calling BaseClass.MyMethod")
    End Sub

    Public Sub UseMe()
        Me.MyMethod()
    End Sub

    Public Sub UseMyClass()
        MyClass.MyMethod()
    End Sub
End Class

Class DerivedClass
    Inherits BaseClass

    Public Overrides Sub MyMethod()
        Console.WriteLine("Calling DerivedClass.MyMethod")
    End Sub

    Public Sub UseMyBase()
        MyBase.MyMethod()
    End Sub
End Class

Class TestClass
    Shared Sub Start()
        Dim TestObj As DerivedClass = New DerivedClass()
        TestObj.UseMe()
        TestObj.UseMyClass()
        TestObj.MyMethod()
        TestObj.UseMyBase()
    End Sub
End Class
```

Calling the *Start* method of *TestClass* will produce the following program output:

```
Calling DerivedClass.MyMethod
Calling BaseClass.MyMethod
Calling DerivedClass.MyMethod
Calling BaseClass.MyMethod
```

If you use *MyClass* or *MyBase* to refer to the method *MyMethod*, *Base-Class.MyMethod* will always be called even if it is overridden in a derived class.

This implies that the overuse of the *MyBase* and *MyClass* keywords can severely limit the flexibility of inheritance and negate the benefits of *Overridable* methods. You should use *MyBase* or *MyClass* only if you want to force the call to the base class method or the method as it is visible in the current class. *Me* is key to inheritance, and there is no reason you should not use it. *Me* allows derived classes to override methods and allows an overridden method to be invoked even if it is called from the base class.

Encapsulation

Encapsulation is defined as the ability to contain and control the access to a group of associated items. Classes are a common way to encapsulate data and implementation logic in OOP languages. Without encapsulation, you would need to declare separate procedures and variables to store and manage information, and it would be difficult to work with more than one object at a time. Encapsulation lets you use the data and procedures in an object as a single unit and allows you to work with multiple objects at the same time without confusion because each object is represented by a separate instance of a class.

Encapsulation also allows you to control how the data and procedures are used. You can use access modifiers, such as *Private* or *Protected*, to prevent outside procedures from executing methods or reading and modifying data in properties and fields. Internal details of a class should be declared as *Private* to prevent them from being used outside your class; this technique is called *data hiding*. A basic rule of encapsulation is that class data should be modified or retrieved only through *Property* procedures or methods. Hiding the implementation details of your classes prevents them from being used in undesired ways and lets you modify such items later without risk of compatibility problems.

Shared Members

The *Shared* keyword indicates that one or more declared class elements are shared across all instances of a class. Shared elements are not associated with a specific instance of a class or structure, but exist on their own and are created only once, regardless of how many classes containing shared members are created.

The *Shared* keyword can be used with

- Variables (the *Dim* statement)
- Properties (the *Property* statement)
- Methods (the *Sub* and *Function* statements)
- Events (the *Event* statement)

Accessing shared members is easy. You can access shared members by qualifying them with the class or structure name or with the variable name of a specific instance of the class or structure. The following example demonstrates how shared members can work:

```
Imports System.Text
Imports Microsoft.VisualBasic

Public Class ApplicationLog
    Private Shared m_log As New StringBuilder()
    Public Shared Sub LogMessage( msg As String )
       m_log.AppendFormat("{0}{1}", msg, vbCrLf )
    End Sub
    Public Shared ReadOnly Property Log() As String
       Get
          Return m_log.ToString()
       End Get
    End Property
End Class

Public Module Module1
    Public Sub Main()
       ApplicationLog.LogMessage("This is a test")
       ApplicationLog.LogMessage("of class' shared members.")
       Console.Write( ApplicationLog.Log )
    End Sub
End Module
```

Notice that we don't need to create an instance of the *ApplicationLog* class. But that only applies to this example. You can create a class that has both shared and instance members if you need to—it's up to you.

Note   Whenever you see a shared variable in a class in this book, you'll notice that it is marked private. This is intentional because public shared variables are dangerous, especially in a multithreaded application. By using properties or methods as indirect ways to manipulate shared variables, you can introduce code to make your shared members thread-safe. We'll cover this and other synchronization-related issues in Chapter 3.

One thing the previous example does not do is demonstrate the shared nature of the *Shared* members. To help clarify this, take a look at the following example, which uses a shared variable to track the number of class instances created:

```vb
Public Class Employee
    Private Shared m_count As Integer = 0

    Public Sub New()
        MyBase.New()
        m_count += 1
    End Sub

    Public Shared Readonly Property EmployeeCount() As Integer
        Get
            Return m_count
        End Get
    End Property
End Class

Public Module Module1
    Public Sub Main()
        Dim emp as Employee
        Console.WriteLine("EmployeeCount = {0}", Employee.EmployeeCount)
        emp = New Employee()
        Console.WriteLine("EmployeeCount = {0}", Employee.EmployeeCount)
        emp = New Employee()
        Console.WriteLine("EmployeeCount = {0}", Employee.EmployeeCount)
        emp = New Employee()
        Console.WriteLine("EmployeeCount = {0}", Employee.EmployeeCount)
    End Sub
End Module
```

If you run this program, you'll see the following output:

```
EmployeeCount = 0
EmployeeCount = 1
EmployeeCount = 2
EmployeeCount = 3
```

The employee count will continue to grow as long as your application continues to call *New Employee()* (or until an integer overflow error occurs). It is important to note that you'll get the same result each time you run your application. The *m_count* variable is reinitialized every time the application is started. Also, the *m_count* variable is shared only within your application's process. If you launch two instances of the application simultaneously, you'll get precisely the same result in each.

Shared Constructors

Shared constructors can be useful for initializing your class's shared variables. Shared constructors have some interesting properties. First, shared constructors are run before any instance of the type is created and before any of the type's shared members are referenced. Shared constructors are also run before any types that derive from that type are loaded. A shared constructor will not be run more than once during a single execution of a program (or application domain). Best of all, they are totally hands-free. You don't have to do anything other than define the constructor itself.

Shared constructors are not the only way to define or initialize shared variables, but they are the most flexible option and are definitely worth considering. Alternatively, you can specify a default value for your shared variables without a shared constructor—this works well for simple initialization needs. If you need to do something more complicated (something that requires file I/O, for instance) you'll probably want to use the shared constructor instead. Visual Basic does automatically create a shared constructor for all of the initialization of shared variables if a shared constructor is not already specified. Even when you define your own shared constructor, Visual Basic will prepend the initialization code for all of your shared variables if necessary.

The following example demonstrates both ways to initialize shared members:

```
Imports System.Data

Public Class Employee
   Private Shared ds As DataSet
   Private Shared Count As Integer = 0 ' Implicitly called

   ' This is called once per application domain
   Shared Sub New()
     ds = New DataSet()
   End Sub
End Class
```

Object Construction

Object construction is all about creating instances of your classes. You cannot create an instance of a class without first calling the class's constructor. The purpose of the constructor is to initialize the class into a known state. Developers often take the opportunity to perform some additional work in the constructor, which can lead to some interesting issues.

The biggest problem with doing too much in a constructor is that it will pose some challenging error-handling issues. A constructor will always return an object reference, regardless of whether the method succeeds. If you have to do something like opening a file handle in your constructor, what do you do if the file doesn't exist? Worse, what if the constructor causes an exception? Yes, you can always handle the exception in the code that calls the constructor. But the problem is that it's already too late. The class has been created and allocated on the heap and is partially initialized. If the class had allocated expensive resources before the exception was thrown, the class will not go away until the next garbage collection. You won't be able to do anything because you won't have a reference to the object, yet it will still exist.

There are two basic approaches to creating an instance of a class. The first is the most obvious: using a public constructor. In this case, you should not do anything that might cause an exception unless you handle the exception in the constructor itself. The second option is more subtle but can be very useful: using a protected or private constructor and a public shared *Create* method. You use the shared member to perform your system checks and validate the parameters before you call the *New* operator. Consider the following example:

```
Public Class Class1
    Public Sub New(filePath as String)
       ' If an exception is thrown and not handled here, you
       ' open yourself up to a lot of trouble.
    End Sub
End Class

Public Class Class2
    Private Sub New()
    End Sub

    Public Shared Function Create() As Class2
    ' Perform your validation logic here.
    ' You can also throw exceptions if you like.

       ' Create the object only if the parameters are valid
       If ValidParams Then
         Return New Class2()
       Else
```

```
        Return Nothing
    End If
End Function
End Class
```

The definition of *Class1* is perfectly fine as long as it can handle invalid construction parameters or it doesn't care. If your class is sensitive to the validity of the construction parameters (bad parameters can result in an unhandled exception), you might want to try static construction. In this case, you can do all of your parameter validation before the object is ever created. This gives you a lot of flexibility without requiring a lot of overhead.

Note   There are whole schools of thought on which approach is ultimately better. We prefer a more pragmatic approach. If a solution makes sense for a single class, great. A one-size-fits-all approach to object construction is a bad idea. Don't take this section as an endorsement of one approach over the other. We just want to make you aware of the options.

Singletons

Singletons are an important part of many applications. Put simply, a singleton is a class for which only one instance can be allowed to exist per application. This is important when you need to have a single resource shared across your entire application. Imagine a situation in which you want to implement custom logging or auditing in an application. To make the task manageable, you'll want a central authority to handle all of the tasks related to logging and auditing. If you were to create multiple instances of a logging class, you would need to implement a great deal of redundant code throughout your application (for creating, initializing, and disposing).

In addition, you want to avoid potential problems with data integrity if, for example, two or more instances might attempt to write to a file at the same time. Who will win? Using a singleton in these cases will make most of the problems go away and will centralize all of the functionality into one place.

There are four requirements for creating a true singleton in an application:

- Your class's constructor must be private. (This prevents direct instantiation.)

- Your class should be marked *NotInheritable*.

- Your class must provide at least one shared method that returns an instance of your singleton class. (This allows access to the singleton.)

- Your class must contain a private shared variable for referencing the singleton instance.

Note   Do you have to follow all of these rules? No. But you should. You should also be concerned about thread safety. Thread safety is covered in the next chapter.

Here's a very basic implementation of a singleton in Visual Basic .NET. Note the behavior of the *GetClass* function.

```
Public NotInheritable Class MySingleton
   Private Shared m_MySingleton As MySingleton

   Private Sub New()
      MyBase.New()
   End Sub

   ' The Shared method that always returns an instance of MySingleton
   Public Shared Function GetClass() As MySingleton
      ' Note we create this if it doesn't exist-but it is only done once
      If m_MySingleton Is Nothing Then
         m_MySingleton = New MySingleton()
      End If

      Return m_MySingleton
   End Function
End Class
```

It is possible to implement singleton behavior without implementing all of the previously stated requirements, but the implementation shown here prevents any other use of the *MySingleton* class. An alternative implementation would not be a "true" singleton because it could be used in a manner not consistent with being a singleton (to create multiple instances or derive classes that could create multiple instances). This is a key concept in projects that involve multiple developers: design your classes and your interface for how they should be used. Never give developers a choice. If a class should not be inherited from, mark it *NotInheritable*. If you intend a class to be used as a singleton, implement it as a true singleton. This prevents inappropriate use of the class. A design that is not explicit in its implementation is open to misuse or abuse.

Whole categories of bugs in systems are the direct result of permissive designs. Don't make the same mistake.

Exception Handling Redux

Mistakes happen. Errors are fact of life. That error handling in applications is important is beyond obvious, but Visual Basic developers have had their own set of challenges. The error handling mechanisms of the past are not really suited to larger-scale applications. Visual Basic .NET supports the classic *On Error* syntax, but it also introduces structured exception handling.

Note   On this subject, we are very biased. Structured exception handling is far more flexible and useful than the "old way." If you're developing a new Visual Basic .NET application, treat any use of *On Error* statement as a bug. I know that many Visual Basic developers like to use what they're most comfortable with, but *On Error* is like a clumsy sledge hammer and really should be avoided at all costs. Chapter 11 discusses the performance problems associated with *On Error*.

Exception Handling Basics

Exception handling is based on a throw-catch metaphor. When an exception is generated by a block of code, we say that it "threw" an exception. If we define an exception handler for that exception type, we say that we "caught" that exception. Visual Basic .NET uses the *Try...Catch...Finally* block to define exceptions handlers. A simple example looks like the following:

```
Public Sub Test()
    Try
        ' Do some work that might cause an exception
    Catch ex As Exception
        MsgBox(ex.ToString())
    End Try
End Sub
```

Of course, you can get more sophisticated in how you handle exceptions. It is important to note that exceptions are just another type of class that all inherits from the base class *System.Exception*. Therefore, you can use the *Catch* statement as an exception filter and specify only the exceptions that you are able to handle:

```
Public Sub Test()
   Try
      ' Do some work that might cause an exception
   Catch ex As FileNotFoundException
      MsgBox("Could not find the file: " + ex.FileName)
   Catch ex As SecurityException
      MsgBox("You do not have permissions to access this object")
   End Try
End Sub
```

Here you can see how it is possible to catch two different types of exceptions and provide custom error handling. Note that if any other exception type is produced in our *Try* block, the exception will not be caught in this code. This is on purpose, and it is how you should approach exception handling in your own code. Generally speaking, you should never catch an exception unless you intend to do something with it. End of story.

The last part of this particular discussion of the *Try...Catch* block has to do with the *Finally* clause. The *Finally* code block contains code that is guaranteed to be executed, no matter what. This allows you to insert cleanup code that will always run.

```
Dim conn As New SqlConnection("A connection string")
Dim cmd As New SqlCommand("Select * from Authors", conn)
Try
conn.Open()
cmd.ExecuteReader()
Catch ex As SqlException
   MsgBox(ex.ToString())
Finally
   ' This always gets called, whether an exception happens or not
   If (Not conn Is Nothing) AndAlso _
      (conn.State = ConnectionState.Open) Then

      conn.Close()
   End If
End Try
```

Alternatively, you can forgo the catch statement altogether and just include the *Finally* block:

```
Dim conn As New SqlConnection("A connection string")
Dim cmd As New SqlCommand("Select * from Authors", conn)
Try
conn.Open()
cmd.ExecuteReader()
Finally
   ' This always gets called, whether an exception happens or not
```

```
    If (Not conn Is Nothing) AndAlso _
       (conn.State = ConnectionState.Open) Then

        conn.Close()
    End If
End Try
```

This is a way of saying that you can't handle the exceptions that might be generated by the code in the *Try* block, but you should always close the connection, regardless. Pretty cool, huh?

Throwing Exceptions

Throwing exceptions yourself is not exactly difficult. The .NET Framework makes it that much easier by defining a whole set of exception classes that you can use:

```
Public Sub ErrorSub()
    ' Do stuff
    Throw new Exception("ErrorSub failed because you made a mistake!")
End Sub
```

Don't use the *System.Exception* class if a more appropriate exception handling type is available to you. If your code is failing because a necessary file does not exist, use an instance of the *FileNotFoundException* class—it has additional properties that can be useful for debugging purposes.

An interesting property of .NET exceptions is that they can contain other exceptions. The *System.Exception* class defines a property called *InnerException* of type *System.Exception*. This property allows you to access an exception that is contained by another. It also potentially allows the development of an exception hierarchy. This allows you to provide better information about what failed and still provide a way to track down the original error. The following code demonstrates how you might use the exception containment mechanism. Using an overload of the *System.Exception* class constructor, we'll create a new exception, passing the previously caught exception:

```
Public Sub ErrorSub()
    ' Do stuff
    Try
        ' Do stuff that might fail.
    Catch ex As SqlException
        Throw new Exception("ErrorSub failed because you made a mistake!", ex)
    End Try
End Sub
```

That's pretty much all there is to throwing. The newly thrown exception will have an *InnerException* that contains the *SqlException* caught by our *Catch* statement.

Now that we've covered the basics of throwing and catching exceptions, it seems appropriate to take a step back and look at exception handling practices you should avoid.

Exception Handling No-Nos

Structured exception handling is no panacea. There are a couple of rules you should follow to maximize the benefits and efficiency of exception handling:

- Never catch an exception unless you intend to do something with it.

- Never catch an exception if you're just going to rethrow it.

- Catch the most specific exception you can.

- Create multiple catch statements for specific exception types if you'll handle them.

It's not unheard of for developers to get exception-handler-happy. When that happens, we see code like this:

```
Public Sub Test()
   Try
      ' Do some work that might cause an exception
   Catch ex As Exception
      Throw ex ' Don't do this!!
   End Try

   Try
      ' Do some more work that might cause an exception
   Catch ex As Exception
      If TypeOf ex Is FileNotFoundException Then
         ' Do something to recover
      Else
         Throw ex ' Don't do this!!
      End If
   End Try
End Sub
```

In the first *Try* block, the exception is caught and immediately rethrown—a bad idea and a waste of resources. If you can't handle the exception, don't catch it. It's that simple. The second *Try* block does something similarly foolish. It catches all possible exceptions and checks the type to see if it is a *FileNot-FoundException* to handle the error. If the caught exception is not a *FileNot-*

FoundException, the method just rethrows the caught exception. This also is very inefficient and unnecessary. You can get the same result by being more specific in your *Catch* statement. Always remember the first rule of exception handling: if you don't do anything with it, don't catch it. Fixing the previous example results in code like the following:

```
Public Sub Test()
    ' Do some work that might cause an exception

    Try
        ' Do some more work that might cause an exception
    Catch ex As FileNotFoundException
        ' Do something to recover
    End Try
End Sub
```

Remember, exceptions are fairly expensive, so as a general rule exceptions should be truly exceptional—avoid overusing them. In many cases, the old standby of returning a success value is perfectly acceptable. On the other hand, if something unexpected happens, the function should throw an appropriate exception. The rule here is based on how often you expect the event to occur. Throw an exception if an error condition is truly exceptional (such as when an expected user record does not exist). If the error happens routinely (for example, an incorrect password), programmatically checking for errors is a much more efficient and appropriate approach.

Custom Exceptions

The .NET Framework defines a wide variety of exceptions types. But sometimes the right kind of exception just isn't available, or you face a whole class of problems that have nothing to do with file or SQL exceptions and are related to specific features in your application. In such cases, you'll probably want to create your own set of exceptions. If you decide to do this, it's best to plan out a hierarchy in advance.

All exceptions in Visual Basic .NET inherit from the *System.Exception* class. The .NET Framework further defines exceptions into two main categories: the *System.ApplicationException* class and the *System.SystemException*. The *System.ApplicationException* class is intended to be the base exception class for all application-specific exceptions you define. Most exceptions defined by .NET Framework derive from *System.SystemException*.

As much as possible, you should use the existing exceptions defined by the .NET Framework. You should define new exceptions only if the existing exceptions don't suffice. When you define a new exception, create your own base exception that's derived from the *System.ApplicationException* class. You can then build your application's exception hierarchy off of this base class. The following example demonstrates creating a base exception class called *MyAppException* that's derived from *System.ApplicationException*. It also shows how to create a specific exception type (*UserConfigException*) from *MyAppException* that provides additional information about the error that occurred.

```
Public Class MyAppException
    Inherits System.ApplicationException

    Public Sub New()
        MyBase.New()
    End Sub

    Public Sub New(ByVal message As String)
        MyBase.New(message)
    End Sub

    Public Sub New(ByVal message As String, _
                ByVal innerException As Exception)
        MyBase.New(message, innerException)
    End Sub
End Class

Public Class UserConfigException
    Inherits MyAppException

    Private m_fileName As String
    Public Sub New(ByVal message As String, ByVal fileName As String)
        MyBase.New(message)
        m_fileName = fileName
    End Sub

    Public ReadOnly Property FileName() As String
        Get
            Return m_fileName
        End Get
    End Property
End Class
```

You'll see many examples of exception handling throughout this book. If you need more information, see the MSDN documentation that comes with Visual Basic .NET.

Resource Management and *IDisposable*

Visual Basic .NET has a new twist on resource management. The CLR provides a resource management mechanism known as *garbage collection* to free the developer from most memory management tasks. But it does not come without a price, nor does it completely free you from dealing with memory management issues. In some ways, garbage collection forces you to be more aware of which objects require manual intervention to ensure that resources are released in an appropriate manner. For the most part, you do not need to worry about when objects are destroyed.

In Visual Basic 6.0, when all object variables that refer to an object are assigned to *Nothing*, the memory and system resources associated with the object are freed immediately. You know exactly when the object was freed (deterministic finalization). The CLR now takes on the responsibility of resource management. This allows developers to concentrate on improving their applications instead of writing lots of resource management and cleanup code.

This requires a change in coding practices. For example, when you set a variable to *Nothing*, the object is not destroyed immediately. It will be destroyed at some later time (to be determined by the garbage collector). For the most part, this shouldn't affect your application. However, in some scenarios (such as when an application is under stress due to low system resources), it can be a real problem that affects both performance and scalability. In a situation in which performance is critical, it is in your best interests to free resources as soon as you're done with them.

Note   Keep in mind that garbage collector collection cycles are expensive. The idea is to prevent the garbage collector from running too frequently. The more you clean up after yourself, the less work it will have to do and the better your application will perform.

The Garbage Collector

If an application uses unmanaged resources (for example, if it explicitly allocates memory, file handles, or other system resources), the CLR garbage collector will usually have no idea how to free them up. Even when the garbage collector can handle some of these resources, it might not necessarily free them in a timely fashion. It is important to do some manual cleanup, especially if what you're working with represents some physical resource on the machine. Override the *Object.Finalize* method and free the resources there. (By default, this method does nothing.) However, be aware that because of way the garbage collector works, using the *Finalize* method affects performance—so don't use it unless you need to. For more information on this, check out MSDN.

Even if *Finalize* is overridden and the resources are freed, you have no control over when the garbage collector will start collecting. You call always call *System.GC.Collect*, but you should never do that in a production environment. CLR resource management is quite complex and the collector knows when to best to run a collection cycle. Your application's performance can be badly hurt if you start calling *System.GC.Collect*. Be aware that the garbage collector starts when there is a need for managed memory. It has no real control over unmanaged resources. The .NET Framework provides a solution to this problem: the *IDisposable* interface (discussed next).

The *IDisposable* Interface

So how can you tell if an object needs additional cleanup on your part? It's actually pretty simple. All classes in the .NET Framework that allocate resources that should be freed immediately should implement the *IDisposable* interface. This interface contains only a single method:

```
Public Interface IDisposable
    Sub Dispose()
End Interface
```

If a class you've instantiated implements this interface, you should call *Dispose* when you're done with it. Pretty simple, right? But what are the advantages of *IDisposable*? *IDisposable* makes it possible to identify all classes that allocate expensive resources, and it provides a simplified, reliable mechanism for freeing all of those resources.

As we already mentioned, many classes in the .NET Framework implement *IDisposable*. Here's an example that uses the *SqlConnection* class:

```
Dim conn As New SqlConnection()
' Do Stuff
conn.Dispose()
```

But this is not necessarily reliable. Errors and exceptions are always possibilities, so putting the *Dispose* call in a *Finally* block of a *Try...Catch...Finally* statement guarantees that your code will always clean up. Our code should look more like this:

```
Dim conn As SqlConnection
Try
    conn = New SqlConnection()
    ' Do Stuff
```

```
Finally ' We skip the catch clause because we don't need it here.
   conn.Dispose()
End Try
```

This makes sense, but what if you need to implement *IDisposable?*

Implementing *IDisposable*

It's an interesting question: when should a class that you create implement *IDisposable?* Here are three common situations in which you should definitely implement the *IDisposable* interface on a class:

- When your class contains other classes that implement *IDisposable*

- When your class contains instances of COM objects

- When your class has a reference to an active Win32 resource handle

The simplest implementation of *IDisposable* would look like the following:

```
Public Class MyDisposableClass
    Implements IDisposable
    ' Other members
    Public Overloads Sub Dispose() Implements IDisposable.Dispose
        ' Release Your Resources Here
    End Sub
End Class
```

However, the simplest implementation is not always the most reliable. A more complete implementation would look like the following:

```
Public Class MyDisposableClass
    Implements IDisposable
    Public Overloads Sub Dispose() Implements IDisposable.Dispose
        Dispose(True)
        GC.SuppressFinalize(Me) ' No need call finalizer
    End Sub

    Protected Overridable Overloads Sub Dispose(ByVal disposing As Boolean)
        If disposing Then
            ' Free managed resources
        End If
        ' Free unmanaged resources
    End Sub

    Protected Overrides Sub Finalize()
        Dispose(False)
    End Sub
End Class
```

Conclusion

Visual Basic .NET is a powerful new language that's built on a very sophisticated platform. It has a lot of features that developers can leverage to produce better-designed applications and systems. In addition, the language and the platform have many aspects that make large-scale development projects more feasible. The introduction of true implementation inheritance alone is a boon to enterprise developers, but other language and compiler features are also important to maintain coding standards in large projects.

We recommend that you take what you can from this chapter (there's a lot here) and run with it. You can always come back to pick up additional snippets, but don't be intimidated by the density of the content. Above all, when you start a project, set standards. Visual Basic .NET has a number of features (some of which we just covered) that can help you do this.

Try to focus on the design practices that will benefit your application. Without a good design, an application is just a pile of code that someone threw together and that creates a maintenance nightmare. This is especially true in larger companies in which people don't necessarily hang around long in the same position. Nobody likes being saddled with someone else's castoffs.

The bottom line is that Visual Basic .NET is an exciting new language and platform, so go forth and code—but have fun, too.

More Info   For more information about using Visual Basic .NET in a team development environment, see Appendix A.

3

Multithreaded Programming

The ability to perform multiple simultaneous tasks is often a critical feature for more sophisticated applications. The Microsoft .NET Framework's threading libraries finally give developers who use Microsoft Visual Basic the freedom to create fully threaded applications. Entire portions of an application can be executed asynchronously, allowing for more efficient designs and more responsive user interaction.

Most introductory Visual Basic .NET books touch on the subject of .NET threading, but they seldom go beyond the simplest of examples. A large amount of information about threading is never included in most practical texts. I'll attempt to address threading concepts at a deeper level. I should state up front, however, that a single chapter can never serve as a comprehensive treatise on a topic such as this. Our discussion will focus on a number of advanced threading concepts without embroiling the reader in nitty-gritty technical details that would be of little use to the more casual reader. In other words, this chapter will provide an introduction to more advanced topics from a practical perspective and at the same time provide some guidance on when, where, and how to use threads in your applications.

Threads can allow you to create sophisticated applications, but not without a cost. More threads do not always mean better performance, and how the threading is implemented will affect your performance and resource usage (either positively or negatively). In this chapter, I'll outline critical methods for implementing threading and other threading-related features and demonstrate how best to use them in your applications. I'll also highlight some practices that are best avoided.

I'll assume that you have at least a passing familiarity with the fundamentals of the technologies under discussion. You should know what threads are and how to create "simple" threads in Visual Basic .NET. But because of the conceptual complexity of threading issues, we'll start with an overview of basic threading concepts and then progress to concepts such as synchronization constructs. I'll provide examples to demonstrate useful techniques and thread usage, which you can build on in your own projects.

An Overview of Basic Threading Concepts

Visual Basic .NET and the .NET Framework provide a full set of threading capabilities that make creating and running simple threads very easy to do. But before we get into doing just that, let's take a step back and review how processes and threads are related and how this relationship can affect your application designs.

Processes and Threads

Applications run in separate processes on a computer. For each new application launched, a new process is created. A process by definition contains at least one execution thread and has its own address space. This serves to isolate applications from each other because processes cannot share memory directly. Isolation prevents one process from trampling over the memory of another process, ensuring, at least in theory, that one application cannot cause another to crash. This also means that applications cannot directly share memory-resident resources (arrays, classes, or variables). Even sharing non-memory-resident resources, such as disk-resident files, can be tricky.

More Info   For ways to share resources across applications, see the discussion of remoting in Chapter 5.

Threads, on the other hand, are the basic unit to which an operating system allocates processor time. The operating system allocates execution time to threads, not (as you might think) processes. A thread requires an owner process and cannot exist on its own. Processes, on the other hand, can contain multiple threads but must contain at least one thread—the main process thread (usually *Sub Main*). When the main process thread exits, the entire process is terminated—any other active threads will be prematurely terminated. Threads can share memory with other threads that are within the same process. A thread also has an associated set of resources that includes its own exception handlers, scheduling priority, and a set of structures that allow the operating system to preserve the thread's context as other threads are given execution time.

The .NET Framework takes this model a step further by introducing the concept of *application domains.* An application domain is a lightweight, managed subprocess that can contain one or more threads. Threads within application domains can create additional application domains.

Execution Time

Threads are granted execution time by the operating system in what are known as *time slices.* The duration of a time slice is system-dependent and varies between operating systems and processors. In the vast majority of environments, only one thread can be given execution control at a time. The exception is when threads are running on a multiprocessor machine.

Limitations of Threads

Any given system will have an upper limit on the number of threads per process. On systems running Microsoft Windows XP, that limit is approximately 2000 threads per process. As a practical matter, the limit is actually much lower. Each thread constitutes real physical resources on a machine. The memory requirements of preserving the thread context information cause the number of possible threads to be bounded by the available memory.

The memory commitment aside, tracking larger numbers of threads creates a significant burden for the operating system, which has to switch between all of the active threads on the system on a regular basis. If there are too many threads, the amount of execution time provided to each thread will not be enough to make significant progress in a reasonable amount of time. This will also affect other applications in the system. Remember that the processor execution time is divided among the active threads. If one application has a single thread and another has three, the first application will get only a quarter of the processing time. As the number of threads in the second application increases, the first application will get increasingly less processor time. This should highlight the need to be a good threading citizen. You can adversely affect other applications on the same machine if you use your threads unwisely.

The bottom line here is that you should create only as many threads as you need and no more. Due to the burden that additional threads impose on the system, you should make careful choices about what tasks belong in separate threads. Here are a couple of additional facts about threads:

- The amount of time given to a thread is not guaranteed.

- The order of thread activation is not guaranteed.

- Events or operations occurring on different threads cannot be assumed to be synchronized; you must perform any synchronization explicitly.

Creating Threads

The core functionality of threading for Visual Basic .NET is contained in the *System.Threading.Thread* class. This class provides all of the operations that can be performed on managed threads. In the managed world, threads are encapsulated by the *Thread* class. You use the *Thread* class to create and manage additional threads within your application. Managed threads, like all other managed objects, are maintained by the .NET runtime environment.

There are three important steps to creating any managed thread in Visual Basic .NET:

1. Create a method to serve as the thread's starting point.

2. Create a *ThreadStart* delegate, using the *AddressOf* operator with the method you want called when the new thread starts.

3. Create a *Thread* object and pass it the *ThreadStart* delegate you created.

After following these steps, you'll have a thread that can be started and run on its own. The following example demonstrates how to create two separate threads and start them. The example is among the chapter's sample files and is named Basic Threading.

```
Imports System.Threading

Module BasicThreading
    Public Const MAX_COUNT As Integer = 200

    Sub Main()
        ' Create the thread objects
        Dim Thread1 As New Thread(New ThreadStart(AddressOf ThreadMethod1))
        ' We can omit the New ThreadStart and just use the AddressOf operator.
        Dim Thread2 As New Thread(AddressOf ThreadMethod2)

        ' Start the threads
        Thread1.Start()
        Thread2.Start()
```

```
      ' Give the user a chance to read the input
      Console.ReadLine()
   End Sub

   ' The respective thread methods
   Public Sub ThreadMethod1()
      Dim i As Integer
      For i = 0 To MAX_COUNT
         Console.WriteLine("ThreadMethod1 {0}", i)
      Next
   End Sub

   Public Sub ThreadMethod2()
      Dim i As Integer
      For i = 0 To MAX_COUNT
         Console.WriteLine("ThreadMethod2 {0}", i)
      Next
   End Sub
End Module
```

When we run this application, the output looks like that shown in Figure 3-1. Both threads print out a repeated set of lines to the console. Note that your results (which thread will actually run first and which will finish first) might vary from run to run and will definitely vary from machine to machine. (Remember the three threading facts mentioned earlier.)

Figure 3-1   Sample output of the Basic Threading sample.

The Basic Threading sample demonstrates the simplest form of threading: the thread class is given the address of a method that it will execute. The method itself has no notion of threads, nor can we pass any parameters to the thread method. One solution to this, given the simplest case, is to declare global variables that are used by your thread methods. This is not very elegant and can be very messy. This does not necessarily present a problem for simple tasks, but it becomes an issue when more threads are involved or if you want to expose that functionality as a library to other developers.

The sample uses a global constant, *MAX_COUNT*, to pass information to the threads. The problem with this is that the mechanism is imprecise—both of the thread methods use the same constant. But what if we want the threads to execute differently? What if we need to have each thread execute with different initial conditions and we want to create an arbitrary number of threads? Obviously, it gets much trickier using dedicated global variables—we have to create specific variables for each thread, which can lead to a maintenance nightmare.

What we need is a way to pass information to the thread execution methods without creating specific global variables for each thread. What we need is a better way to manage thread creation and execution: *encapsulation*.

Encapsulating Threads

To get a better handle on creating, managing, and working with threads, a good strategy is to use encapsulation. Creating a class to encapsulate your threads is not the only answer to the control problem, but it is the cleanest. Being able to handle your threads in an object-oriented manner not only simplifies the management of those threads but prevents misuse by other developers. Remember one of the central themes of this book: always explicitly design your code for how it should be used!

Note   Encapsulating your threads also allows you to implement both synchronous and asynchronous interfaces for greater flexibility, depending on your application's needs. We'll investigate this further in following sections.

Wrapping a Thread with a Class

In the earlier section titled "An Overview of Basic Threading Concepts," all the work to create the threads had to be done, repeatedly, by the main subroutine. From a development standpoint, this is not particularly efficient and can lead to programming errors. (Repetition is rarely desirable.) The solution is to encapsulate the thread's implementation and runtime logic into a separate class, as in the following example:

```
Imports System.Threading

Public Class MyThreadClass

    Private m_Thread As Thread

    Public Sub New()
        Me.m_Thread = New Thread(AddressOf Me.Run)
    End Sub

    Public Sub Start()
        Me.m_Thread.Start()
    End Sub

    Private Sub Run()
        ' The thread's main logic goes here.
    End Sub

End Class
```

This is a good start, but it suffers from a major limitation. We cannot set initial conditions for this thread. We need to find a way to give the *Run* method some information to differentiate one *MyThreadClass* from another. We can do this most simply by providing a parameterized constructor. This makes the class inherently more useful by allowing it to perform different tasks based on different initial conditions. Using the class-based encapsulation scheme, you can pass parameters to the thread through the class's constructor. The constructor will then set some private variables that the thread can access when it needs to.

Warning   You can also use public properties on the class to set or modify the thread conditions, but I won't address how to do this safely until we get to the "Thread Synchronization" section later in the chapter. For the time being, the safest way to implement this is to set the properties before the thread starts. The constructor is the perfect place to do this in an enforceable manner.

If we extend the class we just created to function like the Basic Threading example, we end up with a class that looks something like the following:

```
Imports System.Threading

Public Class MyThreadClass

    Private m_Thread As Thread
    Private m_Id As Integer
    Private m_LoopCount As Integer

    Public Sub New(ByVal id As Integer, ByVal loopCount As Integer)
        Me.m_Id = id
        Me.m_LoopCount = loopCount
        Me.m_Thread = New Thread(AddressOf Me.Run)
    End Sub

    Public Sub Start()
        Me.m_Thread.Start()
    End Sub

    ' This is an instance method.
    ' Note that it can use the 'Me' reference pointer.
    Private Sub Run()
        Dim i As Integer
        For i = 0 To Me.m_LoopCount
            Console.WriteLine("Thread{0} {1}", Me.m_Id, i)
        Next
    End Sub

End Class
```

Now we have a class that can provide information to a thread so it can identify itself, and we can customize its behavior. As a result, we can create several different instances of *MyThreadClass*, all of which will behave according to the supplied initial conditions. We also have made it simple to create new threads, and we've built the requirements for encapsulation into the design itself. With this implementation, it is impossible to create an instance of *MyThreadClass* without supplying the required initial conditions. This allows us to avoid putting in error-handling code or default settings. Take a look at how much simpler the implementation code looks:

```
Module Module1

    Sub Main()
        Dim t1 As New MyThreadClass(1, 200)
        Dim t2 As New MyThreadClass(2, 300)

        t1.Start()
        t2.Start()
```

```
        ' Again, we wait for the threads to finish.
        Console.ReadLine()
    End Sub

End Module
```

Now you see how you can encapsulate threads to simplify implementation and provide better control over how information is passed to the threads. Also note that you can use this mechanism to return information that results from thread execution. This all leads into the discussion of how to control the execution of your threads.

Controlling Thread Execution

All threads have a life cycle. Each thread is created, executes, and dies at some point. Understanding how to manipulate threads through this cycle is essential. Each state has certain implications for the system and thread. Understanding how these states affect your thread and the application that it executes within can make the difference between success and disaster.

The *ThreadState* Property and the Life Cycle of a Thread

The *Thread* class provides an instance property called *ThreadState* that exposes the current state of a thread. The type of this property is the *ThreadState* enumeration, which is defined in the *System.Threading* namespace. Each state listed in the *ThreadState* enumeration corresponds to a specific point in a thread's life cycle. Table 3-1 describes these states.

Table 3-1
***ThreadState* Enumeration Values**

Member	Description
Aborted	The thread is in the *Stopped* state.
AbortRequested	The *Thread.Abort* method has been invoked on the thread, but the thread has not yet received the pending *System.Threading.ThreadAbortException* that will attempt to terminate it.
Running	The thread has been started. It is not blocked, and no *ThreadAbortException* is pending.
Stopped	The thread has stopped.
Suspended	The thread has been suspended.

Table 3-1
***ThreadState* Enumeration Values**

Member	Description
SuspendRequested	The thread is being asked to suspend.
Unstarted	The *Thread.Start* method has not been invoked on the thread.
WaitSleepJoin	The thread is blocked as a result of a call to *Wait*, *Sleep*, or *Join*.

To put this discussion in context, Figure 3-2 shows the thread states in action. You can see how the thread goes from its initial "unstarted" state through running, suspension, and eventual death (*Aborted* or *Stopped*).

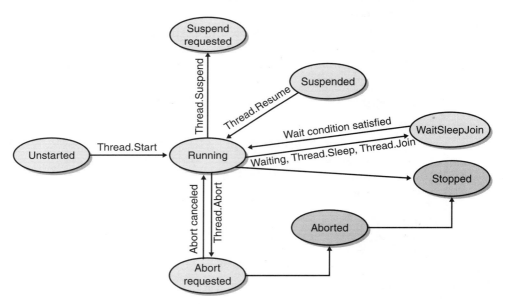

Figure 3-2   The life cycle of a managed thread.

Now let's delve a little deeper into what the individual states really mean and what implications they have for threads and for the system.

Unstarted

This is the initial state of all managed threads. When a thread is in the *Unstarted* state, it has never been run. At this point, the thread is not considered active. Although it consumes memory, which happens as soon as the thread object is constructed, it does not consume any additional processing resources until it is started. Once a thread has been started, it can never return to this state.

You can have a virtually indefinite number of thread objects in your application that are in the *Unstarted* state. In other words, the operating system places no limitation on the number of thread objects as long as the threads have not been started. The number of *Unstarted* threads is limited by the total amount of memory available. Each *Unstarted Thread* object consumes a small amount of memory, which merely contains the type information, the *Thread-Start* delegate for the thread's main method, and some other minor details.

Once you start the thread, things get more complicated. Your thread not only starts to consume processor time, but more memory is allocated to store the thread's state and other relevant information. Ultimately, there is a limit on the number of active threads available to a Windows system. The magic here number is 2000. If you attempt to start any additional active threads once you've reached this limit, you'll run into problems. Thankfully, this is a fairly rare problem because most well-designed applications don't create hundreds, let alone thousands, of active threads.

Note Don't confuse the limit on the number of active threads with a limitation on your ability to start threads. As long as the total active thread count stays below 2000, you can create and start as many new threads as you like. (There are reasons why you'll want to keep the number of active threads to a minimum, but we'll discuss them later in this chapter when we discuss thread pools.

Running

The *Running* state indicates that the thread is active and is executing its main routine. If a thread looks at its own *ThreadState*, it will almost always return *Running*. This should be fairly obvious: the thread has to execute the statement, so it must be running. In more rare cases, *ThreadState* might return *Abort-Requested*, which indicates that another thread has tried to abort the current thread. For the most part, though, a thread is rarely interested in its own state; it is more for the information of other threads.

If a thread evaluates another thread's state, it might return *Running*. On a single-processor machine, this result might seem counterintuitive. After all, only a single thread can be executing at any given time. But ultimately, *Running* does not mean "executing." A thread that is in the *Running* state might or might not be executing. What *Running* means, more that anything else, is that the thread is in an active state—it has been given execution time by the processor, but it might not be the currently executing thread.

Suspended

The *Suspended* state indicates that the thread has been started but is not currently active. This thread will not execute, under any circumstances, until it is told to resume by another thread.

WaitSleepJoin

The *WaitSleepJoin* state is a kind of catch-all thread state. It represents three distinct mechanisms but a single result. The thread is blocked, pending a specific event. The three possibilities are as follows:

■ The thread is waiting for one or more objects (*Wait*).

■ The thread is sleeping for a specific duration (*Sleep*).

■ The thread is waiting on another thread's completion (*Join*).

You can make a thread wait for one or more objects by using the synchronization constructs described in the section titled "Thread Synchronization" later in this chapter. To make a thread sleep for a specific duration or wait for another thread's completion, you can use the *Sleep* and *Join* methods of the *Thread* class. The bottom line is that a thread cannot cause another thread to enter this state. A thread can only enter this state at its own behest.

Stopped

A thread's *ThreadState* is the *ThreadState.Stopped* value when the method pointed to by the thread's *ThreadStart* delegate returns. From the thread's perspective, when that routine returns, everything it was created for has been completed. The *Stopped* state, like the *Aborted* state, indicates that the thread has finished executing. Once a thread is in the *Stopped* state, it can not be restarted. It is, for all intents and purposes, dead. The *Stopped* state indicates that the thread completed executing in a fairly mundane fashion—it was simply done.

Aborted

An aborted thread is a thread that has terminated in an abnormal fashion. The *Aborted* state, like the *Stopped* state, indicates that the thread has finished executing. Once a thread is in the *Aborted* state, it cannot be restarted. It is, for all intents and purposes, dead. If a thread is in the *Aborted* state, its method pointed to by the thread's *ThreadStart* delegate is exiting in an abnormal fashion. This is not necessarily a bad thing, but it does mean that the thread was terminated due to a cause other than simply returning at the end of a task. Once the thread has been completely terminated, the thread will be in the *Stopped* state.

Before we get into how to manipulate the threads using these states, we need a little information on how to access a thread reference.

Referencing the Current Thread

It is often necessary for a thread to obtain a reference to itself. Thanks to the .NET Framework, instead of having to pass around a reference to a thread variable, you can use a *Shared* property of the *Thread* class called *Thread.Current-Thread*:

```
Public Shared ReadOnly Property CurrentThread As Thread
```

This property always returns a reference to the current thread. This allows you to write generic methods that can always have access to the thread they're running on. As you read about the thread control methods in the following section, keep in mind that you can always gain access to and control over the current thread in any part of your code. Accessing different threads is another matter, but accessing the current thread for the sake of control is about as simple as it could be.

Thread Control Methods

Now that I've talked about the states of a thread and how any thread can get a reference to itself, we need to look at how to coax a thread through its life cycle. The methods provided by the *Thread* class give you complete control over the life cycle of threads. Table 3-2 provides an overview of these methods.

Table 3-2
Thread Control Methods

Type	Method	Description
Instance	*Start*	Causes a thread to start running.
Shared	*Sleep*	Pauses the calling thread for a specified time.
Instance	*Suspend*	Pauses a thread when it reaches a safe point.
Instance	*Abort*	Stops a thread when it reaches a safe point.
Instance	*Resume*	Restarts a suspended thread.
Instance	*Join*	Causes the calling code to wait for a thread to finish. If this method is used with a timeout value, it will return *True* if the thread finishes in the allotted time.
Instance	*Interrupt*	Interrupts a thread that is in the *WaitSleepJoin* state.
Shared	*SpinWait*	Causes a thread to wait the number of times defined by the *iterations* parameter. This is equivalent to inserting a simple counter loop in your code.

The purpose of some of these methods is almost painfully obvious, but the in-depth discussion that follows highlights how these methods can and should be used, which is not always so obvious. An excellent example is the concept of safe points. As described by Robert Burns on MSDN, safe points are places in code where it is safe for the common language runtime (CLR) to perform automatic garbage collection. When the *Abort* or *Suspend* methods of a thread are called, the CLR analyzes the thread's code and determines an appropriate location for the thread to stop running.

Thread.Start

```
Public Sub Start()
```

Before a thread can do anything, its *Start* method must be called by another thread. This will cause the thread's *ThreadState* to change to the *Running* state. Repeated calls to *Start* will cause a *ThreadStateException*. *Start* can be called only once per thread and is allowed only when the thread is in the *Unstarted* state.

A thread can never call its own *Start* method because calling *Start* on a thread that's not in the *Unstarted* state will cause a *ThreadStateException* to be thrown. By definition, a thread can reference itself only if it has already been started, so it should never call *Start* on itself (unless, of course, you like catching exceptions for the heck of it).

> **Note**   When you call the *Thread.Start* method, other exceptions might be thrown that have absolutely nothing to do with the current state of the thread. It is entirely possible in extreme conditions to run into an *OutOfMemoryException*. It is also possible for a *SecurityException* to occur if your current security context does not allow you to start the thread.

Thread.Sleep

```
Overloads Public Shared Sub Sleep(Integer)
Overloads Public Shared Sub Sleep(TimeSpan)
```

When a thread is in the *Running* state, it can call the *Sleep* method of the *Thread* class. The *Sleep* method has two distinct uses. First, you can use it to put your thread into the *WaitSleepJoin* state for a specified period of time. By specifying an amount of time in milliseconds or specifying a *TimeSpan*, you cause the operating system to put the thread on an inactive list. This is the most efficient way to introduce delays because it consumes the least amount of resources and the operating system will take care of resuming your thread when the specified time period has elapsed.

> **Warning**   Even though you specify an exact time period of inactivity, the operating system does not guarantee that it will resume your thread immediately once the period has elapsed. Neither Windows 2000 nor the older Windows-based operating systems are real-time operating systems. So it is better to think of this as the operating system promising you that it will resume your thread as soon as possible after the specified time has elapsed. Ultimately, whether a thread resumes in 100 milliseconds or115 milliseconds will not adversely affect most applications. The longer the duration specified in the *Sleep* call, the less important a few milliseconds of delay will generally be. You're more likely to run into problems if you have very tight timing constraints, but this situation is not very common.

The second use of the *Sleep* method is to surrender the thread's execution time without actually having it go into the *WaitSleepJoin* state. By specifying 0 milliseconds or *TimeSpan.Zero*, you tell the underlying operating system that you want to give other threads a chance at the processor. There are advantages to doing this, especially for long-running or processor-intensive tasks. The following example demonstrates both uses of *Thread.Sleep*:

```
' Surrenders execution of the thread.
' Does not cause the current thread to go into the WaitSleepJoin state.
Thread.Sleep(0)
Thread.Sleep(TimeSpan.Zero)

' Surrenders execution of the thread.
' Causes the current thread to go into the WaitSleepJoin state.
Thread.Sleep(100)
Thread.Sleep(New TimeSpan(0, 0, 0, 0, 100))
```

Caution   The *Sleep* method is different from all of the other thread control methods because both overloads are *Shared*. As a result, when a thread calls *Thread.Sleep*, it will affect only the current thread. This can cause some confusion from a code standpoint when a thread attempts to call the *Sleep* method on an instance of another thread object. The code will compile and it will look like you're invoking an instance method on the thread object, but you'll still be invoking the static *Sleep* method and you'll affect only the current thread instance, not the referenced thread instance.

Thread.SpinWait

```
Public Shared Sub SpinWait(ByVal iterations As Integer)
```

SpinWait is almost the polar opposite of the *Sleep* method. It delays the execution of your thread for a specific number of iterations, but it does so by *spinning*. In other words, your thread remains executing rather than marking the thread inactive for a specific period of time. It's the same as creating your own loop that runs continuously until the counter runs out.

This does not mean that your thread will not surrender its execution time on the processor. The operating system will continue to switch between threads, but your thread will spend *x* amount of its execution time spinning and doing nothing productive.

Thread.Suspend

```
Public Sub Suspend()
```

You can call *Suspend* on a thread that's in the *Running* state. This will force the thread into the *Suspended* state. You can call *Suspend* on a thread even if that thread is already in the *Suspended* state. The CLR will not cause an exception. It will figure that you're getting what you want anyway, so why bother you? Calling *Suspend* when the thread is in any other state than *Running* or *Suspended* will cause a *ThreadStateException* to be generated.

If you're calling *Suspend* on another thread, the CLR will attempt to suspend that thread in an appropriate place. This can lead to unexpected behavior because the CLR decides where to suspend the thread and it might not happen where you expect.

If you call *Suspend* on the current thread, the CLR will immediately put your thread into the *Suspended* state. This actually provides an argument in favor of calling *Suspend* only on the owner thread and not on other thread instances. By doing this, you can ensure that a thread will always suspend at a predictable location instead of potentially anywhere in its code.

Thread.Resume

```
Public Sub Resume()
```

When a thread is in the *Suspended* state, another thread can call its *Resume* method. This will cause the thread to move from the *Suspended* state to the *Running* state. If a thread is in the *Suspended* state, it can be resumed only by another, active thread. If no other thread has a reference to the suspended thread, the thread can never be reactivated.

Thread.Abort

```
Overloads Public Sub Abort()
Overloads Public Sub Abort(Object)
```

The *Abort* method has some interesting behaviors. First, calling *Abort* causes a *ThreadAbortException* to be generated on the destination thread. It is up to that thread to handle the consequences of that exception, especially clean-up. To handle the *ThreadAbortException*, you should include exception-handling code in your thread's main *Run* method. This should also highlight the importance of appropriate exception handling, or at least the use of the *Try...Finally* syntax to ensure that file handles and database connections are cleaned up reliably. To that end, your thread's *Run* method might look like this example:

```
Private Sub Run
    Try
        ' Do your stuff here
    Catch ex As ThreadAbortException
```

```
        ' Deal with the exception
    Finally
        ' Clean up your resources here
    End Try
End Sub
```

Warning   An issue can arise when you call the *Abort* method on another thread. As I mentioned, *Abort* causes a *ThreadAbortException* to be generated on the thread. The problem is that it is impossible to guarantee the state of the thread at the time *Abort* is called. Say, for instance, that *Abort* has already been called by another thread. The target thread might be in a catch clause, dealing with the exception. The new *Abort* will cause the catch clause to terminate prematurely, possibly leaving resources unrelinquished. Even though the CLR will attempt to make an intelligent choice about where the *Abort* should occur, some things are beyond its control. Bottom line: try to call *Abort* from within the thread you want to abort. Avoid calling *Abort* directly on another thread. If you need to abort the thread, try one of the signaling mechanisms detailed in "Thread Synchronization" later in this chapter.

Thread.Join

```
Overloads Public Sub Join()
Overloads Public Function Join(Integer) As Boolean
Overloads Public Function Join(TimeSpan) As Boolean
```

Join is the simplest synchronization construct available to developers. When you call the *Join* method on a thread, the calling thread will enter the *WaitSleepJoin* state and will stay there until the called thread has completed (is in the *Stopped* or *Aborted* state). This allows threads to block execution pending the completion of other threads in the system. The following example shows how this might be used:

```
Sub Main()
    Dim t1 As New Thread(AddressOf Thread1Method)
    Dim t2 As New Thread(AddressOf Thread2Method)

    ' Start both threads
    t1.Start()
    t2.Start()

    ' Wait for both threads to complete
```

```
t1.Join()
t2.Join()

' You are guaranteed at this point that both threads have completed
End Sub
```

If a thread has already completed, calling *Join* will have no effect and your application will proceed as normal.

Thread.Interrupt

You can call the *Interrupt* method on another thread to cause it to exit the *Wait-SleepJoin* state. If you call this method while the thread is running, the next time the referenced thread enters the *WaitSleepJoin* state it will be immediately set back to *Running*. I don't recommend this as a common practice—it is appropriate only in the rarest of cases.

Tying It All Together

Now you've seen how to manage a thread through its life cycle. We should spend a little time talking about thread execution and how to tailor your threads to make them run more efficiently and play well with others. Consider the following method:

```
Public Done As Boolean = False

Public Sub MyLongRunningMethod()
    While Not Done
    End While

    Console.WriteLine("Done")
End Sub
```

This is an example of a completely horrendous programming practice. This code will cause the thread to loop interminably while checking a variable that might take minutes, seconds, or even hours to change. This will impose a heavy processing load on a system without achieving anything. Obviously, there should be a better way, and there is. You can use the *Thread.Sleep* method to tell the system to put your thread out of the active thread list until a certain time period has elapsed. Alternatively, you can use the *Thread.Sleep* method to give other threads a chance to execute (still keeping your thread active, of course). This lends itself to two scenarios. The first, like our example above, allows you to use processing resources more efficiently by telling the system how long you can wait before you need to continue. We can recast our previous example as follows:

```
Public Sub MyLongRunningMethod()
   While Not Done
      Thread.Sleep(100) 'Sleep for ~100 milliseconds
   End While

   Console.WriteLine("Done")
End Sub
```

Instead of running this thread continuously and constantly consuming processing resources, we can efficiently poll the status of the done variable 10 times a second.

Now that you know how to manage threads by encapsulating them in classes, let's look at how to make threads work together. What if they need access to a shared resource? What if there are dependencies? How can this all be managed? This is where thread synchronization comes into play.

Thread Synchronization

Synchronization is all about communication and coordination between threads. Throughout the .NET Framework documentation, you'll see references to whether a method is *thread-safe*. For example, if you look at the documentation for the *CollectionBase* class under *System.Collection*s, you'll see a dedicated subsection that discusses thread safety. This essentially tells you whether you have to access that class in a thread-safe manner or whether thread safety is handled for you by the class. This is where synchronization constructs come into play. They allow interthread communication and coordination that can ensure thread-safe access to shared resources. Note that all of the constructs described in this section are required to be programmatically correct. These constructs provide a number of signaling or blocking constructs that enable you to develop code that is thread-safe.

Threads run within the same application domain as their creator, and as such they can share resources. This can present problems if threads have conflicting needs in terms of shared resources. Before we go any further into this topic, let's spend some time discussing how threads and context are related and how this affects synchronization issues.

Race Conditions and You

Predictability is important. You need to be able to control when and where an event happens on a thread. If a critical variable changes at an unexpected time, your application can fail, maybe spectacularly. We typically refer to this as a *race condition*—when timing of events can affect the correctness of your logic.

It is important to avoid race conditions, especially when data integrity or system uptime is critical.

More formally, a race condition is a situation in which multiple threads of execution update or modify shared system resources (objects or variables) in an unsynchronized fashion, leading to unexpected and or undesirable application states. This can manifest itself in different ways. But the core problem can usually be traced to poor assumptions. When multiple threads are involved, timing is simply not guaranteed. In other words, just because two events happen in sequential order in your testing doesn't mean that those events will always happen in that order—unless you've implemented an appropriate synchronization construct to provide a guarantee. Guaranteeing synchronization behavior is most crucial when shared resources (files, network connections, variables, arrays, and so forth) are involved. By implementing synchronization in your code, you can ensure that your code executes in a deterministic fashion.

Synchronization Constructs

As I mentioned, the synchronization classes provide signaling mechanisms that allow you to develop thread-safe code and implement a level of determinism. Table 3-3 describes these classes.

Table 3-3
***System.Threading* Synchronization Classes**

Class	Description
AutoResetEvent	Notifies one or more waiting threads that an event has occurred. This class cannot be inherited.
Interlocked	Provides atomic operations for variables that are shared by multiple threads.
ManualResetEvent	Occurs when one or more waiting threads are notified that an event has occurred. This class cannot be inherited.
Monitor	Provides a mechanism that synchronizes access to objects.
Mutex	A synchronization primitive than can also be used for inter-process synchronization.
ReaderWriterLock	Defines the lock that implements single-writer and multiple-reader semantics.
WaitHandle	Encapsulates operating system–specific objects that wait for exclusive access to shared resources.

The *WaitHandle* Class

The *WaitHandle* class is an abstract type that is used as the base class for the *Mutex*, *AutoResetEvent*, and *ManualResetEvent* classes. To understand how these inherited classes work, it is important to understand what *wait handles* are and how they work.

> **Note** Because the *WaitHandle* class is an abstract class (*MustInherit*), only derived instances of this class can exist. If you need to create your own type of *WaitHandle*, you can inherit from the *WaitHandle* class and provide your own implementation.

A wait handle is a standard threading concept and has to do with resource ownership. A wait handle has two possible states: signaled and nonsignaled. The whole basis of this event signaling relies on a request architecture. Threads can call methods on the *WaitHandle* object and can be blocked until the *WaitHandle* is in a signaled state. *WaitHandle* is an abstract class that provides a standard interface for dealing with all types of wait handles, including the *Mutex*, *AutoResetEvent*, and *ManualResetEvent* classes.

WaitOne The *WaitOne* method of the *WaitHandle* class has three overloads that result in different behaviors. The first overload blocks the current thread until the *WaitHandle* is signaled:

```
Overloads Overridable Public Function WaitOne() As Boolean
```

This will cause the thread to wait indefinitely. If the signal never comes, the thread will never proceed (unless another thread calls this thread's *Interrupt* method).

The other two overloads of *WaitOne* allow you to specify a timeout interval:

```
Overloads Overridable Public Function WaitOne(Integer, Boolean) As Boolean
Overloads Overridable Public Function WaitOne(TimeSpan, Boolean) As Boolean
```

If the *WaitHandle* is signaled within the specified time period, the function will return *True*. Otherwise, the function will return *False*. Threads can use *WaitHandles* to check for specific events on a periodic basis. A timeout of 0 can be specified to check the status of the *WaitHandle* and immediately return with the signaled status of the *WaitHandle*.

WaitAny   The *WaitAny* method of the *WaitHandle* class is a shared method. Unlike the *WaitOne* method, which waits for a single wait handle, *WaitAny* allows a thread to check multiple wait handles. You provide the method with an array of wait handles that the thread is interested in. As its name might suggest, *WaitAny* waits for at least one of the wait handles in the array to be signaled before returning. You have options similar to those provided by the *WaitOne* method. You can wait for a signal, or you can specify a timeout period.

```
Overloads Public Shared Function WaitAny(WaitHandle()) As Integer
Overloads Public Shared Function WaitAny(WaitHandle(), _
                                    Integer, Boolean) As Integer
Overloads Public Shared Function WaitAny(WaitHandle(), _
                                    TimeSpan, Boolean) As Integer
```

WaitAll   *WaitAll*, which is also a shared method of the *WaitHandle* class, takes an array of wait handles. This method differs from *WaitAny* in that it requires all of the passed wait handles to be signaled before it returns.

```
Overloads Public Shared Function WaitAll(WaitHandle()) As Boolean
Overloads Public Shared Function WaitAll(WaitHandle(), _
                                    Integer, Boolean) As Boolean
Overloads Public Shared Function WaitAll(WaitHandle(),
                                    TimeSpan, Boolean) As Boolean
```

As you might have figured out, it is possible to duplicate the behavior of a call to *WaitOne* using *WaitAny* or *WaitAll*. You simply pass a single *WaitHandle* to the method:

```
Sub Wait(handle As WaitHandle)
    ' These three statements are functionally equivalent
    handle.WaitOne()
    WaitHandle.WaitAny(New WaitHandle(){ handle })
    WaitHandle.WaitAll(New WaitHandle(){ handle })
End Sub
```

The *AutoResetEvent* and *ManualResetEvent* Classes

The *AutoResetEvent* and *ManualResetEvent* classes are related—literally. They both derive from the *WaitHandle* class and share a common purpose: to signal the state of one thread to another. These signals are referred to as events, even though they're really just wait handles. These event classes have a signaled state that you can either set or clear (using the *Set* or *Reset* methods). The state is either set (*True*) or not set (*False*). Ultimately the *AutoResetEvent* and *ManualResetEvent* classes differ only in how they behave after a thread has been signaled.

The *AutoResetEvent* class resets the event automatically after a single waiting thread has been signaled. This means that if you have two threads waiting on the same *AutoResetEvent* instance, only one will receive the signal.

The *ManualResetEvent*, as its name suggests, requires manual intervention to reset the signal state. When the signal state is set, all calls to *WaitOne* will always return *True* until some thread resets the signal to *False*. This can be useful if you need to communicate an event to multiple threads at once.

The following sample application, WaitHandleTest, demonstrates how the behaviors of the *AutoResetEvent* and *ManualResetEvent* differ. Note that it is necessary to repeatedly signal the *AutoResetEvent* to make sure that both threads complete; the *ManualResetEvent*, in contrast, requires only a single call to *Set*.

```
Imports System.Threading

Module Module1
    Public Handle As WaitHandle

    Sub Main()
        Dim t1 As Thread
        Dim t2 As Thread

        Console.WriteLine("Starting AutoResetEvent test")
        Handle = New AutoResetEvent(False)
        t1 = New Thread(AddressOf Run1)
        t2 = New Thread(AddressOf Run2)

        t1.Start()
        t2.Start()

        Thread.Sleep(1000)
        Console.WriteLine("Setting the handle")
        CType(Handle, AutoResetEvent).Set()

        Thread.Sleep(1000)
        Console.WriteLine("Setting the handle")
        CType(Handle, AutoResetEvent).Set()

        Console.WriteLine("Starting ManualResetEvent test")
        Handle = New ManualResetEvent(False)
        t1 = New Thread(AddressOf Run1)
        t2 = New Thread(AddressOf Run2)

        t1.Start()
        t2.Start()

        Thread.Sleep(1000)
```

```
        Console.WriteLine("Setting the handle")
        CType(Handle, ManualResetEvent).Set()

        ' Tell the user this is done and give them a chance to read this
        Console.WriteLine("Test complete!!")
        Console.ReadLine()
    End Sub

    Public Sub Run1()
        Console.WriteLine("Starting Run1")
        Handle.WaitOne()
        Console.WriteLine("Run1 Done")
    End Sub

    Public Sub Run2()
        Console.WriteLine("Starting Run2")
        Handle.WaitOne()
        Console.WriteLine("Run2 Done")
    End Sub
End Module
```

Figure 3-3 shows the output from this example.

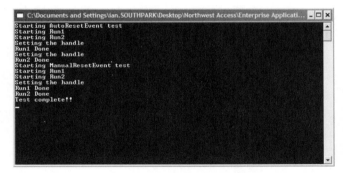

Figure 3-3   The output from the WaitHandleTest sample application.

Note   Note that I did not use a *Join* construct with the child threads to prevent the *Main* method from exiting before the threads have completed. If the *Console.ReadLine* statement were missing from the end of the *Main* method, it's conceivable that the application would summarily exit before either child thread was signaled. In that case, the CLR would destroy the threads and clean up after the *Main* method. If you were to call the *Join* method on both *t1* and *t2*, you would be assured that this example could not exit before the child threads completed their tasks.

The *Mutex* Class

Mutex is another *WaitHandle*-derived class. You use it to coordinate access to a resource that requires exclusive access. In fact, the word *mutex* comes from the term *mutually exclusive*. Unlike other constructs that are geared toward more complex read/write access permissions (the *ReaderWriterLock* class is a good example), the *Mutex* class provides a single thread with exclusive access to a resource or group of resources. The following example uses the *Mutex* class to provide exclusive access to a *Stack* collection:

```
Imports System.Threading

Public Class MutexedStack

    Private m_Mutex As Mutex
    Private m_Stack As Stack

    Public Sub New()
       Me.m_Mutex = New Mutex()
       Me.m_Stack = New Stack()
    End Sub

    Public Sub Add( obj As Object )
       Me.m_Mutex.WaitOne()
       Me.m_Stack.Push(obj)
       Me.m_Mutex.ReleaseMutex()
    End Sub

    Public Function GetItem() As Object
       Me.m_Mutex.WaitOne()
       GetItem = Me.m_Stack.Pop()
       Me.m_Mutex.ReleaseMutex()
    End Sub

End Class
```

When and where you want to use a mutex is up to you. The need for mutually exclusive access is highly dependent on your architecture and the needs of your application. Remember one important point: a mutex cannot enforce access to an object if you do not use the *WaitOne...ReleaseMutex* syntax. If you miss a possible scenario or provide direct access to the underlying object that you want to enforce the access restrictions on, you risk having the object (a *Stack* in the previous example) modified at an improper time.

The *Interlocked* Class

The *Interlocked* class allows you to protect against errors that can occur if the thread scheduler switches contexts while your thread is updating a variable that can be accessed by other threads. Obviously, when you're updating shared variables, it is vitally important that your thread not be interrupted. The *Interlocked* class provides support for what are known as *atomic operations*. There are also performance advantages to using the methods provided by the *Interlocked* class. The operations supported by the *Interlocked* class can often be executed in a single processor instruction, leading to more efficient program execution.

Increment and Decrement   The *Increment* and *Decrement* methods can be used to increment and decrement operations on a variable in a single, atomic operation. Normally, when you increment or decrement a variable, the operation takes three steps. The value is retrieved, the addition or subtraction is performed, and the result is stored in the original variable. The problem is that during any of these operations, your thread might be preempted by the operating system, which can lead to some strange behaviors—if, for example, the same variable is subsequently modified by another thread. The *Increment* and *Decrement* methods protect against this type of error by preventing the operating system from preempting the operations. Consider the following example:

```
Dim x as Integer = 0

' Here is how you would normally increment and decrement x
x = x + 1 ' Increment - This operation can be preempted
x = x - 1 ' Decrement - This operation can be preempted

' These operations are functionally equivalent, but can not be
' preempted by the operating system.
Interlocked.Increment( x )
Interlocked.Decrement( x )
```

What we can see here is that the *Interlocked* class provides a very simple thread-safe mechanism for incrementing variables. But wait…there's more.

Exchange and CompareExchange   Like the *Increment* and *Decrement* methods, the *Exchange* and *CompareExchange* methods of the *Interlocked* class provide support for additional atomic operations on variables. *Exchange* atomically exchanges the values of the specified variables. *CompareExchange* combines two operations: comparing two values and storing a third value in one of the variables based on the outcome of the comparison. The following example demonstrates the use of both methods:

```
Dim oldx, x, y As Integer
x = 5
y = 10
```

```
' Performing an exchange without the Interlocked class
oldx = x
x = y

' Performing an exchange with the Interlocked class
oldx = Interlocked.Exchange( x, y )

'Performing a compare and exchange without the Interlocked class
oldx = x
If x = 10 Then
   x = y
End If

' Performing a compare and exchange with the Interlocked class
oldx = Interlocked.CompareExchange( x, y, 10 )
```

This last example wraps up the *Interlocked* class. Hopefully you can see how useful this class is. I whole heartedly recommend its use in your code. In situation where you need to perform critical operations in an atomic manner, the *Interlocked* class can be a savior.

The *Monitor* Class and *SyncLock*

A *critical section* is a block of code that cannot be executed simultaneously by multiple threads. Imagine you're sharing an object—an *ArrayList*, for example—between multiple threads. Certain operations on an *ArrayList* require exclusive access. For example, if you're sorting the array, you'll want to prevent other threads from accessing the object until the sort is complete.

The *Monitor* class controls access to a block of code by locking an object for a single thread. This prevents other threads from accessing that object in the same block of code (a critical section) while the lock is in place. An interesting side effect is that the *Monitor* class prevents simultaneous entry to a block of code as long as the same object is involved. However, if another object is involved, the *Monitor* class will allow the same block of code to be entered simultaneously. This prevents performing the same operations on one object but allows the same set of operations to execute when multiple objects are involved.

Note   The behavior of the *Monitor* class is quite separate from that of the *Mutex* class. The *Monitor* class enforces mutually exclusive access to a block of code as long as the same object is involved. Otherwise, it will allow unlimited access to a block of code. The *Mutex* class, on the other hand, enforces strict exclusivity for a block of code and is not conditional.

Visual Basic .NET provides simple access to the *Monitor* class by encapsulating it with the *SyncLock* syntax. *SyncLock* is a block-level statement that prevents multiple threads from entering that block simultaneously. Imagine a situation in which you need to perform some operation, such as resizing an array, that will probably fail if two threads try to perform that operation at the same time. By using *SyncLock*, you can prevent the second thread from entering the block of code surrounded by the *SyncLock* statement until the first thread finishes. This vastly simplifies your code and makes it very simple to implement critical sections. The following code illustrates how you can use both the *SyncLock* syntax and the *Monitor* class to achieve the same result:

```
Public MyArrayList As ArrayList

Public Sub Add(obj As Object)
    ' This is a critical section using SyncLock
    SyncLock MyArrayList
      MyArrayList.Add(obj)
    End SyncLock
End Sub
Public Sub Add1(obj As Object)
    ' This is a critical section using Monitor
    Monitor.Enter(MyArrayList)
      MyArrayList.Add(obj)
    Monitor.Exit(MyArrayList)
End Sub
```

The *Monitor* class provides additional flexibility above and beyond that of the *SyncLock* syntax. It allows you to better control the locking behavior, for instance. Imagine a situation in which you want to avoid waiting beyond a certain point in time to enter a critical section. If you use a *SyncBlock*, your code will wait until that lock succeeds. You might decide that you'd rather attempt to enter the critical section and do something else if the lock cannot be obtained in a reasonable amount of time. This level of control is possible through the direct use of the *Monitor* class (but I'll leave it as an exercise for the reader).

The *ReaderWriterLock* Class

Some resources can be shared on a nonexclusive basis under certain circumstances. A resource might require exclusive access only if a thread intends to modify it, and unlimited threads can otherwise have access to view the contents. In this case, the *ReaderWriterLock* can enforce exclusive access to a resource when that resource is being modified. When the resource is being accessed in a read-only manner, the *ReaderWriterLock* allows nonexclusive access.

```
Imports System.Threading

Public Class Counter
    Private m_rwLock As ReaderWriterLock
    Private m_Counter As Integer = 0

    Public Sub New()
        Me.m_rwLock = New ReaderWriterLock()
    End Sub

    Public Sub Increment()
        Me.m_rwLock.AcquireWriterLock(-1)
        Me.m_Counter += 1
        Me.m_rwLock.ReleaseWriterLock()
    End Sub

    Public Sub Decrement()
        Me.m_rwLock.AcquireWriterLock(-1)
        Me.m_Counter -= 1
        Me.m_rwLock.ReleaseWriterLock()
    End Sub

    Public ReadOnly Property Count() As Integer
        Get
            Me.m_rwLock.AcquireReaderLock(-1)
            Count = Me.m_Counter
            Me.m_rwLock.ReleaseReaderLock()
        End Get
    End Property

End Class
```

Thread Pooling

Each thread you create imposes additional system overhead, so you face the inevitable tradeoff between execution efficiency and consumption of system resources. Think of the demands on a Web server. You have very predictable incoming network requests asking for files. You could create a thread to handle each incoming request to make the server perform more efficiently. This would work fine for the first 10 to 100 requests, but then your system would start to bog down because it would have to spend more and more time just switching between threads. Besides, it's not really necessary to create a thread for every incoming request. What you should do instead is create a pool of worker threads that you can reuse to execute incoming requests. You can then queue the incoming requests and dispatch those requests to a thread as soon as one is available. This approach offers a number of benefits:

- You keep new thread creation to a minimum.

- A queued item requires far fewer system resources than a waiting thread.

- You can tune the number of threads you want to create.

- You minimize the resources required by limiting the number of created threads.

You have two thread-pooling options. First, you can implement your own form of thread pooling. This requires you to implement all of the management and retirement functionality. If you need a highly specialized pooling mechanism, this is the way to go, but it's a rare case. Most developers should use the second option.

The second option is to take advantage of the *ThreadPool* class in the .NET Framework. This is usually the best option unless you have specific requirements that are not fulfilled by the implementation of the *ThreadPool* class. Otherwise, the *ThreadPool* class can handle all of the thread management for you.

Caution   You should use the *ThreadPool* class only if you have a large number of discrete tasks that need to be divided up. Do not use it for any persistent, or long running, operations or for threads where there is no expectation of their lifetime. If you need to create a thread that sticks around for monitoring or for serving requests, create your own thread. The *ThreadPool* class is best used when you have a large number of tasks than can be divided up and queued. Longer-running tasks should use more conventional thread management.

The *ThreadPool* Class

Using the *ThreadPool* class is fairly straightforward. The general idea is that you need to queue work items in the pool. A work item is an object that contains the information about the work that needs to be done and a method address that can satisfy that request. The method you provide to the *ThreadPool* must conform to the signature of a *WaitCallback* delegate, which looks like this:

```
Public Delegate Sub WaitCallback(ByVal state As Object)
```

The *state* parameter is for passing information to the thread method that it needs to do its job. The following example shows a simple use of this feature by using an *AutoResetEvent* to synchronize the program's termination with the worker thread's completion:

```
Imports System.Threading

Module Module1
    Sub Main()
        ' We use this to signal the thread completion
        Dim threadDone As New AutoResetEvent(False)

        ' Add the thread method to the queue
        ThreadPool.QueueUserWorkItem(AddressOf Run, threadDone)

        ' Wait for the thread to complete
        threadDone.WaitOne()

        Console.WriteLine("The thread has completed")
    End Sub

    Sub Run(ByVal state As Object)
        Console.Write("Starting the thread...")
        Dim evt As AutoResetEvent = CType(state, AutoResetEvent)

        Thread.Sleep(1000)

        evt.Set()
        Console.WriteLine("done.")
    End Sub

End Module
```

Ultimately, how you use the *ThreadPool* is up to you. It allows you to pass an object to your thread method, so you can pass it any data type you want, including your own custom classes. You can create a class that provides all of the information that your thread method needs to do its work. In the case of the Web server example, you can pass in the requested file path and the network port that the client is connected to.

Conclusion

The ability to create multiple threads in an application is an incredibly powerful tool, but it can add a degree of complexity that makes debugging difficult because of transient conditions. The best way to avoid problems is to sit down and work out how your threads will be used within the application. Identify all of the shared resources and be sure to implement appropriate synchronization mechanisms. Also, design your thread implementation to limit its use to your intended purpose. This offers two benefits. First, your thread will not be used in an unintended way (or will be more difficult to use in an unintended way). Second, if you need to alter the behavior of a thread, this will usually necessitate a design change, which will give the original developer an opportunity to evaluate any potential issues and resolve them.

In this chapter, you learned how to implement threads, communicate between them, share resources, and manage large numbers of threads. Hopefully, you also gained a better appreciation for how threads can and should be used within your applications.

4

Playing Nice with Others: Native Code and COM Interoperability

All Microsoft Visual Basic .NET applications run within the common language runtime (CLR). This should not be news to anyone. The CLR provides what's called a managed runtime environment, which offers a set of services, including garbage collection, to applications that run within that environment. In essence, the CLR is a kind of sandbox—it isolates Visual Basic .NET applications from native (unmanaged) applications that are running on the same computer system. It's been said that no man is an island. That's also true for a runtime environment such as the CLR—it cannot exist on its own. Applications that run in this environment must be able to communicate with the outside world. (They'd be pretty useless otherwise.)

Likewise, enterprise application development often has more to do with playing nice with a company's existing roster of applications, services, and libraries than with creating lots of new, cool code. Backward compatibility and system integration are both the bane and the lifeblood of the enterprise developer. Given this situation, the ability to communicate with legacy systems and components is critically importance. The irony is that these "legacy" components might very well be products under active development. After all, COM sure isn't going away anytime soon.

On the Microsoft Windows platform, two major buckets of native code can be accessed outside of the runtime: native methods and COM objects (as shown in Figure 4-1). Native methods are functions that are contained in native dynamic-link libraries (the entire Win32 API falls into this category). To solve the problem of communicating with native methods, the CLR provides the platform invoke (PInvoke) service. This service lets you define and invoke native methods in a very natural way and gives you the flexibility to work around the functional limitations of the Microsoft .NET Framework. (Yes, there are limitations.)

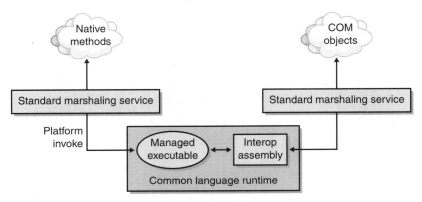

Figure 4-1   The CLR and the unmanaged world.

With COM objects and type libraries, on the other hand, the challenge is to provide a rich type equivalent that you can use in your managed applications and also deal with all of the marshaling and threading complexities in a relatively transparent fashion. After all, COM objects are classes, with methods, properties, interfaces and a whole bunch of other stuff. It's important to be able to treat these objects, for the most part, as managed classes. It's also important to maintain the ease of use of COM objects that classic Microsoft Visual Basic developers are accustomed to.

COM interoperability (COM interop), unlike PInvoke, supports bidirectional communication. In general, COM interop can be considered a bidirectional service that provides a bridge between the .NET Framework and COM. It allows .NET clients to call COM components and COM clients to call .NET Framework components. COM interop is designed to maintain consistency between COM and .NET. It hides the inconsistencies between the two runtime models and makes the differences transparent to both clients and servers (managed or unmanaged).

Note   At the lowest level, PInvoke and COM interop both use the same marshaling service, but the COM interop layer provides a lot of additional functionality.

In this chapter, we'll cover both PInvoke and COM interop. The discussion of PInvoke will cover the basics as well as how to handle more complex data type marshaling situations. The discussion of COM interop will deal with issues related to accessing COM objects from within Visual Basic .NET as well as how to expose managed component through a COM-accessible interface.

Note   To play along with some of the COM interop material, you should probably have Visual Basic 6.0 installed. Creating samples in Visual Basic 6.0 is handy, and Visual Basic 6.0 is also a useful test tool for Visual Basic .NET components that you want to expose to COM clients.

The PInvoke Service

PInvoke allows you to call native, or unmanaged, functions that are implemented in dynamic-link libraries (DLLs). To call a native method, you must first define a prototype in your application, providing the necessary information so the CLR can resolve the function reference. PInvoke can do a lot of the work for you, including marshaling most types and capturing Win32 errors. You can use PInvoke to call Win32 API functions (not a huge surprise)—this is, after all, what the .NET Framework classes do extensively. The other common use of PInvoke is for registering managed callback functions.

Warning   Security issues can arise when you call native methods. The CLR and the .NET Framework largely prevent the infamous buffer overrun security vulnerabilities, but you can easily introduce such problems with improper use of native methods. Also, your application must run in a trusted security environment—otherwise, it will fail.

Calling Native Methods

Visual Basic .NET provides two ways to access native platform methods: the *Declare* statement and the *DllImport* attribute. Most of the samples in this chapter will use the *Declare* statement, but it's important to understand when it might be preferable to use the *DllImport* attribute. To illustrate both of these options, we'll use the *GetUserName* function from the Advapi32 library as an example. This function retrieves the username for the user account the application is running under. The following function definition is from the MSDN documentation that accompanies Visual Studio .NET:

```
BOOL GetUserName(
  LPTSTR lpBuffer,   // name buffer
  LPDWORD nSize      // size of name buffer
);
```

Note   For now, we'll ignore marshaling issues and focus on the syntax of *Declare* and *DllImport*. The code for this example can be found in the GetUserName sample that accompanies this chapter.

Now that we have a function to import, let's do just that—starting with the *Declare* statement.

The *Declare* Statement

The *Declare* statement is the recommended mechanism for importing native methods in Visual Basic .NET. The syntax should be familiar to seasoned Visual Basic developers. For others, the syntax will be mostly easy to understand. The following is the general form of the *Declare* statement syntax:

```
[ Public | Private | Protected | Friend | Protected Friend ] [ Shadows ] _
Declare [ Ansi | Unicode | Auto ] [ Sub | Function ] name Lib "libname" _
[ Alias "aliasname" ] [([ arglist ])] [ As type ]
```

The information you must provide to the *Declare* statement is fairly straightforward: the function name, the library the function comes from, any arguments, and, if necessary, a return type. If the function has a *VOID* return type, you can declare the method as a *Sub*. A method with a specific return type should be declared as a *Function*. The *Declare* statement can be used in two contexts: in a module or a class.

> **Note**   You cannot explicitly define a *Declare* method as *Shared* because all methods that are defined using *Declare* are implicitly *Shared*—they can never be class instance member functions.

You can also provide optional information. The access-level modifiers (*Public*, *Private*, and so forth) should be familiar to you. There are also the string encoding options (*Ansi*, *Unicode*, and *Auto*) and the *Alias* option. Before I discuss these, let's look at how to define the *GetUserName* function:

```
Declare Unicode Function GetUserNameW Lib "advapi32.dll" _
                        (ByVal buffer As StringBuilder, _
                        ByRef size As Integer) As Boolean
```

This is what the *Declare* statement for the aforementioned *GetUserName* function ends up looking like. There's a bit of parameter wizardry going on here. We're using the Unicode version of *GetUserName* and passing a *String-Builder* object—but you can ignore these details for now. The example does, however, illustrate how the *Declare* statement works.

I defined the *GetUserNameW* method as a *Function* because the original function returns a nonvoid: *Boolean*. Otherwise, I would have declared the method as a *Sub*. Because I did not use the *Alias* option, in this example the function name must match the name of the native function. (More on this later.) The only exception to maintaining exact naming is with functions that support platform-specific strings. Most functions in the Win32 API that support strings have two versions: ANSI and Unicode. Typically, if a function definition supports both ANSI and Unicode, the specific native function name will be appended with an *A* (ANSI) or a *W* (Unicode). This segues nicely into the next part of our discussion of the *Declare* syntax: the string encoding options.

> **Note**   The MSDN Platform SDK documentation does not typically list the actual implementation names for specific functions. (See the *GetUserName* function.) Instead, a note in the requirements section indicates that a function is implemented as Unicode and/or ANSI versions.

String-encoding options   Three types of API functions are common throughout the Win32 library: ANSI, Unicode, and platform-dependent. When you need to deal with strings, the difference between an ANSI function and its Unicode equivalent (if one exists) is extremely important. Granted, many functions don't take strings or characters as arguments or return values. I consider these functions to be string-encoding-indifferent, so you can omit the string encoding options for those functions. (This will default the string encoding to *Ansi*—just an interesting technical detail.) For all of the other functions, the string encoding options are extremely important. Here's a quick overview of the options:

- ■ *Ansi*   Converts all strings to ANSI values. If no modifier is specified, *Ansi* is the default. This means that for ANSI functions you can omit this option. If the function deals with strings, you should include it anyway because it makes the declaration easier to read.

- ■ *Unicode*   Converts all strings to Unicode values. If you're calling a Win32 function whose name terminates with a *W*, you must use this option. The *W* suffix indicates a Unicode method.

- ■ *Auto*   Converts the strings according to CLR rules based on the name of the method (or the alias name, if specified) and the targeted platform. This option is very important if your application might run on different platforms. For example, Windows NT, 2000, and XP are all Unicode platforms, but Windows 98 is ANSI by default. If you need to be able to run in both environments, the *Auto* option will give you the flexibility you need. If you specify this option, you do not need to specify the specific ANSI or Unicode function (ending with *A* or *W*). This is especially important when a function takes a platform-dependent string (such as *LPTSTR*). You just specify the function name, and the runtime will handle the rest.

Visual Basic .NET makes it easy to call ANSI or Unicode functions. The only difference you really need to worry about is the string encoding option. It makes sense to use the *Auto* option to ensure that your applications can easily move among multiple platforms. If you use only ANSI functions, you'll limit your application's portability with no noticeable benefit. To ensure that your code will work on most platforms, use the *Auto* option (unless, of course, an API is platform-specific).

```
Declare Auto Function GetUserName Lib "advapi32.dll" _
                    (ByVal buffer As StringBuilder, _
                    ByRef size As Integer) As Boolean
```

The *Alias* option   The *Alias* option of the *Declare* statement allows you to define a method with any arbitrary name while still hooking up to the correct underlying function. The following example illustrates this by defining a function called *GetUserName*, which uses the *GetUserNameW* function:

```
Declare Unicode Function GetUserName Lib "advapi32.dll" _
                    Alias "GetUserNameW" _
                    (ByVal buffer As StringBuilder, _
                    ByRef size As Integer) As Boolean
```

Alias can allow you to clean up your imported method names. Recall that the ANSI Win32 functions have an *A* appended to the function name and the Unicode function have a *W* appended to the function name. Explicitly declaring your functions in this way can be messy and is, frankly, pointless in Visual Basic .NET. You need to know that information only when you create your *Declare* statement. Other methods that call the imported function don't need to know whether you're calling the underlying ANSI or Unicode method—the standard marshaling service handles all of that work for you. In some situations, the actual function name is cryptic or unintuitive, so it is worthwhile to provide an alternate name that indicates what the function actually does.

Caution   I am not recommending that you completely rename any function that you import using *Declare*. Far from it. You'll generally want to maintain a similar naming scheme for the sake of clarity. I'm simply noting that in some situations you might want to rename a function. (You should not do this arbitrarily, however.)

Limitations of *Declare*   The *Declare* statement is powerful and easy to use, but it hides certain implementation details from you, including a whole set of PInvoke options. These options include one for controlling how Win32 errors are handled, one for controlling how DLL entry points are resolved, and one for specifying function-calling conventions. Granted, you'll rarely need to worry about these situations—*Declare* does, after all, handle the vast majority of them. When *Declare* isn't good enough, the *DllImport* attribute will give you all the control you need.

The *DllImport* Attribute

The *DllImport* attribute is a universal mechanism for defining native methods in the .NET world. In languages such as Visual C#, which lack a statement like *Declare*, the *DllImport* attribute is the only means of importing native methods. Of course, Visual Basic developers have never wanted to follow the pack, and the Visual Basic team extended the existing *Declare* syntax to work in Visual Basic .NET. But an unfortunate reality of using *Declare* is that you're not exposed to all of the inner workings of PInvoke. (This is also arguably a tremendous benefit.) For those who are never satisfied with the default or who need more precise control in specific instances, the *DllImport* attribute provides all you need.

Let's look at the previously defined *Declare* statement for the *GetUser-Name* function to see why it doesn't necessarily provide the controls you need. This function has a few strange requirements (note the use of *StringBuilder* as a parameter), but we'll ignore those for a moment.

```
Declare Unicode Function GetUserName Lib "advapi32.dll" Alias _
    "GetUserNameW" (ByVal buffer As StringBuilder, _
                ByRef size As Integer) As Boolean
```

This example defines a method called *GetUserName* and tells the Visual Basic .NET compiler that it uses the *GetUserNameW* API from advapi32.dll and that the *Unicode* keyword indicates that all strings are marshaled as Unicode. Great. Everyone should be on the same page. Now let's take a peek under the covers. In cases such as this, the actual Microsoft intermediate language (MSIL) code produced by the Visual Basic compiler can be very instructive. Here's what's produced when you run the MSIL Disassembler (ILDASM) on the *GetUserName.exe* sample executable:

```
.method public static pinvokeimpl("advapi32.dll" as "GetUserNameW"
nomangle unicode lasterr winapi)
bool  GetUserName(class [mscorlib]System.Text.StringBuilder buffer,
                int32& size) cil managed preservesig
{
}
```

The real magic here is in the *pinvokeimpl* attribute. You can see that the function, the library, and a bunch of options are specified. In fact, you can see some options that are not available through *Declare*: *nomangle, lasterr, winapi,* and *preservesig*. The *unicode* option was specified in the original *Declare* statement (as a part of the *Auto|Ansi|Unicode Declare* syntax), and the *nomangle* option tells the runtime that it must look for the exact function name specified. (It cannot append *A* or *W*.) The *lasterr* option tells the runtime to store the last *Win32* error. This stored error value can be retrieved by calling the

GetLastWin32Error method of the *Marshal* class The *winapi* option is a little more difficult to explain, but suffice it to say that it indicates that the method should be called using the platform's default calling convention. (More on this shortly.) What all of this really means is that the *Declare* statement is doing some work behind the scenes for you. As a result, there are certain defaults (*lasterr* and *winapi*) that you cannot alter and must accept if you're using *Declare*.

ILDASM and You

ILDASM, which is included with the .NET Framework SDK, can be run on any .NET assembly (DLL or executable) to generate a human-readable form of the compiler-generated MSIL output. As you gain familiarity with developing in Visual Basic .NET, you'll come across situations where you have several implementation options and you want to know which is the most efficient. Comparing the compiler output can be an instructive way to determine an efficient alternative. I use ILDASM quite frequently to confirm that Visual Basic is doing what I expect it to do. It's also a great learning tool for understanding how MSIL works.

The easiest way to access the Ildasm.exe tool is to run the Visual Studio .NET command prompt. From the Start menu, choose All Programs, Microsoft Visual Studio .NET, Visual Studio .NET Tools. For more information about using ILDASM, consult the documentation that accompanies Visual Basic .NET. I highly recommend the ILDASM tutorial.

The *DllImport* attribute allows you to fully customize the PInvoke attributes to meet your needs. A verbose equivalent to the above *Declare* statement follows. (A number of the properties specified for the *DllImport* attribute are already defaults, but we're listing them to show you their usage.)

```
<DllImport("advapi32.dll", EntryPoint:="GetUserNameW", _
 CharSet:=CharSet.Unicode, ExactSpelling:=True, _
 CallingConvention:=CallingConvention.Winapi, PreserveSig:=True, _
 SetLastError:=True)> _
Public Shared Function GetUserName2(ByVal buffer As StringBuilder, _
                                    ByRef size As Integer) As Boolean
    ' No code here but us chickens!
End Function
```

Notice also that the *DllImport* attribute is applied to an empty function. This is because the function is needed to provide the signature for the underlying function, and the *DllImport* attribute causes all calls to the *GetUserName2* function to be forwarded to the *GetUserNameW* library function. As a result, any code contained in the *GetUserName2* function would never be called, and the Visual Basic .NET compiler will generate an error if any executable code is contained within the method. Table 4-1 lists the properties supported by the *DllImport* class.

Note You must define your *Sub* or *Function* as *Shared*; otherwise, you'll get a compiler error. The only exception is if the *Function* or *Sub* is defined in a module (implicitly shared).

Table 4-1
***DllImport* Attribute Properties**

Property	Type	Description
CallingConvention	*CallingConvention*	Specifies how a native method is invoked by the runtime. The default value is *CallingConvention.StdCall*. The *Declare* default is *CallingConvention.Winapi*.
CharSet	*CharSet*	Controls name mangling and indicates how to marshal string arguments to the method. This is essentially what allows conversions to and from ANSI and Unicode character sets.
EntryPoint	*String*	Indicates the name or ordinal of the DLL entry point to be called. Ordinal values are prefixed with the # character. You'll generally provide a method name, but ordinals can be useful if the entry point is known but the function name is not.

Table 4-1
DllImport **Attribute Properties**

Property	Type	Description
ExactSpelling	*Boolean*	Indicates whether the name of the entry point in the unmanaged DLL should be modified to correspond to the *CharSet* value specified in the *CharSet* field. If this is set to *True* and the *CharSet* property is set to *Ansi* or *Unicode*, an *A* or a *W* will be appended to the name of the function specified in the *EntryPoint* property.
PreserveSig	*Boolean*	Allows you to work with functions that return an *HRESULT* and have out parameters. (A lot of COM methods fall into this category.) The default value for *PreserveSig* is *True*, which means that the function is used as defined. If you're invoking a method that returns an *HRESULT*, you might want set this property to *False* so you can call the method in a more natural way. See the MSDN documentation if you're interested in pursuing this further.
SetLastError	*Boolean*	Indicates that the callee will call the Win32 API *SetLastError* before returning from the attributed method. The runtime will then call the *GetLastError* Win32 API and cache the value returned, making it accessible to your application through the *Marshal.GetLastWin32Error* function.

The *CallingConvention* property definitely gives you a peek under the covers. Table 4-2 describes the possible values of the *CallingConvention* enumeration. You can pretty much gloss over this material—it's probably more than you want to know—but we've provided it here for the sake of completeness. What you really need to know is this: if you're calling methods from the Win32 library, either always use *Declare* or specify the *Winapi CallingConvention*. The *Winapi* option is the most flexible because it will adapt to the platform your application is running on. (Different Windows platforms use different calling conventions.) Of course, your own custom libraries or legacy code might require a different calling convention. In this case, the default *StdCall* is most likely to suit your purpose.

Table 4-2
***CallingConvention* Enumeration Members**

Member	Description
Cdecl	The caller cleans the stack. This enables the calling of functions with a variable number of arguments.
StdCall	The callee cleans the stack. This is the default convention for calling unmanaged functions from managed code.
ThisCall	The first parameter is the *this* pointer, which is stored in register ECX. Other parameters are pushed on the stack. This calling convention is used to call methods of classes exported from an unmanaged DLL.
Winapi	Uses the default platform calling convention. For example, on Windows it's *StdCall* and on Windows CE it's *Cdecl*.

You can see that there's a lot to the *DllImport* attribute. Not to worry, though—as we've mentioned, the defaults for *DllImport* are designed to address the most common cases. If you do need to fiddle with the settings, however, you need a good understanding of what exactly you're trying to target.

Now we get to take a look at a subject I've only skirted up until this point: marshaling.

Marshaling Types

Marshaling, for the uninitiated, is the process of moving data across process boundaries. In the Visual Basic .NET context, this can also mean moving data across managed and unmanaged process boundaries. Marshaling is essential when you need to translate the Windows API function definitions into their Visual Basic .NET equivalents, using either the *Declare* or *DllImport* syntax. Marshaling can get tricky, especially when you're defining the function parameters and return types for imported functions. There's often more than one way to define individual parameters, and the differences are not always obvious. We'll start with a summary of generic marshaling and then look at some specific examples that demonstrate how to put this information into practice.

Basic Types

Many value types have the same managed and unmanaged memory layout, which allows the default interop marshaler to take care of everything for you. The .NET Framework documentation refers to these types as *blittable* types. They include the signed and unsigned varieties of *Byte*, *Short*, *Integer*, and *Long*. The CLR provides two additional types that are exclusively for dealing with unmanaged pointers and handles: *IntPtr* and *UIntPtr*. One-dimensional arrays of blittable types and structures that contain only blittable types can also be considered blittable types (in that you do not have to worry about marshaling issues). Table 4-3 compares these types. More complex types with more complex memory layout considerations—*Boolean*, arrays of more than one dimension, arrays of nonblittable types, *Class*, *String*, and *Structure*—usually require some special handling.

Table 4-3
A Comparison of Basic Types

Native Type	Visual Basic .NET Equivalent	Size (in Bytes)
SHORT	Short, Int16	2
WORD	*Short, Int16*	2
DWORD	*Integer, Int32, UInt32*	4
INT	*Integer, Int32*	4
UINT	*Integer, UInt32*	4
LPXXX	*IntPtr, UIntPtr*	4 (on 32-bit platforms)
		8 (on 64-bit platforms)
HANDLE	*IntPtr*	4 (on 32-bit platforms)
		8 (on 64-bit platforms)

Of course, this table doesn't tell the whole story. I haven't yet addressed the difference between *ByVal* and *ByRef* parameters.

ByRef vs. ByVal   In Visual Basic .NET, the default for parameters is *ByVal*. This makes a lot of sense, but sometimes you need to pass a pointer to a basic type instead of just the pointer value. In this case, you must define your function parameter as *ByRef* instead of *ByVal*. The CLR will ensure that the parameter is properly marshaled. This applies to all value types, including structures.

You can also decorate parameters with the *In* and *Out* attributes, which control whether the parameter is for read only (*In*), for output only (*Out*), or for both input and output (*In, Out*). Because Visual Basic considers *In* as a protected keyword, you must specify the attribute as either *[In]* or *InAttribute*. Passing a *ByVal* parameter with *In, Out* attributes is equivalent to passing *ByRef*. If necessary, you can also decorate a parameter with the *MarshalAs* attribute. This attribute allows you to explicitly specify how the interop marshaler should handle the data. Let's revise our previous example, replacing the *ByVal* and *ByRef* syntax with *In, Out* attributes to demonstrate how they work.

```
<DllImport("advapi32.dll", EntryPoint:="GetUserNameW", _
 CharSet:=CharSet.Unicode, ExactSpelling:=True, _
 CallingConvention:=CallingConvention.Winapi, PreserveSig:=True, _
 SetLastError:=True)> _
Public Shared Function GetUserName2( _
                       <[In]> buffer As StringBuilder, _
                       <InAttribute, Out> size As Integer) As Boolean
    ' No code here but us chickens!
End Function
```

Note how I've used both forms of the *In* attribute and shown how to decorate your function parameters with them. Pretty easy to understand. Realize, however, that you do not need to specify these attributes—*ByVal* and *ByRef* are usually sufficient.

Dealing with constants   The Win32 API is rife with constants and predefined values, which are used as parameters to all sorts of functions. Therefore, when we import functions, we naturally have to deal with constants and predefined values, often redefining the constants in our own code. Take the following example of the *MessageBeep* function from the User32 library:

```
BOOL MessageBeep(
  UINT uType   // sound type
);
```

This function takes an unsigned integer as a parameter. The valid constants for this function are listed in Table 4-4. In the WinUser.h header file, these constants are defined using a series of *#define* statements. When you work with a function that requires constant parameters, such as *MessageBeep*, you have three options for defining these constants when you import the function into Visual Basic .NET:

■   Pass the integer equivalent of the constant. (This works, but the result is hard to read and, more importantly, harder to understand.)

- Define the constant in your code and pass the constant to the function. (This is better, but it's still not very .NET-ish.)

- Create an *Enum* to contain the constant values and define the method parameter as the *enum* type. (This looks a lot better.)

Table 4-4
The *MessageBeep* Constants

Value	Sound
-1	Simple beep. If the sound card is not available, the sound is generated using the speaker.
MB_ICONASTERISK	SystemAsterisk
MB_ICONEXCLAMATION	SystemExclamation
MB_ICONHAND	SystemHand
MB_ICONQUESTION	SystemQuestion
MB_OK	SystemDefault

Digging into the WinUser.h header file, I was able to find the definitions for each of these constants. For completeness, here they are:

```
#define MB_OK                 0x00000000L
#define MB_ICONHAND           0x00000010L
#define MB_ICONQUESTION       0x00000020L
#define MB_ICONEXCLAMATION    0x00000030L
#define MB_ICONASTERISK       0x00000040L
```

Now we need to consider how to deal with these constants in our applications. Using the first option, we don't need to do anything out of the ordinary—just pass the integer value to the function. Using the second option, we can define a set of constants:

```
' This would satisfy the second option
Const MB_SIMPLE As Integer = -1
Const MB_ICONHAND As Integer = &H10
Const MB_ICONQUESTION As Integer = &H20
Const MB_ICONEXCLAMATION As Integer = &H30
Const MB_ICONASTERISK As Integer = &H40
Const MB_OK As Integer = &H0
```

Taking this example even further, as in the third option, we can group the constants into an enumerated type. This doesn't look terribly different but is somewhat cleaner than the previous two options.

```
' This would satisfy the third option
Public Enum SystemBeeps As Integer
    Simple = -1
    OK = &H0
    IconHand = &H10
    IconQuestion = &H20
    IconExclamation = &H30
    IconAsterisk = &H40
End Enum
```

The following example shows how you might define the *MessageBeep* function using these three options. We first define a *Function* that takes an *Integer* as the sole parameter. This allows us to pass either a variable (constant or otherwise) or just an integer value, and it basically satisfies the requirements for both the first and second options. The second function is far more interesting. You've seen the enumerated type *SystemBeeps* that specifies members with the same values as the argument constants. We then define the function prototype as taking an argument of type *SystemBeeps*. Because the *SystemBeeps* structure was defined as an *Integer*, it is equivalent to the declaring the parameter as an *Integer* but has the added benefit of enforcing specific values on the parameter type. You can play with this and other examples in the SimplePInvoke sample project included with this book's sample files.

```
' For first and second option
Declare Function MessageBeep Lib "User32.dll" _
                            (ByVal type As Integer) As Boolean
' For third option
Declare Function MessageBeep Lib "User32.dll" _
                            (ByVal type As SystemBeeps) As Boolean
```

The following example shows how different each calling method looks. Ask yourself which option leads to more readable and maintainable code.

```
' Option 1 - Ugly
MessageBeep(-1)

' Option 2 - Better
MessageBeep(MB_SIMPLE)

' Option 3 - Makes sense to me!
MessageBeep(SystemBeeps.Simple)
```

By far the best option is to handle the constant parameters as enumerated types. There are exceptions, of course. If you have only a single constant to worry about, say *MAX_SIZE*, declaring a constant is the best way to go. Using enumerations generally gives you much more control and flexibility than simple constants. By defining a function parameter as an enum, you eliminate the possibility that someone will provide an invalid parameter value. It also allows you to better control the allowed parameters by eliminating certain options (through omission) or creating additional custom options.

The cool thing here is that enums are always implemented as a basic type. This means you really don't have to worry about any marshaling issues. Plus, you can customize your enums to represent *Byte*, *Integer*, *Long*, or *Short*. This gives you a lot of flexibility, helps organize the constant values into a single location, provides a type-safe way to ensure valid function parameters, and generally makes your code easier to read. What more could you ask for?

Marshaling Strings

Dealing with strings is a bit tricky. If you've worked with APIs, you might know what I mean. As I've mentioned, strings cannot always be marshaled in a conventional way. When you're importing native methods that sport *String* parameters or return types, you must be mindful of the requirements imposed by the function's behavior. It is important to understand where the strings are allocated and who is responsible for releasing that memory. Recall the *GetUserName* example:

```
BOOL GetUserName(
    LPTSTR lpBuffer,   // name buffer
    LPDWORD nSize      // size of name buffer
);
```

The question is, how do we translate this function definition into something Visual Basic .NET can work with? The trick here is that the *GetUserName* function expects the calling method to allocate a string and pass a pointer to that memory and a pointer to a *DWORD* containing the allocation size of the string. In this case, you must use *StringBuilder* as the first argument because *GetUserName* modifies the string passed to it—which is not normally allowed. (Note that strings are immutable objects in Visual Basic .NET—you cannot modify the contents of a *String* object.) Thankfully, *StringBuilder* provides the necessary functionality. Furthermore, because the *StringBuilder* class is a reference type, you must pass it *ByVal* instead of *ByRef*. (Otherwise, it would be a reference to a reference type.) The second argument can be defined as an *Integer* (a *DWORD* is 4 bytes—see Table 4-3) and must be passed as a *ByRef* (because the function requires a pointer, not just a copy of the value).

```
Declare Auto Function GetUserName Lib "advapi32.dll" _
    (ByVal buffer As StringBuilder, ByRef size As Integer) As Boolean

...
' Using the imported method
Const MAX_UNLEN As Integer = 257
```

```
Dim sb As New StringBuilder()
Dim length As Integer
length = MAX_UNLEN
sb.Capacity = MAX_UNLEN
GetUserName(sb, length)
Console.WriteLine(sb.ToString())
```

There are very specific rules related to marshaling strings. The two situations that you need to be most concerned with are passing string parameters and functions that return strings. We'll look at these in turn.

Strings as parameters   You might be surprised at the number of ways that strings can be passed to methods. Sometimes a string is passed as a read-only parameter, and other times a method requires a pointer to a string buffer so the string can be modified. (Recall the *GetUserName* function used in several examples so far.) Table 4-5 shows how to specify parameters given certain parameter requirements.

Table 4-5
String Marshaling Rules

Parameter Requirement	Equivalent Visual Basic .NET Parameter
A pointer to a string for input; string will not be modified.	ByVal … As String
A string that can be replaced with another string. (The caller owns memory or is responsible for deallocating memory.)	*ByRef … As String*
A pointer to a string that you don't own.	*ByVal … As IntPtr*
A pointer to a pointer (handle) to a string that you don't own.	*ByRef … As IntPtr*
A pointer to a string buffer that can be read and written to.	*ByVal … As StringBuilder* (You can also use *ByVal … As String* if the function is imported using the *Declare* statement.)
An array of strings.	*ByVal strAry As String()*
A pointer to an array of strings.	*ByRef strAry As String()*

Ultimately, you must understand what the requirements are for the function you're importing. Whether the function needs to modify the string will influence your choice of *StringBuilder* versus *String*. (This applies mainly to functions imported with the *DllImport* attribute.) Always keep in mind, however, that importing functions with the *Declare* statement will simplify string marshaling for you. *Declare* will handle marshaling strings back to the caller, which lets you avoid using *StringBuilder* as a parameter type altogether. Now let's take up the issue of string ownership.

Functions that return strings   Functions that return strings pose some interesting challenges. When you deal with strings, you must pay special attention to who is allocating the string and who is responsible for releasing it. This information will allow you to define the correct declaration of the function in your code. There are two possibilities for string ownership.

- A function returns a string, and you own the result.
- A function returns a string but retains ownership of the resource.

If the function returns a string that you own (that is, if you're responsible for destroying it when you're done with it), you should declare the function return type *As String*. This allows the CLR to handle the string cleanup for you, and you can use this function and the returned string in a normal fashion.

```
Function ... As String
```

If, on the other hand, a function returns a pointer to a string that resides in a memory location that you do not own, you must be careful. Defining the return type as a string is unacceptable because the CLR would eventually attempt to release that memory. This could cause some interesting problems if, say, the memory were kernel resident. In this situation, you're better off not dealing with the string directly as a managed *String* object. Instead, deal with it as a pointer:

```
Function ... As IntPtr
```

An example will definitely help. Let's consider the *GetCommandLine* function from the Kernel32 library. The function prototype looks like this:

```
LPTSTR GetCommandLine(VOID);
```

Note   This scenario is contrived. You should never use this API via PInvoke; instead, you should use *System.Environment.CommandLine* to read the parameters. In general, always use the managed equivalent if one is available.

GetCommandLine is a pretty simple function. It returns the command-line arguments for your application. It takes no arguments and returns a pointer to a string. Easy, right? When you import the function, you might assume that, because a platform-dependent string is being returned, you can define the *Declare* statement like this:

```
Declare Auto Function GetCommandLine Lib "Kernel32.dll" () As String
```

Makes sense, right? But there's a problem. It might not be obvious, but I just made an error. I made an assumption about the return type. Think about it. Who allocates the returned string? There are only two possibilities: the *GetCommandLine* function allocated the string or I did. In this situation, it must have been the *GetCommandLine* function (actually, it's the operating system in this case, but the point is still valid) because I sure didn't give it anything to work with. This raises the question of who's responsible for releasing the memory associated with the returned string.

If you delve deeper into the definition of the *GetCommandLine* function, you'll find out that it returns a pointer to a string that's created by the operating system at the application's startup. The caller is supposed to use the pointer to read the string, which represents the program's arguments, but the caller is not supposed to modify or release the underlying string. If we define the function return value as a string object, the CLR will try to free the memory represented by that string. If this happens and some other function depends on the existence of this string, bye-bye application.

The proper way to handle this situation is to not explicitly treat the return value as a string object. Instead, you define the return type as a pointer to a memory location (*IntPtr*). This allows you to have a pointer to the memory location of the string without giving the CLR the impression that it needs to clean up anything for you. Great, problem solved. But this raises another question. Once you have a pointer to the string, how do you access it? Not to worry. That particular quandary is solved by the *Marshal* class (from the *System.Runtime.InteropServices* namespace). Check out the following example:

```
Declare Auto Function GetCommandLine Lib "Kernel32.dll" () As IntPtr
...
Dim param As IntPtr = GetCommandLine()
Dim commandLine As String = Marshal.PtrToStringAuto(param)
```

You can see how I used the *Marshal.PtrToStringAuto* method to convert the *LPTSTR* (a platform-dependent string) to a Visual Basic .NET string. (There are other methods for dealing with ANSI and Unicode strings.) Generally, if you need to deal with strings in this way, the specific *Marshal.PtrToString* method you use should depend on the underlying string type. Also, remember that this example applies only to the situation in which we're not responsible for releasing the returned string's memory. If a function returns a pointer to a string and assumes that the caller will free it, it's perfectly acceptable to declare the return type as *String* and everyone will be happy.

Note   You should get familiar with methods of *Marshal* class; this class is used wherever manual marshaling is needed. A common mistake is using inappropriate managed types for the supposed native equivalent. (For example, managed *Long* is 64 bits and unmanaged *long* is only 32 bits.) This gets even more complicated when you're dealing with structures. Thankfully, you can check the size of a structure using the *Marshal.SizeOf* method. Before you ever try to call a native DLL from Visual Basic .NET, first check whether the code works correctly in the unmanaged world and then convert it into a Visual Basic .NET equivalent.

This wraps up our discussion of string marshaling. Now let's look at *Structure* and *Class* marshaling.

Marshaling Structures

Structures can present a variety of marshaling challenges. The structure, which is a value type, often requires little additional manipulation—the default marshaling is usually sufficient. This frees you from having to worry about a lot of implementation details. When you pass structures or classes to a function, the default marshaler takes care of the layout of its members. However, if the function expects a specific layout, you might need to alter the memory of the structure to conform to what the API expects. You can do this using the *StructLayout* attribute (which we'll describe later).

Strings tend to present a basic problem with structures. Recall that structures that contain only basic types can usually be marshaled by the standard marshaling service without your having to specify any additional layout information. Strings are a big exception.

Structures and strings   Strings can present some interesting marshaling challenges for structures (surprise, surprise). There are, of course, several variations on the theme. Typically, you'll see one of the following scenarios:

- A string as a pointer to a string (*LPSTR*, *LPTSTR*, or *LPWSTR*).

- A string as a pointer to character buffer (*CHAR*, *TCHAR*, or *WCHAR*). The size of the buffer is usually passed as another member of the structure.

- A string as an embedded fixed-size character array (*CHAR[]*, *TCHAR[]*, or *WCHAR[]*).

To handle these situations, you can use the *MarshalAs* attribute to control how the individual elements of a structure (including strings) are marshaled. Let's work through an example to see how to handle strings in a structure. An interesting example, yet again from the Win32 API, is the *OSVERSIONINFO* structure, which is used in conjunction with the *GetVersionEx* function from the Kernel32 library:

```
BOOL GetVersionEx(
  LPOSVERSIONINFO lpVersionInfo // version information
);
```

This function fills an existing structure with information about the current operating system. This Visual C++ structure looks like this:

```
typedef struct _OSVERSIONINFO{
  DWORD dwOSVersionInfoSize;
  DWORD dwMajorVersion;
  DWORD dwMinorVersion;
  DWORD dwBuildNumber;
  DWORD dwPlatformId;
  TCHAR szCSDVersion[ 128 ];
} OSVERSIONINFO;
```

Most of the members of the *OSVERSIONINFO* structure are fairly straight-forward and easy to understand, but the last element raises a question. The *szCSDVersion* element is defined as a fixed array of *TCHAR* (platform-dependent) characters. You might be tempted to specify a *StringBuilder*, but you'd be incorrect. You should specify the element as a string and decorate it with the *MarshalAs* attribute. This will allow you to specify how the string should be marshaled (in this case, as a *ByValTStr* with a size of 128 characters). Check out the following example:

```
Public Structure OSVersionInfo
    Public OsVersionInfoSize As Integer
    Public majorVersion As Integer
```

```
      Public minorVersion As Integer
      Public buildNumber As Integer
      Public platformId As Integer
      <MarshalAs(UnmanagedType.ByValTStr, SizeConst:=128)> _
      Public version As String
End Structure
```

This is only a single example, and unfortunately space is limited. You can play around with the *MarshalAs* attribute for the other scenarios you're likely to encounter.

More Info   See the GOTDOTNET Web site (*http://www.gotdotnet.com*) for utilities and samples to help you with marshaling issues.

Now that we've looked at strings, let's spend a little time looking at the *StructLayout* attribute.

The *StructLayout* attribute   *StructLayout* provides a set of options (described in Table 4-6) for controlling the physical layout of a given structure. (Sounds obvious, right?) If you omit the *StructLayout* attribute for any structure, the runtime will default to the *StructLayout.Automatic* setting. This means that the standard marshaling service will be used and assumptions will be made about the structure's memory layout.

Table 4-6
The *StructLayout* Attribute Options

Options	Type	Values	Description
LayoutKind (constructor)	Enum	Auto	Controls the layout of an object when it's exported to unmanaged code.
		Explicit	
		Sequential	
CharSet	*Enum*	*Ansi*	Indicates how string data fields within the class should be marshaled.
		Auto	
		Unicode	

Table 4-6
The *StructLayout* Attribute Options

Options	Type	Values	Description
Pack	*Integer*	0, 1, 2, 4, 8, 16, 32, 64, or 128	Controls the alignment of data fields of a class or structure in memory. Used in conjunction with the *LayoutKind.Sequential* option. A value of 0 indicates that the packing alignment is set to the default for the current platform. The default packing size is 8.
Size	*Integer*	Unrestricted	Indicates the absolute size of the structure or class. This is primarily for use by compiler writers and should generally be avoided.

Alternatively, you can define your structure's layout explicitly. This is more common when you have odd-member byte offsets and need to conform to an explicit layout. The following example is directly equivalent to the previous definition of the *OSVersionInfo* structure. The only difference is that we specify all of the member element's byte offsets.

```
<StructLayout(LayoutKind.Explicit)> _
Structure OSVersionInfo
   <FieldOffset(0)> Public OsVersionInfoSize As Integer
   <FieldOffset(4)> Public majorVersion As Integer
   <FieldOffset(8)> Public minorVersion As Integer
   <FieldOffset(12)> Public buildNumber As Integer
   <FieldOffset(16)> Public platformId As Integer
   <FieldOffset(20), MarshalAs(UnmanagedType.ByValTStr, SizeConst:=128)> _
   Public version As String
End Structure
```

There's a lot more you can control in a structure's layout, but that's a matter for you to explore on your own. Now let's look at everyone's favorite topic: shortcuts.

Structure definition shortcuts   You'll often run into structures that contain other structures. In other words, some structures are composites. A good example is the *CONSOLE_SCREEN_BUFFER_INFO* structure shown below. This structure contains multiple instances of two additional structure types: *COORD* and *SMALL_RECT*. You might think that if you want to properly define the *CONSOLE_SCREEN_BUFFER_INFO* structure, you must also define the contained structures. This is not the case. In fact, you don't have to worry about contained structures in this situation.

```
typedef struct _CONSOLE_SCREEN_BUFFER_INFO {
  COORD       dwSize;
  COORD       dwCursorPosition;
  WORD        wAttributes;
  SMALL_RECT  srWindow;
  COORD       dwMaximumWindowSize;
} CONSOLE_SCREEN_BUFFER_INFO ;

typedef struct _COORD {
  SHORT X;
  SHORT Y;
} COORD;

typedef struct _SMALL_RECT {
  SHORT Left;
  SHORT Top;
  SHORT Right;
  SHORT Bottom;
} SMALL_RECT;
```

Confused? The trick is to recognize that the contained structures take up space in a very standard way. You can substitute basic types without having to worry about defining the other contained structures. The only limitation is that you must preserve the memory layout. Recall the basic types shown in Table 4-3 on page 119. Because we know the size of each of these types, we should be able to get away with substitutions.

Take the *COORD* structure as an example. *COORD* contains two members, both of type *SHORT*. We know that the *SHORT* type is 2 bytes in size, so the total size of the *COORD* structure must be 4 bytes. It just so happens that the *Integer* type is also 4 bytes. Logically, we could replace any definition of *COORD* with an *Integer*, and everyone would be happy. By extension, the *SMALL_RECT* structure takes up 8 bytes (4 × 2 byte *SHORT* values). We could then substitute a *Long* (also 8 bytes) and still maintain the correct structure layout—sort of. The only problem with this structure definition is there is a *Short* field right in the middle of the other fields: *wAttributes*. When you want to simplify your layouts, the easiest case is when all the fields are even multiples of 4 bytes. (This is a consequence of running on 32-bit [4-byte] processor architectures.) Unfortunately, a *Short* is 2 bytes and that complicates the memory layout story. Consequently, to maintain our correct in-memory layout, we need to use the *StructLayout* attribute to tell the runtime what the structure's memory layout should look like. Our new definition for *CONSOLE_SCREEN_BUFFER_INFO* might look like this:

```
<StructLayout(LayoutKind.Sequential, Pack:=4)> _
Public Structure CONSOLE_SCREEN_BUFFER_INFO
  Public dwSize As Integer
  Public dwCursorPosition As Integer
  Public wAttributes As Short
  Public srWindow As Long
  Public dwMaximumWindowSize As Integer
End Structure
```

Of course, there are certain disadvantages to performing the substitution. The most important is that you lose the ability to access the data contained by the structure. By defining the contained structures as basic types, we cannot access the data as if they were contained structures. This is not a problem if we have no interest in the structure member, but it can be a pain if we want to work with a *COORD* or a *SMALL_RECT* structure. In that case, we must define the structures and change the definition of the containing structure to contain those specific types. We can then access the members using dot notation—a big convenience. Of course, nothing can prevent you from substituting a basic type at first and then defining one or more of the contained types on an as-needed basis. It's just that having to define all structures and substructures at once can be a pain—especially if you aren't interested in the information. This method can give you an expedient workaround.

The *Marshal* Class

You will see the *Marshal* class many times in this book. The reason is obvious: it's so darn useful. You saw it before when I discussed returning strings from functions. Here you'll get a broad overview of the class. Table 4-7 lists some of the methods specific to platform invoke operations. The *Marshal* class provides many utilities that allow you to read and write unmanaged memory, convert types, copy managed arrays to unmanaged memory, and much, much more. Whenever you get stuck in a marshaling jam, remember this class.

Table 4-7
Selected Shared Methods of the *Marshal* Class

Method	Description
AllocHGlobal	Overloaded. Allocates a block of memory using *GlobalAlloc*.
Copy	Overloaded. Copies data between a managed array and an unmanaged memory pointer.
DestroyStructure	Frees all substructures pointed to by the specified native memory block.

Table 4-7
Selected Shared Methods of the *Marshal* Class

Method	Description
FreeBSTR	Frees a *BSTR* using *SysFreeString*.
FreeHGlobal	Frees memory previously allocated from the unmanaged native heap of the process using *AllocHGlobal*.
GetExceptionCode	Retrieves a code that identifies the type of the exception that occurred.
GetExceptionPointers	Retrieves a machine-independent description of an exception and information about the machine state for the thread when the exception occurred.
GetLastWin32Error	Returns the error code returned by the last unmanaged function called using platform invoke that had the *SetLastError* flag set.
PtrToStringAnsi	Overloaded. Copies all or part of an ANSI string to a managed *String* object.
PtrToStringAuto	Overloaded. Copies an unmanaged string to a managed *String* object.
PtrToStringBSTR	Copies a Unicode string stored in native heap to a managed *String* object.
PtrToStringUni	Overloaded. Copies an unmanaged Unicode string to a managed *String* object.
PtrToStructure	Overloaded. Marshals data from an unmanaged block of memory to a managed object.
ReadByte	Overloaded. Reads a single byte from an unmanaged pointer.
ReadInt16	Overloaded. Reads a 16-bit integer from native heap.
ReadInt32	Overloaded. Reads a 32-bit integer from native heap.
ReadInt64	Overloaded. Reads a 64-bit integer from native heap.
ReadIntPtr	Overloaded. Reads a processor native sized integer from native heap.
ReAllocHGlobal	Resizes a block of memory previously allocated using *AllocHGlobal*.

Table 4-7
Selected Shared Methods of the *Marshal* Class

Method	Description
SizeOf	Overloaded. Returns the unmanaged size of a class used via *Marshal* in bytes.
StringToBSTR	Allocates a *BSTR* and copies the string contents into it.
StringToHGlobalAnsi	Copies the contents of a managed *String* object into native heap, converting into ANSI format as it copies.
StringToHGlobalAuto	Copies the contents of a managed *String* object into native heap, converting into ANSI format if required.
StringToHGlobalUni	Copies the contents of a managed *String* object into native heap.
StructureToPtr	Marshals data from a managed object to an unmanaged block of memory.
WriteByte	Overloaded. Writes a single-byte value into native heap.
WriteInt16	Overloaded. Writes a 16-bit integer value into native heap.
WriteInt32	Overloaded. Writes a 32-bit integer value into native heap.
WriteInt64	Overloaded. Writes a 64-bit integer value into native heap.
WriteIntPtr	Overloaded. Writes a processor native-sized integer value into native heap.

This table contains a somewhat abbreviated list of the members. We've omitted most of the COM-related members for the sake of simplicity, but you're more than welcome to investigate those on your own.

To wrap up our marshaling section, let's look at how to implement callback functions.

Implementing Callback Functions

Some interfaces require that a pointer to a function be passed, usually to handle events or generic tasks. To show this in action, I developed the ExtendedConsole sample (included with this book's sample files) to, in part, enable a console application to handle control-key events. For example, how do you handle the situation when the user hits the Ctrl+C key combination? This is not something that is provided by the *System.Console* class. Searching the MSDN library,

I found the function *SetConsoleCtrlHandler*, which allows you to register a call-back function (or a series of callbacks) that is called whenever a specific set of control events occurs (including Ctrl+C). Here's what *SetConsoleCtrlHandler* looks like:

```
BOOL SetConsoleCtrlHandler(
    PHANDLER_ROUTINE HandlerRoutine,   // handler function
    BOOL Add                           // add or remove handler
);
```

Of course, this leads us down the merry old dependency trail. We need the definition of the *HandlerRoutine* parameter (the following example), and consequently the possible values for the *dwCtrlType* specified by the *Hander-Routine* prototype (from WinCon.h).

```
#define CTRL_C_EVENT          0
#define CTRL_BREAK_EVENT      1
#define CTRL_CLOSE_EVENT      2
// 3 is reserved!
// 4 is reserved!
#define CTRL_LOGOFF_EVENT     5
#define CTRL_SHUTDOWN_EVENT  6

BOOL WINAPI HandlerRoutine(
    DWORD dwCtrlType   //  control signal type
);
```

So what do we do here? We simply start off by creating an *Enum* called *ConsoleEventKey*, which contains the constant values. Then—and this is the interesting part—we create a delegate (remember them from Chapter 2?), *ControlHandler*, that roughly matches the prototype for the *HandlerRoutine* function. (Note that we don't have to worry about exact function naming—just the function's signature.) Because the *ConsoleEventKey* enum is declared as an *Integer*, we can substitute that enum for the *DWORD* argument for *ControlHandler*. Now all that needs to be done is to declare the *SetConsoleCtrlHandler* method:

```
' The control event that occurred. (from wincom.h)
Public Enum ConsoleEventKey As Integer
    CTRL_C = 0
    CTRL_BREAK = 1
    CTRL_CLOSE = 2
    CTRL_LOGOFF = 5
    CTRL_SHUTDOWN = 6
End Enum' This is the definition of the callback function
```

```
' Handler to be called when a console event occurs.
Private Delegate Function ControlHandler _
    (ByVal key As ConsoleEventKey) As Integer

' Here is the function we need to call to register a callback
Private Declare Function SetConsoleCtrlHandler Lib "kernel32.dll" _
    (ByVal e As ControlHandler, ByVal add As Boolean) As Boolean
```

The declaration of *SetConsoleCtrlHandler* is straightforward. We specify the function's first argument as a *ControlHandler* delegate type. Everything else should be self-explanatory at this stage. The ExtendedConsole sample shows this in action. The *ConsoleControlEvents* class provides the functionality for hooking up a *ControlHandler* delegate. We also define a *ConsoleEvent* event that clients can subscribe to and handle:

```
' Event fired when a console event occurs
Public Event ConsoleEvent As ControlEventHandler

Private eventHandler As ControlHandler

Public Sub New()
    MyBase.New()

    ' save this to a private var so the GC doesn't collect it...
    eventHandler = New ControlHandler(AddressOf Me.OnConsoleEvent)
    SetConsoleCtrlHandler(eventHandler, True)
End Sub

Protected Function OnConsoleEvent(ByVal eventKey As ConsoleEventKey) _
        As Integer
    Dim e As New ControlEventArgs(eventKey)
    RaiseEvent ConsoleEvent(Me, e)
    If e.Cancel Then
        Return 1
    Else
        Return 0
    End If
End Function
```

That takes care of the callback function. It really isn't that complicated. Essentially, all you need to do is define a delegate method, following most of the same rules as for the *Declare* statement. Visual Basic .NET really can't make it much easier than that!

Wrapping Things Up

Ultimately, both the *Declare* statement and the *DllImport* attribute use the same underlying mechanism to do their jobs. The major difference between the two is the accessibility of certain PInvoke settings. In most situations, the loss of flexibility of the *Declare* statement is perfectly acceptable, given its ease of use and simple syntax. I recommend that you use the *Declare* statement whenever possible. Granted, in some situations it might be necessary to use *DllImport* (for legacy libraries that use alternate calling conventions, for instance). But those situations should be relatively rare.

We've encountered a lot of marshaling issues already, but we've still barely scratched the surface. You'll be glad to know that most of the information about PInvoke marshaling can be applied to COM interop, but there's much more than can be adequately addressed in a single chapter. If you need to delve further, take a look at *.NET and COM* by Adam Nathan (Sams Publishing, 2002).

COM and Visual Basic .NET

Working with COM components is almost a given for any major application built today. Admittedly, most, if not all, of the Win32 API and COM objects will eventually be published with managed interfaces. But even then, there will always be some need to work directly with COM components. Legacy COM components can be expected to live for many years before they're upgraded or replaced.

What Is COM Interop?

Some people get confused when they discuss COM interop. We're sorry to say that some of the more reputable technical publications don't always do much better. The confusion often seems to surround the difference between calling native methods from Visual Basic .NET and calling COM objects. Part of the problem might be that an implicit assumption that any calls that cross the native/managed barrier must be COM interop. This is simply not the case. COM interop implies a whole nasty set of requirements and possibly thread marshaling overhead that is simply not necessary when you call a native Win32 method. To keep it simple, think of it this way. If you need to import a type library or create a COM reference in your project, it's COM interop. If you use the *Declare* statement or the *DllImport* attribute, on the other hand, you're just calling native methods—no COM interop involved.

COM vs. .NET

COM differs from the .NET Framework object model in several fundamental ways. First and foremost, COM is based on binary standard. The internal binary layout of classes must comply with COM rules. In contrast, .NET is based on a type standard. Its common type system establishes a framework that enables cross-language integration, type safety, and high-performance code execution. We'll look at each of the other major differences in turn.

Type Libraries vs. Assemblies

COM uses type libraries to store type information. A type library contains only the public types the designers wanted to be made available. Moreover, in COM a type library is optional. In the managed world, type information is stored as metadata and is mandatory for all types public, private or otherwise. This metadata is embedded inside assemblies to ensure that the type information is always present.

Interfaces and Inheritance

Unmanaged (COM) objects always communicate through interfaces. Period. COM requires the implementation of the *IUnknown* interface for all objects. This interface supports the *QueryInterface* method, which retrieves pointers to interfaces implemented by an object. Managed objects and classes can pass classes and interfaces around indiscriminately. You can get an interface supported by a managed object simply by casting to the desired type.

.NET also allows both implementation and interface inheritance. It also supports cross-language inheritance—classes can inherit from other classes regardless of what .NET language the base class was written in. COM allows interface inheritance only and does not support implementation inheritance.

New vs. *New*

The Visual Basic .NET *New* operator is used to create instances of new classes. You can, however, use the *CreateObject* method to specifically create new instances of COM objects. COM relies on the *CoCreateInstance* API or *IClassFactory* interface to create new instances of COM objects. (That's what Visual Basic 6.0's *New* operator did.)

Object Identity

Uniquely identifying COM classes requires the definition and use of globally unique identifier (GUID) values (really big numbers). Each public interface is assigned a GUID, including the COM class itself. Each GUID must be stored in the registry to allow other clients to access the classes and interfaces. Whenever an interface changes, it must be given a new GUID. The CLR, on the other hand, uses fully qualified names or strong names (names with a digital signature) to uniquely identify types.

Error Handling

All COM methods that can generate an error usually return an *HRESULT*. This value indicates whether that method call succeeded or failed. It can also indicate various failures or error information. All managed objects implement exceptions using structured exception handling for the vast majority or errors. There are certainly no *HRESULT* values.

Object Lifetimes

COM objects manage their own object lifetimes via a mechanism called reference counting. This is supported through the *IUnknown* interface methods *AddRef* and *Release*. Whenever a copy of an object's interface is made, a call must be made to *AddRef*, which increments a simple counter. When a client is done with an interface, it must call *Release* on the underlying object. When the reference count eventually reaches zero, the object is destroyed. In this way, we describe COM objects as having a deterministic lifetime. As soon as the objects are not in use, they are destroyed.

In .NET, things work a little differently. The CLR manages the lifetime of objects through garbage collection, which is a nondeterministic memory model. Essentially what this means is that when an object is no longer in use, it will be destroyed—but not necessarily immediately. In fact, when garbage collection occurs is completely up to the garbage collector. This can lead to some interesting and problematic cleanup issues, but more on that later.

IDispatch vs. Reflection

COM Automation is implemented through the *IDispatch* interface. This is intended to provide a flexible way to access COM objects without your having to know the interface layout in advance. All Visual Basic 6.0 COM components implement the *IDispatch* interface by default. This mechanism also allows scripting languages such as VBScript to talk to COM classes. Late binding in Visual Basic 6.0 is also implemented using the *IDispatch* interface.

In contrast, Visual Basic .NET supports late binding through reflection. Reflection is a mechanism by which a client can discover virtually anything about a type. Through reflection, you can inspect fields, properties, methods, interfaces, and inheritance hierarchies of any type. In addition, you can use reflection to inject MSIL code at run time and alter method contents or add new methods. (Emitting MSIL code at run time isn't a common practice, nor is it for the faint of heart, but it sure is powerful.)

What COM Interop Does

Given these huge differences between COM and .NET, you can only imagine the complexities involved in having them coexist in same application. Worry not—Microsoft made huge investments in COM interop to make this as seamless as possible. So what exactly does COM interop do for you? In a nutshell, it provides the following basic services:

- **Marshaling and type translation**   Handles data type conversion between managed and unmanaged data types.

- **Lifetime management for COM objects**   Managing object references to ensure that objects are either released or eventually marked for garbage collection. You can do your own object cleanup to guarantee a more deterministic release of underlying COM objects.

- **Object identity**   Enforces and maintains COM identity rules.

- **Type binding**   COM interop supports both early bound interface and late-bound (IDispatch) interfaces.

- **Error handling**   The COM interop provides translation for COM *HRESULT* return values to .NET exceptions. It also supports translating .NET exceptions to *HRESULT* values for COM to .NET communication.

Let's see how all of this comes together to produce a usable application.

Using COM from Visual Basic .NET

To call a COM component from Visual Basic .NET, you must do a couple of things. First, you must obtain a managed wrapper for the underlying COM type library. In .NET parlance, this wrapper is called a *runtime callable wrapper* (RCW), or *interop assembly*. Note that the interop assembly is merely a wrapper for the COM component and does not contain any of the component's functionality. The interop assembly's purpose in life is to make accessing the underlying COM component as seamless as possible. In other words, it does all of the standard marshaling stuff for you. This means that all of the machines your application runs on will still need the COM component to be properly registered before it can be used.

Creating an RCW

As we've stated, to access a COM component through Visual Basic .NET you must have an interop assembly. There are two ways to get this assembly. First, and preferably, the original developer of the component should publish what we call a *primary interop assembly* (PIA). You can think of this as the definitive, or vendor-approved, interop assembly. If this is not available (which is highly likely at this point), you can create your own interop assembly in one of the following ways:

- By adding a COM reference to your Visual Basic .NET project.

- Using the Type Library Importer (Tlbimp.exe) utility (which ships with the .NET Framework SDK).

- Programmatically generate your own wrapper using the *System.Runtime.InteropServices.TypeLibConverter* class, which also supports generating primary interop assemblies.

- Defining types manually in your own assembly.

The most common approaches are the first two. The last option, baking your own assembly, is way beyond the scope of this book; I recommend that you think carefully before going down that path.

Primary Interop Assemblies

You can obtain interop assembly in two ways. The first choice is to use primary interop assembly from the vendor, if available. Primary interop assemblies (PIAs) do not currently exist for most COM components, but expect more vendors to provide them in the future. Visual Studio .NET provides primary interop assemblies for some of the standard COM components and are installed by default in *<Drive>*:\Program Files\Microsoft.NET\Primary Interop Assemblies. Of course, a PIA need not be placed in a specific location, and you certainly do not need to store it along with all the other included PIAs.

To create a primary interop assembly, you must take these steps:

1. Create a public/private key pair with using sn.exe tool (for example, *sn.exe –k keys.snk*)

2. Run Tlbimp.exe against the COM DLL or type library, specifying the */primary* and */keyfile:[filename]* options.

We start by creating a public/private key pair because this is a requirement of any primary interop assembly. The key pair is used to generate a signed library for registering in the GAC. This provides a unique identity for the assembly that is absolute. In other words, the runtime cannot possibly confuse your assembly for another assembly that might contain identical namespaces and classes.

At this point, you have a primary interop assembly, and all you need to do is register it. All primary interop assemblies are registered using the Regasm.exe utility. Note that it is never a good idea to generate a primary interop assembly for a component you don't own. Keep an eye on the MSDN Web site—more and more primary interop assemblies for existing COM components should be published as time goes on.

Tlbimp and RCWs   Tlbimp.exe is a command-line utility for importing COM type libraries. It generates a runtime callable wrapper for your COM type library. This RCW can then be referenced in your Visual Basic .NET project, and the objects contained in the type library can be used as if they were any other .NET objects. You can also use Tlbimp to generate PIAs. (See the earlier sidebar on PIAs.)

Tlbimp is fairly simple to use and works well for the vast majority of cases. It is easily accessible through the Visual Studio .NET command prompt shortcut. From the Start menu, choose All Programs, Microsoft Visual Studio .NET, Visual Studio .NET Tools. All you need to do, in the simplest case, is to point the utility at a COM type library—either a DLL, if the type library is included, or a TLB file—and it will generate an RCW.

More Info   For more information on how to use Tlbimp, see the .NET Framework SDK documentation.

For all of Tlbimp's ease of use, it should come as no surprise that it doesn't necessarily do everything that you need. In these cases, you can crack the generated interop assembly and customize the MSIL code. I won't cover that subject here, but I'll mention some limitations so you can at least understand what you'll need to work around. Tlbimp needs a little help in the following situations:

■ **Success *HRESULT* values**   All failure *HRESULT* values cause exceptions in managed code. However, success *HRESULT* values other than *S_OK* (such as *S_FALSE*) that are returned from unmanaged code are not reported to managed callers of that code. If you don't need to differentiate between various success *HRESULT* values, this limitation does not present a problem. If you do need to differentiate between two success *HRESULT* values (such as *S_OK* and *S_FALSE*), use *PreserveSigAttribute*.

■ **C-style arrays**   Tlbimp cannot generate the proper marshaling attributes because there is no *size_of* information present in the input. To marshal C-style arrays, you need to do custom marshaling and specify the additional parameter *SizeParamIndex* to indicate the length of the array.

■ **Passing null to *ByRef* or out parameters**   This subject can get quite involved. Suffice it to say that currently there is no way to pass null to *ByRef* parameters.

■ **Multidimensional arrays**   Type libraries can contain definitions of methods that have variable-length array arguments. In such cases, the size of the array is typically passed as a separate method argument (for example, *HRESULT SomeMethod(int size, byte* buffer);*). Because the type library has no information to tie the two arguments together, the runtime cannot marshal the array correctly. To correct the problem, you must do custom marshaling and provide the array size using the *MarshalAs* attribute.

■ **Unions with reference types**   In .NET, structures marked with the explicit layout attribute can't contain reference types. If the type library contains a union with a reference type (such as *CHAR** or *VARIANT**), it will be converted to a structure with size and packing information but without any members.

Caution   The type library might itself also contain errors or incorrect information, which might become apparent only when it is converted to .NET metadata. In this case, you must correct the original COM type library by modifying the Microsoft Interface Description Language (MIDL) or Object Definition Language (ODL) used to produce it and recompiling it with the MIDL compiler. For more information, search on MIDL and ODL in the Platform SDK.

In any of the above situations, it is a good idea to generate the defaults using TLBIMP, open the MSIL using ILDASM.exe, edit the MSIL to get the desired output, and then use ILASM.exe to regenerate the assembly. This is also an opportune time to remove unused types, set *PreserveSig* for a success *HRESULT*, change *ref* to arrays, and change parameters to *IntPtr*. But this is really for advanced developers—you shouldn't attempt this without a decent understanding of MSIL and the ILASM and ILDASM tools.

Using Your RCW

Using an interop assembly in your application is just about as simple as working with COM objects from Visual Basic 6.0. For the most part, the objects are virtually indistinguishable from other .NET classes. Once you have an interop assembly (primary or otherwise), invoking the COM object is pretty simple. You reference the assembly or type library in your project and use the contained types as you would any other managed type.

Garbage collection and reference counting   In most cases, you don't need to worry about when the garbage collector gets around to cleaning up your COM object, but in some situations it is of critical importance. If it is vital that your application release a particular object at a specific time, you can take advantage of a method of the *Marshal* class (remember it?): *Marshal.ReleaseComObject*. *Marshal.ReleaseComObject* essentially forces the release of a COM object's interface. This can bring about the object's destruction. This method, by definition, decrements the RCW's reference count. Much like in COM, when the RCW's reference count hits zero, the object is toast.

That's about all I'll cover about using COM from Visual Basic .NET. It's mostly so simple that there really isn't much to talk about. Things get a little more interesting, however, in the next section, which covers using Visual Basic .NET from COM.

Using Visual Basic .NET from COM

The key to creating a Visual Basic .NET component that is visible to COM clients is to create a *COM callable wrapper* (CCW). At a very basic level, creating classes in Visual Basic .NET that are visible to COM clients is simple. Every .NET object is potentially a COM-accessible object, provided you take the step of registering the .NET assembly containing your object. If you're using Visual Basic .NET, all you need to do is select the Register For COM Interop option on the project's property page (as shown in Figure 4-2). Alternatively, you can manually run the Regasm.exe utility on your managed assembly.

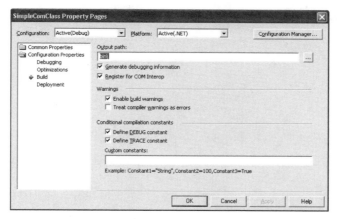

Figure 4-2   The project settings and registering an application for COM interop.

.NET is a paradigm shift from COM, but building .NET objects is probably the easiest way to build COM objects. Every .NET object is potentially a COM object—all you need to do is create a CCW. The CCW provides a whole host of features. It has a class factory, it has a type library, it implements *IUnknown* and *IDispatch*, and it is *CoCreatable*. However, not all features of the CLR types are exposable to COM through the wrapper. Shared methods and parameterized constructors are not exposed. Overloaded methods are renamed, and the inheritance hierarchy is flattened.

Creating a More Sophisticated COM Class

Visual Basic makes it easy to create more sophisticated classes. The default mechanism described above works, but it isn't easy to control. You have no way to define the GUID associated with your types, and everything defaults to supporting only the *IDispatch* interface. That might work, but it doesn't address every possible scenario in which you'd want to expose a class or set of classes to COM. At times, you'll need to emulate an existing COM component or interface for the sake of backward compatibility. In this case, you probably want to start with a Visual Basic .NET COM Class file, which is available through the Add New Item dialog box (shown in Figure 4-3).

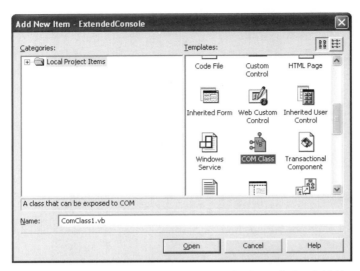

Figure 4-3   The COM class file is available through the Add New Item dialog box.

This COM class file does several things. First, it creates an empty class in a new file. Second, it applies the Visual Basic .NET specific *ComClass* attribute to that class and provides a set of autogenerated GUIDs. All you need to do is add public methods to the new class. (You can add private members, but they just won't be visible to the COM world). Your class file might look something like this:

```
<ComClass(ComClass1.ClassId, ComClass1.InterfaceId, ComClass1.EventsId)> _
Public Class ComClass1

#Region "COM GUIDs"
    ' These  GUIDs provide the COM identity for this class
    ' and its COM interfaces. If you change them, existing
    ' clients will no longer be able to access the class.
    Public Const ClassId As String = "3A6B5582-9A72-438F-8B66-C0832FEE6AA3"
    Public Const InterfaceId As String = _
                    "42D21B6F-D962-4552-8104-C4291B07E3ED"
    Public Const EventsId As String = "74DE4086-EB18-4243-9AFD-061CD36A127C"
#End Region

    ' A creatable COM class must have a Public Sub New()
    ' with no parameters, otherwise, the class will not be
    ' registered in the COM registry and cannot be created
    ' via CreateObject.
    Public Sub New()
        MyBase.New()
    End Sub
End Class
```

This is a pretty simple way to create your own COM components. But it is also very powerful. You should look into the documentation for the *ComClass* attribute to find out what else you can do to customize your components.

There are many ways to create COM components from Visual Basic .NET. We've only touched on some of the Visual Basic .NET–specific mechanisms. A plethora of attributes are available in the .NET Framework that you can use to customize marshaling, interfaces, GUIDs, and everything in between.

COM Threading Models

COM supports two threading models: multithreaded apartment (MTA) and single-threaded apartment (STA). Of course, CLR-based languages are free threaded by default—which creates a potential problem. STA components don't play nicely (or sometimes at all) in a free-threaded environment. Thankfully, a simple solution is available: the *MTAThread* and *STAThread* attributes.

The simple rule for COM threading models is that STA components should be used by STA threads but MTA components can be used universally. There are a great many STA threaded components (mostly built by Visual Basic 5.0 and 6.0).

Threading Concerns

By default, .NET components are free-threaded. The Visual Basic .NET compiler, on the other hand, will mark your main program threads as STA threads. The documentation for the *STAThread* attribute can be misleading. It states the following: "Threading models only pertain to applications that use COM interop. Applying this attribute to an application that does not use COM interop has no effect." This might lead you to ask why the compiler defaults to STA threads for the main application method. It turns out that in the .NET Framework, COM interop is used in many instances. The *Windows.Forms* namespace is full of examples of this. This should not create a major problem for your applications—you can always create additional free threads. All you need to be concerned about is whether any spawned threads need to talk to STA components. If so, they must be marked with the *STAThread* attribute.

Performance Considerations

All of the features I've described in this chapter allow you to publish your .NET components to the wide world of COM, but not without a price. Transitions—from PInvoke or COM interop—always imply additional associated overhead, however small. The overhead penalty for PInvoke is roughly 10 native (assembly) instructions per call; for COM interop, it is roughly 30 to 50 instructions per call. For the most part, you can consider the calling overhead to be constant. This should lead you to ask certain questions about how you use functions or COM objects.

More Info   More information on COM interop and performance issues can be found on the MSDN Web site in an article titled "Microsoft .NET /COM Migration and Interoperability." The URL is *http://msdn.microsoft.com/library/ default.asp?url=/library/en-us/dnbda/html/cominterop.asp*.

What it boils down to is this: you should do substantial work whenever you cross the boundary between the unmanaged and managed world. Think of it this way. A simple property on a COM object might have only a four- or five-instruction overhead. If you call that property through COM interop, you've increased the calling overhead to roughly 55 instructions—a potentially noticeable difference, if you invoke the property frequently. This can lead to horrendous performance degradation in your application.

On the other hand, if there is a method that you can call that not only sets the property but does additional needed work, you can potentially reduce the effect of the interop overhead. The longer the method takes to run, the less noticeable the COM interop overhead will be. I consider frequent calls to lightweight methods to be *chatty*, while less frequent calls to methods that do a significant amount of work are *chunky*. In the distributed application model, chunky calls are vastly preferable. Also keep in mind that data marshaling adds additional overhead. The amount of additional overhead will depend greatly on the type and size of the data to be marshaled. Wherever possible, try to pass only blittable types, rather than more complex nonblittable types, because they result in significantly less marshaling overhead.

Memory Considerations

Remember that when you use native methods to create unmanaged data structures, these structures are created outside of the managed environment. In other words, the CLR has no idea that this memory has been allocated and if you don't clean it up yourself, the CLR never will (at least until the application is terminated and all memory is released). You can appreciate that keeping objects and resources lying around until application termination is wasteful at best. At worst, it can seriously affect the runtime behavior of your application. Be a good developer and clean up after yourself.

Conclusion

The subject of native and COM interop is almost overwhelming in its scope. You'll notice that I've barely touched on the topics of PInvoke and COM interop. Instead, I've attempted to cover the basics and point you down the right road. The path you choose is up to you.

As time goes on, you should have to do less and less interop with native code and COM. Microsoft is certainly making a huge commitment that all new Windows APIs will support a managed interface. As more of the Win32 API functionality makes its way into the .NET Framework classes and other managed assemblies, the less work you'll need to do to take advantage of those features.

Of course, you'll have your own legacy issues to contend with. Corporations are notorious for keeping around old code that no one has the time, expertise, or inclination to upgrade. (Sometimes the original source code no longer exists.) System integration issues will always pose challenges that will ensure a solid future for the likes of PInvoke and COM interop.

Part II

Building an Enterprise Infrastructure

5

Distributed Programming in .NET

Applications need to be able to communicate with each other. This has always been possible using technologies such as shared memory and network socket communication, but using these technologies in a way that preserves types and type fidelity has always been a challenge for developers. Subsequent technologies such as COM and DCOM have provided Windows developers with some of the necessary functionality, but COM and DCOM don't play well in the world of the Internet. DCOM, especially, has suffered because most network administrators restrict the number of TCP/IP ports that Internet traffic can use to get through their firewalls. Unfortunately, the ports used by DCOM usually don't make the cut for security and performance reasons, so DCOM applications rarely work across the Internet (at least not with corporate customers).

With the .NET Framework, Microsoft has completely revised its interapplication communication. In place of DCOM are .NET Remoting and XML Web services. XML Web services seem to get more press, but .NET Remoting is an equally formidable technology that solves certain problems that XML Web services simply cannot. In this chapter, we'll look at both of these technologies and explore the advantages and disadvantages of each.

You've seen the basic demonstrations of XML Web services and how they're supposed to change the Web. You might also have heard of .NET Remoting. But how should these services be integrated into real applications? How do you enforce permissions and referential security across the enterprise and over the Internet? These are among the questions this chapter will address.

We need to begin, however, with a discussion of object serialization. The topic of serialization is relevant to both XML Web services and Remoting and is crucial to understanding distributed interapplication communication.

Serialization

Simply put, serialization is the process of deconstructing information about a type into some basic format. The reverse process, deserialization, reconstructs the original object from the serialized data. The advantages of serialization include the ability to persist in-memory objects to disk, to marshal object across process boundaries, and to marshal objects over network connections.

Imagine an application that over time builds up a set of in-memory objects. It might be desirable for these objects to persist even if the application itself is terminated. Using serialization to persist these objects to a file or database would be extremely useful. Another possibility might be a custom user state maintained by a Web site. Using serialization, you can store an object in a database for easy retrieval.

Serialization has many uses within an application, including the following:

- Sharing objects through the Clipboard

- Persisting in-memory objects to disk

- Marshaling data over Remoting and XML Web services

- Serializing a type to a stream

Before we continue our discussion on the uses of serialization, we'll look at the available serialization formats.

Serialization Formats

Three major forms of serialization formats are available through the .NET Framework: binary, SOAP, and XML. Binary and SOAP serialization preserves complete type fidelity. This means that the deserialized objects preserve all of the type details of the original objects. Binary serialization is not available for use with marshaling XML Web service parameters or return types. XML serialization, on the other hand, serializes only public read/write types and fields of a type. (It does also support read-only collections.) SOAP and binary serialization are the most applicable to Remoting and XML Web services. XML serialization (using the *Xml.Serialization* namespace) is most applicable to custom serialization needs, so I won't cover that topic here.

As long as a type supports serialization—we'll look at how you do this shortly—you can use either SOAP or binary serialization, which provide a great deal of flexibility. Remoting supports both the binary and XML serialization formats, and XML Web services support only the SOAP serialization format. Binary serialization is performed using the *BinaryFormatter* class from the *System.Runtime.Serialization.Formatters.Binary* namespace. SOAP serialization is performed with the *SoapFormatter* class from the *System.Runtime.Serialization.Formatters.Soap* namespace.

The following sample demonstrates how to manually serialize an *Integer* array—a type that does support serialization—using both the *BinaryFormatter* and *SoapFormatter* classes:

```
Option Strict On

Imports System.IO
Imports System.Xml.Serialization
Imports System.Runtime.Serialization.Formatters
Imports System.Runtime.Serialization.Formatters.Binary
Imports System.Runtime.Serialization.Formatters.Soap

Module Module1
    Sub Main()
        Dim iAry() As Integer = New Integer(9) {0, 1, 2, 3, 4, 5, 6, 7, 8, 9}

        Dim bf As New BinaryFormatter()
        Dim sf As New SoapFormatter()

        Console.WriteLine("Serializing the array using BinaryFormatter")
        Dim binaryMs As New MemoryStream()
        bf.Serialize(binaryMs, iAry)
        Dim binaryBytes() As Byte = binaryMs.GetBuffer()
        Console.WriteLine(BitConverter.ToString(binaryBytes))
        binaryMs.Close()

        Console.WriteLine("Serializing the array using SoapFormatter:")
        Dim soapMs As New MemoryStream()
        sf.Serialize(soapMs, iAry)
        Dim soapBytes() As Byte = soapMs.GetBuffer()
        Console.WriteLine(System.Text.Encoding.UTF8.GetString(soapBytes))
        soapMs.Close()

        Console.WriteLine("Deserializing the array with BinaryFormatter:")
        binaryMs = New MemoryStream(binaryBytes)
        Dim bAry() As Integer = CType(bf.Deserialize(binaryMs), Integer())

        Console.WriteLine("Deserializing the array with SoapFormatter")
```

```
        soapMs = New MemoryStream(soapBytes)
        Dim sAry() As Integer = CType(sf.Deserialize(soapMs), Integer())

        Console.WriteLine(vbCrLf & "Serialization statistics")
        Console.WriteLine(vbTab & "Soap Size  : {0}", soapBytes.Length)
        Console.WriteLine(vbTab & "Binary Size: {0}", binaryBytes.Length)

        Console.WriteLine("The deserialized arrays matched")
        Console.ReadLine()
    End Sub
End Module
```

The code starts by defining the array we want to serialize. All blittable types (that is, those types that do not require conversion when passed between unmanaged and managed code) and arrays of blittable types are serializable. We then created instances of a *BinaryFormatter* and *SoapFormatter* class to do all of the work. The rest of the sample consists of variations on calling the *Serialize* and *Deserialize* methods on the formatters.

If you run the sample ObjectSerialization project, you'll immediately see the differences between binary and XML serialization. First of all, the binary representation of the array is 68 bytes and looks like the following:

```
00-01-00-00-00-FF-FF-FF-FF-01-00-00-00-00-00-00-00-0F-01-00-00-00-0A-00-00-
00-08-00-00-00-00-01-00-00-00-02-00-00-00-03-00-00-00-04-00-00-00-05-00-00-
00-06-00-00-00-07-00-00-00-08-00-00-00-09-00-00-00-0B
```

The SOAP representation is much larger—in fact, larger by an order of magnitude (655 bytes versus 68 bytes for the binary representation). The nice thing about it is that you can at least read it. Check this out:

```
<SOAP-ENV:Envelope xmlns:xsi="http://www.w3.org/2001/XMLSchema-instance"
xmlns:x
sd="http://www.w3.org/2001/XMLSchema" xmlns:SOAP-ENC=
"http://schemas.xmlsoap.org
/soap/encoding/" xmlns:SOAP-ENV="http://schemas.xmlsoap.org/soap/envelope/"
xmln
s:clr="http://schemas.microsoft.com/soap/encoding/clr/1.0" SOAP-ENV:
encodingStyl
e="http://schemas.xmlsoap.org/soap/encoding/">
<SOAP-ENV:Body>
<SOAP-ENC:Array SOAP-ENC:arrayType="xsd:int[10]">
<item>0</item>
<item>1</item>
<item>2</item>
<item>3</item>
<item>4</item>
<item>5</item>
<item>6</item>
```

```
<item>7</item>
<item>8</item>
<item>9</item>
</SOAP-ENC:Array>
</SOAP-ENV:Body>
</SOAP-ENV:Envelope>
```

Pretty easy, right? What I've demonstrated here is how to manually serialize types using the *BinaryFormatter* and *SoapFormatter* classes. When you use either Remoting or XML Web services, the serialization is done for you. You can, however use the formatter classes whenever you need to perform your own serialization.

The *Serializable* Attribute

All types in Visual Basic .NET are inherently serializable, but that doesn't mean they automatically support serialization. All types that are support serialization must first be marked as serializable. This is done by using the *Serializable* attribute. Many objects within the .NET Framework support serialization, but such support is far from universal. Your own custom types (classes and structures) do not support serialization by default—you must explicitly use the *Serializable* attribute.

Here's a simple class that has the *Serializable* attribute specified:

```
<Serializable> _
Public Class Employee
    Public FName As String
    Public LName As String
    Private SSN As String
End Class
```

Surprisingly, that's it. You do not need to do anything else. Pretty darn easy, isn't it? Of course, this doesn't give you much control. What if you want to control what is and isn't serialized? You have two options: selective serialization and custom serialization.

Selective Serialization

Selective serialization is the simplest way to control serialization of an object. Since the default behavior of binary serialization with the *Serializable* attribute is all-inclusive (it causes everything to be serialized), the designers of the .NET Framework decided to provide a simple exclusion mechanism: the *NonSerialized* attribute. You can control whether an individual member field is serialized by simply applying the *NonSerialized* attribute to that field. You might need this, for example, for fields that represent pointers to memory that cannot be serialized, for information that would not be meaningful in a different context, or information that for security reasons you do not want to be transportable or persistable. The following example demonstrates how this works:

```
<Serializable> _
Public Class Employee
    Public FName As String
    Public LName As String

    <NonSerialized> Public SSN As String
End Class
```

This is, again, a simple approach that does not necessarily work for every situation. What if you want even more control over how your type is serialized? You need to look at implementing a custom serialization solution for your type.

Custom Serialization

Custom serialization gives you complete control over how a type is serialized, although it requires more work to implement. To understand how custom serialization works, you must understand how the *SerializationInfo* class and the *StreamingContext* structure fit into the picture.

Generally speaking, the *SerializationInfo* class is the most important part of implementing custom serialization. This class provides methods for storing and retrieving member information (name, type, and value). You add members to a *SerializationInfo* class at serialization time. When you deserialize an object, members are retrieved from this class. The *StreamingContext* structure is also available during serialization and deserialization; it provides information about the context of the serialization event.

To support custom serialization on a custom type, you must do all of the following:

- Mark your class or structure with the *Serializable* attribute

- Implement the *ISerializable* interface

- Provide a serialization constructor with the following syntax: *Public Sub New(ByVal info As SerializationInfo, ByVal context As Streaming-Context)*

The following class, which you can find in the CustomSerialization project, demonstrates how to implement custom serialization that fulfills the three requirements listed above:

```
Option Strict On

Imports System.Runtime.Serialization
```

```
<Serializable()> Public Class Person
    Implements ISerializable

    Public FirstName As String
    Public LastName As String
    Public BirthDate As Date
    Public SSN As String
    Public Children() As Person

    Public Sub New(ByVal info As SerializationInfo, _
                ByVal context As StreamingContext)

        FirstName = info.GetString("FirstName")
        LastName = info.GetString("LastName")
        BirthDate = info.GetDateTime("BirthDate")
        SSN = info.GetString("SSN")
        Children = CType(info.GetValue("Children", GetType(Object)), _
                    Person())
    End Sub

    Public Sub GetObjectData(ByVal info As SerializationInfo, _
                        ByVal context As StreamingContext) _
                        Implements ISerializable.GetObjectData

        info.AddValue("FirstName", FirstName)
        info.AddValue("LastName", LastName)
        info.AddValue("BirthDate", BirthDate)
        info.AddValue("SSN", SSN)
        info.AddValue("Children", Children)
    End Sub

    Public Sub New(ByVal fName As String, ByVal lName As String)
        MyBase.New()

        Me.FirstName = fName
        Me.LastName = lName
        Me.SSN = "123-45-6789"
        Me.BirthDate = New Date(1976, 6, 27)
    End Sub

    Public Overloads Overrides Function ToString() As String
        Return Me.ToString(0)
    End Function

    Private Overloads Function ToString(ByVal indentLevel As Integer) _
                                    As String

        Dim sb As New System.Text.StringBuilder()
```

```
    Dim indent As New String(CChar(vbTab), indentLevel)

    ' Print the type
    sb.AppendFormat("{0} {1} {2}", indent, Me.GetType(), vbCrLf)

    ' Print the properties
    indent &= " "
    sb.AppendFormat("{0} FirstName = {1} {2}", _
                indent, Me.FirstName, vbCrLf)
    sb.AppendFormat("{0} LastName  = {1} {2}", _
                indent, Me.LastName, vbCrLf)
    sb.AppendFormat("{0} SSN       = {1} {2}", _
                indent, Me.SSN, vbCrLf)
    sb.AppendFormat("{0} BirthDate = {1} {2}", _
                indent, Me.BirthDate, vbCrLf)
    sb.AppendFormat("{0} Children  = {1} {2}", _
                indent, Me.Children, vbCrLf)

    ' Print the children
    If Not Me.Children Is Nothing Then
      Dim p As Person
      For Each p In Me.Children
         sb.Append(p.ToString(indentLevel + 1))
      Next
    End If

    Return sb.ToString()
  End Function
End Class
```

When this class is to be serialized, the *GetObjectData* method is called. As you can see from this example, storing fields in the *SerializationInfo* class is trivial. The only thing you need to be careful about is that you must store the member with a string representation of the name of that member. When the number of properties on a class becomes larger, maintaining a consistent naming scheme becomes more challenging. Since your goal should be minimizing confusion, I'd recommend that you provide a string that matches the name of the field being stored. This might lead to a lot of typing, but you'll greatly reduce the chances for confusion.

The *Person* class demonstrates another interesting serialization aspect. Notice how it supports the *Children* property. This property is a *Person* array, which means that an instance of the *Person* class represents a hierarchy of other *Person* objects. This example also helps demonstrate how to serialize nested classes. Notice that this is not difficult—the *SerializationInfo* class essentially takes care of calling the *GetObjectData* methods on the classes contained in the *Children* field.

Deserialization happens when the public constructor is called. Here all of the stored members are extracted from the *SerializationInfo* class. For most of the standard built-in types (such as *Byte*, *Char*, *Double*, and *String*), the *SerializationInfo* class provides a set of overloads that allow you to extract those types directly. Thus, for most of our fields in the *Person* class, we call the *GetString* method. The exception is the *Children* property, which is an array of *Person* objects. In this case, you must call the generic *GetValue* method, passing *GetType(Object)*. (I'm not sure why a *GetObject* method isn't supported.) You can then cast the returned object to the correct type.

Note   You should be able to pass the specific type to the *GetValue* method, but it really won't help you. You need to do the cast anyway, and in the first release of the .NET Framework, passing a specific type to this method will result in an exception if the type doesn't support *IConvertible*. This is a bug and should be fixed in future versions of the .NET Framework.

Limitations of the *Serializable* Attribute

It should be no great surprise that the *Serializable* attribute has limitations. Here are the major ones:

- The *Serializable* attribute cannot be inherited and must be explicitly specified for each class that you want to make serializable.

- Serialization cannot be added to a class after it has been compiled. (Modifying a class through reflection won't work.)

More Info   If you're interested in learning more about serialization, see the documentation that accompanies Visual Basic .NET and the Framework SDK—both contain lots of great information about serialization and associated topics.

XML Web Services

XML Web services is a distributed communications protocol based on SOAP. SOAP can be loosely defined as XML over HTTP. SOAP, among other things, provides a standard that supports the transfer of data in the form of XML messages. Other forms of distributed communication technologies require communication in a much more tightly-coupled fashion, often using platform-specific binary protocol formats. SOAP, thanks to its use of XML and HTTP, frees the client and server from any platform-specific implementation restrictions, allowing much greater flexibility and the use of Web services in a heterogeneous (nonuniform) computing environment.

What ties together the client and a server is a contract. When you develop a Web service, a contract is created that specifies all of the supported headers, methods, parameters, and return types. (This contract is generated automatically by the Visual Basic .NET compiler when you build an ASP.NET Web Service project.) As long as a client honors the contract, that client will be able to successfully communicate with the server. This makes Web services language-independent and platform-independent. Also, because of the flexibility of the XML format, you can add more methods to your service without breaking the functionality of your clients. Unlike tightly-coupled applications, which break easily with the smallest changes, XML Web services are extremely flexible and tolerant of change.

Getting Started

Creating Web services is almost trivial in Visual Basic .NET using the ASP.NET framework. A Web service has access to virtually all of the .NET Framework, including authentication, caching, state management, threading, and COM+. To differentiate Web services from regular ASP.NET applications, which use the .aspx file extension, the .asmx file extension was introduced.

Creating a Web service is as simple as creating a new ASP.NET Web services project through the Visual Basic .NET IDE. From there, all you need to do is customize the default ASMX file created by the IDE. The basic requirements for a Web service in a Web service project include:

- A class that inherits from the *WebService* class
- A method that is marked with the *WebMethod* attribute

That's about it. Using the default example created by the Visual Basic .NET IDE, a simple Web service might look like this:

```
Imports System.Web.Services

<WebService(Namespace := "http://tempuri.org/")> _
Public Class Service1
    Inherits System.Web.Services.WebService

#Region " Web Services Designer Generated Code "

    <WebMethod()> Public Function HelloWorld() As String
```

```
        HelloWorld = "Hello World"
    End Function

End Class
```

That's about it. All you need to do is compile the Web service, which will generate all of the contract and discovery information needed for a client to consume this service.

Consuming an XML Web Service

To consume a Web service in Visual Basic .NET, you must add a Web reference to your project. A Web reference is a design-time-generated proxy class. This class provides the methods exposed by a *WebService* and marshals all method calls to the actual Web service at run time. This allows the developer to access the Web service as if it were a local component. This provides several advantages, including support for code completion (IntelliSense) for the methods and properties provided by the service. This proxy class implementation is responsible for enforcing the SOAP contract details for the target Web service. You can add a Web reference to any kind of project.

At run time, every call to the proxy object is converted to a SOAP request and sent to the Web service. The target Web service translates the SOAP request and invokes the specified target method. If the target method returns any information, that data is first translated into a SOAP message and then sent back to the client. On the client, the proxy class is responsible for converting the SOAP message back to a native format before returning the type back to the calling code.

Note   You can use the *URL* property of the proxy class to specify the destination URL of the XML Web service. The Add Web Reference dialog box defaults the proxy target to the URL of the XML Web service originally selected. This is useful if you need to change the target of a Web service at run time. For example, you might be using one Web service while developing your application but need to easily specify a different service when the application is deployed.

SOAP Header Extensions

Recall that all Web services are based on the SOAP protocol. One interesting feature of SOAP is the ability to support a variable number of headers—known as SOAP headers—that can be sent with each SOAP request. SOAP headers offer a way to pass information to and from an XML Web service method without affecting the actual method being invoked. The header can contain user authentication details or other information that you think is important. You can thus send all sorts of information back and forth without having to change the definition of your methods to accept additional parameters.

You can define as many SOAP headers as your application needs, and headers will be applied to individual methods contained within a service. You can easily change what headers are required for which method calls.

To incorporate a SOAP header in the design of your Web service, you must follow these steps:

1. Create a class that inherits from *SoapHeader*. This class should contain all of the members that have the information you want to include. You can implement additional header classes to process different types of information. From a design perspective, you should logically group related information into a single SOAP header class.

2. Add a member your XML Web service class of the type of your new SOAP header class.

3. Apply a *SoapHeaderAttribute* to your XML Web service method, specifying the name of the new member variable representing your SOAP header.

4. In your XML Web service method, add code to process your header (that is, to process the information contained in the incoming header and possibly populate additional information for response back to the client).

5. In your XML Web service client code, add code to process your header (that is, to populate the header with the information you want to send and possibly process the contents of the header after the method call).

To see how this works, let's walk through a simple implementation using user credentials. First, let's define a class that represents our SOAP header:

```
Public Class MyHeader
    Inherits SoapHeader

    Public UserName As String
    Public Password As String
End Class
```

Fairly simple so far. You can see that the header class *MyHeader* contains the necessary information to authenticate a user. Now we need to create a Web service that implements this header:

```
<WebService(Namespace:="http://tempuri.org/")> _
Public Class Service1
    Inherits System.Web.Services.WebService

#Region " Web Services Designer Generated Code "

    Public UserCredentials As MyHeader

    <WebMethod(),SoapHeader("UserCredentials", Required:=True)> _
    Public Function HelloWorld() As String

    End Function
End Class
```

I defined a service called *WebService1* that supports a Web method called *HelloWorld*. Using the *SoapHeader* attribute, I also indicated that the *HelloWorld* method supports the *UserCredentials* SOAP header and, in fact, requires that it be passed. This is a simple way of preventing a client from calling the method without providing the header. Now we need to process the header on the *Web-Services* side to determine whether the user is allow to use this method. The code I added to the *HelloWorld* method looks like this:

```
If Me.UserCredentials.UserName = "bob" And _
   Me.UserCredentials.Password = "password" Then

    Return "Hello World"
Else
    Throw New Exception("Invalid user.")
End If
```

Simple enough, right? Now all we need to do is set up the client application to call this method and provide the header. First, we need to have an application that contains a Web reference to our service. Once we have that and the *MyHeader* and *Service1* classes are defined, all we need to do is use them. We must create the header class and populate it with the user information:

```
Dim hdr As New localhost.MyHeader()

hdr.UserName = "bob"
hdr.Password = "password"
```

All that's left to do at this point is create an instance of the Web service, assign the header, and call the Web method. Note that *MyHeader* is implemented as a member variable named *UserCredentials* on the *Service1* class in the Web service but is missing from the *Service1* class in the client. What's going on here? This is just a quirk. The header is available through the *MyHeader-Value* property on the client. This actually makes sense because it prevents you from declaring the same header type more than once. It also provides the client with an obvious member to store the *MyHeader* value. Given this information, the following code should make more sense:

```
Dim ws As New localhost.Service1()

ws.MyHeaderValue = hdr
Console.WriteLine(ws.HelloWorld())
```

You can use this same methodology to implement all sorts of additional headers.

Warning   You should never pass user credentials (name and password) in the clear like this in a real application. This is example is meant to illustrative SOAP headers only. Also, you should always use a strong password. Never use an easily guessed password, especially not the word *password*. See the upcoming section on security and Chapter 9 for additional information about good security practices.

Performance

Web services and performance can go hand-in-hand. Because Web services are hosted in the IIS application, you automatically get a lot of performance features Granted, you can do all sorts of things to kill your performance, but IIS inherently provides built-in scalability. You can also use operating system features such as clustering—see Figure 5-1—to improve your application's performance by moving to a multimachine system. This is simple to do with Web services, but it is much more problematic with Remoting (unless you also host your remote objects in IIS). You also benefit from the fact that IIS scales well on multiprocessor systems.

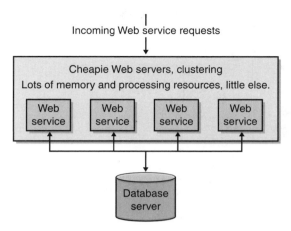

Figure 5-1   An example of a clustered Web service.

Calling Overhead

The flip side of the performance benefits of Web services is that they incur a lot of calling overhead. This means that each call to a Web service is a relatively expensive process. Recall our discussion of chunky versus chatty COM calls in Chapter 4. The same rationale applies here: the calling overhead is significant, so you should design your Web service to minimize the number of necessary calls. Figure 5-2 illustrates the difference between calling methods in a chatty versus chunky way. The first bar indicates the overhead of a single method call. Note that the network overhead is substantial compared to the amount of time spent executing the actual method.

The third bar demonstrates what the performance picture looks like if you call the same method five times. The overhead of the network calls quickly becomes overwhelming—notice the performance penalty. The center bar shows what happens if you redesign your method to require only a single call. In this case, you realize a performance benefit because you've increased the amount of work accomplished by that method while keeping the overhead at a fixed cost. This is the best way to handle the situation. You should use serialization, whenever possible, to pass the necessary information back and forth to minimize the total number of remote method invocations.

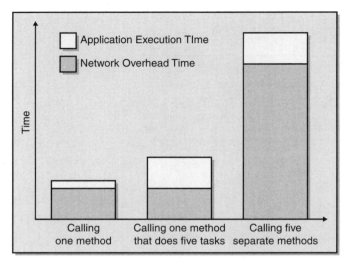

Figure 5-2   The effects of calling overhead.

Limitations of Web Services

Unfortunately, Web services cannot support Interop to single-threaded apartment (STA) COM objects. Unlike ASP.NET, which supports an ASPCOMPAT option to execute the page on an STA thread, Web services cannot alter their executing thread model. All Web services run on free threads, and you cannot change this. This is intentional because high performance of Web services is essential.

Security

Web service security relies on the security features of IIS, including built-in user authentication and content security. You can take advantage of these features, or you can roll your own security implementation. We'll look at each of these options in turn. All of these features are accessible through the IIS MMC plug-in from the Computer Management console or under Administrative Tools on the All Programs menu.

User Authentication

IIS provides full support for authenticating users for any resource available through IIS. You can disallow anonymous access to prevent unauthenticated users from accessing specific resources or all resources by turning off anonymous access at the Web-site level. The authentication methods supported by IIS include the following:

■ Anonymous access (no authentication)

■ Digest authentication (sends a hash value over the network instead of the password)

■ Basic authentication (clear-text password)

■ Integrated Windows authentication (built-in secure challenge-response domain-based security)

Supporting each authentication type is as easy as selecting a check box in a dialog box. All of these authentications mechanisms rely in some way on Windows security and permissions.

Content Security

IIS supports a technology called Secure Sockets Layer (SSL), which is intended to provide secure communication for HTTP. The combination of HTTP and SSL is referred to as *HTTPS*. HTTPS is essentially content-level encryption—all communication between the client and server is encrypted. It is not an authentication technology. When a client connects to a server, it establishes a secure connection; you must then authenticate your client. If you're using an authentication method such as Basic authentication, you're strongly advised to use SSL. Period. Whenever you send user credentials over the network in a clear-text format, you run the risk that someone will poach that information directly off the wire. (Yes, it can be done quite easily by someone with the know-how.)

In the IIS administration utilities, you can also indicate what content must use SSL. Typically, if you only enable SSL for a Web site, you can still access the site's content through both HTTP and HTTPS. By marking content as requiring SSL, you prevent user access over HTTP. Not only will this help isolate a potential set of security bugs (typos are easy to introduce when all you're typing is HTTP or HTTPS), but it will completely prevent intentional misuse of that content.

Custom Security

From a pure security perspective, it is always extremely risky to implement your own custom solution. Custom solutions can be more vulnerable than a provided solution, although the vulnerabilities might be less obvious. If you choose to implement a custom solution, you should be aware of the potential consequences. You should also plan for extensive testing of your security features, preferably by someone who's very experienced with computer security and potential vulnerabilities.

Custom authentication   It is not uncommon for Internet-based services to have their own user databases that are separate from standard user authentication mechanisms. Implementing your own authentication methods in this case is essential—the standard IIS authentication methods will not suffice. Many avenues are available, including using SOAP header extensions.

In a custom SOAP header extension, you can pass a set of security credentials. These credentials can take several forms, including a user ID and password or a session ID. Passing a user ID and password with each call is inherently dangerous. If you do this, you should at least encrypt the header, if not the entire communication (by using SSL). Preferably, you should authenticate once and obtain a session-specific ID over a secure channel. You then pass that session ID in lieu of actual security information. Yet again, the session ID should be encrypted in some manner to ensure that the ID cannot be spoofed.

Custom content security   You can manually encrypt the contents of your Web service requests by combining object serialization with some form of encryption (probably using one of the Crypto service providers from the *Cryptography* namespace). This offers some performance advantages by allowing you to encrypt only information that needs to be secure, but it requires a lot of extra work when you can simply use SSL. But, this may just fit the bill for you anyway.

Remoting

.NET Remoting is an extremely flexible interapplication communication technology provided by the .NET Framework. It provides a tightly coupled communication model that also supports connecting to distributed systems. One major difference between remoting and Web services is that you can pass objects by reference to the target of a remoting call, which enables the target to actively communicate back to the originator of the call. This known as *bidirectional communication*. Remoting provides several specific features:

■   The flexibility to publish or consume services in any type of application, including console and Windows applications, Web applications (hosted in IIS), XML Web services, and Windows services

■   The preservation of type fidelity (tightly coupled)

■   The ability to pass objects and return objects by reference (bidirectional communication)

■   The implementation and use of custom communication channels or protocols

■   The customization of the communication process to provide additional functionality

The general concept behind remoting is you have the client and a service. The service registers types to be available to clients. Clients register types in order to be able to bind to types provided by the service. Type registration applies only to an application instance; to host a remoting service, you must have a process. You then have two choices: create your own process (application or service) to host your remoting service, or host your remoting service in IIS (more on this later).

The client and service do not need to be on separate machines. Remoting can be used in a distributed environment, but it is a generic interprocess communication technology. Much like the DCOM technologies it replaces, remoting lets you create and invoke remote objects and marshal data, objects, and references.

Remoting is most useful for communication between machines on the same network. It is not really intended as an Internet communication technology. For that purpose, Microsoft recommends XML Web services.

Getting Started

The key to providing a class through remoting is the *RemotingConfiguration* class. This class provides all of the necessary methods to configure and monitor the remoting services provided and consumed by a process. Table 5-1 lists the properties supported by this class that provide information specific to the current application and process.

Table 5-1
Public Shared Properties of the *RemotingConfiguration* Class

Property	Description
ApplicationId	Gets the ID of the currently executing application
ApplicationName	Gets or sets the name of a remoting application
ProcessId	Gets the ID of the currently executing process

The methods that control the registration of service and client types are listed in Table 5-2. These methods give a process control over how services provided by that application behave. In addition to the ability to register types, you can also find out whether a type has been registered, which types have been registered (for both service and client), and which types have been activated on the client.

Table 5-2
Public Shared Methods of the *RemotingConfiguration* Class

Method	Description
Configure	Reads the configuration file and configures the remoting infrastructure
GetRegisteredActivatedClientTypes	Retrieves an array of object types registered on the client as types that will be activated remotely
GetRegisteredActivatedServiceTypes	Retrieves an array of object types registered on the service end that can be activated on request from a client
GetRegisteredWellKnownClientTypes	Retrieves an array of object types registered on the client end as well-known types
GetRegisteredWellKnownServiceTypes	Retrieves an array of object types registered on the service end as well-known types
IsActivationAllowed	Returns a Boolean value indicating whether the specified type is allowed to be client-activated
IsRemotelyActivatedClientType	Checks whether the specified object type is registered as a remotely activated client type
IsWellKnownClientType	Checks whether the specified object type is registered as a well-known client type
RegisterActivatedClientType	Registers an object type on the client end as a type that can be activated on the server
RegisterActivatedServiceType	Registers an object type on the service end as one that can be activated on request from a client
RegisterWellKnownClientType	Registers an object type on the client end as a well-known type (single call or singleton)
RegisterWellKnownServiceType	Registers an object Type on the service end as a well-known type (single call or singleton)

To have an application host a service through remoting, you must do the following:

1. Create a type that you want to make available as a service.

2. Create a communication channel (*TcpChannel* or *HttpChannel*).

3. Register your type as a *Service* type, using the *RegisterActivated-ServiceType* or *RegisterWellKnownServiceType* method

For a client to consume a service through remoting, the following must happen:

1. The client must have a reference to the type to be remoted.

2. Register the type as a client type (using the *RegisterActivatedClient-Type* or *RegisterWellKnownClientType* method), specifying the host name of the service, the channel used, and the desired port. The client registration method you call must match the corresponding server registration method for this to work.

3. Create, or otherwise obtain, an instance of the registered type.

Remoting Activation Models

Two activation models are supported by remoting: activated and well-known. The activated model causes a new instance of a remoted class to be created in the service process when a client creates an instance of the type. The client can then make multiple calls to the remote class, all to the same class instance.

The well-known activation model is quite different. Essentially, the service publisher has a choice: have a new class instance created for each method invocation from a client or make the class available as a singleton to all remoting clients.

Picking the Right Channel

Remoting offers a performance advantage over XML Web services because it provides a choice of communication channels. The two channel classes provided with the .NET Framework are *TcpChannel* and *HttpChannel*.

The *TcpChannel* Class

TcpChannel offers by far the best performance. In an intranet scenario, where security is not an issue, this is the best-performing option. A remoting call through *TcpChannel* is generally five to seven times faster than an equivalent call through *HttpChannel*.

You cannot use *TcpChannel* when a remote object is hosted in IIS, so *TcpChannel* is a remoting-only solution. You must create your own process to host objects with *TcpChannel*.

The *HttpChannel* Class

HttpChannel has benefits as well. The overhead for a remoting call through *HttpChannel* is greater than that for *TcpChannel*, but if you host the remote object in IIS (a requirement if you are using *HttpChannel*), you gain a whole host of scalability benefits. In other words, by hosting your remote objects in IIS, you can take advantage of features such as clustering, robust scaling, session state, and farming.

Sometimes you'll have to use *HttpChannel*, which is less efficient than *TcpChannel*. To make things less painful, you can force the use of binary encoding for all object marshaling instead of the default marshaling.

Marshaling Data

When you pass parameters to or receive values from remote methods, you're marshaling data (in much the same way that Web services work). The important twist for remoting is the ability to pass variables by value or, more significantly, by reference. The default, as for Visual Basic .NET in general, is to marshal all of your parameters and return types by value.

Marshaling Types By Value

The fact that the default marshaling of types is by value is not a major problem. In fact, you don't even need to think twice about it when you're using standard types that support serialization. If, on the other hand, you want to marshal a custom type, you must implement a form of serialization (as described earlier).

Marshaling Types By Reference

If you want a class to be passed by reference instead of by value, you must take a different approach. A class that supports by reference marshaling through remoting must derive from the *MarshalByRef* class. This class provides all of the functionality required to allow manipulation of a remote object. Objects that are marshaled by reference can support remote events and calls to methods and properties. This is pretty slick, and you get it virtually for free just by deriving a class from *MarshalByRef*.

To support having a service call a method on a client object passed by reference, the client must also register a communications channel. Otherwise, any method invocation on the passed object will fail. (The client would essentially not be listening for a request.)

Caution   Bidirectional communication using pass-by-reference is a great feature but generally should not be used in a distributed application environment. The overhead of calling back to the client just to get the value of properties is a complete waste of resources. You're better off serializing the data. Pass-by-reference is most useful when you want remote systems to be able to trigger events or perform some other specific operation.

Using a Separate Interface

You have a choice when designing your remoting implementation. You can remote a class and provide the client with a copy of that class—you need a reference to the type you want to consume, after all—or you can provide a reference to an interface supported by your remote class. Which one do you choose? Of course, it depends.

Remoting an interface instead of a class has certain advantages. You can put the interface into a separate assembly from the class that implements it. Designing in this manner allows the publisher to distribute an assembly that allows clients to talk to their remoting objects, without publishing any real code. If you were to remote a class, you'd have to provide all clients with a definition of that class (or at least a base class). Unfortunately, that class would contain all of the implementation code for the remoted class.

It is often desirable to have the client application be completely unaware of the implementation details of your remoted object. By using an interface (that's available, say, in a separate assembly, as shown in Figure 5-3), you can allow the client to consume a service, without providing any of the implementation details.

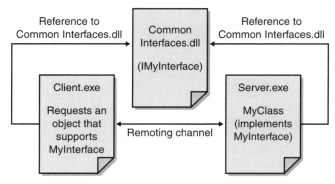

Figure 5-3   Using a common interface to hide implementation details.

Remember that if you ship out an assembly containing a remoted class, any customer can run ILDASM on the assembly (or one of the other reverse-engineering tools) and extract the implementation code. If you distribute only an interface, there's nothing to reverse-engineer.

Remoting Singletons

You've seen a remoting method that results in new object instances being created on the server for each incoming client request. This is not always desirable. Sometimes you might want to allow only a single object to exist—a singleton.

Remoting an object as a singleton is fairly simple. In the same way that we registered other types through remoting, we can also register singletons. Unlike with true singletons, you must define your class with a public constructor because the remoting infrastructure is responsible for creating and maintaining the singleton throughout its lifetime and will only allow a single instance of the class to be created through the remoting channel.

The only thing you really need to worry about is when your singleton is targeted for garbage collection. That's where lifetime leases come into play.

Lifetime Leases

When you define a singleton for remoting, you must carefully consider how the object is going to be used. More specifically, you need to know whether it is acceptable for the singleton object to be recycled (garbage-collected and then re-created) even if there are connected clients. Every remote object has a lifetime lease. A singleton can, and most likely will, exceed the default lifetime lease and be destroyed. This is not normally desirable behavior for a singleton—it should last the entire lifetime of the application. If you don't want to deal with this, you must change the default lifetime lease to something more appropriate. In this case, an infinite lifetime lease.

Creating a infinite lifetime lease is simple and straightforward. The *MarshalByRef* class defines a method called *InitializeLifetimeService* for retrieving the lifetime service object that controls the lifetime of the current class's instance. By overriding *InitializeLifetimeService*, you can provide and control your own lease information. The simplest case, returning a reference to *Nothing*, results in a remoting object with an infinite lifetime lease. You can thus implement a true singleton through remoting. The following example illustrates how to do this:

```
Public Overrides Function InitializeLifetimeService() As Object
    Return Nothing ' Specify an infinite lifetime lease
End Function
```

That's all there is to it. You can see similar code at work in the remoting example toward the end of the chapter.

Security

Remoting itself provides no features that directly support secure communication. Instead, three general approaches are available for securing your communication: securing the communication channel itself, securing the message's content, or both. We'll look at each of these options in turn.

Note   Generally, as more security features are implemented, an application's performance will get worse. And although absolute security is a desirable goal, it is never practical technically or financially unless you bury your application in a bunker! Compromises are commonplace, and you must balance the need to provide security with the overall cost of implementing it.

Securing the Communications Channel

As you know, only two remoting channels are available out of the box: *HttpChannel* and *TcpChannel*. *TcpChannel*, a channel implementation over the low-level TCP protocol, does not natively provide support for secure communications. You can use *TcpChannel* if the network environment your application is running in supports wire-level protection (such as IPSec). Unfortunately, this is not common. It generally leaves *TcpChannel* as a high-speed but insecure communications channel.

Internet Protocol Security Extensions (IPSec)

IPSec is a set of security extensions to the Internet Protocolv4 (IPv4) standard. IPSec is a protocol for negotiating both encryption and authentication at the wire level. Other security protocols secure specific sockets or communication, but IPSec secures all communication between hosts. IPSec is a required part of the IPv6 standard. (Support is available in version 1.1 of the .NET Framework). To communicate via IPSec, both hosts involved must support the IPSec protocol.

The alternative, of course, is *HttpChannel*. Recall that remoting hosts that use *HttpChannel* must reside in IIS. IIS provides a lot of goodies for free (although features are rarely free where performance is concerned), including SSL and user authentication. In fact, hosting remote objects in IIS allows you to support complex security solutions with little coding required on your part.

Securing the Message's Content

You secure a message's content by encrypting it. In Chapter 9, I'll explain how to use the .NET Framework's CryptoService providers to properly encrypt data. However, you'll need to consider some issues with this approach. First, you must manually encrypt and decrypt the contents of your messages. This requires a lot of additional work but might make sense if you're using the remoting *TcpChannel*. You'll take a performance hit, but probably less of one than if you use *HttpChannel* over SSL (as discussed in the previous section).

Ultimately, the choice is up to you. Depending on your performance requirements, you might try several different combinations just to see what fits. Remember that implementing your own security strategy is not for the fainthearted. More often than not, you're far better off taking advantage of built-in technologies that free you from many of the implementation details. Using IIS to host your remote objects is an excellent example. The services provided by IIS—including user authentication, secure sockets, and a scalable performance architecture—are nothing to sniff at.

Tying It All Together

To tie together most of the topics discussed so far, I created a remoting sample that does a little bit of everything. The sample, which is simply called Remoting, does the following:

- Registers a type as a singleton
- Passes a custom type by value (supports serialization)
- Passes a custom type by reference (inheriting from *MarshalByRef*)
- Creates channel sinks

To start with, we'll define the following custom marshaling types in a common assembly:

```
Public Class MyClient
    Inherits MarshalByRefObject

    Public Sub PostMessage(ByVal msg As String)
        MsgBox(msg)
```

```
      End Sub
End Class

<Serializable()> Public Structure MachineData
   Public Name As String
   Public ProcessID As Integer
   Public IPAddresses() As System.Net.IPAddress
End Structure
```

Next, we'll define an interface, also in the shared common assembly:

```
Public Interface IMachine
   ReadOnly Property Name() As String
   ReadOnly Property ProcessID() As Integer
   ReadOnly Property IPAddresses() As System.Net.IPAddress()

   Function GetMachineData() As MachineData
   Sub SendMeAMessage(ByVal c As MyClient)
End Interface
```

In the server application, we'll implement the *IMachine* interface with the *Machine* class. To simplify debugging and to illustrate how this works, we'll include a *Console.WriteLine* call in each of the methods. When you run the host application, you'll see printed statements documenting all of the remoting activities:

```
Imports RemoteInterfaces
Imports System.Collections
Imports System.Net

Public Class Machine
   Inherits MarshalByRefObject
   Implements IMachine

   Public Sub New()
      MyBase.New()

      Console.WriteLine("Machine object created")
   End Sub

   Public ReadOnly Property Name() As String Implements IMachine.Name
      Get
         Console.WriteLine("Machine.Name called")
         Return Dns.GetHostName()
      End Get
   End Property

   ReadOnly Property IPAddresses() As IPAddress() _
      Implements IMachine.IPAddresses
```

```vb
      Get
          Console.WriteLine("Machine.IPAddresses called")
          Return Dns.GetHostByName(Dns.GetHostName()).AddressList
      End Get
  End Property

  Public ReadOnly Property ProcessID() As Integer Implements _
      IMachine.ProcessID
      Get
          Console.WriteLine("Machine.ProcessID called")
          Return System.Diagnostics.Process.GetCurrentProcess.Id
      End Get
  End Property

  Public Function GetMachineData() As MachineData Implements _
      IMachine.GetMachineData
      Console.WriteLine("Machine.GetMachineData called")

      Dim md As New MachineData()

      md.Name = Dns.GetHostName()
      md.IPAddresses = Dns.GetHostByName(Dns.GetHostName()).AddressList
      md.ProcessID = System.Diagnostics.Process.GetCurrentProcess.Id

      Return md
  End Function

  Public Sub SendMeAMessage(ByVal c As MyClient) Implements _
      IMachine.SendMeAMessage
      c.PostMessage("Hello")
  End Sub

  Public Overrides Function InitializeLifetimeService() As Object
      Return Nothing
  End Function
End Class
```

Once we've implemented the *Machine* class, all we need to do is register it. In this case, we want to register the class as a singleton—because there's no need for more than one copy of the class to exist. In this case, the decision was simple. To see how the host process is set up, check out the following example:

```vb
Imports System.Runtime.Remoting
Imports System.Runtime.Remoting.Channels
Imports System.Runtime.Remoting.Channels.Tcp
Imports System.Runtime.Remoting.Channels.Http

Module Module1
    Public Sub Main()
```

```
        Dim channel As TcpChannel
        channel = New TcpChannel(8085)
        ChannelServices.RegisterChannel(channel)

        RemotingConfiguration.RegisterWellKnownServiceType( _
            GetType(Machine), "Machine", WellKnownObjectMode.Singleton)

        Console.WriteLine("Remoting setup complete")
        Console.ReadLine()
    End Sub
End Module
```

We now have a host process for our remote object. (See Figure 5-4.) To enable our client, all we need to do is create a *TcpChannel* (because we want to support bidirectional communication—it's not necessary on the client otherwise), register the *IMachine* type, and use the *Activator.GetObject* method to get instances of our remote object.

Figure 5-4   The remoting client example's form.

The implementation code for this form looks like the following:

```
Imports RemoteInterfaces
Imports System.Runtime.Remoting
Imports System.Runtime.Remoting.Channels
Imports System.Runtime.Remoting.Channels.Tcp

Public Class Form1
    Inherits System.Windows.Forms.Form

#Region " Windows Form Designer generated code "

    Private Sub Form1_Load(ByVal sender As Object, _
                        ByVal e As System.EventArgs) Handles MyBase.Load

        Dim c As New TcpChannel(8086)
        ChannelServices.RegisterChannel(c)
```

```vb
                RemotingConfiguration.RegisterWellKnownClientType( _
                            GetType(IMachine), _
                            "tcp://localhost:8085/Machine")
    End Sub


    Private Sub MachineButton_Click(ByVal sender As System.Object, _
                            ByVal e As System.EventArgs) _
                            Handles MachineButton.Click

        Dim m As IMachine = _
            Activator.GetObject(GetType(IMachine), _
                            "tcp://localhost:8085/Machine")

        MsgBox(m.Name)
    End Sub

    Private Sub AddressButton_Click(ByVal sender As System.Object, _
                            ByVal e As System.EventArgs) _
                            Handles AddressButton.Click

        Dim m As IMachine = _
            Activator.GetObject(GetType(IMachine), _
                            "tcp://localhost:8085/Machine")

        MsgBox(m.IPAddresses)
    End Sub

    Private Sub ProcessButton_Click(ByVal sender As System.Object, _
                            ByVal e As System.EventArgs) _
                            Handles ProcessButton.Click

        Dim m As IMachine = _
            Activator.GetObject(GetType(IMachine), _
                            "tcp://localhost:8085/Machine")

        MsgBox(m.ProcessID)
    End Sub

    Private Sub EverythingButton_Click(ByVal sender As System.Object, _
                            ByVal e As System.EventArgs) _
                            Handles EverythingButton.Click

        Dim m As IMachine =
            Activator.GetObject(GetType(IMachine), _
                            "tcp://localhost:8085/Machine")

        MsgBox(m.GetMachineData().ToString())
    End Sub
```

```
    Private Sub MessageButton_Click(ByVal sender As System.Object, _
                                    ByVal e As System.EventArgs) _
                                    Handles MessageButton.Click

        Dim m As IMachine = _
           Activator.GetObject(GetType(IMachine), _
                                "tcp://localhost:8085/Machine")

        Dim c As New MyClient()
        m.SendMeAMessage(c)
      End Sub
End Class
```

More Info   To look further at the remoting technology, start with the .NET Framework SDK quick-start samples and tutorials.

Conclusion

Both Web services and remoting provide a wealth of features for applications. Your choice should be based purely on design considerations. Web services work well in an environment in which you have to consider supporting diverse platforms. SOAP is, after all, an open standard, and Web services can be consumed by any platform that understands the Microsoft WebServices XML schema. Web services also provide a great deal of scalability and performance features, thanks to IIS.

Remoting is obviously more platform-centric, but it provides for the more generic interapplication communication scenarios. Combining speed with less overhead, remoting definitely fits the bill for local interapplication communication. When a distributed network is involved, you have the option of hosting your remote objects in IIS to improve performance as well as gain scalability features. In addition, the ability to use a variety of communication channels is extremely powerful and can accommodate all sorts of custom remoting scenarios.

In the end, you must choose the solution that best fits your application's needs. Remoting and Web services are not always mutually exclusive options, so you can also use them in concert if necessary.

6

Custom Network Communication

The last chapter covered the distributed technologies that enable you to tie together sophisticated applications. While XML Web services and .NET Remoting are really the major connectivity technologies, they are high-level communication mechanisms. If you have to implement a Web server, an e-mail client, or a TCP/IP-based gaming system, neither Remoting nor Web services can help you. It's time to start exploring the Microsoft .NET Framework's *System.Net* namespace.

In the .NET Framework, the *System.Net* namespace is where all of the lower-level networking technologies can be found. Included are classes that support a wide variety of communication technologies, from low-level socket communication to higher-level networking protocols such as HTTP. Many of these objects are extensible, allowing you to develop custom protocol implementations. In this chapter, I'll introduce you to most of the these technologies and demonstrate how to use some of the important classes. Unfortunately, however, much of the subject of network programming is beyond the scope of this book.

This chapter will provide an overview of lower-level network communication in Microsoft Visual Basic .NET and the .NET Framework, but you should not expect a complete reference. If you're familiar with some elements of network programming, you should be off to a great start. For everyone else, I'll kick things off with a discussion of networking protocols. From there, we'll work through the *System.Net* namespace, starting with the higher-level classes and working our way down to the lower-level protocol and communication classes.

An Overview of Network Communication

We live in an increasingly networked world. From our computers to our cell phones, the Internet (including custom intranets) is becoming almost unavoidable. This means, of course, that the importance of communicating over these networks is more important and necessary than ever. Technologies such as remoting and XML Web services provides high-level distributed communication frameworks, but they are not the complete solution. Besides, those technologies must at some point be implemented, and that involves using a lower-level communications protocol. (They are both built on TCP/IP, after all.)

Network Architectures

Before we get into too much detail, we should take a step back and look at what role network architectures play into today's applications. There are effectively two types of communication architectures in common use today:

- Client/server

- Peer-to-peer

The vast majority of applications are based on the client/server application architecture. Web-based applications are a client/server model. A client/server model is typically a centralized networking architecture with communication in only one direction. (See Figure 6-1.) Applications that fall into this category include e-mail server, Web server, database server, and Telnet.

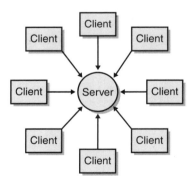

Figure 6-1   The client/server application architecture.

The traditional client/server model has been challenged in recent years by the popular peer-to-peer (P2P) networks. Peer-to-peer communication architectures have been around for years. The earliest P2P networks in wide use were based on the AppleTalk networking protocol; these were closely followed by the SMB protocol used by Microsoft for Windows file sharing. Unfortunately, neither of these technologies is suitable for large-scale (such as Internet-scale) P2P networks. Napster and all of the subsequent P2P file-sharing networks heralded a much more sophisticated form of P2P network—one that allowed true online communities to be built. These P2P networks are based on the idea that each computer represents a communications node within the network. In many ways, these nodes provide functionality and additional robustness to the network they join.

In true P2P networks—see Figure 6-2—nodes communicate directly with other nodes on the network, forming a weblike structure (that's *web* as in spider, not browser). Nodes continually come on line and drop off, but the network maintains itself by requiring each node (computer) to maintain links to multiple clients. This creates a robust network that does not have a single failure point.

Note   In terms of a distributed architecture, the Napster P2P network did not have a strict P2P architecture because it had a single failure point. Napster maintained a set of central servers that held song indexes and user lists. File transfers happened in a P2P fashion, but the server was needed to find the peers with the desired content. This was the architectural Achilles' heel of the Napster network—you take out the servers, and the network is toast.

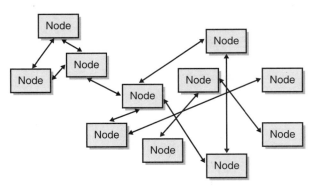

Figure 6-2   The P2P network architecture.

Application architectures can be tricky to define. Rarely are applications a pure form of one architecture or another. Increasingly, we see applications that are a distinct mixture of the two, and that's probably a good thing. Mixing the Client/server and P2P architectures allows a great deal of flexibility when your development requirements allow it.

Communications Protocols

Protocols in the computer world are the basic rules of communication between two devices, or endpoints. You can think of the English language as a protocol of sorts; You have greetings, phrases, questions, and, most important, interaction. Protocols define how you communicate and in what language. Protocols can be built off of other protocols (forming compound protocols), and they can flexible or rigid. It's all up to the originator of the protocol.

Probably the most common protocol in use today is HTTP, the backbone of the World Wide Web. HTTP is built on the foundation of TCP, which is, in turn, based on IP. Figure 6-3 illustrates how some of the network protocols build off each other.

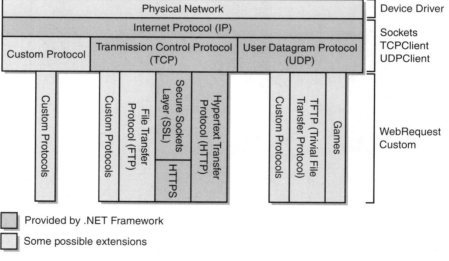

Figure 6-3   Sample hierarchy of IP network communication protocols.

> **More Info** For more details about network architectures and communications, consult the Open Systems Interconnection (OSI) routing protocol documentation at *http://www.cisco.com/univercd/cc/td/doc/cisintwk/ito_doc/osi_prot.htm*.

To give you a better understanding of how some of these protocols interact, we'll first look at IP and at the two most common IP-based protocols in use today.

The IP Protocol

IP is the protocol by which all data is sent on the Internet. Each computer, or host, on the Internet has at least one IP address. This address uniquely identifies the host among all other hosts on the network. For two devices to communicate, both the sender and recipient IP addresses must be known in advance. These two IP addresses constitute the two endpoints of the communications link. Communication between these two endpoints is done in a connectionless fashion. The sender does not open a connection to the recipient; rather, it sends a set of "packets" to the recipient that the recipient can either accept or refuse.

All data that are sent or received over the Internet is first divided into these packets, which contain both the sender's and recipient's Internet addresses. As a packet is sent out, it hits a gateway computer. This gateway determines where to send that packet (usually to another gateway). Each packet makes a series of hops, from gateway to gateway, until it reaches a gateway that is responsible for the recipient machine's address space. This final gateway forwards the packet directly to the computer designated as the recipient in the packet.

Because messages are divided into many packets, it is possible, and even desirable, for each packet to trace a different route across the Internet. This can mean that packets arrive in a different order than the order in which they were sent. IP doesn't care—all it cares about is delivering the packets. It's usually the job of another protocol built on top of IP, typically TCP, to restore the packets to their original order.

IPv4 vs. IPv6 It shouldn't be surprising that there are different versions of the IP protocol. The version of IP that is most widely used today is version 4 (IPv4). The problem with IPv4 is that the address space is limited, leading to a shortage of addresses. To the rescue comes version 6 of the IP protocol (IPv6). IPv6 provides support for many more IP addresses, which is crucial as more and more devices are connected to the Internet. The IPv6 protocol is a functional superset of IPv4; by extension, any device that supports IPv6 packets can also support IPv4 packets.

Note Support for IPv6 was introduced to the .NET Framework in version 1.1, which was included in the Microsoft Visual Studio .NET 2003 release.

IP-Based Protocols

A low-level protocol such as IP isn't really that much fun. It's very lightweight, but it requires you to do an awful lot of work. Thankfully, you'll rarely need to deal with IP at all. Instead, you'll deal with two common protocols that are based on IP:

- Transmission Control Protocol (TCP)

- User Datagram Protocol (UDP)

Most network applications use the TCP protocol (TCP over IP, or TCP/IP). The UDP protocol has found its use in several kinds of applications, most notably multiplayer gaming systems.

TCP TCP is considered a connection-oriented protocol. This means a connection is established and maintained until the information to be exchanged between endpoints has been transferred.

TCP is a protocol built on IP to send data between computers. IP handles the actual delivery of the data, while TCP handles breaking down the data into packets for transmission and reordering and reassembling packets upon receipt. For example, when you request a Web page from a server, the TCP layer in that server divides the page into one or more packets, numbers the packets, and then forwards them individually to the IP layer. Recall that although each packet has the same destination IP address, it might travel a different route through the network. At the other end (your Web browser), the TCP layer reassembles the individual packets and waits until they have all arrived before forwarding them to your browser as a complete Web page.

UDP UDP provides significantly fewer features than TCP. UDP is considered an alternative to TCP. Like TCP, UDP uses IP to transmit packets from one endpoint to another. Unlike TCP, however, UDP does not provide the service of dividing a message into packets or reassembling and reordering them at the other end. In other words, UDP doesn't provide any facility for maintaining proper sequencing of IP packets. This means that an application that uses UDP is responsible for ensuring that the entire message has arrived and in the correct order. Applications that want to save processing time might favor UDP over

TCP. Typically, applications benefit from UDP if they have very small amounts of data to exchange (and therefore little reassembling to do at the other end).

UDP does provide two services not provided by the IP layer. To start with, UDP provides port numbers to help distinguish different user requests. Second, it provides an optional checksum capability to verify that the data arrived intact.

Pluggable Protocols

A tremendous number of protocols run over TCP/IP. Only the most common ones have been provided with the first revisions of the .NET Framework. Given that you might need to communicate using a protocol that has not be provided, it seems reasonable that you would want to write your own communication layer. Taking this a step further, it would be desirable to have a single object model that could be used for multiple protocols. The *WebRequest* and *WebResponse* classes are the .NET Framework classes that provide the basis for pluggable protocols in the .NET Framework.

In my opinion, the *WebRequest* and *WebResponse* classes are poorly named. They are designed as abstract classes (*MustInherit*) that are designed to make a request to a give Uniform Resource Identifier (URI). These classes do not need to be specifically tied to a requests using the HTTP protocol. In fact, you can specify additional protocol handler classes (create your own or share with your buddies) or override existing handlers.

What's in a URI

A URI is simply the combination of a protocol and an address, either an IP address or DNS host name. When you enter **http:// www.microsoft.com** in your Web browser, you're specifying that you want to connect to the *www.microsoft.com* server by using the HTTP protocol. Conversely, if you enter **file://c:\pagefile.sys**, you're specifying a file on your local system.

The .NET Framework supports only three URI protocols out of box for the *WebRequest* mechanism: http, https, and file. The Machine.config file contains the following definitions for the *webRequestModules* object in the *<system.net>* section:

```
<webRequestModules>
  <add prefix="http" type="System.Net.HttpRequestCreator" />
  <add prefix="https" type="System.Net.HttpRequestCreator" />
  <add prefix="file" type="System.Net.FileWebRequestCreator" />
</webRequestModules>
```

You're not limited to just these default protocols. You're free to add your own *webRequestModules*. For example, you can easily add support for File Transfer Protocol (FTP). In the current version of the .NET Framework, if you try to pass a URI with the FTP protocol, you'll get a *NotSupportedException*. However, creating an FTP *webRequestModule* is easy. On the other hand, implementing it might not be so easy. Regardless, you'll need to inherit your new classes from both the *WebRequest* and *WebResponse* classes and then register the new classes with the *WebRequest.RegisterPrefix* method. Alternatively, you can modify the App.Config file to specify your own handler. Typically, you'll distribute the App.Config file with the application, and you can have only your custom protocol in it rather than make it globally available on your machine. (This is exactly what would happen if you added the handler to the machine.config file.)

The *WebRequest* Class: More Than Meets the Eye

The *WebRequest* class is designed to fulfill a network request to a particular URI. The network request consists of the information you'll be sending to server; an instance of a *WebResponse* class will be produced that consists of the response data stream from the server. To illustrate how these two classes work together, look at the following example, which simply reads a page and dumps the output to the console:

```
Imports System
Imports System.Net
Imports System.Text
Imports System.IO

Module HelloInternet
    Sub Main()
        Dim req As WebRequest = _
            WebRequest.Create("http://www.gotdotnet.com/")

        Dim res As WebResponse = req.GetResponse()
        Dim sr As StreamReader = New StreamReader(res.GetResponseStream())
        Dim resChar(256) As Char
        Dim charCount As Integer = sr.Read(resChar, 0, resChar.Length)
```

```
        Do While charCount > 0
            Dim str As String = New String(resChar, 0, charCount)
            Console.Write(str)
            charCount = sr.Read(resChar, 0, resChar.Length)
        Loop

        res.Close()
    End Sub
End Module
```

The sample starts off with a call to *WebRequest.Create*, a static method of the *WebRequest* class, which creates a *WebRequest* instance of this class using the *webRequestModule* defined for the specified URI—in this case, the HTTP protocol. What's really happening under the covers is that the *WebRequest.Create* method looks at the protocol defined in the specific URI. It then checks the machine.config file's defined *webRequestModules* for the specified protocol. (See the following excerpt from the machine.config file.) In this case, the *HttpRequestCreator* is defined for the HTTP protocol, so the *Create* method uses the *HttpRequestCreator* class to create an instance of an *HttpRequest* class. Because *HttpRequest* inherits from *WebRequest*, you do not need to treat it any differently.

Note   The *HttpWebRequest* and *HttpWebResponse* classes support most of the HTTP 1.1 protocol's feature set.

```
<webRequestModules>
    <add prefix="http" type="System.Net.HttpRequestCreator" />
    ...
</webRequestModules>
```

Once we have an instance of our *WebRequest* class, we call the *GetResponse* method, which returns an instance of a *WebResponse* class. This class contains the response data in a *Stream*, which can be obtained by calling the *GetResponseStream* method. To easily read the data in the stream, we create a new *StreamReader* class, passing the response stream to the constructor. We then read characters from the stream until we reach the end of the stream. As a last act before we're done, we close the *StreamReader* instance. Easy.

> **Note**   *GetResponse* is a synchronous method: the calling thread is
> blocked until the response is returned by the server. In the real world,
> where response times can be slow, it's not a good idea to block the
> thread—especially if the thread is a user interface thread, which can
> result in a unresponsive user experience during the time it takes to
> make the call to *GetResponse*. To avoid this problem, you can use the
> *BeginGetResponse* and *EndGetResponse* methods instead.

Supporting Client Authentication

You often need to provide some client authentication when communicating
with a Web server. You can provide this by using the *Credentials* property of
the *WebRequest* class. The simplest case requires you to create an instance of a
NetworkCredential class and then assign it to the *Credentials* property. This
mechanism supports Basic, Digest, NTLM, and Kerberos authentication. It also
stores appropriate information (name, password, domain, and so forth). This
property can contain an instance of the *NetworkCredentials* class (if there is
only one credential) or an instance of the *CredentialCache* class (if there are
multiple sets of credentials tied to specific sites). The following sample demonstrates how you might use the *Credentials* property:

```
Dim wr As WebRequest
...
' Option 1: create a credential, then assign it
Dim nc As New NetworkCredential( "tony", "wong" )
wr.Credentials = nc

' Option 2: Create a set of credentials, add them to the cache, then
' assign the cache to the Credentials property
Dim cache As New CredentialCache()
cache.Add( New Uri("www.microsoft.com"), "Basic", nc )
cache.Add( New Uri("msdn.microsoft.com"), "Basic", nc )
wr.Credentials = cache
```

Managing Your Connections

Resource management is an important part of all well-designed applications.
Network connections, like any other physical resource, should be tightly controlled and considered a relatively scarce resource. Thankfully, most of the connection management work for the *WebRequest* class is handled for you. You can

customize a number of supported connections through the App.Config or Machine.Config files. The following excerpt demonstrates how this works:

```
<connectionManagement>
    <add address="*" maxconnection="2" />
</connectionManagement>
```

This section of the configuration file defines the maximum number of connections to a server or group of servers. The default entry means there can be a maximum of two simultaneous connections in your application to each server. If you exceed this limit, you'll start encountering exceptions. By adjusting this setting in the application configuration file, you can override the default and also add server-specific settings, as shown here:

```
<connectionManagement>
    <add address="*" maxconnection="5" />
    <add address="www.microsoft.com" maxconnection="10" />
</connectionManagement>
```

In this example, I've overridden the default maximum connections and set it to 5; the *www.microsoft.com* server has been allowed up to 10 simultaneous connections.

Note   Connection limits are per host or server or URI. They are protocol- and domain name–specific. That is, it doesn't matter whether the resource you're using is on the same server. (You can exceed the number of connections to a single machine if you're using different protocols.)

System.Net also provides the *ServicePoint* and *ServicePointManager* classes for programmatically managing connection limits. If you don't want to rely on the configuration file for setting your connection limits, use the *ConnectionLimit* property of the *ServicePoint* class for a particular host. The following example demonstrates how you can customize the connection limits for a specific host dynamically at runtime:

```
Dim uri As New Uri("http://www.microsoft.com")
Dim sp As ServicePoint = ServicePointManager.FindServicePoint()
sp.ConnectionLimit = 20
```

To change the setting programmatically for all hosts, change the *Default-PersistentConnectionLimit* property of the *ServicePointManager* class (*Default-*

NonPersistentConnectionLimit when you use HTTP 1.0). You usually don't need be bothered with these classes unless you're hitting the connection limit and want to change it right away.

Note   The default value of the *KeepAlive* property of *HttpWebRequest* is *true*, which means that all the connections will remain open and will be reused for subsequent requests to same server unless a timeout occurs (specified by the *MaxIdleTime* property of the *ServicePoint*).

Extending this concept, the *WebRequest* class's *ConnectionGroupName* property lets you group connections. It is mainly relevant for middle-tier components that want to reuse existing connections to a server.

Note   Reusing existing connections is a recommended best practice for increasing network performance. A certain amount of overhead is associated with establishing a network connection. If you can make the connection only once and reuse the open connection, you'll improve the efficiency of your application. For example, The SqlClient ADO.NET provider uses connection pooling for all connections to SQL servers to achieve greater responsiveness and application throughput.

Creating Custom *WebRequestModules*

This section is really an extension of our earlier discussion of pluggable protocols. The *WebRequest/WebResponse* model allows for the creation of custom protocol handlers and even overriding existing default handlers. For example, consider a design for creating an FTP protocol handler (ignoring the actual protocol details):

1.   Create a *FileWebRequestCreator* class that inherits from the *IWebRequestCreate* class. In the *Create* method, return an object of *FtpWebResponse* (mentioned below).

2.   Register this class using the *RegisterPrefix* method of the *WebRequest* class, as follows. By registering the class, you are making it known that there is an object called *ftp* that handles all *ftp:* requests.

3.   Create *FtpWebRequest*, which inherits from the *WebRequest* class and overrides all needed members: the *ConnectionGroupName*, *Content-Length*, *ContentType*, *Credentials*, *Headers*, *Method*, *PreAuthenticate*, *Proxy*, *RequestUri*, and *Timeout* properties; and the *Abort*, *BeginGet-RequestStream*, *EndGetRequestStream*, *BeginGetResponse*, *EndGetResponse*, *GetRequestStream* and *GetResponse* methods.

4.   Create an *FtpWebResponse* class that inherits from the *WebResponse* class and overrides all necessary members: the *ContentLength*, *ContentType*, *Headers*, and *ResponseUri* properties; and the *Close* and *GetResponseStream* methods.

Note   It's a good idea to program in terms of *WebRequest* and *WebResponse* classes wherever possible so that any new protocols that are added by the .NET Framework or new protocols that you add will continue to be used with minimal (if any) changes to the code.

Here's what the skeleton code for a new *WebRequest* handler might look like:

```
Imports System.Net

Public Class FtpWebRequestCreator
    Implements IWebRequestCreate

    Function Create(ByVal uri As Uri) As WebRequest _
        Implements IWebRequestCreate.Create

        Return New FtpWebRequest(uri)
    End Function
End Class

Public Class FtpWebRequest
    Inherits WebRequest

    Private m_Uri As Uri

    Friend Sub New(ByVal uri As Uri)
        MyBase.New()

        m_Uri = uri
    End Sub
```

```
End Class

Public Class FtpWebResponse
    Inherits WebResponse

    Friend Sub New()
        MyBase.New()
    End Sub
End Class
```

Advanced *WebRequest* Features

Now that we've covered the basics of *WebRequest* and *WebResponse*, let's look at the some of the more advanced features. As you've seen, the *Create* method of the *WebRequest* determines which protocol will be used, and any new protocols can be registered via the *RegisterPrefix* method of *WebRequest*. Here's how you would typically use the *WebRequest* and *WebResponse* classes:

1. Create a request using *WebRequest.Create*. Depending on the protocol being used, you can typecast this into an appropriate protocol-specific class.

2. Fill in *Credentials* property of the *WebRequest*. You can use *CredentialCache.DefaultCredentials* for NTLM, negotiate, and Kerberos-based authentication or use *NetworkCredential* to specify a specific username/password.

3. If you're using a proxy that requires authentication, create and set *Credentials* for the *WebProxy* class.

4. Fill in protocol-specific properties (such as the user agent and client certificates for HTTP requests).

5. Call the *GetResponse* method of the *WebRequest* class. This will cause a blocking request. If you need asynchronous calls, use *BeginGetResponse* and *EndGetResponse* instead (as noted below).

6. Typecast the *WebReponse* returned to appropriate protocol class and access any protocol-specific methods. Get the stream using the *GetResponseStream* method. Close the stream and the *Response* class.

The following sample puts all of the previous steps into practice:

```
Imports System
Imports System.Net
Imports System.IO
Imports System.Text
```

```vb
Imports System.Security.Cryptography.X509Certificates

Module WebRequestSample
    Sub Main()
        Dim sb As New System.Text.StringBuilder()
        Try
            Dim wreq As WebRequest = _
                WebRequest.Create("https://SomeServer/SomePage.aspx")
            wreq.Credentials = CredentialCache.DefaultCredentials
            Dim myProxy As New WebProxy("ProxyServer:Port")
            myProxy.Credentials = New NetworkCredential("UserID", _
                                                        "Password", _
                                                        "Domain")
            CType(wreq, HttpWebRequest).ClientCertificates.Add( _
                X509Certificate.CreateFromCertFile("") _
                )

            Dim wrep As WebResponse = wreq.GetResponse()
            Dim s As Stream = wrep.GetResponseStream()

            Dim buffer() As Byte = New Byte(1024) {}
            Dim count As Integer = 0

            While (count < s.Read(buffer, 0, buffer.Length))
                sb.Append(Encoding.Default.GetString(buffer, 0, count))
            End While

            s.Close()
            wrep.Close()
        Catch we As Exception
            sb.Append(we.ToString())
        End Try

        Console.WriteLine(sb.ToString())
    End Sub
End Module
```

That's a more complete implementation using *WebRequest*. Next, we'll look at another important feature: asynchronous operations with *WebRequest*.

Asynchronous Operations

As I mentioned earlier, you can use the *BeginGetResponse* and *EndGetResponse* methods of the *WebRequest* to initiate and complete requests in an asynchronous manner. An important point to keep in mind is to not mix asynchronous and synchronous operations. The *WebRequest* classes were not designed to support both types of communication simultaneously, and you might end up with strange results if you try it. Do it one way or the other, but never mixed.

This includes dealing with the *Stream* data returned by the *WebResponse* class. In other words, if you use the asynchronous *BeginGetResponse* method, you should also use the *BeginRead/EndRead* asynchronous methods of the resulting *Stream* object.

Now let's take a closer look at the *BeginGetResponse* method of the *WebRequest* class. The *BeginGetResponse* has following prototype:

```
Public Overridable Function BeginGetResponse( _
    ByVal callback As AsyncCallback, _
    ByVal state As Object _
    ) As IAsyncResult
```

Note   If you implement your own pluggable protocol, you must override the *BeginGetResponse* method.

The first parameter is an *AsyncCallback* delegate. The callback method that implements it will use the returned *IAsyncResult* interface to obtain the status of this asynchronous request and complete the request by calling the *EndGetResponse* method. This function returns an *IAsyncResult* that uniquely identifies the asynchronous request. The second parameter represents the state of the asynchronous request. When you perform asynchronous operations, you must pass and preserve data across asynchronous calls. This state parameter can be any object, but it often makes sense to create a specific class to help maintain the state information of the *Request* and eventual stream so that the class can be used with the *Stream* reader callback functions as well. Our sample defines the following *State* class:

```
Public Class State
      Const BufferSize As Integer = 4096 ' default buffer size
      Public Request As WebRequest ' Store the WebRequest class
                                   ' for calling EndGetRequest
      Public Response As WebResponse ' Store for closing out
                                     ' Response when done
      Public ResponseStream As Stream ' For calling BeingRead/EndRead
      Public Data As StringBuilder ' Actual data of interest
      Public Buffer() As Byte ' array to read bytes from Response

      Public Sub New()
          Request = Nothing
          Response = Nothing
          ResponseStream = Nothing
          Data = New StringBuilder()
```

```
        Buffer = New Byte(BufferSize) {}
      End Sub
  End Class
```

Now that we've discussed the implementation of asynchronous requests, it's time to see it in action. Building on the earlier examples, following is an example of asynchronously downloading a file using the *WebRequest* class. (See also the AsyncWebRequest sample project.)

Note   This example uses a *ManualResetEvent* to prevent the application from exiting prematurely.

```
Imports System
Imports System.Net
Imports System.IO
Imports System.Text
Imports System.Threading

Module AsyncWebRequest
   Public Class State
      Const BufferSize As Integer = 4096 ' default buffer size

      ' Store the WebRequest class for calling EndGetRequest
      Public Request As WebRequest

      ' Store for closing out Response when done
      Public Response As WebResponse
      Public ResponseStream As Stream ' For calling BeingRead/EndRead
      Public Data As New StringBuilder() ' Actual data of interest
      Public Buffer() As Byte ' array to read bytes from Response

      Public Sub New()
         Buffer = New Byte(BufferSize) {}
      End Sub
   End Class

   Private allDone As New ManualResetEvent(False)

   Sub Main()
      Dim requestState As New State()
      requestState.Request = WebRequest.Create("http://www.microsoft.com")
      Dim r As IAsyncResult = _
         CType(requestState.Request.BeginGetResponse( _
            New AsyncCallback(AddressOf RequestCallback), _
            requestState), IAsyncResult)
```

```vbnet
        ' Don't exit till ManualResetEvent is set in Callback
        allDone.WaitOne()
    End Sub

    Sub RequestCallback(ByVal ar As IAsyncResult)
        Try
            Dim requestState As State = CType(ar.AsyncState, State)
            requestState.Response = requestState.Request.EndGetResponse(ar)
            requestState.ResponseStream = _
                requestState.Response.GetResponseStream()

            Dim iarRead As IAsyncResult = _
                requestState.ResponseStream.BeginRead( _
                    requestState.Buffer, _
                    0, _
                    requestState.Buffer.Length, _
                    New AsyncCallback(AddressOf StreamCallback), _
                    requestState)
        Catch ex As Exception
            Console.Error.WriteLine(ex.ToString())
        End Try
    End Sub
    Sub StreamCallback(ByVal ar As IAsyncResult)
        Try
            Dim requestState As State = CType(ar.AsyncState, State)
            Dim bytesRead As Integer = requestState.ResponseStream.EndRead(ar)

            If (bytesRead > 0) Then
                requestState.Data.Append( _
                    Encoding.Default.GetString(requestState.Buffer, _
                                               0, _
                                               bytesRead))
                requestState.ResponseStream.BeginRead(requestState.Buffer, _
                    0, _
                    requestState.Buffer.Length, _
                    New AsyncCallback(AddressOf StreamCallback), _
                    requestState)

            Else
                requestState.ResponseStream.Close()
                requestState.Response.Close()
                Console.WriteLine(requestState.Data.ToString())
                allDone.Set()
            End If
        Catch ex As Exception
            Console.Error.WriteLine(ex.ToString())
        End Try
    End Sub
End Module
```

> **Note**   The synchronous *WebRequest.GetResponse* method actually uses the asynchronous methods (*BeginGetResponse* and *EndGetResponse*) internally.

That wraps up our discussion of the *WebRequest* and *WebResponse* classes. Now on to a related class: *WebClient*.

The *WebClient* Class

Why, you might ask, are there two completely different sets of classes for making "Web" requests in the .NET Framework? We've already covered the *WebRequest/WebResponse* architecture. What value does the *WebClient* class add? For one, it provides a simple, single object model for making similar requests. In fact, like the *WebRequest* class, the *WebClient* class processes generic URI requests. There's a reason for this. The *WebClient* class is implemented using the *WebRequest* and *WebResponse* classes—it just hides them. For simple scenarios, the *WebClient* class might just fit the bill.

> **Warning**   The *WebClient* class does not provide any support for asynchronous operations.

To get an idea of what the *WebClient* class can do for you, check out the following code example. It performs the same function as our original *WebRequest* example, but it uses less code.

```
Imports System
Imports System.Net
Imports System.Text
Imports System.IO

Module WebClientTest
    Sub Main()
        Dim client As WebClient = New WebClient()
        Dim resStream As Stream = _
            client.OpenRead("http://www.gotdotnet.com/about_new.aspx")
        Dim sr As StreamReader = New StreamReader(resStream)
        Dim resChar(256) As Char
```

```
            Dim charCount As Integer = sr.Read(resChar, 0, resChar.Length)
            Do While charCount > 0
                Dim str As String = New String(resChar, 0, charCount)
                Console.Write(str)
                charCount = sr.Read(resChar, 0, resChar.Length)
            Loop
            resStream.Close()
        End Sub
    End Module
```

As I mentioned, internally the *WebClient* class uses both the *WebRequest* and *WebResponse* classes. The *WebClient* exposes methods both for sending and reading data. However, because it is designed to keep things simple, it provides support for synchronous (blocking) calls only. Table 6-1 describes the major methods of interest for the *WebClient* class.

Table 6-1
Selected Methods of the *WebClient* Class

Method	Description
DownloadData	Downloads a byte array from the server
DownloadFile	Downloads data from an URI to a local file
OpenRead/OpenWrite	Opens a stream from an URI for reading/writing
UploadData/UploadFile	Uploads data or local file to an URI
UploadValues	Uploads name/value pairs to an URI

Apart from the fact that all *WebClient* method calls are synchronous, other potential disadvantages include:

■ You can't maintain cookies between the calls. You must use the *Http-WebRequest* object's *CookieContainer* property.

■ *ResponseHeaders* contains name/value header pairs, but there is no way to catch response code unless there is an error. In case of an error, a *WebException* will be thrown and its response property will contain the *HttpWebResponse* that was returned in error; there you can see the *StatusCode*. If you need to check nonerror status codes, you have to use the *HttpWebRequest* class.

■ You can't know the download status (the amount of data that has been processed and copied). You must instead use the *WebRequest/WebResponse* objects.

When you deal with downloads in general, and *WebClient* in particular, you should be aware of the classes described in Table 6-2. These classes can help your application work through proxy servers and handle authentication and credentials.

Table 6-2
Useful Classes for Making Web Requests

Class	Description
WebProxy	If the request goes through a proxy, you must specify this.
Credentials	This is a property of *WebProxy* and *WebClient* that you must specify with the *NetworkCredential* or *Credential-Cache* of the proxy and the server, respectively.
GlobalProxySelection	This contains the default proxy settings for all HTTP requests. Assign the *WebProxy* created to this *Global-ProxySelection*.

Here's a sample that uses some of the other useful methods of the *Web-Client* class. Note the use of the *DownloadData* and *DownloadFile* methods.

```
Imports System
Imports System.Net
Imports System.Text
Imports System.Collections.Specialized

Module WebClientSample
   Public Sub Main()
      Try
         Dim client As New WebClient()
         Dim pageData As Byte() = _
            client.DownloadData("http://www.gotdotnet.com")
         Dim pageHtml As String = Encoding.ASCII.GetString(pageData)
         Console.WriteLine(pageHtml)
         client.DownloadFile("http://www.gotdotnet.com", "C:\Temp.html")
      Catch webEx As WebException
         Console.WriteLine(webEx.ToString())
      End Try
      Console.WriteLine("Hit any key to continue...")
      Console.Read()
   End Sub
End Module
```

Most of the information about the *WebClient* is pretty much a rehash of the *WebRequest* material, so I won't spend any further time on it. The MSDN documentation is quite helpful on this topic, and the information contained here should be more than enough to get you up and running.

Socket Programming

Sockets are the meat of the low-level network communication programming model. Everything we've discussed so far is great when you use the standard request/response communication architecture. However, at times you'll need to get down to the nitty-gritty network infrastructure details. Members of *System.Net.Sockets* support a wide range of functionality and granularity. I'll focus first on the *TCPClient*, *TCPListener*, and *UDPClient* classes, which are built on the lower-level *System.Net.Sockets.Socket* class. Then I'll briefly dig into the *Socket* class itself and take you on a tour of an implementation of the ping functionality in Visual Basic .NET.

Getting Started with Addressing

The socket-level network classes require a different form of addressing than the one used by the *WebClient* and *WebRequest* classes. Don't let this frighten you. The scheme is not particularly daunting; it's just different. Recall from our discussion of the IP and TCP protocols that we defined the source and recipient computers (hosts) as endpoints. The .NET Framework continues the use of this terminology. You use an *IPEndPoint* class with your sockets. But before you can define an endpoint, you must get an IP address for that host. That's what this section is all about.

Creating Simple Addresses

As I've mentioned, the *IPAddress* class represents an IP address and is needed for creating an instance of an *IPEndPoint* class. To create an instance of *IPAddress*, you need the IP address of the target machine. The following example shows how simple it is to create an *IPAddress* class that you can use to define an endpoint:

```
Dim address As IPAddress = IPAddress.Parse("207.46.228.80")
```

Simple right? Not entirely. What if you don't know the physical IP address? In that case, you need to look at the DNS resolution capabilities of the .NET Framework.

DNS Host Name vs. IP Address

The Domain Name Service (DNS) is the backbone of the current Internet addressing scheme. Generally speaking, DNS is designed to provide human-friendly addresses that are mapped to physical IP addresses. In this situation, a single site—say, Microsoft's Web site—essentially has two valid addresses (from the user's point of view). The first is the human-readable *www.microsoft.com*. When a user enters this in a Web browser, the browser must resolve the address to a more machine-friendly IP address (*10.10.0.123*). DNS provides this necessary link, much like a large telephone book. A very large telephone book.

We generally know the host name (DNS name) of a machine but not the IP address. This is useful because the physical IP address can change without affecting a user's ability to access a Web site. However, you need to resolve this host name to a physical address before you can use any of the socket classes to access the site, which is where the *System.Net.Dns* class comes into play.

The *System.Net.Dns* class is a kind of catchall utility for DNS resolution issues. It provides a set of shared methods that can help you resolve host name and IP address to *IPHostEntry* objects. With methods such as *GetHostByAddress*, *GetHostByName*, *GetHostName*, and *Resolve*, the *Dns* class gives you the ability to perform all sorts of name and IP address resolutions. (See Table 6-3.)

Table 6-3
Synchronous Methods of *System.Net.Dns*

Method	Description
GetHostByAddress	Retrieves an *IPHostEntry* instance based on the specified IP address
GetHostByName	Retrieves an *IPHostEntry* instance based on the specified DNS host name
GetHostName	Retrieves an *IPHostEntry* instance for the local computer
Resolve	Retrieves an *IPHostEntry* instance based on the specified IP address or DNS host name

For added flexibility, the *Dns* class also supports asynchronous methods. You'll generally be most interested in the asynchronous methods when you expect the name/IP resolution operation to take a significant amount of time. Given that these requests are not instantaneous and are subject to transient network conditions (or slowdowns), you're likely to be interested in these methods at some point. The asynchronous methods of the *Dns* class are described in Table 6-4.

Table 6-4
Asynchronous Methods of *System.Net.Dns*

Method	Description
BeginGetHostByName	Starts an asynchronous request for resolving a host by name. Returns a reference to an *IAsyncResult* interface that provides a unique reference for this request. You must provide a callback that is signaled when the request is complete. Your callback must call *EndGetHostByName* to retrieve the result of this request.
EndGetHostByName	Retrieves an instance of the *IPHostEntry* class that represents the result of the original *BeginGetHostByName* request.
BeginResolve	Starts an asynchronous request for resolving a host name or IP address. Returns a reference to an *IAsyncResult* interface that provides a unique reference for this request. You must provide a callback method that is signaled when the request is complete. Your callback must call *EndResolve* to retrieve the result of this request.
EndResolve	Retrieves an instance of the *IPHostEntry* class that represents the result of the original *BeginResolve* request.

But enough of playing with addresses. Let's start digging into the real meat of our subject.

Using the *TcpClient*, *TcpListener*, and *UdpClient* Classes

TCPClient and *TCPListener* aren't hugely complicated wrappers. For example, they don't provide any asynchronous methods. They do, however, take care of setting up and managing the IP socket for TCP. *UDPClient* is designed differently to accommodate the different role that UDP plays in networks. Essentially, the design of *UDPClient* is geared toward sending and receiving data over IP multicast.

TcpClient and *TcpListener*

The *TcpClient* and *TcpListener* classes are built on top of the *Socket* class. These classes are simple to use and provide simpler access to the network—much like *WebClient* does. Both classes serve a special purpose. The *TcpClient* class is designed for initiating a connection with another host. The *TcpListener* class is designed to support other hosts that connect to the local machine (receive incoming requests).

Both the *TcpClient* and *TcpListener* classes uses synchronous (blocking) methods. If you need to make asynchronous method calls or access other features not exposed by these classes, you must use the *Socket* class directly. One way of getting access to a raw *Socket* is through the *TcpListener* class, by calling the *AcceptSocket* method.

Let's get our hands dirty and look at some real code. A typical implementation of the *TcpListener* functionality might look like the following:

```
Imports System
Imports System.Net.Sockets
Imports System.Text

Module TcpServerApp
    Sub Main()
        Dim server As New TcpListener(65535)
        server.Start()
        ' Keep listening
        While True
            Console.WriteLine("Waiting for connection")
            Dim client As TcpClient = server.AcceptTcpClient()
            Console.WriteLine("Client connected")
            Dim ns As NetworkStream = client.GetStream()
            Dim buffer(1024) As Byte
            Dim bytesRead As Integer = ns.Read(buffer, 0, buffer.Length)
            Console.WriteLine("Client says: {0}", _
                            Encoding.ASCII.GetString(buffer, 0, bytesRead))
            buffer = Encoding.ASCII.GetBytes("Hello from server!")
            ns.Write(buffer, 0, buffer.Length)
            ns.Close()
            Console.WriteLine("Disconnecting from client...")
            client.Close()
        End While
        server.Stop()
    End Sub
End Module
```

This sample is a console application that waits infinitely for client connections and echoes the incoming status and received message, if any. *AcceptTcpClient* is the key method—it blocks the server while waiting for clients to connect. The rest of the sample is all reading and writing to various streams.

Note   Be sure to not step on other ports in use, and use your port number correctly. Refer to *http://www.iana.org/assignments/port-numbers* for an official list of ports.

Here's an example of a *TcpClient* application that opens a connection to the above server:

```
Imports System
Imports System.Net.Sockets
Imports System.Text
Imports System.IO

Module TcpClientApp
    Sub Main()
        Dim client As New TcpClient("Sarath", 65535)
        Dim ns As NetworkStream = client.GetStream()
        Dim sw As StreamWriter = New StreamWriter(ns)
        sw.Write("Hello from client!")
        sw.Flush()
        Dim bytes(1024) As Byte
        Dim bytesRead As Integer = ns.Read(bytes, 0, bytes.Length)
        Console.WriteLine("Server says: {0}", _
                        Encoding.ASCII.GetString(bytes, 0, bytesRead))
    End Sub
End Module
```

Again, the code here is not rocket science—just use the correct server name and port number and read/write to *Stream*-appropriate information.

The above scenario is relatively trivial. However, it demonstrates the potential of the *TcpClient* and *TcpListener* classes. You can, for example, convert the server to a Windows service, have multiple threads depending on the number of clients connecting, and so forth.

More Info For an example of using the *TcpClient* and *TcpListener* classes, see Chapter 7.

UdpClient

UDP services are provided through the *UdpClient* class, which is also built on the *Socket* class. The most common use of this class is for broadcasting messages to a group of machines—for example, sending a message to your whole group to take a break. Unlike TCP, UDP is connectionless, which means there's no guarantee if/when the datagram (packets) will arrive. The *UDPClient* class does make it easier to send and receive data over IP multicast. It does this by providing group management APIs such as *JoinMulticastGroup* and *DropMulticastGroup*.

To get a broadcast, a host must listen to a specific IP multicast address. The *UdpClient* class supports the *JoinMulticastGroup* method, and once you're done, it is possible to disjoin by calling the *DropMulticastGroup* method. Alternatively, you can connect to a remote host using the *Connect* method. After you join a multicast group or connect to a machine, you use one of the *Send* overloaded methods to send the datagram. For listening, you must rely on the *Receive* method of *UdpClient* or directly use the *Socket* class.

Let's look at some sample code. The following sample sends messages to a particular server over UDP:

```
Imports System
Imports System.Net.Sockets
Imports System.Text

Public Class UDPSender
    Public Shared Sub Main()
        Dim updSender As New System.Net.Sockets.UdpClient()
        Try
            updSender.Connect("Sarath1", 8080)
            Dim sendBytes As Byte() = _
                Encoding.ASCII.GetBytes("Time to go home?")

            updSender.Send(sendBytes, sendBytes.Length)
            updSender.Close()
        Catch e As Exception
            Console.WriteLine(e.ToString())
        End Try
    End Sub
End Class
```

Similarly, we can use the *Receive* method to receive the datagram (packet):

```
Imports System
Imports System.Net
Imports System.Net.Sockets
Imports System.Text

Public Class UDPReceiver
    Public Shared Sub Main()
        Dim updReceiver As New UdpClient()

        ' read datagrams sent from any source
        Dim ipSender As New IPEndPoint(IPAddress.Any, 8080)

        Try
            ' This call blocks
            Dim receiveBytes As Byte() = updReceiver.Receive(ipSender)

            Dim returnData As String = Encoding.ASCII.GetString(receiveBytes)
            Console.WriteLine("From {0} {1}", _
                        ipSender.Address.ToString(), _
                        returnData.ToString())
        Catch e As Exception
            Console.WriteLine(e.ToString())
        End Try
    End Sub
End Class
```

That's the simple overview of using TCP and UDP. Now let's get even more detailed. I've already said several times that most, if not all, network communication in the .NET Framework can be traced all the way down to a socket implementation. Now we'll see what this looks like.

Down to the Wire: Socket-Level Network Programming

The *System.Net.Sockets* namespace is intended to give programmers who are familiar with sockets programming an interface they can use from managed code. The *Socket* class provides the foundation for most of the classes in the *System.Net* namespace.

Deciding where to begin with this subject is more than a little challenging. This material is definitely not for the faint-hearted. Your best bet for gaining a good understanding of packet-level network programming is probably to pick up a book on the subject. Many of the details that are far beyond the scope of this book. However, I'll show you how to do packet-level network communication using a simple example. With additional background, you should be able to implement anything you need.

The *Socket* Class

The *Socket* class exposes methods such as *Send*, *SendTo*, *Receive*, and *Receive-From* (and their asynchronous variants) for sending and receiving data. There are three basic types of send and receive methods: synchronous (blocking), select, and asynchronous. The following example demonstrates a synchronous network operation using the *Socket* class:

```
Imports System
Imports System.Net
Imports System.Net.Sockets
Imports System.Text.Encoding

Module SocketBlocking
    Sub Main()
        Try
            Dim serverIPHostInfo As IPHostEntry = Dns.Resolve("BobsMachine")
            Dim serverIPAddress As IPAddress = serverIPHostInfo.AddressList(0)
            Dim serverIPEndPoint As New IPEndPoint(serverIPAddress, 8080)

            Dim serverSocket As New Socket(AddressFamily.InterNetwork, _
                SocketType.Stream, ProtocolType.Tcp)

            serverSocket.Connect(serverIPEndPoint)
            Dim buffer As Byte() = ASCII.GetBytes("Testing Socket Blocking")
            Dim bytesSend As Integer = serverSocket.Send(buffer)
```

```
        Dim bytesReceived As Integer = serverSocket.Receive(buffer)
        Console.WriteLine("Received from server = " + _
            ASCII.GetString(buffer, 0, bytesReceived))
        serverSocket.Shutdown(SocketShutdown.Both)
        serverSocket.Close()
    Catch se As SocketException
        Console.WriteLine("SocketException : {0}", se.ToString())
    Catch e As Exception
        Console.WriteLine("Unexpected exception : {0}", e.ToString())
    End Try
  End Sub
End Module
```

> **Note**   In this example, a listener is expected to be running on the server at the specified port; otherwise, the exception "No connection could be made because the target machine actively refused it" will occur.

Blocking calls are great for simple scenarios. However, if you need multiple reading and writing, you might have to launch multiple threads, and having blocking calls on each of them can increase complexity of your program. A better approach is to use *Select*, which allows you to manage multiple sockets for sending and receiving from a single thread. What happens is that you give a list of sockets that you test for readability and writability. The following code sample demonstrates how you might test the sockets for readability:

```
Dim Socket1 As Socket
Dim Socket2 As Socket
' code that creates Socket1 and Socket2.
Dim checkReadSockets As Socket() = {Socket1, Socket2}
Socket.Select(checkReadSockets, Nothing, Nothing, 2000)
' Now checkRead contains only those sockets that need to be read
' Others have timeout or are not ready to Read
Dim counter As Integer
Dim buffer(1024) As Byte
For counter = 0 To (checkReadSockets.Length - 1) - 1
   checkReadSockets(counter).Receive(buffer)
   Console.WriteLine("Socket " + counter.ToString() + _
      " has the message" + ASCII.GetString(buffer))
Next counter
```

Even better than *Select* is the *Asynchronous* model. It works in a similar way to asynchronous methods of *WebRequest/WebResponse*. The main methods of interest here are listed in Table 6-5.

Table 6-5
Asynchronous Methods of the *Socket* Class

Method	Description
BeginAccept	Begins an asynchronous request to accept an incoming connection request
EndAccept	Completes or terminates an asynchronous request to accept an incoming connection request
BeginConnect	Initiates an asynchronous request to connect to a host
EndConnect	Completes or terminates an asynchronous request to connect to a host
BeginReceive	Initiates an asynchronous receive operation from an already-connected socket
EndReceive	Completes or terminates an asynchronous receive operation from an already-connected socket
BeginSend	Initiates a send operation to a connected socket
EndSend	Completes or terminates a send operation to a connected socket
BeginSentTo	Initiates an asynchronous send to a specific remote host
EndSendTo	Completes or terminates an asynchronous send to a specific remote host

System.Net.Sockets also exposes some other cool classes. *NetworkStream* gives developers a consistent, stream-based mechanism to read and write data over the network. Its value goes beyond the utility of a *Stream* object. This is a base type supported throughout our framework classes, so you can do all sorts of cool things with a *NetworkStream*, such as pass it into an *XmlTextReader* and read XML data. Or you can use it in conjunction with the encoding classes.

Example: Creating Ping

To see the *Socket* class in action, I developed a sample that demonstrates how you can implement a custom protocol on top of the *Socket* class. For this example, I chose to implement a bare-bones ping client. This system has two components. The first is the Internet Control Message Protocol (ICMP) packet that contains the information needed to perform a ping. This class, called *Icmp-Packet*, is designed to do three things. First, it contains all of the information necessary to describe the ping packet. Second, it contains the logic to serialize the contents of the packet into a *Byte* array. Third, it computes a checksum for the packet; otherwise, the receiver will assume that the packet has become corrupted in transport and the packet will be rejected. The following is my implementation of the *IcmpPacket* class:

```vb
' Internal Class representing the ICMP Packet sent over the wire
Public Class IcmpPacket
    ' Our public members representing the actual data contained
    ' by the packet
    Public Type As Byte              ' packet type
    Public SubCode As Byte           ' sub code
    Public CheckSum As UInt16        ' binary complement checksum
                                     ' of the structure
    Public Identifier As UInt16      ' packet identifier
    Public SequenceNumber As UInt16  ' packet sequence number
    Public Data() As Byte

    ' Internal Members/Constants
    Private buffer() As Byte
    Private Const ICMP_ECHO As Integer = 8
    Private Const PingData As Integer = 32 ' Size Of IcmpPacket - 8

    Public Sub New()
        ' Construct the packet to send
        Me.Type = ICMP_ECHO
        Me.SubCode = 0
        Me.CheckSum = Convert.ToUInt16(0)
        Me.Identifier = Convert.ToUInt16(45)
        Me.SequenceNumber = Convert.ToUInt16(0)

        Me.Data = New Byte(PingData - 1) {}

        Dim i As Integer

        ' Initilize the Data Array
        For i = 0 To PingData - 1
            Me.Data(i) = CByte(Asc("#"))
        Next
    End Sub

    Private Sub ComputeCheckSum()
        Dim i As Integer
        Dim cksum As Integer = 0

        ' Add up the values for all of the bytes in the array
        For i = 0 To 39 Step 2
            cksum += Convert.ToInt16(BitConverter.ToUInt16(buffer, i))
```

```
        Next

        ' Add the high and low words
        cksum = (cksum / (2 ^ 16)) + (cksum And &HFFFF)

        ' Invert and clear the high bits
        cksum = (Not cksum) And &HFFFF

        Me.CheckSum = Convert.ToUInt16(cksum)
    End Sub

    Public Function GetBytes() As Byte()
        If buffer Is Nothing Then buffer = New Byte(39) {}

        Dim index As Integer = 0

        Dim bType() As Byte = New Byte(0) {Me.Type}
        Dim bCode() As Byte = New Byte(0) {Me.SubCode}

        Dim bCksum() As Byte = New Byte(1) {0, 0}
        Dim bId() As Byte = BitConverter.GetBytes(Me.Identifier)
        Dim bSeq() As Byte = BitConverter.GetBytes(Me.SequenceNumber)

        ' Copy the data into the buffer
        bType.CopyTo(buffer, 0)
        bCode.CopyTo(buffer, 1)
        bCksum.CopyTo(buffer, 2)
        bId.CopyTo(buffer, 4)
        bSeq.CopyTo(buffer, 6)
        Me.Data.CopyTo(buffer, 8)

        ' Compute the Checksum
        Me.ComputeCheckSum()

        ' Update the byte array with the checksum
        bCksum = BitConverter.GetBytes(Me.CheckSum)
        bCksum.CopyTo(buffer, 2)

        Return buffer
    End Function
End Class
```

Now that we have a packet defined, we need to send it. The following code demonstrates how to send the packet over the network. Notice how we first define our *IPEndPoint* classes and then worry about all of the other socket setup issues.

```vbnet
Imports System.Net
Imports System.Net.Sockets

' The Ping Class
Public NotInheritable Class Ping
    'Declare some Constant Variables
    Private Const SOCKET_ERROR As Integer = -1

    'This method takes the "hostname" of a machine
    'and then ping's that host.
    Public Shared Function PingHost(ByVal hostName As String) As Boolean
        Dim destEndPoint As EndPoint
        Dim srcEndPoint As EndPoint

        ' Get the source and destination IP endpoints
        Try
            destEndPoint = GetEndPoint(hostName)
            srcEndPoint = GetEndPoint(Dns.GetHostName())
        Catch
            ' Return False if any exception occurs.
            Return False
        End Try

        ' Initilize a new ICMP Socket
        Dim pingSocket As New Socket(AddressFamily.InterNetwork, _
                                SocketType.Raw, _
                                ProtocolType.Icmp)

        ' Set the socket's Timeout values
        pingSocket.SetSocketOption(SocketOptionLevel.Socket, _
                                SocketOptionName.SendTimeout, _
                                1000)
        pingSocket.SetSocketOption(SocketOptionLevel.Socket, _
                                SocketOptionName.ReceiveTimeout, _
                                1000)

        Try
            ' send the packet over the socket
            Dim nBytes As Integer = 0
            Dim packet As New IcmpPacket()
            If (nBytes = pingSocket.SendTo(packet.GetBytes, _
                                    packet.GetBytes.Length, _
                                    0, _
                                    destEndPoint)) = SOCKET_ERROR Then
                Return False
            End If

            Dim ReceiveBuffer() As Byte = New Byte(255) {}
```

```
            nBytes = pingSocket.ReceiveFrom(ReceiveBuffer, _
                                            256, _
                                            0, _
                                            srcEndPoint)

        If (nBytes = SOCKET_ERROR) Or (nBytes = 0) Then
            Return False
        End If
    Catch
        Return False
    Finally
        pingSocket.Close()
    End Try

    Return True
End Function

Private Shared Function GetEndPoint(ByVal hostName As String) _
                                    As IPEndPoint

    ' Get the host entry of the specified host
    Dim hEntry As IPHostEntry = Dns.GetHostByName(hostName)

    ' Create an IPEndPoint for the default address for the HostEntry
    Dim ePoint As EndPoint = New IPEndPoint(hEntry.AddressList(0), 0)

    Return ePoint
End Function
End Class
```

Conclusion

If you've gotten this far, you could probably used a good coffee break right about now. This chapter's material is probably the densest in the entire book. If you're having some difficulty understanding it, don't worry—this stuff isn't easy. It sure isn't all about Remoting and Web services either. But I find it exciting to have this level of network functionality and capability in such an accessible package.

I hope you now have a sense of how much you can do with the .NET Framework's networking classes. At almost every level, you have the opportunity to slap on your own protocol or extend existing ones. From an enterprise perspective, all of this is crucial when you have preexisting custom protocols that your brand-spanking-new Visual Basic .NET application must interoperate with.

7

Windows Services

Windows services are an important concept in Windows development. A service is a long-running application that typically executes in its own user session. A service can be set to automatically start when the operating system boots and can run without the user having to be logged in. Services can run under separate user accounts that do not require an actual user to be logged into the operating system. This makes services ideal for applications that must run all the time because they do not interfere with other users working on the same system. Services are usually server-specific.

In this chapter, we will discuss creating, interacting with, installing, and debugging Windows services created with Visual Basic .NET. The Visual Basic .NET language, coupled with the Microsoft .NET Framework, provides a wonderful platform for developing Windows services. For those who are new to Windows services, a quick introduction follows.

Windows Services and Visual Basic 6

Visual Basic 6 developers have long awaited the day in when they can easily, confidently, and reliably create and deploy Windows NT services. Of course, several "hacks" have been available to help you get a service up and running in Visual Basic 6, but most have been fairly inflexible, inelegant, and unreliable. These have included ActiveX controls, third-party components or libraries, and services that are essentially hand-rolled with Win32 API calls. The latter have proved problematic due to the threading behavior inherent in Visual Basic 6. We now have reason to celebrate because the Microsoft

.NET Framework has built-in support for Windows services, so Visual Basic programmers can finally create Windows services in an easy, recommended, and supported manner.

Introduction to Windows Services

Windows services are background processes that need to run for an extended period of time. This is usually the entire time the computer is up and running— although a user with the appropriate permissions can control the lifetime of the service if necessary. Examples of common Windows services include applications such as Microsoft Internet Information Services (IIS), Index Server, and the Telnet service. You can see and control a complete list of services via the Services Management Console (MMC) snap-in; you can load this add-in by clicking on the Services icon under the Administrative Tools section of the Control Panel (as shown in Figure 7-1).

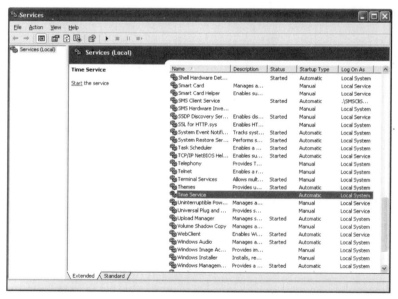

Figure 7-1   The Services Management Console.

Because services run as background processes, they do not require a user to log into the operating system in order to run. Typical applications are launched by users logged into the computer, and they run under the credentials of that user's account. A service is launched by the Service Control Manager

(SCM). Figure 7-2 shows the basic life cycle for a service based on the commands sent from the SCM.

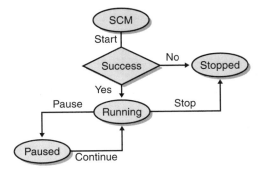

Figure 7-2   The life cycle of a Windows service.

Individual services are configured to run under specific user accounts—either a domain user's account or a local machine account (a local user or one of the many predefined system accounts: LocalSystem, LocalService, or NetworkService). Table 7-1 describes the account options for a service.

Table 7-1
Accounts That Services Can Run Under

Account	Account Capabilities
User Specific	Runs with the credentials of a local or network domain user account.
LocalSystem	An account with extensive privileges on the local computer. It can interact with the desktop but has limited access to the network because it has null credentials.
LocalService	Has minimum privileges on the local computer. Uses anonymous credentials for network requests.
NetworkService	Has minimum privileges on the local computer. Can access network resources to allow access to the Everyone or Authenticated Users groups.

Services are, by definition, background processes, but they can contain user interface elements (with design limitations). If a service needs to interact with the desktop, it must run under the LocalSystem account and be set to allow the service to interact with the desktop. (This is done by selecting a check box on the Logon tab of the Properties dialog for the service, as shown in Figure 7-3.) If the service is not set to interact with the desktop, any dialog boxes or message boxes on the main thread will simply cause the service to block because they will not be visible to anyone. The only option is to kill the service process because the SCM will be unable to communicate with the service. A service should not contain any user interface elements (Windows Forms, expected or unexpected dialog boxes, system tray icons, and so forth). If you need an interface with your service, we recommend giving strong consideration about whether the service should be a Windows service or simply a Windows-based application.

Figure 7-3   Service properties dialog box.

If a service lacks a user interface, it is common and recommended for the service to register and log events to the Windows Event Log. We would not recommend treating the Event Log as a general-purpose log file—primarily for performance reasons—however, logging the starting, stopping, and other various diagnostic-related events of services is the standard approach. The Event Log will be discussed in further detail later in this chapter.

As mentioned earlier, using the Services Management Console is the most common method for controlling a Windows service. The following section contains a discussion on the .NET Framework class which contains properties and methods for programmatically manipulating Windows services.

The *ServiceController* Class

Interaction with Windows services is made possible through the *ServiceController* class. Using this class, you can essentially control all aspects of a Windows service, including starting and stopping, pausing and continuing, and sending custom commands to the service.

The *ServiceController* class resides in the *System.ServiceProcess* namespace, which is where you'll find all classes that deal with Windows services. The use of the *ServiceController* class couldn't be much easier. Starting a service involves three steps:

1. Create an instance of the *ServiceController* class by dragging a *ServiceController* component from the Toolbox to the designer. You can also easily create a *ServiceController* instance in code, as in the following code example, or by dragging a specific service from the *Services* node in the Visual Studio .NET Server explorer for a specific machine.

2. Set the *ServiceName* property of the *ServiceController* instance. You can also optionally set the *MachineName* property if the service resides on another machine.

3. Call the *Start* method.

    The following subroutine starts a service:

```
Imports System.ServiceProcess

Private Sub StartService(ByVal serviceName As String)
    Dim myController As New ServiceController(serviceName)

    Try

        myController.Start()
        myController.WaitForStatus(ServiceControllerStatus.Running, _
                            New TimeSpan(0, 0, 30))
        MsgBox(String.Format("The {0} Service has Been Started", _
            serviceName))

    Catch ex As System.InvalidOperationException

        MsgBox(String.Format( _
            "The {0} Service could not be Started. Details : {1}", _
            serviceName, ex.ToString()))

    Catch ex As System.ServiceProcess.TimeoutException

        MsgBox(String.Format( _
            "The {0} Service Timed out Attempting to Start. Details : {1}", _
            serviceName, ex.ToString()))

    Finally
        myController.Close()
    End Try

End Sub
```

As you can see, the *ServiceController* class also provides a method named *WaitForStatus*. This method contains two overloads—one that simply blocks until the service reaches the specified status and another that takes a second argument, which is a *TimeSpan* argument. If a *TimeSpan* is specified and the value of the *TimeSpan* expires before the service reaches the desired state, a *TimeoutException* is thrown.

The code for stopping a Windows service is almost identical to that for starting the service, with one additional comment. The *ServiceController* class has properties such as *CanStop* and *CanPauseAndContinue* so you can avoid throwing unnecessary exceptions if a service doesn't support a particular action. The following code checks the *CanStop* property of the service before attempting to stop it.

```
Imports System.ServiceProcess

Private Sub StopService(ByVal serviceName As String)
   Dim myController As New ServiceController(serviceName)

   Try
      If (myController.CanStop) Then
         myController.Stop()

         'Wait 30 seconds for the Service to Stop
         '
         myController.WaitForStatus(ServiceControllerStatus.Stopped, _
                        New TimeSpan(0, 0, 30))
         MsgBox(String.Format("The {0} Service has Been Stopped", _
                     serviceName))
      Else
         MsgBox(String.Format( _
            "The {0} Service does not support Stopping", serviceName))
      End If

   Catch ex As System.InvalidOperationException

      MsgBox(String.Format("The {0} Service could not be Stopped." & _
                     " Details : {1}", serviceName, ex.ToString()))

   Catch ex As System.ServiceProcess.TimeoutException

     MsgBox(String.Format("The {0} Service Timed out Attempting to Stop." _
               & " Details : {1}", serviceName, ex.ToString()))

   Finally
      myController.Close()
   End Try

End Sub
```

The code for pausing or continuing a service using the *ServiceController* class is similar to that for stopping the service. The *ServiceController* class will be discussed further in the next section. This will include a sample application which provides buttons to control the non-device-driver services on the machine the application is running on.

The Service Manager Application

The Service Manager sample application provides buttons that allow the user to start, stop, pause, and continue services running on the local machine.

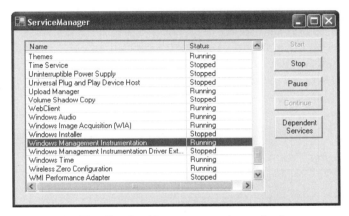

Figure 7-4   The Service Manager sample application.

Note   Another button, the Dependent Services button, invokes a simple system dialog box that lists the dependent services for the currently highlighted service in List View.

The following code shows how the application does this:

```
' Displays a Message box which shows the DependentServices of the
' currently selected Service

Private Sub depButton_Click(ByVal sender As System.Object, _
                ByVal e As System.EventArgs) Handles depButton.Click
    Dim serviceName As String = GetServiceName()
    Dim namesList As String
    Me.Cursor = Cursors.WaitCursor
    If serviceName <> "" Then
```

```
      Dim service As ServiceController = New ServiceController(serviceName)
      Dim depService As ServiceController
      ' Iterate over the array to get the Display name of each Service
      For Each depService In service.DependentServices
         namesList = namesList & depService.DisplayName & vbCrLf
      Next
      If namesList <> "" Then
         MsgBox(namesList)
      End If
      service.Close()
   End If
   Me.Cursor = Cursors.Default
End Sub
```

Notice the call to *service.Close()*. It is good practice to call the *Close* method after you finish with a *ServiceController* object that you created. The *Close* method disconnects from the service, freeing handles and other resources that were allocated when the *ServiceController* was created.

Tables 7-2 and 7-3 describe the properties and the methods of the *Service-Controller* class, respectively.

Table 7-2
***ServiceController* Properties**

Property	Description
CanStop	Specifies whether the service can be stopped (*True* or *False*).
CanShutdown	A value of *True* specifies that the service should be notified when the computer is shutting down.
CanPauseAndContinue	A value of *True* specifies that the service supports *Pause* and *Continue* commands. *OnPause* and *OnContinue* base class methods should be overridden if this property is *True*.
DependentServices	Returns an array of *ServiceController* instances that depend on this service.
DisplayName	The name that is used to identify the service.
MachineName	The name of the machine that the service resides on.
ServiceName	Set or gets the short name of the service.
ServicesDependedOn	Returns an array of *ServiceController* instances that a service depends on.

Table 7-2
ServiceController **Properties**

Property	Description
ServiceType	Returns a bitwise *Or* combination of the *ServiceType* enum member. These include *Adapter*, *FileSystemDriver*, *InteractiveProcess*, *KernelDriver*, *RecognizerDriver*, *Win32OwnProcess*, and *Win32ShareProcess*.
Status	An enum that depicts what state the service is in: *Running*, *Stopped*, *Paused*, *PausePending*, *StopPending*, *StartPending*, or *ContinuePending*.

Table 7-3
ServiceController **Methods**

Method	Description
Close	Closes the *ServiceController* instance and frees all resources that it allocated
Continue	Resumes a paused service
ExecuteCommand	Sends a custom command to the service
GetDevices (Shared)	Returns an array of *ServiceController* instances that represent the device-driver-specific services on the machine
GetServices (Shared)	Returns an array of *ServiceController* instances that represent services that are not device drivers
Pause	Pauses the service
Refresh	Resets the *ServiceController* instance properties back to their defaults
Start	Starts the service
Stop	Stops the service
WaitForStatus	Waits for the service to reach a particular status or time-out period

The majority of services log the starting, stopping, and other state transitions to the Windows Event Log. Before diving into creating a service, a brief overview of the Windows Event Log will be given, with code examples that write to the Windows Event Log using Visual Basic .NET.

The Windows Event Log

An *event* is anything of significance or importance in an application or operating system that requires users to be notified via an entry added to a log file. The Windows Event Log is a service on Windows NT, Windows 2000, and Windows XP that runs automatically when the computer boots. The Event Log service is responsible for recording these significant application, security, and system events to a log file. The Event Viewer allows you to examine the events logged to a given event log. By default, Windows contains System, Security, and Application Event logs, although custom event logs can be created by an application. Event logs can help you identify and diagnose system or application problems.

Writing to the Windows event log is a must when you deal with a service because it is one of the best and easiest ways to debug and trace the execution of a service. An event log can be created from within an application in three ways. We'll briefly discuss each option and show a fairly trivial example of creating a custom log on the computer, setting the log source, and writing to the log. Creating an event log is extremely simple using the .NET Framework *EventLog* class. These three approaches all yield the same result—an instance of an *EventLog* class:

- Add an *EventLog* component from the Components tab of the Toolbox by dragging it to the designer.

- In Server Explorer, find the specific event log on the machine and drag it onto your designer.

- Create the *EventLog* instance in code, as in the following example:

```
Public Module Logger

    Private m_log As EventLog

    Public Sub LogEvent(ByVal message As String, _
                        ByVal eventType As EventLogEntryType)

        ' Check to see if we have a valid EventLog object
        '
        If (m_log Is Nothing) Then

            If Not EventLog.SourceExists("TimeService") Then
                EventLog.CreateEventSource("TimeService", "Utilities")
            End If

            ' Create an EventLog instance and assign its source.
            '
```

```
        m_log = New EventLog("Utilities")
        m_log.Source = "TimeService"
    End If
    m_log.WriteEntry(message, eventType)

End Sub

End Module
```

The *LogEvent* sub shown in the preceding example takes the textual message for the event as an input parameter. If the *EventLog* instance has not been created, the code checks to see whether the *"TimeService"* source exists on the computer. If the source does not exist, a new custom event log called *Utilities* is created. The code then creates an instance of the *EventLog* in the private *m_log* variable and sets the *Source* property of this log instance to the *TimeService* event source.

Caution   If you don't call *CreateEventSource* in your code, the first time you call *WriteEntry*, it will call CreateEventSource for you to create the event source. If the log property has not previously been set, then the event will be written to the *Application* log by default.

Finally, the code writes the event to the custom log as the type specified by the *eventType* parameter. Many overloads are available for the *WriteEntry* method, including parameters for setting the *EventLogEntryType*, registered event source, and application-defined event identifiers and categories, as well as parameters for appending binary data.

The following snapshot of the Event Viewer shows the *Utilities* custom event log after the service has inserted an entry.

The *EventLog* class has several other properties, methods, and events for managing a Windows event log. This class includes methods for retrieving an array of event logs on a specific computer, deleting event logs and *EventLog* sources, reading from an event log, and an event which signals when an entry has been written to a log.

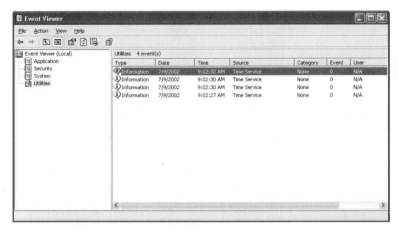

Figure 7-5 The *Utilities* custom event log.

A Simple Service

Visual Studio .NET makes it extremely easy to create a Windows service. If you've mastered the primary mouse-button click, you're well on your way to creating your first service. The following example shows part of the code that Visual Studio .NET inserts when you create a new Visual Basic Windows Service project. Here are the steps for creating a bare-bones service:

1. Derive your class from the *System.ServiceProcess.ServiceBase* class.

2. Pass an instance of this derived class to the shared *ServiceBase.Run* method. (Alternatively, you can pass an array of derived *ServiceBase* instances to the overloaded *ServiceBase.Run* method—multiple services can reside in a single executable file.)

3. Override the *OnStart* and *OnStop* methods.

```
Imports System.ServiceProcess

Public Class Service1
    Inherits System.ServiceProcess.ServiceBase

    <MTAThread()> _
    Shared Sub Main()
        Dim ServicesToRun() As System.ServiceProcess.ServiceBase

        ServicesToRun = _
            New System.ServiceProcess.ServiceBase() {New Service1}
        System.ServiceProcess.ServiceBase.Run(ServicesToRun)
    End Sub
```

```
Protected Overrides Sub OnStart(ByVal args() As String)
   'Add initialization code here.
End Sub

Protected Overrides Sub OnStop()
   'Add cleanup code here.
End Sub

End Class
```

The *OnStart* method is where you should place any initialization code and code that is necessary for starting and running the service. When the *ServiceBase.Run* method is called, the service is loaded into memory and the constructor is called. When the service is started, the Service Control Manager (SCM) sends a *Start* command to the service, which in turn invokes the *OnStart* method in the service. The *OnStop* method is where you should dispose of any resources your service allocated.

Warning   Do not place any initialization code in the class constructor that must be executed each time the service is started. The class constructor is called only once by the Service Control Manager—the first time the service is loaded. Subsequent attempts to start the service will most likely fail because this initialization code will not be executed.

Warning   Do not perform a long-running or blocking command in the *OnStart* method. This method should simply start a timer or another thread and then return immediately; otherwise, the service will fail to start.

ServiceBase also defines several properties and other methods that can be overridden. Tables 7-4 and 7-5 list the properties and the protected methods of the *ServiceBase* class, respectively.

Table 7-4
***ServiceBase* Properties**

Property	Description
CanStop	Specifies whether the service can be stopped (*True* or *False*).
CanShutdown	A value of *True* specifies that the service should be notified when the computer is shutting down.
CanPauseAndContinue	A value of *True* specifies that the service supports *Pause* and *Continue* commands. *OnPause* and *OnContinue* base class methods should be overridden when this property is *True*.
CanHandlePowerEvent	If *True*, the *OnPowerEvent* method is triggered when the computer goes into an alternate power state.
AutoLog	If *True* (the default), status information for the service will automatically be logged when actions occur (such as starting and stopping).
EventLog	An *EventLog* object with a source already registered with the *Application* log.
ServiceName	Set or gets the short name of the service.

Table 7-5
***ServiceBase* Overridable Methods**

Method	Description
OnStart	Invoked when the service is started by the SCM or when the operating system boots (if the service is set to run automatically)
OnStop	Invoked when the service is being stopped by the SCM
OnPause	Invoked when a *Pause* command is sent to the service from the SCM
OnContinue	Invoked when a *Continue* command is sent to the service from the SCM
OnPowerEvent	Called when the computer's power changes state (to hibernation or system standby mode, for example)

Table 7-5
***ServiceBase* Overridable Methods**

Method	Description
OnShutdown	Invoked before the operation system shuts down
OnCustomCommand	Invoked when a custom command is sent to the service by the SCM

The *OnCustomCommand* method can be overridden in your derived *ServiceBase* class. This method takes one parameter—an integer whose value must be between 0 and 256. Values below 128 correspond to system-reserved values. If the *AutoLog* property is set to *true*, custom commands will log an entry to the event log to report the failure or success of the method execution.

One interesting characteristic of services is that they can share a process with other services. Visual Studio .NET is capable of creating two types of services. These correspond to the *Win32OwnProcess* and *Win32ShareProcess ServiceType* enumerations. In Visual Studio .NET you cannot create service types that relate to hardware, file system, or other device drivers. With the basics of creating a service covered, we will now move on to creating an actual service.

A Timely Example of a Service

As mentioned earlier, services are an excellent candidate for utility-style applications that run in the background and periodically poll data. This might include monitoring a process executing on the computer or on a network computer, or simply waiting for some other process or system to contact the service.

For example, let's assume that we need a way to synchronize the time of day on several machines. These machines reside on a private LAN and are not part of a domain and therefore can't reach out to the Internet to synchronize their time. These computers can, however, reach a machine on the network with access to the Internet. Let's create a time synchronization service, which we also included as the TimeService sample in the book's sample files. The sample uses the Network Time Protocol (NTP) to synchronize the time of the computer to another reference source somewhere on the Internet. The sample use a fairly well-known NTP host located at *time.nist.gov*. Let's examine the four primary functions of the service:

- **Communicate with the service**   Accept remote TCP connections on port 37 and upon connection respond with a 4-byte value representing the number of seconds since 1/1/1900, and then immediately close the connection. (This is basically what an NTP server does.)

■   **Accept remoting calls through a predefined *ITime* interface**
This interface supports one method, which returns the current time.

■   **Update the date and time**   Connect to an NTP time server once a
day and update the time on the local machine.

■   **Read from a local file a list of machines on the network that
need to have their time updated periodically**   Synchronize the
time on these machines with the time on the local machine running
the service.

Communicating with the Service

One method of communicating with a service is to use the classes and methods
contained in the *System.Remoting* namespace. Remoting simply allows for communication across application and application domain boundaries. Applications
can reside on the same computer, the same LAN, or on networks on opposite
sides of the world. Remoting uses a specified channel to transport messages to
and from applications and uses formatters for encoding and decoding the messages before they're transported via the channel.

To see how extremely simple yet powerful remoting can be, take a look at
the following code, which includes the *OnStart* method of the *TimeService* class:

```
Public Class TimeService
    Inherits System.ServiceProcess.ServiceBase

    Private m_time As Time
    Private m_tmr As System.Timers.Timer
    Private m_listener As Thread

    Protected Overrides Sub OnStart(ByVal args() As String)

        'Read the remoting configuration from the <app>.exe.config file.
        '
        Dim configFile As String = Windows.Forms.Application.StartupPath & _
                        "\TimeService.exe.config"

        LogEvent("The TimeService is Starting", _
            EventLogEntryType.Information)
        Try
            m_time = New Time()
            RemotingConfiguration.Configure(configFile)
            ' Start the thread to listen for connections on port 37
            '
            m_listener = New Thread(New ThreadStart(AddressOf Listen))

            ' Make sure it is a background thread so it doesn't keep the
```

```
    ' process hanging around after the service stops.
    '
    m_listener.IsBackground = True
    m_listener.Name = "Listener Thread created at " & _
                    DateTime.Now.ToString()
    m_listener.Start()

    m_tmr = New System.Timers.Timer(1000)
    AddHandler m_tmr.Elapsed, AddressOf OnTimer
    m_tmr.Enabled = True

  Catch ex As Exception
    LogEvent("The TimeService Encountered an Error: " & _
            ex.ToString(), EventLogEntryType.Error)
  End Try
End Sub
```

The *OnStart* method starts out by logging an event to the event log to show that the service is starting. The service then creates a new instance of a custom *Time* class (which we'll discuss in detail a little later). The next line is interesting: one line simply reads in everything the service needs in order to remote out an interface. The *RemotingConfiguration* class contains many static methods, such as the *Configure* method, that allows you to use XML to define your remoting infrastructure. It is highly recommend to use this feature if you want to communicate with a service via remoting. No recompiling is necessary to change the mode, channel, port, and so on—you just restart your service. How cool is that!

```
<?xml version="1.0" encoding="utf-8"?>
<configuration>
  <system.runtime.remoting>
    <application>
      <service>
        <wellknown mode="Singleton"
                  type="TimeService.Time,TimeService"
                  objectUri="TimeServiceUri" />
      </service>
      <channels>
        <channel ref="tcp" port="9000" />
      </channels>
    </application>
  </system.runtime.remoting>
</configuration>
```

In this service, we're remoting out the *TimeService.Time* type from the *TimeService* assembly as a singleton object, which is made available on a TCP channel at port 9000.

How do you get an instance of this object from outside of the application? We recommend that you create another Visual Basic .NET project and define your interfaces as shown in the following example. This is a fairly trivial example—it contains only one method which clients will use to retrieve the current date and time.

```
Public Interface ITime
    Function CurrentTime() As DateTime
End Interface
```

You then build this interface into its own assembly, named TimeLib.dll. This assembly contains only the definition for the *ITime* interface. The *ITime* interface is then implemented by the *TimeService.Time* class. The code for the *ITime.CurrentTime* method is shown here:

```
' Implements the ITime.CurrentTime method and returns the Current DateTime
' for this computer
'
Public Function CurrentTime() As Date Implements ITime.CurrentTime
    Return DateTime.Now()
End Function
```

Now for the client code. The first step is to reference the TimeLib.dll assembly we created above, and then the following function calls the static *Get-Type* method of the *Type* class to retrieve an instance of the *ITime* type. Next, we call *Activator.GetObject*, passing the *ITime* type and the URL to the server-activated well-known object. This URL is a concatenation of the protocol, server, channel, and *objectURI* we defined earlier in the *TimeService* application configuration file. *Activator.GetObject* creates a proxy for the well-known object which we cast to the *ITime* interface. From here, we can call methods directly on the interface.

```
Dim time As ITime
Dim t As Type = Type.GetType("TimeLib.ITime,TimeLib")

If Not (t Is Nothing) Then
    time = CType(Activator.GetObject(t, _
            "tcp://localhost:9000/TimeServiceUri"),  ITime)
    If (time Is Nothing) Then
        MsgBox("Could not Contact TimeService")
    Else
        MsgBox("The Time is Currently: " & time.CurrentTime())
    End If
End If
```

That's about it for basic communication via remoting. Remoting is covered in more detail in Chapter 6. The good thing about separating out the interface and placing it in its own assembly, is that you can simply deploy this assembly to any clients that need to communicate with the service. You can do this without having to deploy any implementation code for the underlying class that does all the work.

We can't verify that this service abides totally by the specification for an NTP server, so we won't call it one, but it does return 4 bytes that represent the number of seconds since January 1, 1900. So, looking back at the *TimeService* example, the *OnStart* method creates a new thread (*m_listener*) and points the *ThreadStart* at the *Listen* function:

```
' Listens on Port 37 and Sends the number of elapsed seconds
' since 1/1/1900
'
Public Sub Listen()
    Dim listener As Socket
    Dim socket As Socket
    Dim host As IPEndPoint
    Dim seconds As Integer
    Dim buffer() As Byte
    Trace.WriteLine("Listen Starting")
    Try

        ' Create a New IP EndPoint on port 37 for the localhost

        host = New IPEndPoint(Dns.Resolve("127.0.0.1").AddressList(0), 37)
        listener = New Socket(AddressFamily.InterNetwork, _
                        SocketType.Stream, _
                        ProtocolType.Tcp)

        listener.Blocking = True
        ' Bind the Listening socket to the host IP EndPoint
        listener.Bind(host)

        ' Allow up to 10 connections to queue up.
        listener.Listen(10)

        ' Call Accept which blocks waiting for a remote connection
        While True
            socket = listener.Accept()

            ' If we have a valid connection then send the number of seconds
            '   since 1/1/1900 on the socket and then close it.
            If Not (socket Is Nothing) Then
                Trace.WriteLine("Remote socket connection on port 37. " & _
                        "AddressFamily = " & _
                        socket.RemoteEndPoint.AddressFamily.ToString())
                Dim ts As TimeSpan = DateTime.UtcNow.Subtract( _
                                New DateTime(1900, 1, 1, 0, 0, 0))
                buffer = _
                    BitConverter.GetBytes(Convert.ToUInt32(ts.TotalSeconds))
```

```
           Array.Reverse(buffer)
           socket.Send(buffer)
           socket.Shutdown(SocketShutdown.Both)
           socket.Close()
       End If
     End While
     listener.Close()
   Catch ex As Exception
     LogEvent("An exception occurred in Listen() : " & _
                   ex.ToString(), EventLogEntryType.Error)
   Finally
       socket.Close()
       listener.Close()
   End Try

End Sub
```

The *Listen* function binds a listener socket to *IPEndPoint* of the localhost on port 37. It sets the socket to blocking and adjusts the size of the queue to handle up to 10 simultaneous connections. The service enters an infinite loop and blocks on the *Accept* call in the loop.

When a connection comes in, a socket is returned from the *Accept* method. After making sure the socket is still valid, the function calculates the number of seconds since 1/1/1900, stuffs the number into a 4-byte array, and sends the bytes out via the socket. Finally, it disables receiving and sending on this socket and then closes it out.

Updating the Date and Time

Now that we can communicate with our service, we need to make sure that our service maintains the correct date and time. Let's look again at the *OnStart* method for our service. It creates an instance of a server-based timer by instantiating an instance of the *System.Timer* class. Timers are the typical approach that most Windows services use to deal with monitoring or polling at specified intervals. It is simple to create a timer, set the interval, set up an event handler, and enable it.

Warning   The .NET Framework has two timers: the Windows Forms timer and the server-based timer in the *System.Timers* namespace. The Windows Forms timer is the familiar timer that is optimized for the user interface—it requires a message pump in order to work. You should use the server-based timer in a Windows service because it has built-in thread safety and is optimized for the multithreaded environment.

The *OnTimer* event handler is triggered after the initial one second of life and then it adjusts the interval to every 24 hours.

```
Public Sub OnTimer(ByVal source As Object, _
                   ByVal e As System.Timers.ElapsedEventArgs)
    ' Set this to update the local time every 24 hours from now on
    m_tmr.Interval = 86400000

    If m_time Is Nothing Then
        m_time = New Time()
    End If
    m_time.Update()
    UpdateClients()
End Sub
```

With the timer in place, let's take a look at the code for updating the time on the local machine. The following code connects to a well-known time server on the Internet, *time.nist.gov*, on port 37:

```
Public Sub Update()
    Dim tcp As New TcpClient()
    Dim netStream As NetworkStream
    Dim buffer(3) As Byte
    Dim bytesRead As Integer
    Dim seconds As Long
    Dim dtime As DateTime

    Try
        ' Attempt to connect to a well-known Time Server on port 37
        tcp.Connect("time.nist.gov", 37)
        netStream = tcp.GetStream()
        If netStream.CanRead Then
            ' Attempt to read 4 bytes from the Connection
            bytesRead = netStream.Read(buffer, 0, 4)
            If (bytesRead = 4) Then
                ' Turn this into the number of seconds since the 1/1/1900
                Array.Reverse(buffer)
                seconds = Convert.ToDouble(BitConverter.ToUInt32(buffer, 0))
                dtime = New DateTime(1900, 1, 1, 0, 0, 0)
                dtime = dtime.AddSeconds(seconds)
                'Set the time on the localmachine
                m_localhost.SetDateTime(dtime.ToLocalTime)
                LogEvent("Successfully Set the time on the local" & _
                         " machine to " & dtime.ToLocalTime(), _
                         EventLogEntryType.Information)

            Else
                LogEvent("Unable to Set the time on the local" & _
                         " machine from server time.nist.gov", _
                         EventLogEntryType.Error)
```

```
        End If
    End If

Catch ex As Exception
    LogEvent(String.Format("Unable to Update the Time on" & _
                " the Server. Error : {0}", ex.Message), _
                EventLogEntryType.Error)
Finally
    ' Close the network stream
    netStream.Close()
End Try

End Sub
```

Some of this code is like the code for our listener thread, except it converts the bytes back into seconds and then computes the date and time by adding the value (in seconds) to 1/1/1900. The code initiates a new instance of the *TcpClient* class, connects to the host on port 37, and gets the resulting network stream. Next, it reads the first 4 bytes off of the stream and verifies that the connection was successful. Finally, after the conversion to the *DateTime* object, the time in Universal Time Coordinate (UTC) format is converted to *LocalTime* before being passed to the *SetDateTime* method of the *Machine* object represented by the private class variable *m_localhost*.

The *Machine* class defines a method that takes a *DateTime* variable and uses Windows Management Instrumentation (WMI) to set the date and time on the particular computer. It does this by formatting the path, which includes the host name of the computer, and then passes it along to the newly created *ManagementScope* object. The following code shows this in action:

```
Public Class Machine

    Private m_name As String
    Public ReadOnly Property Name()
        Get
            Return m_name
        End Get
    End Property

    Public Sub New(ByVal machineName As String)
        m_name = machineName
    End Sub

    ' WMI Win32_OperatingSystem SetDateTime method exists only on
    ' Windows XP.
    '
    Public Sub SetDateTime(ByVal dtLocal As DateTime)
```

```
    Dim retval As System.UInt32
    Dim path As String = String.Format("\\{0}\root\CIMV2", m_name)
    Dim dtBegin As DateTime = Now()
    Dim tsElapsed As TimeSpan
    Dim osColl As WMI.OperatingSystem.OperatingSystemCollection
    osColl = WMI.OperatingSystem.GetInstances( _
                                New ManagementScope(path), "")
    Dim os As WMI.OperatingSystem
    Dim elapsed As Integer

    For Each os In osColl
        tsElapsed = Now.Subtract(dtBegin)
        dtLocal = dtLocal.Add(tsElapsed)
        retval = os.SetDateTime(dtLocal)
        If System.Convert.ToInt32(retval) <> 0 Then
            Logger.LogEvent(String.Format( _
                "Error Setting Time on {0}. Error Code = {1}", _
                m_name, retval), EventLogEntryType.Error)
        End If
    Next
  End Sub

End Class
```

WMI and Generating Management Strongly Typed Classes

The .NET Framework comes with a handy tool that generates source code for a strongly typed class from a particular WMI class. This tool makes it much easier to access properties and call functions defined within WMI classes.

For those of you that are new to WMI, here is a brief overview. WMI is a set of classes built into the Windows operating system. The classes make it easier for developers to author applications that monitor, manage, and detect failures in most aspects of the operating system, the computer, and applications running on the computer. Using WMI, you can retrieve a list of processes running on a machine, determine the free disk space on the primary partition, and retrieve a list of installed applications, among other tasks.

The syntax used to call WMI methods to obtain properties of WMI classes is typically not easy and can lead to errors. The mgmtclassgen.exe utility provided by the .NET Framework makes the code much simpler to write when accessing properties and invoking functions defined within the WMI classes. This utility has several command-line options; here are a few that was used to generate a file named os.vb which is included in the TimeService project:

```
mgmtclassgen Win32_OperatingSystem /n root\cimv2 /l VB /p c:\os.vb
```

Finally, we need to update the date and time on a set of clients from our computer hosting the service. In the *OnTimer* method, a call is made to the *UpdateClients* method:

```
' Reads the machine names from the clients.txt file, creates a new
' Machine object instance for each and adds them as a worker item
' to a ThreadPool.
'
Private Sub UpdateClients()
    Dim path As String = Windows.Forms.Application.StartupPath & _
                         "\clients.txt"
    Dim rdr As StringReader
    Dim strm As StreamReader
    Dim client As String
    Dim machine As Machine

    ' Make sure the clients.txt file exists
    '
    If (File.Exists(path)) Then
        Trace.WriteLine("Loading Clients from file " & path)
        Try

            ' Open the Text file returning a StreamReader and create a
            ' StringReader to iterate over each line in the file
            '
            strm = File.OpenText(path)
            rdr = New StringReader(strm.ReadToEnd())

            ' Get the first line in the file
            '
            client = rdr.ReadLine()
            Do While Not (client Is Nothing)
                ' Create a new machine object for the client and queue up
                ' another thread to handle setting the time for this client.
                machine = New Machine(client)
                ThreadPool.QueueUserWorkItem(AddressOf ThreadFunc, machine)
                client = rdr.ReadLine()
            Loop
        Catch ex As Exception
            LogEvent("An Error occurred in UpdateClients : " & _
                     ex.ToString(), EventLogEntryType.Error)
        Finally
```

```
        rdr.Close()
        strm.Close()
     End Try
   Else
     LogEvent(path & " does not exist.", _
                     EventLogEntryType.Information)
   End If

End Sub
```

This code is pretty straightforward. The service opens the clients.txt file and reads the entire file into a string variable. A *StringReader* then iterates through the file, grabbing each host name in the file, and creates a new a *Machine* object for it. The next line in the code queues a work item in the *ThreadPool*, passing each *Machine* object along for the ride.

The *WaitCallBack* delegate, shown in the following code, is called for every work item that hits the thread pool queue. This code casts the object to a *Machine* object and then calls the *SetDateTime* method on the instance, handling any exceptions along the way by logging to the event log.

```
' Call Back Function which initiates setting the time of the remote
' client machine
'
Public Sub ThreadFunc(ByVal obj As Object)
   Dim client As Machine = CType(obj, Machine)
   Try
      LogEvent("Setting Time on Machine " & client.Name, _
                        EventLogEntryType.Information)
      client.SetDateTime(DateTime.Now())
   Catch ex As Exception
      LogEvent("An Exception was Thrown attempting to Set the Time on " _
            & client.Name & " Details : " & ex.ToString(), _
            EventLogEntryType.Error)

   End Try
End Sub
```

Finally, the *OnStop* event handler is defined in the service and is called when the service shuts down. The code in the *OnStop* event handler, disables the timer and logs an event to indicate that the service is shutting down.

```
Protected Overrides Sub OnStop()
   ' Add code here to perform any tear-down necessary to
   ' stop the service.
   Timer1.Enabled = False
   LogEvent("The TimeService is Stopping", _
                     EventLogEntryType.Information)
End Sub
```

Installing a Service

A Windows service must be registered with the system and the SCM before it can be started or debugged. (We'll talk about debugging a service in the next section.) The .NET Framework ships with the InstallUtil tool, which helps you quickly and easily install a Windows service.

The first step in the process is to add a *ServiceInstaller* class to the Windows service project. An easy way to do this is to click the Add Installer link at the bottom of the Properties dialog box for the Windows service component. You end up with a bare-bones *ProjectInstaller* class, which is added to your existing Windows service project. The *ProjectInstaller* class has the *RunInstaller(True)* attribute defined, which is what the InstallUtil.exe utility looks for when it attempts to invoke the *Install* or *Uninstall* method.

Before you run the InstallUtil application, you need a separate *ServiceInstaller* component for every service in the application. You'll want to change several properties for each *ServiceInstaller* component. The Properties dialog box for the component allows you to specify the display name, startup type, and dependent services and give the service a name. Looking at the designer-generated code, you can see that it simply adds these component instances to the *System.Configuration.Install.InstallerCollection* at run time to start the installation process.

The *ServiceInstaller.DisplayName* name will show up as the friendly name in the SCM. The *ServiceName* property should have the same name as the class that inherits from *ServiceBase* because when the service is installed, an *EventLog* source with that name is created in the Windows application event log. The *ServicesDependedOn* property allows for an array of strings—clicking the ... button next to this entry will allow you to define the set of services that this service is dependent on. Finally, the *StartType* of the service can have a value of *Automatic*, *Manual*, or *Disabled*, which will determine the behavior of the service when the machine boots up. Figure 7-6 shows the Properties dialog box for the *ServiceInstaller* class.

Along with the *ServiceInstaller* component comes a *ServiceProcessInstaller* component, which is needed for each assembly that contains Windows services. For each instance of a *ServiceProcessInstaller*, you can specify that a service application is run with specific account credentials other than the credentials of the logged-on user. This is done by specifying a username and password combination and setting the *Account* property to *user*. If the username and password are *Nothing,* at installation time a dialog box will appear prompting you for them. You can also set the *Account* property so the service will run under the computer's *System* account or a local/network service account.

Figure 7-6   The *ServiceInstaller* Properties dialog box.

The following code is the designer-generated code for the *InitializeComponent* method of the *ProjectInstaller* class. This code is essentially all there is to creating an installer for a service.

```
Friend WithEvents ServiceInstaller1 As ServiceProcess.ServiceInstaller

<System.Diagnostics.DebuggerStepThrough()> _
Private Sub InitializeComponent()
   Me.ServiceProcessInstaller1 = _
                  New ServiceProcess.ServiceProcessInstaller()
   Me.ServiceInstaller1 = New System.ServiceProcess.ServiceInstaller()
   '
   'ServiceProcessInstaller1
   '
   Me.ServiceProcessInstaller1.Account = _
                     ServiceProcess.ServiceAccount.LocalSystem
   Me.ServiceProcessInstaller1.Password = Nothing
   Me.ServiceProcessInstaller1.Username = Nothing
   '
   'ServiceInstaller1
   '
   Me.ServiceInstaller1.DisplayName = "Time Service"
   Me.ServiceInstaller1.ServiceName = "TimeService"
   Me.ServiceInstaller1.StartType = _
                  ServiceProcess.ServiceStartMode.Automatic
   '
   'ProjectInstaller
   '
```

```
Me.Installers.AddRange( _
    New System.Configuration.Install.Installer() _
    {Me.ServiceProcessInstaller1, Me.ServiceInstaller1})

End Sub
```

The *Installer* class, which is a base class for the *ServiceInstaller,* has built-in transactional support for rolling back installations that fail and thus resetting registry and other settings to their previous values. It exposes methods for installing, rolling back, and uninstalling applications as well as several methods for defining public events that can be handled to customize the installation of your service. These include *AfterInstall, AfterRollback, AfterUninstall, BeforeInstall, BeforeRollback, BeforeUninstall, Committed,* and *Committing.*

The InstallUtil application takes several command-line parameters, but simply accepting the defaults yields the output for the *TimeService* executable shown in Figure 7-7.

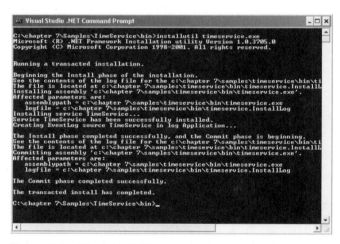

Figure 7-7 The InstallUtil.exe output.

Debugging a Service

Debugging a Windows service is not as straightforward as debugging your run-of-the-mill Windows Forms application. The difficulty stems from the context in which the service runs. As previously noted, the SCM handles starting, stopping, and essentially controlling the lifetime of the service. An attempt to run a Windows service project from within Visual Studio will result in the failure dialog box shown in Figure 7-8.

Figure 7-8   The message box that appears if attempting to start a Windows service project within the IDE.

To debug a Window service, you must start the service and then attach to the process hosting the service with Visual Studio .NET. After installing the service, you can start, stop, pause, and continue the service by right-clicking the service in the Server Explorer window in Visual Studio .NET.

Note   Another quick way to start and stop a service is via the command prompt. At the Windows command prompt, you can issue *Net Start TimeService* or *Net Stop TimeService* to start or stop a service, respectively.

Once the service is running, choose Debug Processes from the Tools menu. In the dialog box that appears, locate the Show System Processes check box and select it, then select the service process name in the list. Click the Attach button to see the Attach To Process dialog box, as shown in Figure 7-9. Be sure that the Common Language Runtime check box is selected , and then click OK. Click the Close button in the Processes dialog box.

If all has gone well, you can set breakpoints within the service and have the debugger break into the code when the service hits the area of code around the breakpoint. You can also send the service Stop, Pause, and Continue commands to coax it into a section of code that you want to debug.

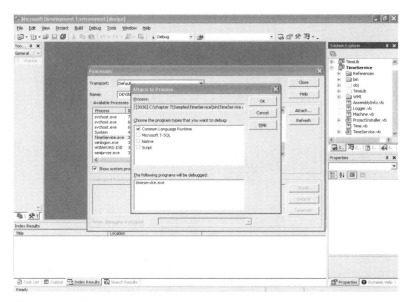

Figure 7-9   Attaching the Visual Studio .NET debugger to a process.

Debugging the *OnStart* Method

Debugging the *OnStart* method can be a little more difficult because the SCM imposes a 30-second timeout on starting the service and the debugger must be attached to the process before you can debug. Realistically, you shouldn't be doing much of anything in the *OnStart* method other than some occasional initialization. The initialization might need to be debugged, however. The "Debugging Windows Service Applications" topic in the Visual Studio .NET MSDN collection discusses creating a second "dummy" service and then simply adding this to the same Windows service project. This service will exist primarily to aid in the debugging of the other service. Here's the general idea:

1.   Add a dummy service to the existing Windows service project.

2.   Install both services.

3.   Start the dummy service so the process is loaded into memory.

4.   Attach the debugger to the running process, as described earlier.

5.   Set a breakpoint in the *Main* or *OnStart* method of the service that you want to debug.

6.   Start the service.

The *Trace* Class

The *Trace* class in the *System.Diagnostics* namespace provides another alternative for debugging with either debug or release code and is especially useful with Windows services. Sure, the event log is useful in debugging and tracing to some degree, but it can definitely be easier to watch trace to a text file or output to a debug monitor, rather than attempting to wade through a ton of log entries. For basic functionality, call the *Trace.WriteLine* function throughout your code.

The Visual Basic .NET compiler supports the *Trace* and *Debug* conditional compilation constants. By default, the *Debug* statements are omitted in release builds, but the *Trace* statements are not. This makes it easy for a user to attach a debug window to your released code and then send a log file back to you, without you having to recompile your code. As shown in Figure 7-10, you can set the *Trace* and *Debug* constants in the Build Configuration property page.

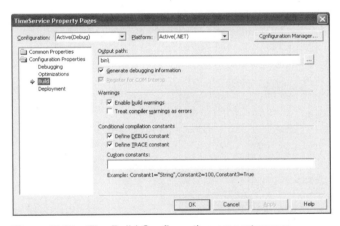

Figure 7-10   The Build Configuration property page.

After enabling tracing via the conditional compilation flag, you'll need a viewer of some sort to examine the trace statements at run time. The Web site at *http://www.sysinternals.com* has a collection of great diagnostic tools. One of these tools is a debug viewer named DebugView for capturing such trace statements. Figure 7-11 shows the DebugView tool in action.

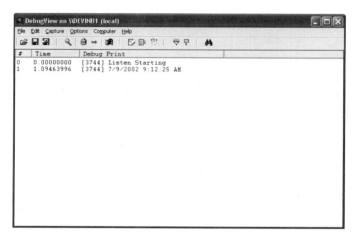

Figure 7-11   The DebugView tool.

Conclusion

As you've seen, Windows services (formerly known as Windows NT services) are not just for C/C++ developers anymore. The .NET Framework provides several classes in the *System.ServiceProcess* namespace that allow for the easy creation and manipulation of Windows services. The *ServiceController* class provides the essentials for controlling, monitoring, and interacting with Windows services, and the *ServiceBase* class provides a base class that all services must derive from. It is highly recommend that you use the Event Log for recording significant events that occur during the lifetime of the service. You can do this by simply setting the *AutoLog* property on the service to *true*.

Debugging a service can prove to be a more difficult than debugging standard Windows-based applications, so the *Trace* class was introduced as another option for tracing the execution of a service. Finally, if your service requires a user interface, you should attempt to separate the user interface from the service and place it into a secondary application that communicates with the service or the data generated by the service.

8

Integrating Enterprise-Level Services

As we've discussed in earlier chapters, applications for the enterprise typically have strict requirements regarding reliability, performance, and scalability—reliability usually being the most important of the three. Enterprise applications are typically considered mission-critical. In days gone by, developers were on their own trying to build these kinds of systems, with varying degrees of success. With Microsoft Visual Basic .NET, you have access to a whole host of services that provide a stable foundation on which to build your applications.

In this chapter, I'll address two major topics relating to these services. The first is the COM+ application model and how you can implement basic services through your application. The second topic is Windows Messaging and how to implement communication between systems. The material should give you a solid foundation for building systems using these services. From there, you should be able to dig even deeper into the technologies to further extend your applications.

Understanding COM+ and Enterprise Services

You can think of COM+ as a foundation for your enterprise applications. COM+ was designed as a services framework with built-in features such as transaction processing, synchronization, and object pooling that developers can use instead of having to roll their own solutions. COM+ relieves the developer from having to worry about the core technologies and lets them focus on the actual problems being solved by their applications. In other words, COM+ services provide a solid foundation on which to build scalable and robust enterprise applications.

The subject of COM+ services is huge, and I cannot possibly do it justice in one chapter. So I will focus on a core set of features that most developers can leverage in their applications.

At the core of all of the COM+ technologies in Visual Basic .NET is the *System.EnterpriseServices.ServicedComponent* class. Deriving your objects from this class puts a whole set of COM+ services at your fingertips, including just-in-time activation, object pooling, and transactions.

You'll find that all classes derived from the *ServicedComponent* class are known as *serviced components*. Any serviced component can be hosted by a COM+ application and use services provided by COM+. Table 8-1 lists some of the COM+ services that can be supported by serviced components.

Table 8-1
Some COM+ Services That Can Be Supported by Serviced Components

COM+ Service	Description
Automatic Transaction Processing	Allows you to designate a class at design time that participates in transactions.
Just-In-Time Activation	Allows you to create an inactive object. The object remains inactive until a client invokes one of its methods. The runtime then creates and initializes the full object. When the call returns, COM+ deactivates the object but retains the context in memory. Once an object is deactivated, it releases all resources it has obtained during its lifetime.
Object Construction	Allows you to specify class instance initialization information, eliminating the need to hardcode this information.
Object Pooling	Allows you to reduce the overhead of working with serviced components. You can create a minimal number of components and then reuse them to service additional incoming requests.
Private Components	Allows you to protect specific serviced components from accessibility by other processes. By default, services components are accessible and published to all available clients. This service provides a mechanism for controlling the availability of your components.
Queued Components	Provides an easy way to invoke and execute components asynchronously by clients. Processing of the requests can occur regardless of the availability of the originator or the recipient of the requests.

Table 8-1
Some COM+ Services That Can Be Supported by Serviced Components

COM+ Service	Description
SOAP Services	Allows you to take an existing serviced component and publish it as an XML Web service. The component will continue to be accessible through standard COM+ activation mechanisms, with the added bonus of being accessible through Web Services Description Language (WSDL) and SOAP.
Synchronization	A mechanism that prohibits components from being called by more than one client at a time. The access can flow from object to object.

Services such as transactions and queued components are configured through the use of attributes of the serviced component class. These features must be specified at design time. You can implement other services by calling methods of other serviced components or overriding methods of your own component. Some services can flow from one component to another. Transactions are an excellent example of this flow.

COM+ Requirements

To take advantage of COM+, a component must meet all of the following requirements:

- It must inherit from the *ServicedComponent* class or from another class derived from *ServicedComponent*.

- It must apply attributes that specify the COM+ services supported by that component.

- The assembly containing the component must have a strong name.

Creating a Serviced Component

Serviced components can be contained in any application or assembly type. You must perform a few basic steps to implement a serviced component in your applications. You start with a new project in Visual Basic .NET and then do the following:

1. Add a reference to System.EnterpriseServices.dll.

2. Add an *ApplicationName* attribute to your project, specifying the desired name of your COM+ application.

3. Create a class derived from the *ServicedComponent* class.

4. Create a public/private key pair using the sn.exe tool by calling *sn –k myKeyPair.snk* in your project's directory.

5. Add an *AssemblyKeyFile* attribute to your project that specifies the key file you created.

I've already explained why you need to use the *ServicedComponent* class, but the last two steps need some explanation. When you create a serviced component, it must be registered with Component Services before it can be used. Any component that is available through Component Services is globally available on your system. As a result, you must provide a strong name for your assembly. When we discussed primary Interop assemblies (PIAs) in Chapter 4, I introduced the Strong Name tool (sn.exe). Using this tool, you can generate a key file for signing your assembly (specified by the *AssemblyKeyFile* attribute). This provides a unique identity for your assembly that prevents any potential assembly and namespace confusion and makes COM+ and the .NET runtime happy.

Note You can share a key file between multiple projects in your application if you want.

Let's see what this looks like in code. You can find this class in the SimpleComponent sample application. Our class definition is pretty simple:

```
Imports System.EnterpriseServices

Public Class MyServicedComponent
    Inherits ServicedComponent
End Class
```

When you create a new Visual Basic .NET project, the IDE creates a file called AssemblyInfo.vb. This is usually the best place to store all of your assembly-level attributes. You are by no means required to store all of your assembly attributes, but doing so helps keep things organized and makes your life easier. So our minor addition to this file would look like this:

```
Imports System.EnterpriseServices
Imports System.Reflection

<Assembly: ApplicationName("COMPlus Sample")>
<Assembly: AssemblyKeyFile("myKeyFile.snk")>
```

To test our application, I've created a form with a single button. (See Figure 8-1.) This button simply creates an object and then disposes of it:

```
Dim c As New MyServicedComponent()
ServicedComponent.DisposeObject(c)
```

This demonstrates two things. First, creating an instance of a COM+ object is simple and easy. Second, when a client is done with a component, it should call *DisposeObject* to ensure that the reference is correctly released.

Tip   Calling *DisposeObject* is critical if you need your application to be able to scale well. If you don't you call it, you'll make extremely poor use of your system's computing resources (both memory and CPU).

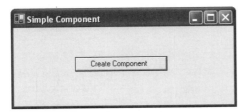

Figure 8-1   The SimpleComponent sample application.

What is not immediately obvious from this sample is that your COM+ components are self-registering. When you click the button, your application will try to create an instance of the *MyServicedComponent* class. When COM+ realizes that the application hasn't yet been registered, it will add your application to the COM+ catalog before completing the construction of your component. To see the results of this registration process, you can check out the Component Services management console, as shown in Figure 8-2.

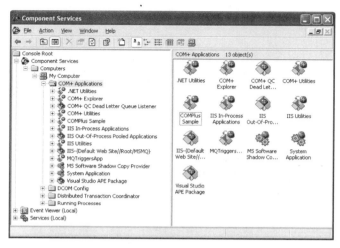

Figure 8-2   Checking the Component Services console for our sample application.

You have other options for registering your COM+ applications. In some situations, self-registration is not feasible—for example, if you have a component library that contains COM+ components. In this case, you need to register the component using the Service Registration utility (regsvc.exe).

Note   Registering your COM+ application causes your assembly to be added to the local machine's Global Assembly Cache (GAC). This makes the public components available to all applications on the system.

Understanding Application Activation

COM+ supports two forms of component activation: library activation and services activation. The activation dictates how your clients work with your components, and it can have a critical effect on performance. Put simply, library activation causes your component to be created within the process of the client application itself (in-process). Server activation, on the other hand, causes the components to be created in an out-of-process host application. This means that all client calls to your COM+ components are out-of-process.

In-process calls are, by definition, less expensive than equivalent out-of-process calls because an out-of-process call requires a lot of marshaling overhead to make it happen and in-process calls are directly accessible to your client's process. Another way to look at this is that library COM+ applications are duplicated for each process they're created in. If the process exits, so does the COM+ application. Server applications stand alone from all other processes on the system, regardless of what the client applications do. In addition, server applications are shared between all clients on the machine instead of being re-created for each client application. This can have certain advantages, especially when you're implementing something like object pooling—your object pools can be global, which allows you to retain greater control over the performance of your application. (See Figure 8-3.)

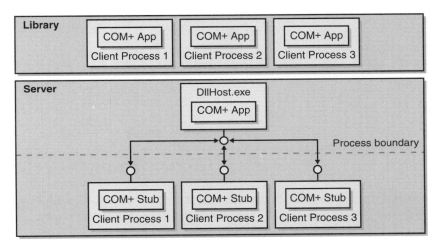

Figure 8-3   How server and library applications work.

You can control the way a COM+ application is activated by using the *ApplicationActivation* assembly-level attribute. The two possible settings are *ActivationOption.Library* and *ActivationOption.Server*. In our previous example, we didn't define this attribute at all, and you might wonder how I got away with that. It turns out that the default application activation for a COM+ application in Visual Basic .NET is library. That's why I didn't need to define it explicitly. However, to be pedantic I could add a line to the AssemblyInfo.vb file that looks like this:

```
<Assembly: ApplicationActivation(ActivationOption.Library)>
```

If you look at the SimpleComponent sample application, you'll find that I did define this attribute, if only for completeness.

Understanding COM+ Contexts

Every COM+ component has a *context*. The context contains all of the information regarding the current state of an instance of a component. This context information is stored by COM+ in a context object. It is usually created when a component is activated and destroyed when it is deactivated. The context also provides information about the environment the component is running in and represents everything the component needs to know about its world. Once the context has been created, it is immutable until the context is invalidated (either through object deactivation or destruction).

When creating a context for a component, the COM+ runtime evaluates your component's attributes to determine what services are supported. These services, and their requirements, become a part of the context and represent a contract between the client and the component. This contract includes information about transactional requirements and security settings, all of which must be satisfied to allow the component to be used.

To access your component's COM+ context, you must use the *ContextUtil* class from *System.EnterpriseServices*. This class provides a host of shared properties and methods that provide information about your current context and allow you to manipulate the context in specific ways. Table 8-2 lists the shared properties supported by the *ContextUtil* class. All of the members of the class are shared for one important reason: your component can have access only to its own context. COM+ does not allow one component to access another component's context, so you can never have more than one instance of a context object. The only possible exception is when contexts are permitted to flow from one component to another. In that case, however, the shared context is still the only context accessible by those components. This renders the distinction moot: a component can have access to only one context at a time.

Table 8-2
Shared Properties of *ContextUtil*

Property	Description
ActivityId	A GUID identifying the activity containing the component. You can think of an activity, or a task, as a single logical thread of execution. A COM+ activity can span processes and machines.
ApplicationId	Gets a GUID for the current application. Each COM+ application has an associated GUID.
ApplicationInstanceId	Gets a GUID for the current application instance.

Table 8-2
Shared Properties of *ContextUtil*

Property	Description
ContextId	Gets a GUID representing the current context.
DeactivateOnReturn	Gets or sets the done bit in the COM+ context.
IsInTransaction	Gets a value indicating whether the current context is transactional.
IsSecurityEnabled	Gets a value indicating whether role-based security is active in the current context.
MyTransactionVote	Gets or sets the consistent bit in the COM+ context. The consistent bit signifies the status of a transaction—either success or failure. If this value is *Commit*, the transaction has been successful and the consistent bit is set to *true*. If the value is *Abort*, the COM+ context will vote to abort the current transaction and set the consistent bit to *false*.
PartitionId	Retrieves the GUID identifying the current partition.
Transaction	Retrieves an object describing the current COM+ Distributed Transaction Coordinator (DTC) transaction.
TransactionId	Gets the GUID of the current COM+ DTC transaction.

Most of the properties are read-only because they merely indicate the current state of your component's context. You manipulate the context by using one of the shared methods of *ContextUtil* (described in Table 8-3). These methods allow you to manipulate the current state of your transactions, evaluate security state, and retrieve any application-specific variables. (ASP.NET provides a set of IIS intrinsic objects that are accessible if your component is called by ASP.NET.)

Table 8-3
Shared Methods of *ContextUtil*

Method	Description
DisableCommit	Sets both the consistent bit and the done bit to *false* in the COM+ context.
EnableCommit	Sets the consistent bit to *true* and the done bit to *false* in the COM+ context.
GetNamedProperty	Returns a named property from the COM+ context.

Table 8-3
Shared Methods of *ContextUtil*

Method	Description
IsCallerInRole	Determines whether the caller is in the specified role.
SetAbort	Sets the consistent bit to *false* and the done bit to *true* in the COM+ context.
SetComplete	Sets the consistent bit to *true* and the done bit to *true* in the COM+ context.

COM+ Object Construction

A difficulty arises when you try to configure a *ServicedComponent*. The component is activated by the COM+ runtime environment, so you have no opportunity to provide constructor parameters. This presents some challenges when you want to configure a component for use on multiple machines. The solution to this is object construction. COM+ supports an activation model that enables the passing of object construction parameters without using the object's physical constructor.

You need to do two things to support object construction. First, you must specify the *ContructionEnabled* attribute on your component. Second, you need to override the *Construct* method of the *ServicedComponent* class. The following example, also found in the ObjectConstruction sample, illustrates how this works:

```
Imports System.EnterpriseServices

<ConstructionEnabled([Default]:="Hello")> _
Public Class MyContructedObject
    Inherits ServicedComponent

    Protected Overrides Sub Construct(ByVal s As String)
        ' Do stuff
    End Sub
End Class
```

The *Construct* method will be called only if you first specify the *ConstructionEnabled* attribute. Using this attribute, you can also specify a default setting for the construction parameter. The above example provides a default value for the construction string in the attribute itself. I set the *Default* property of the *ConstructionEnabled* attribute to *"Hello"*. That's it.

Once we have this component, we should register it. This chapter's samples include the ObjectContruction project to demonstrate this. The project itself is just a component library, so you must manually register the assembly to see it in action. Running the regsvcs.exe tool on the assembly generates output that looks much like the following:

```
Microsoft (R) .NET Framework Services Installation Utility Version 1.0.3705.0
Copyright (C) Microsoft Corporation 1998-2001.  All rights reserved.

Installed Assembly:
        Assembly: C:\Samples\ObjectConstruction\bin\ObjectConstruction.dll
        Application: ObjectConstruction Sample
        TypeLib: c:\samples\objectconstruction\bin\ObjectConstruction.tlb
```

After we register this component, we can view its properties through the Component Services management console, shown in Figure 8-4.

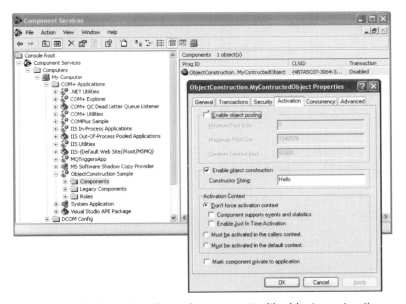

Figure 8-4   Our newly registered component with object construction enabled and the correct default settings.

You can open the properties sheet for your component, and on the Activation tab you can see, among other things, the settings for object construction. Notice that the Constructor String text box is automatically filled in with the default construction string that we specified in our code. By changing this value in the text box, you can customize the string passed to the *Construct* method. These things often include connection strings, the machine name, and any other configuration settings you might think appropriate.

Object Pooling

Object pooling is a mechanism that allows you to create a reusable "pool" of certain COM+ objects. Pooling is typically used to save CPU resources by creating a set number of objects and reusing them again and again. When you have an object that requires significant startup and initialization time, being able to create it once and then reuse it allows you to amortize the original startup costs across multiple uses. It also helps improve your application's response time and general throughput because less time is spent on object creation and more time is spent doing real work.

Object pools are created on a component-by-component basis. If I want five components to be pooled, five component pools will be created. Each pool is managed independently and can be configured differently. A COM+ object pool support three parameters: *MinPoolSize*, *MaxPoolSize*, and *CreationTimeout*. The *MinPoolSize* setting specifies the minimum number of objects in the pool. On startup, COM+ will create as many objects as needed to satisfy the minimum requirement, regardless of whether there are enough clients to use them. Similarly, if an object, once used, cannot be returned to the pool, COM+ will create a new instance to take its place in the pool if it is necessary to maintain the minimum number of pooled objects.

The *MaxPoolSize* property sets the upper bound on the number of components allowed in a pool. Typically, if a client request comes in and there are no available objects in the pool (they are all in use), COM+ will create a new instance of the component and attempt to add it to the pool when the client is done with it. This causes the pool size to grow over time. The *MaxPoolSize* prevents COM+ from growing the pool to an arbitrarily large size and consuming excessive resources. If the pool reaches the maximum size, COM+ will queue incoming requests and wait for a pooled object to be made available.

The *CreationTimeout* property works in conjunction with the *MaxPoolSize* property. Because incoming requests are queued, if there are no available objects, you can use the *CreationTimeout* property to manage how long COM+ will wait until a pooled object is made available. If the queued request exceeds the timeout setting, an exception will be thrown.

The Life Cycle of a Pooled Object

A pooled object has a definite and predicable lifecycle starting with its creation. (See Figure 8-5.) There are two reasons for a poolable object to be created. First, a poolable object can be created by COM+ to satisfy the minimum pool size requirement. This creation is not in response to a client invocation and can happen when the pool is first created or when an already existing object cannot be returned to the pool and must be destroyed. In this case, the newly created object will be put directly into the pool and await a client request.

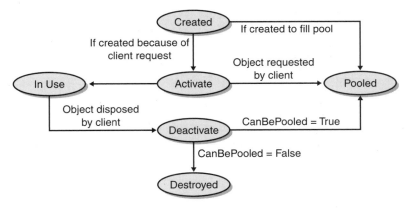

Figure 8-5   The life cycle of a pooled object.

The other possibility is that an instance of the object is created by COM+ to satisfy an incoming client request when no other pooled objects are currently available. In this case, the object is created, activated, and then passed back to the client. Otherwise, an incoming request will be satisfied by an existing unused object residing in the pool.

Regardless of why an object is created, at some point before it is passed to a client, it must first be activated. This is a way to signal the object that it must immediately perform whatever client-specific initialization is needed. Then the object reference is passed to the client and is used just like any other object. When the client is done with the object, COM+ signals it to deactivate. This is when the object performs whatever operation is necessary to eliminate any client-specific state or other information it has acquired since it was activated. This also gives the object a chance to evaluate whether it is still poolable.

Note   If an object cannot recover its original state, it should not be returned to the pool. Returning an object to a pool that hasn't reverted to its original state might result in unpredictable behavior. Not good!

Once the object has been deactivated, COM+ will ask it whether it can be returned to the object pool. If the object replies in the affirmative, it is merrily returned to the pool to await another incoming request. If the object states that it cannot be pooled, COM+ will destroy it.

Requirements for Pooled Objects

An object that supports COM+ object pooling must do several things. First and foremost, it must specify the *ObjectPooling* attribute in the class definition. This attribute allows you to specify not only that an object supports pooling but also various properties of the pool itself. In addition to the *ObjectPooling* attribute, two key methods of the *ServicedComponent* class that are related to pooling: *Activate* and *Deactivate*. By overriding these methods, you can customize your object's behavior as it is activated and deactivated by COM+.

A poolable object must also be stateless. This means a poolable object can retain no client-specific state between activations. This is necessary to maintain proper security, consistent behavior, and isolation. You can perform any context-specific initialization in your *Activate* method, but you must clean up and eliminate any context-specific state in your *Deactivate* method.

Your object must also be threading-model-agnostic. A poolable object can assume that it will run on a single thread at any given time. Poolable objects must run as free threads (the default) or in a multi-threaded apartment. You cannot mark a poolable object as running in an apartment-threaded thread. Poolable objects also should not use such things as thread local storage (TLS).

Other Pooling Considerations

When you define a pooled component, you must also consider what the configuration settings of the pool should be. We've already discussed the three main properties of any pool: *MaxSize*, *MinSize*, and *CreationTimeout*. Each of these properties has defaults, but I can't say I'd recommend them. When you create your pool, there are typically several considerations:

- How many pooled objects should be available at startup? If your component serves in a high-performance environment, you might want it to be able to service a large number of requests right away. By specifying a pool with a minimum size, you cause that number of objects to be created when the pool is first initialized. This means you have a ready set of components to handle incoming requests when the application first starts up.

- How long can your application take to start up? The idea behind pooling is to create expensive components once and then reuse them. The problem is that the larger the minimum size of your pool, the longer it takes to get everything initialized. Increasing the minimum pool size will cause your application to take longer to start up. Decreasing the size will cut the initialization time. This is probably something you can experiment with, and your choice will depend highly on what your requirements are.

■   How large should your pool be? Each object in the pool consumes memory, if not processing resources. Obviously, the more objects that are in the pool, the greater the impact on your application's working set. You need to understand how much in the way of system resources you can devote to a pool to help set the upper bound. Also, there are performance considerations. The larger the number of pooled objects, the greater the number of possible concurrent operations. This can consume significant computing resources, and you might need to test to find your ideal threshold. Typically, you want to limit the pool size to where you get a decreasing rate of return on additional pooled objects.

■   How long can a client wait for an object? Remember that all object requests that exceed the maximum available pooled objects will be queued until a pooled object is available. The default timeout setting is an infinite wait time, but this might not work for you, especially when a client application might be hung, waiting for the request to complete. So you have to ask yourself (or your application architects): what is a reasonable timeout value?

Creating a Poolable Object

I've already discussed the requirements for a pooled object, but let's look at the steps for creating a basic, well-behaved poolable component:

1.   Apply the *ObjectPooling* attribute to your class, providing the desired settings for your object pool.

2.   Override the *Activate* method and add your custom activation logic.

3.   Override the *Deactivate* method and add your custom cleanup logic.

4.   Override the *CanBePooled* method to indicate your object's ability to be returned to the pool.

Here's what a pooled object might look like:

```
' Enable pooling with a minimum size of 10 and a maximum size of 20
' CreationTimeout is left at its default of infinite.
<ObjectPooling(True, 10, 20)> _
Public Class MyComponent
    Inherits ServicedComponent

    Protected Overrides Sub Activate()
        ' Perform any initialization you need here
    End Sub
```

```
Protected Overrides Sub Deactivate()
    ' Clean up your object and eliminate any client-specific state
End Sub

Protected Overrides Function CanBePooled() As Boolean
    ' Return a value to indicate your ability to be placed back
    ' into the pool
    Return True
End Function
End Class
```

Of course, this sample doesn't do anything. In this respect, it is a perfect pooled component because it retains no client state. Unfortunately, that's not particularly useful. So I created a sample called ObjectPooling (Figure 8-6) that demonstrates how object pooling works.

Figure 8-6 The ObjectPooling sample application.

When you launch the application and click the Cleanup button, you cause an instance of the *MyPooledObject* class to be created, among other things. The code is as simple as the following three lines:

```
Dim myObj As New MyPooledObject()
myObj.HelloWorld()
ServicedComponent.DisposeObject(myObj)
```

The other button does exactly the same thing but omits the call to *Serviced-Component.DisposeObject*. What actually happens under the covers at this point is interesting. Of course, the first time you run this, the COM+ application is registered—you know that part already. What's also interesting is the pooling mechanism's behavior. But before I get into that, let's take a look at the pooled object in question, *MyPooledObject*:

```
Imports System.EnterpriseServices

<ObjectPooling(5, 10)> _
Public Class MyPooledObject
    Inherits ServicedComponent
```

```vb
        Private Shared s_Count As Integer = 0

        Private m_Count As Integer

        Private m_CanBePooled As Boolean = True

        Public Sub New()
            MyBase.New()

            ' Because more than one instance may be created at once,
            ' we implement synchronization to ensure correctness
            m_Count = System.Threading.Interlocked.Increment(s_Count)
            Debug.WriteLine(m_Count & " MyPooledObject:New Created ")
        End Sub

        Protected Overrides Function CanBePooled() As Boolean
            Debug.WriteLine(m_Count & " MyPooledObject:CanBePooled called")
            Return m_CanBePooled
        End Function

        Protected Overrides Sub Activate()
            ' Perform activation code
            Debug.WriteLine(m_Count & " MyPooledObject:Activate called")
        End Sub

        Protected Overrides Sub Deactivate()
            ' Perform deactivation code
            Debug.WriteLine(m_Count & " MyPooledObject:Deactivate called")
        End Sub

        Public Function HelloWorld() As String

            Return "Hello World"
        End Function
End Class
```

What's going on here? The ObjectPooling sample is intended to do one thing: demonstrate the actual behavior of COM+ object pooling. To this end, the *MyPooledObject* does a couple of things. First, it keeps track of the number of instances of the class and assigns each new instance a unique ID. This is implemented in the class's constructor and uses the shared variable *s_Count* and the member variable *m_Count*.

> **Note**   You'll notice that the constructor uses the method *Interlocked.Increment* to increment the shared member *s_Count*. This is for thread safety reasons—to prevent incorrect incrementing behavior (which can happen if two instances of *MyPooledObject* are created concurrently). For more information on the *Interlocked* class, see Chapter 3.

To make the code easier to debug, I added debug statements to each method and displayed the object's ID with each statement. I also configured the COM+ application as a library application, which means that the object pool is created in the process of the calling application. This makes it easy to see the results of the debug statements—you only need to view the contents of the Output window in the IDE.

When I first run the application and click the Cleanup button, I get the following output:

```
1 MyPooledObject:New Created
2 MyPooledObject:New Created
3 MyPooledObject:New Created
4 MyPooledObject:New Created
5 MyPooledObject:New Created
1 MyPooledObject:Activate called
1 MyPooledObject:Deactivate called
1 MyPooledObject:CanBePooled called
```

This demonstrates well how the pool works. When I first try to create *MyPooledComponent*, COM+ sees that there's no pool and creates one. It then fills the pool with objects. (This is the reason for five consecutive calls to *New*.) Then COM+ activates the first component and returns it to the client. The client then calls *DisposeObject* when it is done. COM+ deactivates the component and calls *CanBePooled*. The object is then returned to the pool.

If I click the same button again, I can see that the same object is being returned again and again. Here I click the Cleanup button twice:

```
1 MyPooledObject:Activate called
1 MyPooledObject:Deactivate called
1 MyPooledObject:CanBePooled called
1 MyPooledObject:Activate called
1 MyPooledObject:Deactivate called
1 MyPooledObject:CanBePooled called
```

Something different happens when I click the Don't Cleanup button. As I mentioned before, this button omits the call to *DisposeObject*. This keeps the reference to the COM+ object around (at least until the next garbage collection happens—and who knows when that will be). This is easy to see; the only calls are to *Activate*:

```
1 MyPooledObject:Activate called
```

If I keep clicking this button, I'll quickly go through all of the objects in the pool until I run out. Then a new object will be created and returned—just like this:

```
2 MyPooledObject:Activate called
3 MyPooledObject:Activate called
4 MyPooledObject:Activate called
5 MyPooledObject:Activate called
6 MyPooledObject:New Created
6 MyPooledObject:Activate called
```

If you keep clicking this button, the application will eventually hang because it will exceed the pool size and wait indefinitely in the request queue for an object that might never be made available. This helps highlight two things: how the pooling mechanism works, and why it is so important to call *DisposeObject*.

The only other thing I would point out is the way the *CanBePooled* method is implemented. I used a member variable to track the ability of the object to be pooled. This object might conceivably have performed an operation that it cannot cleanly recover from, thereby preventing reuse. In this situation, I would cause *CanBePooled* to return *false*—which means the object instance will be destroyed instead of just deactivated. So any method in the class could detect an unrecoverable error that effectively invalidates the class forever. By setting this member variable to *false*, the object will be destroyed rather than reused.

Next, we'll move on to a related topic: JIT activation.

Just-in-Time Activation

JIT activation is another service provided by COM+. JIT activation can enable more efficient use of computing resources, especially when you're implementing a system that is intended to be scalable. If a component is marked as JIT-activated, COM+ can deactivate an instance of the object while a client still has a reference to it. Each time the client calls a method of that object, COM+ will transparently reactivate the object. In other words, objects are activated and reactivated just in time to service the incoming client request.

Clients can thus obtain references to objects and retain them for as long as needed. At the same time, server resources can be freed up on an as-needed basis. So, from the client perspective, JIT activation makes its life easier. The client doesn't need to be concerned about how it uses server resources and the potential expense. JIT activation frees the client from needing to be aggressive about releasing server resources.

Note JIT activation isn't a substitute for cleaning up after your components. You should still call *DisposeObject*. But it does free you from worrying whether you should dispose of an object between method calls. (This has been done in the past to improve system scalability.)

The benefits of JIT combined with long-lived object references become greater the farther the client is from the server. Without JIT activation, the cost of activating and marshaling the object, opening the communications channel, setting up the object proxy and stubs, and so forth becomes an overwhelming performance hit. Doing whatever you can to minimize the number of expensive round-trips to the server is extremely advantageous. Each time you create an instance of a COM+ component remotely requires a round-trip, so using JIT activation with a single long-lived object reference (rather than multiple short-lived references) offers a definite performance advantage.

Note JIT activation is often combined with object pooling because they complement each other quite nicely. One allows pooling and reuse of expensive objects, and the other allows efficient use of the allocated objects. This significantly speeds object reactivation while retaining whatever resources they might be consuming.

Creating a JIT-Activated Component

Like most of the COM+ features in Visual Basic .NET, JIT activation is enabled with the use of a class-level attribute, in this case *JustInTimeActivation*. There is little else you need to worry about. You can override the *Activate* and *Deactivate* methods because they are called by COM+ before and after the component is activated and reactivated. That is where you should provide any code that you need to reestablish any resources you might be using.

The following example demonstrates how you can enable a class to implement both JIT activation and object pooling:

```
Imports System.EnterpriseServices

<ObjectPooling(5, 10), JustInTimeActivation()> _
Public Class MyJitPooledObject
    Inherits ServicedComponent

    Private Shared s_Count As Integer = 0

    Private m_Count As Integer

    Private m_CanBePooled As Boolean = True


    Public Sub New()
        MyBase.New()

        ' Because more than one instance may be created at once,
        ' we implement synchronization to ensure correctness
        m_Count = System.Threading.Interlocked.Increment(s_Count)
        Debug.WriteLine(m_Count & " MyJitPooledObject:New Created ")
    End Sub

    Protected Overrides Function CanBePooled() As Boolean
        Debug.WriteLine(m_Count & " MyJitPooledObject:CanBePooled called")
        Return m_CanBePooled
    End Function

    Protected Overrides Sub Activate()
        ' Perform activation code
        Debug.WriteLine(m_Count & " MyJitPooledObject:Activate called")

        ' This obj can't be pooled until it is deactivated
        m_CanBePooled = False
    End Sub

    Protected Overrides Sub Deactivate()
        ' Perform deactivation code
        Debug.WriteLine(m_Count & " MyJitPooledObject:Deactivate called")

        ' I am re-allowing pooling of this object
        m_CanBePooled = True
    End Sub
```

```
Public Function HelloWorld() As String

    Return "Hello World"
  End Function
End Class
```

Modeled after the *MyPooledObject* class from the Object Pooling section, the *MyJitPooledObject* provides many of the same debugging features you've already seen. You can find this class in the JustInTime sample application.

Now let's move on to the granddaddy of all COM+ technologies: transactions.

COM+ Transactions

A transaction is a collection of tasks that must all succeed, or else they will have no effect. If any part of a transaction fails, the transaction must be aborted, returning the system to its original, pre-transaction, state. Consider a situation in which you need to perform a series of actions that are highly dependent on each other—say, transferring money from one bank account to another. In this scenario, there are two steps. First, you must deduct the correct amount from the source account. Then you need to add the correct amount to the destination account.

What if the first operation succeeds but the second fails? What happens? If you took no precautions, the money would probably be lost in the ether, never to be found again. However, if you used a transaction, both steps would be a part of a larger, single (or atomic) operation. If the second step were to fail, you would abort the transaction, which would cause the original account deduction to be undone (rolled back).

If, on the other hand, the second operation were to succeed, the transaction would go into a commit phase. This happens when all participants in a transaction agree that any changes they have made should be permanent. This is handled through a voting scheme. Each participant performs some action. When that action is completed, the participant votes to either commit or abort. If all participants vote to commit, the transaction is committed.

A transaction can be confined to a single resource (for example, a database or a message queue) or can span multiple resources (more than one database or message queue or any combination thereof). Distributed transactions allow you to integrate a series of distinct operations that span multiple systems into a single transaction. This provides a great deal of reliability in a complex system. It doesn't prevent system failures, but it can help you manage complex systems, ensure data consistency, and avoid corruption issues.

The ACID Rules

Transactions are not a new concept. In fact, the notion has been around for many years. As with anything that's been around long enough, common rules have developed that all transactions must obey. This set of rules, commonly referred to as the *ACID rules*, identify the role that transactions play in mission-critical applications. ACID stands for atomicity, consistency, isolation, and durability:

- **Atomicity**   A transaction is a single unit of work in which a series of operations occur. A single transaction executes exactly once, and all work done in a transaction is atomic. All operations contained in a transaction must succeed or all fail. There is no middle ground.

- **Consistency**   A transaction preserves the consistency of data. Transactions transform one consistent state of data into another consistent state of data.

- **Isolation**   Each transaction is isolated from other transactions. This permits multiple, concurrent, transactions to behave as if each is the only transaction running. As a result, each transaction will appear to be the only transaction manipulating a data store, regardless of whether or not there exist other concurrent transactions. This requires that any of the intermediate changes to a system during a transaction are not visible to any other transaction, until the entire operation has been committed.

- **Durability**   If a transaction is successful, the system guarantees that its updates will persist. Period. Regardless of whether the system crashes immediately afterwards, if the transaction has been committed, the information has been stored and will be preserved.

Creating a Transactional Component

Getting started with a transactional component is fairly straightforward. Let's walk through an example of transferring money from one bank account to another. We'll modify the previous example of a simple serviced component:

```
Imports System.EnterpriseServices

<Transaction()> Public Class MyTransactionalComponent
    Inherits ServicedComponent
End Class
```

We first indicate that the component supports transactions. You can do this by using the *Transaction* attribute. This attribute has five options: *Disabled*, *NotSupported*, *Supported*, *Required*, and *RequiresNew*. Each option implies a different set of rules for client applications. Table 8-4 describes each of these transactional configuration options. You can get away without specifying a transaction type because the default type, with a parameterless constructor, is *Required*.

Table 8-4
Values for the *Transaction* Attribute

Value	Description
Disabled	Eliminates the control of automatic transactions on the object. An object with this attribute value applied can engage the Distributed Transaction Coordinator (DTC) directly for transactional support.
NotSupported	Indicates that the object does not run within the scope of transactions. When a request is processed, its object context is created without a transaction, regardless of whether a transaction is active.
Supported	Indicates that the object runs in the context of an existing transaction, if one exists. If no transaction exists, the object runs without a transaction.
Required (default)	Indicates that the object requires a transaction. It runs in the scope of an existing transaction, if one exists. If no transaction exists, the object starts one.
RequiresNew	Indicates that the object requires a transaction, and a new transaction is started for each request.

We now have a basic class that supports transactions. Unfortunately, we don't seem to be doing much with it. We need to correct this. Let's look at a real example to see how we can do this.

Building a Transactional Component

The scenario I have concocted is a simple bank account application. (See Figure 8-7.) The purpose of the application is to transfer money from one account to another. To this end, I created an MSDE database called Bank that contains two user tables: Accounts and Transactions. The general idea is that a monetary transfer between accounts consists of three individual actions: a deduction from the source account, an addition to the destination account, and a new record inserted into the Transactions table. None of these operations can be performed independently. They must all succeed or all fail. Otherwise, you could end up with a database whose contents are suspect. In other words, we need to treat all three actions as a single, atomic super-action. If any part of the transaction fails, no data is affected. Period.

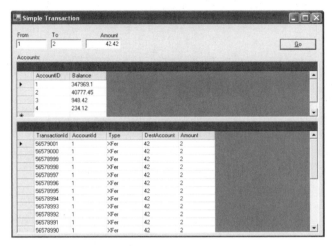

Figure 8-7   The Simple Transaction sample application.

So how do you preserve data integrity? Thankfully, you don't really need to track individual values or previous states. This sample communicates with a system that supports transactions. (MSDE, like SQL Server, supports transactions.) Therefore, if I make a call to MSDE, SQL Server, or any other DTC provider, my transactional context will automatically flow to the system. I leave the actual task of preserving the original data up to the underlying system (in this case) MSDE.

Note   If I were manipulating a custom data store, I'd have to implement my own transactional support.

The *MyTransactionalClass* Object

To support the features I need in the SimpleTransaction sample application, I created the *MyTransactionalClass* class to implement the transaction. Let's walk through it step by step.

First, we have the class definition. As you might expect, I used the *Transaction* attribute. The default value for the transaction type is *Required*, so the class supports two different scenarios. The first possibility is that the class methods are called by a client that is not part of a transaction. In this case, *Required* forces a new transaction to be created when the client calls into the *MyTransactionalClass* object. Once that initial call is completed, the transaction is either committed or aborted, depending on what happened during the transaction. The other possibility is that this class is called by a client that's already part of an existing transaction. In this case, method calls on this class will participate as a part of the larger transaction. If I decide that I don't want my class to participate in any other transaction, I can specify *TransactionOption.RequiresNew*, which will force a new transaction to be created each time.

I also take advantage of object construction for the connection string to the database. Rather than hardcoding the value, I decided to show one useful way to use the *ConstructionEnabled* attribute:

```
<Transaction(), ConstructionEnabled(Default:="server=(local)\NetSdk; " & _
    "Trusted_Connection=yes;database=Bank")> _
Public Class MyTransactionalClass
    Inherits ServicedComponent
    ...
End Class
```

Now that I have a class definition, I need this class to actually do something. First, I create a set of three private methods that actually do the work. Remember that we're trying to tie together three separate operations: deduct, add, and insert. To implement this, I created the following methods: *Deduct*, *Add*, and *InsertTransaction*.

```
<AutoComplete()> _
Private Sub Deduct(ByVal acctId As Integer, ByVal amount As Single)
    Dim sql As String
    sql = String.Format("Update Accounts " & _
                        "Set Balance = Balance - {0} " & _
                        "Where AccountId = {1}", amount, acctId)

    Dim cmd As New SqlCommand(sql, m_connection)

    'Throw New Exception("This is a manual failure")

    cmd.ExecuteNonQuery()
End Sub

Private Sub Add(ByVal acctId As Integer, ByVal amount As Single)
    Dim sql As String
```

```
    sql = String.Format("Update Accounts " & _
                        "Set Balance = Balance + {0} " & _
                        "Where AccountId = {1}", amount, acctId)

    Dim cmd As New SqlCommand(sql, m_connection)
    cmd.ExecuteNonQuery()

    'Throw New Exception("This is a manual failure")

    ContextUtil.SetComplete()
End Sub

<AutoComplete()> _
Private Sub InsertTransaction(ByVal sourceAcctId As Integer, _
                        ByVal type As String, _
                        ByVal Amount As Single, _
                        ByVal destAcctId As Integer)

    ' Insert a record in the transaction table
    Dim sql As String
    sql = "Insert into Transactions " & _
        "( AccountID, Type, Amount, DestAccount ) "
    sql &= String.Format("Values( {0}, '{1}', {2}, {3} )", _
                        sourceAcctId, type, destAcctId, Amount)

    Dim cmd As New SqlCommand(sql, m_connection)
    cmd.ExecuteNonQuery()

    'Throw New Exception("This is a manual failure")
End Sub
```

The same basic principle applies to all of these methods. Each performs an operation on the database using the SqlClient managed providers. The methods use a shared *SqlConnection* object (shown later) to do all of their work. Notice that I don't have to do anything explicit to pass the transaction context to the *SqlConnection*; it's done transparently. It's actually pretty easy to forget that it is happening at all—but it is.

You'll also notice the use of a method attribute called *AutoCommit*. This attribute is used to specify methods that will automatically vote to commit a transaction, unless the method terminates abnormally (generates an exception). This is handy because it frees you from having to explicitly add commit code. You can still vote to abort the transaction—by calling the *ContextUtil.SetAbort* method—if you need to. I designed these three methods to demonstrate how you can implement a method both with and without the *AutoCommit* attribute. You can always use the *ContextUtil.SetCommit* and *ContextUtil.SetAbort* methods explicitly if you want to, but if you can let the environment do some of the work for you, why do it yourself?

You'll also notice that all of these methods are declared as *Private*. This is for a good reason. No external client should be able to directly call any of these methods. I made one *Public* method available to allow the client to perform the balance transfer that can then call the methods that do the actual work: *Transfer*.

```
<AutoComplete()> _
Public Function Transfer(ByVal sourceAcctId As Integer, _
                         ByVal destAcctId As Integer, _
                         ByVal amount As Single) As Boolean

    Deduct(sourceAcctId, amount)
    Add(destAcctId, amount)
    InsertTransaction(sourceAcctId, "Xfer", amount, destAcctId)

    'Throw New Exception("This is a manual failure")
End Function
```

Yet again, I used the *AutoComplete* attribute of this method and then called each private method. Note how easy it is to deal with transactions. The transactional context flows transparently from method to method. You don't need to do anything other than call the methods. Also note that, in most cases, the *Transfer* method represents the top-level method in the transaction. This means that when the method terminates normally, the transaction will commit. If, on the other hand, an exception is thrown in this method even after the other methods have been called, the transaction will still fail. Each part of the chain must succeed.

Each method includes something a little odd: a commented *Throw* statement. I added it because it allows you to play with the sample by uncommenting certain exceptions and seeing how it affects the transaction. You should notice that whenever an exception occurs in the transaction call hierarchy, the transaction is automatically aborted and no data is changed.

The following is the complete *MyTransactionalClass* so you can see everything in place. (This is also available in the SimpleTransaction sample application.)

```
Imports System.Data.SqlClient
Imports System.EnterpriseServices
Imports System.Reflection

<Transaction(), ConstructionEnabled(Default:="server=(local)\NetSdk; " & _
  "Trusted_Connection=yes;database=Bank", ObjectPooling())> _
Public Class MyTransactionalClass
    Inherits ServicedComponent
```

```
Private m_ConnectionString As String

Protected Overrides Sub Construct(ByVal s As String)
   m_ConnectionString = s
End Sub

Private m_connection As SqlConnection

Protected Overrides Sub Activate()
   m_connection = New SqlConnection(m_ConnectionString)
   m_connection.Open()
End Sub

Protected Overrides Sub Deactivate()
   m_connection.Close()
End Sub

<AutoComplete()> _
Public Function Transfer(ByVal sourceAcctId As Integer, _
                         ByVal destAcctId As Integer, _
                         ByVal amount As Single) As Boolean

   Deduct(sourceAcctId, amount)
   Add(destAcctId, amount)
   InsertTransaction(sourceAcctId, "Xfer", amount, destAcctId)

   'Throw New Exception("This is a manual failure")
End Function

<AutoComplete()> _
Private Sub Deduct(ByVal acctId As Integer, ByVal amount As Single)
   Dim sql As String
   sql = String.Format("Update Accounts " & _
                       "Set Balance = Balance - {0} " & _
                       "Where AccountId = {1}", amount, acctId)

   Dim cmd As New SqlCommand(sql, m_connection)

   'Throw New Exception("This is a manual failure")

   cmd.ExecuteNonQuery()
End Sub

Private Sub Add(ByVal acctId As Integer, ByVal amount As Single)
   Dim sql As String
   sql = String.Format("Update Accounts " & _
                       "Set Balance = Balance + {0} " & _
                       "Where AccountId = {1}", amount, acctId)
```

```
        Dim cmd As New SqlCommand(sql, m_connection)
        cmd.ExecuteNonQuery()

        'Throw New Exception("This is a manual failure")

        ContextUtil.SetComplete()
    End Sub

    <AutoComplete()> _
    Private Sub InsertTransaction(ByVal sourceAcctId As Integer, _
                                  ByVal type As String, _
                                  ByVal Amount As Single, _
                                  ByVal destAcctId As Integer)

        ' Insert a record in the transaction table
        Dim sql As String
        sql = "Insert into Transactions " & _
            "( AccountID, Type, Amount, DestAccount ) "
        sql &= String.Format("Values( {0}, '{1}', {2}, {3} )", _
                            sourceAcctId, type, destAcctId, Amount)

        Dim cmd As New SqlCommand(sql, m_connection)
        cmd.ExecuteNonQuery()

        'Throw New Exception("This is a manual failure")
    End Sub
End Class
```

That's it for the sample. Go ahead and run it. (You'll first need to attach the database to an instance of MSDE or SQL Server.) You can play with the sample by commenting out different exceptions and seeing what effect that has.

Messaging

Messaging allows an application to enable asynchronous communication between two systems in a robust manner. These systems can reside in the same process, in separate processes on the same machine, or in separate processes on distributed machines. Messaging hides these complexities so the sender of a message doesn't care where the receiver is. The two components to messaging are messages and message queues.

Messages

A message is simply a packet of information. You can send a string as a message, or you can send a serialized object (or set of objects). Messages can have priorities, which allow them to skip ahead of preexisting messages in a queue. Table 8-5 lists the available message priorities.

Table 8-5
Available Message Priorities

Priority	Description
Highest	Highest message priority
VeryHigh	Between *Highest* and *High* message priority
High	High message priority
AboveNormal	Between *High* and *Normal* message priority
Normal	Normal message priority
Low	Low message priority
VeryLow	Between *Low* and *Lowest* message priority
Lowest	Lowest message priority

A message can contain not only information about itself, but information about what it expects the receiving queue to do. This category of functionality includes features such as acknowledgements, where the message fits into a transaction (first or last, or in the middle), the response queue, and the source machine.

> **More Info** For more information about serialization, see Chapter 5. I will refer to many of the concepts covered in that chapter as we work with our upcoming messaging example.

Message Queues

A message is sent by an application to a specific queue. This can be a local queue or a queue on another machine. Where this queue resides is not important. The message is received by the queue and is stored in an ordered list, which preserves the original arrival ordering of messages (ignoring the concept of priority for the moment).

Note Regardless of whether there exists a client process that is retrieving the messages, if the message queue exists, messages will be stored. This helps protect against process failures, which can happen from time to time.

Another process, or possibly the same process, retrieves messages from the queue. All messages are retrieved in a first-in-first-out (FIFO) manner. The process retrieving the queue entries processes each entry in turn until the queue is exhausted (empty). Simple, right? Not quite. Messaging can also provide certain guarantees. So you can send a message and guarantee, within reason, that the message will arrive. Even if the network connection between the systems goes down, the message will be stored and eventually sent when the connection is reestablished.

In addition to the standard queuing functionality, a robust communication mechanism is provided. This allows you to ensure, within reason, eventual delivery of a message regardless of application failures, transient network conditions, power failures, and so forth. As long as a message has been queued, you can ensure that it will be delivered. This reliability feature, also called *recoverability*, causes your message to be stored on the local machine before it is sent to the destination message queue. Recoverability is the default but is optional—for reasons of performance. Enabling recoverability reduces the number of messages per second that your system can generate. Yet again, you have the choice of sacrificing optimal performance for reliability.

There are two basic types of message queues: public and private. Public queues are published in Active Directory and require more time and disk space to set up. One advantage of public queues is that they can all be administered and controlled centrally. You can set your security policies and other information in a single location. Private, or local, queues are not globally published. However, private queues are available to other systems on the network. Private queues must be administered on a machine-by-machine basis.

There are also four types of what are known as *auxiliary queues*:

- **Response queues** These are queues designated for responses. When you send a message, you can specify a desired response. That response from the target queue ends up in a response queue.

- **Journal queues** You can think of a journal queue as a kind of a subqueue. It allows you to keep a log, or journal, of received messages, which is typically used as an auditing mechanism. You cannot create standalone journal queues.

- **Dead letter queues**   These queues are repositories for messages that could not be delivered. Messages can end up here for a variety of reasons. The target queue might have refused the message, or a message's expiry timeout might have been exceeded. You cannot create dead letter queues. These queues are also used for auditing.

- **Administration queues**   Administration queues are another way to provide an explicit auditing trail and retain more information than might be found in either a journal queue or a dead letter queue. You can create your own administration queues.

Transactional Queues

Transactional queues are designed to ensure exactly-once delivery of messages. When you create a queue, you have the option of making it a transactional queue. Messages in the same transaction arrive in the same order they were sent. If multiple transactions are sending messages at the same time, they will likely be interleaved in the same queue, but the ordering of the messages within a transaction is guaranteed. One downside to transactional queues is that they cannot provide support for message priorities—all messages are priority 0.

Transactional queues include support for both internal and COM+ transactions. This means that if you have implemented a transactional component in COM+ that also uses a transactional queue, your transactional context will automatically flow to the messaging system, much like it did with our database example.

Queued Components

A queued component is a COM+ component that transparently uses messaging as an invocation mechanism. You can create a client-side object from a queued component and invoke method calls as you would normally. Under the covers, the method calls are translated into a series of messages and are sent to a special queue. From this queue, the messages are retrieved and translated into the intended method with the passed parameters and executed.

Messaging in Visual Basic .NET

Messaging in Visual Basic .NET is implemented in the *System.Messaging* namespace. This namespace and its classes are contained in the *System.Messaging.dll* assembly. The two major classes that you need to be familiar with are *Message* and *MessageQueue*.

The *Message* Class

As I've said, a message is simply a packet of information. Messages are sent to, and retrieved from, message queues. The *Message* class encapsulates everything about a message and makes the configuration options and content easily accessible. You can specify all sorts of information about a message, including encryption algorithms, security options, and digital signatures. The message class is what is sent by clients to queues and what is returned.

The *MessageQueue* Class

The *MessageQueue* class allows you to manage and manipulate messaging queues. An instance of the *MessageQueue* class represents a single queue. You can create more than one *MessageQueue* object that points to a single queue, if you want to. Here are some of the things you can do using the *MessageQueue* class:

- Create new queues.

- Send and retrieve messages from queues.

- Set the default properties for messages set to the queue. (This is valid only for the current instance of the *MessageQueue* class.)

- Create an object reference to deal with a remoted component. (This is the mechanism that provides support for Queued Components.)

- Administer a queue's properties (if the user context has permissions).

- Asynchronously retrieve messages.

All of this a just a bunch of generalities. What we need is a good, solid example. First, we'll create a real message queue.

Creating Your First Queue

Manually creating messaging queues is a snap, thanks to the Visual Basic .NET IDE. The Server Explorer feature is often overlooked but is extremely powerful (See Figure 8-8.) From this window, you can inspect all of the queues available on a machine, as well as create new ones.

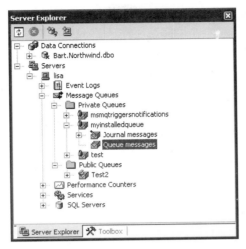

Figure 8-8   Using Server Explorer to manage queues.

Note   You must install the message queuing software through the Windows Installer if you have not already done so. Without it , you cannot use any of the *System.Messaging* features.

Selecting an existing queue in Server Explorer also exposes a number of properties through the Properties window, shown in Figure 8-9. From here, you can manipulate the following queue properties:

■ **Authentication**   The Boolean *Authenticate* property allows to you specify whether the queue accepts only authenticated messages.

■ **Encryption**   The *EncryptionRequired* property has three possible values. *None* indicates that received messages cannot be encrypted (that is, the message appears in clear text). *Optional*, the default for new queues, allows both encrypted and unencrypted messages to be received. Setting the property to *Body* requires all received content to be encrypted to be accepted.

■ **Queue size**   The *MaximumQueueSize* property specifies the maximum size of the queue.

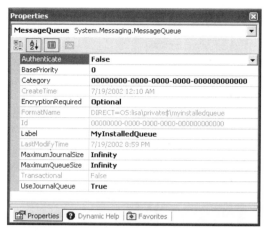

Figure 8-9   The Properties window for a queue selected in Server Explorer.

Manually creating your own queue is a snap. To create your own messaging queue—in this case, a private non-transactional one—just follow these simple steps:

1.   Open the Visual Basic IDE.

2.   Expand Server Explorer.

3.   Expand the node for your local machine, expand Message Queues, and then expand Private Queues.

4.   Right-click on the Private Queues node, and click Create Queue.

5.   Enter a name for the Queue (in this case, MyQueue), and click OK.

That's it. You now have a real messaging queue. Now let's try using it.

Working with Your Queue

To work with any queue, you must first add a reference to the *System.Messaging.dll* assembly to your project to have access to the *System.Messaging* namespace. To help clarify what else you need to do, let's take a look at a simple messaging example:

```
Console.WriteLine("Attaching to the Message queue")
Dim mq As New MessageQueue(".\Private$\MyQueue")

Console.WriteLine("Sending a message...")
mq.Send("This is a test")

Console.WriteLine("Detaching from the queue")
mq.Dispose()
```

You can see how easy it is to send a message. You create an instance of a *MessageQueue* class, specifying the path to the queue. In this case, we're accessing the local private queue called MyQueue that you created earlier. We then send a *String* object to the queue. The *MessageQueue* class obscures the fact that the *String* is first serialized, then added to a newly created message, and then sent to the target queue. As soon as we send the message, we dispose of the *MessageQueue* object (which doesn't affect the target queue—it just releases the resources of the *MessageQueue* object).

On the receiving side, things are only a little more complicated:

```
Console.WriteLine("Attaching to the Message queue")
Dim mq As New MessageQueue(".\Private$\MyQueue ")

Dim formatter As XmlMessageFormatter = CType(mq.Formatter, _
    XmlMessageFormatter)
formatter.TargetTypeNames() = New String() {"System.String"}

m = mq.Receive()
Console.WriteLine(m.Body())

Console.WriteLine("Detaching from the queue")
mq.Dispose()
```

Here you can see some similarities. We still create an instance of the *MessageQueue* class, pointing to the same queue as in our previous example. The next step is a little different, however. Because the message contents have been serialized, we must first provide a formatting mechanism to deserialize the object. In this case, we know that the *XmlMessageFormatter* is used (because it's the default), so all we have to do is tell the formatter what kind of object it is trying to deserialize (in this case, a *System.String* object).

Note   Two other formatters are available besides *XmlMessageFormatter: ActiveXMessageFormatter* and *BinaryMessageFormatter*. The *BinaryMessageFormatter* is the same binary serialization mechanism we encountered in Chapter 5; we'll use it again later with more complex messages.

Once we have the formatting issues out of the way, all we have to do is retrieve the *Message* by calling *Receive*. Calling the *Body* method of the *Message* object will retrieve the original object using the specified message formatter.

Next, we detach from the queue. Easy. But wait—there's a problem. How do you know if there's a message in the queue? What if there are more messages? This way of retrieving messages isn't really that helpful because it ties up a thread waiting for a message. You can specify a timeout parameter for receive, but that still doesn't really solve the problem. It would be much more interesting if the queue could tell us when a message is available rather than your application continuously polling for messages that might or might not be in the queue. This is where receiving messages asynchronously comes into play.

Receiving Messages from a Queue Asynchronously

The *MessageQueue* class provides support for receiving messages and processing messages asynchronously. The two methods of interest are *BeginReceive* and *EndReceive*. To begin an asynchronous read, you need to do the following:

1.   Create a method to process a message. It must correspond to the signature of a *ReceiveCompletedEventHandler* delegate.

2.   Create a *MessageQueue* object.

3.   Use *AddHandler* to add the message processing method to the *ReceiveComplete* event of the *MessageQueue* class.

4.   Call *MessageQueue.BeginReceive*.

If a message arrives or one already exists in the queue, the *MessageQueue* class will signal your application by calling your message-handling method. The event will be fired only once for each call to *BeginReceive*, so if you want to receive a continuous set of messages, your message handler method should call *BeginReceive* before it exists. This will cause your handler method to be called repeatedly as long as there are messages in the queue. If the queue is emptied, your method will be called as soon as a new message is received. Here's what this looks like in action:

```
Sub Main()
    Console.WriteLine("Attaching to the Message queue")
    Dim queue As New MessageQueue(".\Private$\MyInstalledQueue")

    Dim formatter As XmlMessageFormatter = _
        CType(queue.Formatter, XmlMessageFormatter)
    formatter.TargetTypeNames() = New String() {"System.String"}

    AddHandler queue.ReceiveCompleted, AddressOf MessageReceived
    queue.BeginReceive()
```

```
    Console.ReadLine()

    queue.Dispose()
End Sub

Public Sub MessageReceived( _
        ByVal source As Object, _
        ByVal asyncResult As ReceiveCompletedEventArgs)

    ' Store the source in a MessageQueue reference for easy access
    Dim queue As MessageQueue = CType(source, MessageQueue)

    ' Get the message and complete the receive operation
    Dim m As Message = queue.EndReceive(asyncResult.AsyncResult)
    Console.WriteLine(m.Body())
    ' Restart the asynchronous receive operation.
    queue.BeginReceive()
End Sub
```

Sending More Sophisticated Messages

So far, I've demonstrated only how to send strings in the message content, which is pretty boring and not very useful. Let's look at a something more interesting: a complex type. Imagine you're designing an ATM-based application. A customer walks up to the ATM and withdraws 100 dollars. The ATM first checks the account balance and then delivers the money to the customer. Now the ATM must post the result of the transaction to its central data store to update the customer's bank balance. You'd probably want to provide some degree of assurance that, regardless of what happens, the transaction will be posted to the account. Let's look at what information we need to provide.

First, we define the *Account* object (which would typically be in a database):

```
Public Class Account
    Public Sub New(ByVal name As String, ByVal id As Integer, _
        ByVal balance As Single)
        Me.Name = name
        Me.Id = id
        Me.Balance = balance
    End Sub

    Public Name As String
    Public Id As Integer
    Public Balance As Single
End Class
```

Now we define a base transaction class called, strangely enough, *Transaction*. All of our real transaction classes, *Deposit* and *Withdrawal*, derive from this base class. This allows our message handler to deal with transactions in a generic way rather than special-casing every possibility. Each class, including the base *Transaction* class, is marked with the *Serializable* attribute because I intend to use binary serialization (the most efficient serialization method) to serialize these types.

```
<Serializable()> Public MustInherit Class Transaction
    Public m_AccountId As Integer
    Public m_Amount As Single

    Public Property AccountId() As Integer
      Get
          Return m_AccountId
      End Get
      Set(ByVal Value As Integer)
          m_AccountId = Value
      End Set
    End Property

    Public Property Amount() As Single
      Get
          Return m_Amount
      End Get
      Set(ByVal Value As Single)
          m_Amount = Value
      End Set
    End Property

    Public MustOverride Sub Update(ByVal acct As Account)
End Class

<Serializable()> Public Class Deposit
    Inherits Transaction

    Public Overrides Sub Update(ByVal acct As Account)
      acct.Balance += Amount
      Console.WriteLine( _
        "Depositing ${0} To Account '{1}' Ending Balance: ${2}", _
        Amount, acct.Name, acct.Balance)
      Return
    End Sub
End Class

<Serializable()> Public Class Withdrawal
    Inherits Transaction
```

```
      Public Overrides Sub Update(ByVal acct As Account)
         acct.Balance -= Amount
         Console.WriteLine( _
            "Withdrawing ${0} From Account '{1}' Ending Balance: ${2}", _
            Amount, acct.Name, acct.Balance)
         Return
      End Sub
   End Class
End Class
```

Now that we have our types defined, we need to be able to send them. This really isn't that big a deal. In fact, it is trivial. I've created a sample application (actually, two applications—one a message sender and the other a receiver). (See Figure 8-10.) The first application is the Account Viewer, which is a console application that receives messages and processes the results. The second is a Windows Form application, called ATM, that sends messages to Account Viewer. Shared between the two is a component library, called Bank-Library, that contains the definitions for the transactions we just looked at.

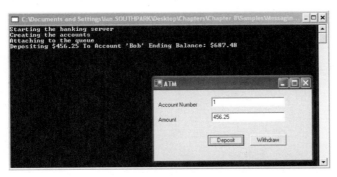

Figure 8-10   The ATM application and Account Viewer running side-by-side.

When the ATM application first loads, it initializes a private *MessageQueue* object and specifies a *BinaryMessageFormatter*. This ensures that all of the messages sent to the queue will use binary serialization.

```
Dim queue As MessageQueue

Private Sub Form1_Load(ByVal sender As System.Object, _
                       ByVal e As System.EventArgs) Handles MyBase.Load
   queue = New MessageQueue(".\Private$\BankQueue")
   queue.Formatter = New BinaryMessageFormatter()
End Sub
```

The ATM application allows you to specify an account number, an amount, and whether you want to cause a deposit or withdrawal. The implementation code is pretty simple for both possibilities:

```
Private Sub DepositButton_Click(ByVal sender As System.Object, _
                                ByVal e As System.EventArgs) _
                                Handles DepositButton.Click

    Dim d As New Deposit()

    d.AccountId = CInt(AccountNumber.Text)
    d.Amount = CSng(Amount.Text)

    queue.Send(d)
End Sub

Private Sub WithdrawButton_Click(ByVal sender As System.Object, _
                                ByVal e As System.EventArgs) _
                                Handles WithdrawButton.Click

    Dim w As New Withdrawal()

    w.AccountId = CInt(AccountNumber.Text)
    w.Amount = CSng(Amount.Text)

    queue.Send(w)
End Sub
```

This is pretty easy. So what does the receiving code look like? Not much more complicated than what we're used to, other than that the application uses asynchronous message processing. (You wouldn't expect anything less, would you?) Ignoring some of the initialization code, you can see that the asynchronous read stuff is nothing to write home about—you've seen it already. The action is really in the *MessageReceived* method:

```
Option Strict On

Imports BankLibrary
Imports System.Messaging

Module Module1
    Dim accounts() As BankLibrary.Account

    Public Sub Main()
        Console.WriteLine("Starting the banking server")

        Console.WriteLine("Creating the accounts")
        Dim acct1 As New Account("Bob", 1, 231.23)
        Dim acct2 As New Account("Alice", 2, 654.01)
        Dim acct3 As New Account("Roy", 3, 984.65)
        accounts = New Account() {acct1, acct2, acct3}
```

```vb
        Console.WriteLine("Attaching to the queue")
        Dim queue As New MessageQueue(".\Private$\BankQueue")

        AddHandler queue.ReceiveCompleted, AddressOf MessageReceived
        queue.BeginReceive()

        ' Wait for the user to terminate the application
        Console.ReadLine()

        queue.Dispose()

    End Sub

    Public Sub MessageReceived( _
        ByVal source As Object, _
        ByVal asyncResult As ReceiveCompletedEventArgs)

        ' Store the source in a MessageQueue reference for easy access
        Dim queue As MessageQueue = CType(source, MessageQueue)

        queue.Formatter = New BinaryMessageFormatter()

        ' Get the message and complete the receive operation
        Dim m As Message = queue.EndReceive(asyncResult.AsyncResult)
        Dim t As Transaction

        Try
            t = CType(m.Body(), Transaction)
        Catch ex As Exception
            Console.WriteLine(ex.ToString())
        End Try

        Dim i As Integer
        For i = 0 To accounts.Length - 1
            If accounts(i).Id = t.AccountId Then
                t.Update(accounts(i))
                Exit For
            End If
        Next

        ' Restart the asynchronous receive operation.
        queue.BeginReceive()
    End Sub
End Module
```

You can see from this sample that you need to explicitly set the *Message-Formatter* each time you come through the *MessageHandler* method. Other than that minor complexity, there's nothing in here that should surprise you. The message body is cast to a *Transaction* class (we don't care what type of transaction), and then its *Update* method is executed on the proper account. Done. The transaction is responsible for updating the account and spitting the account information to the console.

Automating Queue Installation

Manually creating your queues works just fine when you're developing your application. Deployment, however, is a completely different story. Some applications must be able to create a new messaging queue on a machine. Thankfully, there is a solution for this. The *MessageQueueInstaller* class in the *System.Messaging* namespace is intended to be used by the InstallUtil.exe utility for installing and uninstalling message queues from a machine.

As I explained in Chapter 7, the reasons for using the installer services instead of a more manual process are simple. While you might need to install your own messaging queue, you absolutely need to provide some way of cleaning up after yourself. If you use the installer services, cleanup becomes much simpler. The following sample illustrates how you can use this class to define a queue that can be installed using the InstallUtil.exe utility:

```
Imports System.ComponentModel
Imports System.Messaging

<RunInstaller(True)> _
Public Class MyQueueInstaller
    Inherits MessageQueueInstaller

    Public Sub New()
        MyBase.New()

        Me.Authenticate = False
        Me.BasePriority = 5
        Me.EncryptionRequired = EncryptionRequired.Optional
        Me.Label = "MyInstalledQueue"
        Me.Path = ".\Private$\MyInstalledQueue"
    End Sub
End Class
```

Do you have to create your own installer to set up queues? Obviously not. We manually created one earlier. You can also use the *MessageQueue* class to programmatically create your own queues. The problem is that this process is unnecessarily messy and presents a deployment nightmare. You can use the *MessageQueueInstaller* class to define all the queues that your application needs in a structured and well organized fashion. Why mess around with manual installation when you can easily take care of all of the installation and uninstall issues in one go?

Conclusion

This chapter has offered a taste of some of the more advanced capabilities of Visual Basic .NET. When you implement mission critical applications, the services provided by Windows Messaging and COM+ can be invaluable. There is much more to both of these subjects than I've been able to cover here, but you should now have a basic grasp of the technologies.

Security is a major part of enterprise-level and mission-critical applications, so I would expect that you noticed its absence here. This is for several reasons, not least of which is that security is a complex issue that requires a lot of discussion. The next chapter deals more with general security issues.

9

Adding Security to Your Applications

In the days preceding the Internet, computing devices were islands of functionality with little interconnectivity. Nowadays, it is hard to tell whether a device is "on the network" even if all cables to it are unplugged. In order for the device to be useful, at least one software entity must be running—and then this device is a candidate for attack via the same channels and primitives that enable connectivity for that software entity.

When computing devices were invented, software functionality and features were the prime areas of consumer interest. Today, the same consumers seek trust in the feature-rich software that they use.

Management in application development houses has traditionally viewed security as a non-revenue-generating component of the development process. But with the paradigm shift to seamless connectivity à la Web services, security has become an important component of software return on investment because compromises in this area can hurt a company's reputation.

This chapter touches on Visual Basic .NET security programming concepts and techniques—some of which are specific to the .NET Framework. For a broad treatment of security programming, including application threat modeling using the STRIDE model, see *Writing Secure Code, Second Edition* by Michael Howard and David LeBlanc (Microsoft Press, 2003).

Security Features in .NET

Security architectures that predate .NET provide isolation and access control based on user accounts. One approach has been to isolate code on a per-user basis, but this doesn't always sufficiently protect one program from another if both programs are running on the same user's behalf. Another approach has been to relegate code that is not fully trusted to a sandbox model of execution, in which code is run in an isolated environment, with no access to most services. The .NET Framework security model attempts to strike a balance between these two models of security by providing access to resources in order for useful work to be done and by requiring finer control of application security to ensure that code is identified, examined, and given an appropriate level of trust.

We'll look at the following key features of the .NET security model:

- Role-based security

- Web application security

- Evidence-based security

- Cryptography

- Buffer overrun detection

Role-Based Security

Sometimes it is appropriate for authorization decisions to be based on an authenticated identity or on the role associated with the context of the code's execution. For example, bank tellers might be allowed to process requests up to a certain dollar amount, whereas anything larger will require the role of a supervisor. The .NET Framework provides the infrastructure that enables applications to incorporate such logic, building it around the concept of identities and principals. Role information might not necessarily be limited to the user's "group" as defined by the operating system.

For managing user identity, role-based security provides a unified model for authorization and authentication of principals based on identity and roles. ASP.NET also provides customization and functionality (such as Microsoft Passport cookie authentication and IIS-based impersonation) that are specifically targeted at Web application security requirements.

Authentication is the process of examining credentials (such as name and password) and establishing the identity of the principal. A principal might also have zero or more roles to which it belongs, representing authorizations. Application code can then learn the identity of the current principal or query it for a particular role to perform some privileged operation.

For enterprises, the Windows logon identity of users is an important form of identity for security, so the *WindowsPrincipal* class is provided to handle the authentication. The Windows username becomes the principal identity, and the groups the user belongs to are the names of the roles assigned.

You can define a generic principal object for applications that define their own authentication and authorization, such as by looking up passwords and a list of roles in an application-specific database. You can also define custom principals, providing further customization.

Web Application Security

ASP.NET was built with security in mind. It leverages IIS to provide strong support for common HTTP authentication schemes, including Basic, Digest, NTLM, Kerberos, and SSL/TLS client certificates. ASP.NET also supports Passport authentication and provides a convenient implementation of Forms-based (cookie) authentication. Regardless of which authentication scheme is employed, developers get a consistent programming and authorization model.

ASP.NET supports traditional methods of performing access control and also provides URL authorization, which allows administrators to provide XML configuration that allows or denies access to URLs based on the current user or role. Developers can easily code explicit authorization checks into their application or take advantage of the .NET common language runtime's support for declarative security to include control access to methods based on the calling user or role.

ASP.NET has an extensible security architecture that allows the developer to write custom authentication or authorization providers. These providers can handle authentication and authorization events in the application-level global.asax file; alternatively, a developer can write a module that can be reused across applications. In addition to built-in support for doing role-based security with Windows users and groups, ASP.NET applications can easily provide application-defined roles.

Evidence-Based Security

For all managed code on the platform, server, or client, evidence-based security applies different levels of trust to all running code and enforces security accordingly. This enables semitrusted code to be safely executed, subject to restrictions that can be controlled by the administrator. In addition to the trust of users, the trust of code with appropriate restrictions enforced on it is also critical to achieving good security in the .NET application space. Managed code running on the .NET Framework can be restricted at the interface level, which allows security to be effectively enforced on the code. As a result, large applications composed of many components can be safely deployed, with varying degrees of security enforced against the various components, all running in-process. This enables a number of possibilities not formerly available to applications:

- Mobile code can be downloaded from unsecured sources and executed safely with restrictions.

- Server hosts can run different site applications together in-process safely, improving performance.

- Server applications can be extended with user-written code that is constrained to not interfere with overall server operation.

- Programmable applications can safely run macro script associated with user documents.

Before any managed code runs, the security policy system determines what permissions to grant it based on evidence about the code assembly and what the code itself requests. Evidence can be anything known about the code, such as any valid digital signatures or the URL, site, or zone the code comes from. Security policy configured by the administrator or user specifies rules of using evidence to determine permissions to grant to code. After ensuring that the minimum permissions the code requests can be given, and excluding permissions the code does not want, the security policy system grants permissions and the code runs, limited by what the permissions allow it to do. If the policy would grant code less than the minimum it requests, the code is not run. The permission request also allows you to examine the code at deployment time to learn what permissions the developer declared it needs.

Most application code does not need to explicitly use evidence-based security, which is usually handled by the lowest levels of the standard class libraries. Nonetheless, all this application code benefits from the security being there. For example, when you run low-trust code from the Internet, you are protected against that code somehow calling into more trusted code installed on the machine and using it in a malicious way.

The one thing that many such applications will want to do with security is to include a permission request. This ensures that your code will run only if it gets the permissions it expects it will have, and no more. Other situations in which evidence-based security can help you include the following:

- **Limited access public API**   You can decorate a type or method with an attribute identifying it as requiring specific permissions or evidence in order to call or subclass it. For example, you can use this technique to create a public API that only other code from your Web site can call or only code signed with a certain key can use.

- **Resource protection**   When you define a class library that exposes a resource that needs protection, you can define a permission (as shown in a later example) that acts as a gatekeeper to the resource and use the security policy system to restrict access.

Cryptography

Cryptography is the art and science of keeping messages secure. It involves converting a plain-text message into a secret/ciphertext (otherwise known as *encrypting*) and converting that secret/ciphertext back into the original plain text (this process is called decryption). In addition to providing confidentiality, cryptography is used in authentication, integrity and nonrepudiation. For more information, see *Applied Cryptography* by Bruce Schneier (John Wiley and Sons, 1996).

Cryptographic Algorithms

A *cryptographic algorithm* (also called a *cipher*) is the mathematical function used for encryption and decryption. Cryptographic *keys* are used by the cipher to perform the encryption and decryption operations.

A *symmetric cipher* is an algorithm based on a single encryption key. Symmetric ciphers are designed to be efficient algorithms and are intended to encrypt large amounts of data. Examples are the Data Encryption Standard (DES), International Data Encryption Algorithm (IDEA), and Rivest Cipher 4 (RC4).

Asymmetric ciphers (public-key algorithms) are designed so that the key used for encryption is different from the key used for decryption—a stranger can use the encryption key (public key) to encrypt a message, but only a person with the corresponding decryption key (private key) can decrypt the message. Asymmetric ciphers are more suited to key management and protocol security. Examples are RSA, Diffie-Hellman, and DSA.

Security protocols use a hybrid of symmetric/asymmetric algorithms. The session key (symmetric) is set up using an asymmetric cipher in which the public key (contained in a certificate) bootstraps the secure communication.

A *hash function* is a cryptographic algorithm that produces a compressed unique output (or message digest) for each blob of data supplied to it. The MD5 algorithm creates a 128-bit digest, and SHA-1 creates a 160-bit digest. Cryptographic operations rely on hashing for a couple of reasons—to work on a smaller set of representative data (for efficiency, typically to verify signed data) and because it is computationally infeasible to use hashing to determine the original data given the message digest. (This raises the security bar when storing secrets—for example, when the hash of a password is stored and compared rather than the password itself.) When a cryptographic hash is used to render secrets into a digest (as in the latter case described above, to avoid storing cleartext passwords), another technique can be used: "salting" the hash so a random number is stored unencrypted with the hash. This eliminate the risks associated with dictionary attacks (whereby an attacker tries every possible secret key to decrypt the encrypted data). As much as possible, secrets should not be stored—instead, get the secret each time from the user. *Writing Secure Code* has more information on how to use Data Protection API (DPAPI) when storing a secret is unavoidable. Note that you can use Win32 DPAPIs (such as CryptProtectData/CryptUnprotectData) via PInvoke to store and retrieve secrets.

Random Number Generation

Random numbers are used in cryptographic operations—for example, to generate keys. Clearly, if this process is predictable, encryption and the math behind are both rendered useless. Hence, you should avoid using *rand()* or any such naïve generator and instead use a cryptographically strong random number generator. In particular, you should use the *RNGCryptoServiceProvider* class via the *GetBytes()* method.

Validating data   Data must be validated as it crosses the boundary between untrusted and trusted environments because data can be purposely crafted to fault your application. Many server vulnerabilities are due to poor validation—all input is suspect until proven otherwise—so you should use the *RegularExpressionValidator* control.

The *RegularExpressionValidator* control confirms that the entry matches a pattern defined by a regular expression. This type of validation allows you to check for predictable sequences of characters, such as those in social security numbers, e-mail addresses, telephone numbers, postal codes, and so on, and it lets you eliminate invalid input that might be intentionally malicious to exploit a software flaw.

RegularExpressionValidator uses two key properties to perform its validation: *ControlToValidate*, which contains the value to validate, and *ValidationExpression*, which contains the regular expression to match.

Digital Signatures

To verify that a message originating from a particular sender has not been tampered with, digital signatures are used. Signatures can also be chained (with the data being encapsulated) to verify intermediate originators.

A digital signature verifies that a message has not been tampered with. The sender encrypts a hash of the message (which is more performant than encrypting the whole message) with his secret key and sends it with the message *(M, Pr(h(M))*. The receiver can compute the hash of the message using *h(M)* and *M* and apply the sender's public key to the hash, thus decrypting the hashed message *Pu(Pr(h(M)))* and yielding *h(M)*. If the *h(M)*s computed in the two ways are the same, the message has not been tampered with. Such a conclusion can be reached because it is not possible to create two messages with the same hash (hence the term *one-way function* for *h()*).

Digital Signatures and XML

The XML Digital Signature specification (XMLDSIG), which is currently under development by the IETF and the W3C, provides an easy way for application programmers to sign XML documents and fragments. Signed (and, in the future, encrypted) XML will become increasingly important as a means for securely sending messages over the Internet. XrML is also gaining popularity as a standard for expressing security policies.

Cryptography and Visual Basic .NET

The .NET Framework provides classes that implement a variety of cryptographic functions for encryption, digital signatures, hashing, and random number generation. Supported algorithms include asymmetric encryption (RSA and DSA), symmetric encryption (DES, TripleDES, RC2), and hashes (MD5, SHA1). The implementation uses a stream-based model—for example, a stream of data from a file can be routed into an encryption object and the resulting stream will be sent over the network. A new managed library of cryptography functions is provided; it includes direct support for XML digital signatures.

Here's an example of using a block cipher to encrypt/decrypt a file stream using DES. This is a symmetric cipher.

```
Private Sub EncryptOrDecryptFile(ByVal sInputFile As String, _
                                 ByVal sOutputFile As String, _
                                 ByVal byteDESKey() As Byte, _
```

```vbnet
                                        ByVal byteDESIV() As Byte, _
                                        ByVal Direction As CryptoAction)

        'Create the file streams to handle the input and output files.
        Dim fsInput As New FileStream(sInputFile, _
                        FileMode.Open, FileAccess.Read)
        Dim fsOutput As New FileStream(sOutputFile, _
                        FileMode.OpenOrCreate, FileAccess.Write)
        fsOutput.SetLength(0)

        'Variables needed during encrypt/decrypt process
        Dim byteBuffer(4096) As Byte 'holds a block of bytes for processing
        Dim nBytesProcessed As Long = 0 'running count of bytes encrypted
        Dim nFileLength As Long = fsInput.Length
        Dim iBytesInCurrentBlock As Integer
        Dim desProvider As New DESCryptoServiceProvider()
        Dim csMyCryptoStream As CryptoStream
        Dim sDirection As String

        ' Set up for encryption or decryption
        Select Case Direction
            Case CryptoAction.actionEncrypt
                csMyCryptoStream = New CryptoStream(fsOutput, _
                    desProvider.CreateEncryptor(byteDESKey, byteDESIV), _
                    CryptoStreamMode.Write)
                sDirection = "Encryption"
            Case CryptoAction.actionDecrypt
                csMyCryptoStream = New CryptoStream(fsOutput, _
                    desProvider.CreateDecryptor(byteDESKey, byteDESIV), _
                    CryptoStreamMode.Write)
                sDirection = "Decryption"
        End Select

        sbEncryptionStatus.Text = sDirection + " starting..."

        'Read from the input file, then encrypt or decrypt
        'and write to the output file.
        While nBytesProcessed < nFileLength
            iBytesInCurrentBlock = fsInput.Read(byteBuffer, 0, 4096)
            csMyCryptoStream.Write(byteBuffer, 0, iBytesInCurrentBlock)
            nBytesProcessed = nBytesProcessed + CLng(iBytesInCurrentBlock)
            sbEncryptionStatus.Text = sDirection + _
                            " in process - Bytes processed - " + _
                            nBytesProcessed.ToString
        End While

        sbEncryptionStatus.Text = "Finished " + sDirection + _
                ". Total bytes processed - " + nBytesProcessed.ToString
```

```
        csMyCryptoStream.Close()
        fsInput.Close()
        fsOutput.Close()

    End Sub
```

Buffer Overrun Detection

Buffer overruns occur when a buffer (a stack or a heap) is overwritten because data larger than the buffer is copied into the buffer location. Variables declared on the stack are located next to the return address for the function's caller, and in the case of a stack overrun, this return address for the function gets overwritten by an address chosen by the attacker. Malicious code can then be executed. Typically, attackers supply malicious input that the program consumes unintentionally—the malicious code runs under an intentionally privileged context. Heap overruns are similar, but they are trickier to exploit.

Microsoft intermediate language (MSIL) is a CPU-independent machine language that you can think of as an object-oriented machine language. However, to execute a method, the intermediate language is first converted to native CPU instructions by the CLR's Just-In-Time (JIT) compiler. During JIT compilation, the CLR verifies code to ensure memory type safety. This minimizes the risk of code unexpectedly circumventing security checks. A new compile-time option (the */GS* option) adds special data called a *canary* into the stack between local data and the return address of functions. The canary value is random and is determined in the startup code for a binary. During code execution, when the function returns, the canary is checked—if it has changed, a special error handler is called that halts program execution. You can customize the default security error handler by calling *_set_security_error_handler* with a pointer to the custom handler.

Enterprise Security Scenarios

The following sections offer enterprise application development scenarios that implement the concepts we've discussed thus far in the chapter.

Code Security

Windows security is based on a user's identity, and code access security is based on an assembly's identity. We'll delve into two important aspects of the Visual Basic .NET code security model: code access security and requesting code permissions.

Code Access Security

Code access security is all about control access to assemblies (or individual methods contained in assemblies). Every assembly loaded by the CLR is assigned evidence that describes its identity. This evidence can be the path or URL from which the assembly was loaded, or it can be a digital signature given to the code by its publisher. To control access to your code, you can simply demand that your caller have a specific identity. For example, to limit access to a shared component to only code from the same publisher, the publisher will sign all its code and then place a demand for that signature within its shared component.

The identity permissions found under the *System.Security.Permissions* namespace are used for this purpose. Identity permissions are provided for the following types of assembly identity: strong name, Authenticode publisher certificate, URL of origin, site of origin, and Internet Explorer security zone. All identity permissions support three types of identity demands, which are described in Table 9-1.

Table 9-1
Types of Identity Demands

Identity	Description
Demand	All callers on the call stack are required to have the specified identity. This check is performed at run time.
LinkDemand	Only the code's immediate caller is required to have the specified identity. The caller must be trusted to not allow misuse of the called code by its own callers. This check is performed during loading.
InheritanceDemand	Requires the specified identity of any code that attempts to inherit from or override a method on the protected code. This check is performed during loading.

Because *LinkDemand* and *InheritanceDemand* are performed when assemblies are loaded, they can be specified only declaratively using attributes at compile-time. The compiler places the declarative security in an assembly's manifest, where the CLR can read and act upon it when loading that assembly. A straight demand, on the other hand, occurs at run time and can be specified imperatively or declaratively.

The following example demonstrates how to make a link demand on a method based on a strong-named method. The public key has been abbreviated for readability.

```
<StrongNameIdentityPermission(SecurityAction.LinkDemand, _
   PublicKey := "002400000...")> _
Public Shared Sub ProtectedMethod()
   'do something
End Sub
```

The *StrongNameIdentityPermission* attribute supports the additional properties *Name* and *Version*. By specifying *Name*, *Version*, and *PublicKey*, a client can reliably demand an exact version of an assembly. If the client specifies only *Name* and *PublicKey*, the demand will succeed if the assembly name and signature match, regardless of the assembly version. If the client specifies only *PublicKey*, as in the code example above, the security system will look for only the required signature; this is useful when you want to limit access to a group of code signed by the same key.

Attaching a strong name signature to your code involves two steps: creating the strong name key and compiling your assembly with that key. The first step is accomplished by using the SN (strong name) utility provided with the .NET Framework SDK. Below is the command-line syntax for creating a key pair and viewing the public key portion. (You must make an identity demand for code signed with the corresponding private key.)

```
sn -k keypair.dat
sn -p keypair.dat publickey.dat
sn -tp publickey.dat
```

More Info   For more information about the strong name tool, see Chapter 8.

The second step requires adding a declaration to the assembly to indicate the location of the file generated in step 1:

```
<Assembly: AssemblyKeyFile("keypair.dat")>

Public Class MyClass
    'something interesting
End Class
```

You can also delay-sign an assembly. Delayed signing reserves room for the signature in an assembly's manifest but does not actually sign the assembly. It is used when the author of the assembly does not have access to the private key that will be used to generate the signature. You can implement delayed signing by using the *AssemblyDelaySign* attribute class.

More Info For more information about delayed signing, check out the Framework SDK documentation that accompanies Visual Studio .NET.

Requesting Code Permissions

You do not necessarily have control over what permissions are assigned to the code you write, so the CLR provides a mechanism for requesting the permissions code needs in order to run properly. If the code is not granted the required permissions, it will not run. And, because permission requests are stored in an assembly's manifest, the end user can run the SDK tool called PERMVIEW to determine what permissions have been requested by the assembly author and then take the appropriate steps to grant those permissions if she needs the code to run on her machine. Table 9-2 lists the three types of permission requests supported by the .NET runtime.

Table 9-2
Permission Request Types

Type	Description
RequestMinimum	The permissions the code must have to run properly. If these permissions cannot be granted, the code will not be executed.
RequestOptional	The permissions that should be granted if allowed by policy. The runtime will attempt to execute code even if permissions it requests as optional have not been granted.
RequestRefuse	The permissions that code should never be granted. Code will not receive these permissions even if they would normally be granted to it. This is an extra precaution you can take to prevent your code from being misused.

Permission requests can be made only in a declarative fashion and must always be at the assembly level. (The assembly is the unit to which permissions are granted by the security system.) The following code is a request stating that an assembly must have unrestricted access to the file system in order to function:

```
<Assembly: FileIOPermission(SecurityAction.RequestMinimum, _
    Unrestricted := True)>
Public Class FileMover
    'something interesting
End Class
```

You can make several requests of the same type, in which case the final permission set requested will be the aggregate of all requests of that type. In the following example, *RequestMinimum* is used twice with different permissions to state that the assembly must have the ability to use *Reflection Emit* and perform serialization in order for it to function.

```
<Assembly: ReflectionPermission(SecurityAction.RequestMinimum, _
    ReflectionEmit := True)>
<Assembly: SecurityPermission(SecurityAction.RequestMinimum,_
    SerializationFormatter := True)>

Public Class CodeGenerator
    'something interesting
End Class
```

The same permission can also appear in requests of different types. For instance, the following example program uses an *EnvironmentPermission* in each of its three requests (*Minimum, Optional,* and *Refuse*). Using requests of different types is useful when a permission encompasses a number of operations and you want to ensure that your assembly has the ability to perform some of those operations while being prevented from performing others.

Note   Any permission you refuse using *RequestRefuse* will not be granted to your assembly even if you request that same permission using *RequestMinimum*.

In addition to requesting individual permissions, you can also request entire sets of permissions in a compact fashion. The following example shows two requests: one stating that an assembly must have unrestricted access to the file system in order to function, and one stating that it will take any and all other permissions that the security system is willing to grant it.

```
<Assembly: FileIOPermission(SecurityAction.RequestMinimum, _
    Unrestricted := True)>
<Assembly: PermissionSet(SecurityAction.RequestOptional, _
    Name := "FullTrust")>

Public Class FileMover
    'something interesting
End Class
```

The example shows how to request a permission set by name, but it is also possible to use a custom permission set representing the exact permissions you want. For more information on how to do this, search on *PermissionSetAttribute* in the .NET Framework SDK Reference.

The PERMVIEW tool is useful for verifying that your permission requests are correct. You can run PERMVIEW on a compiled assembly to read the permission requests out of the assembly's manifest and display them, as shown here:

```
C:\>permview filemover.exe
Microsoft (R) .NET Framework Permission Request Viewer.  Version 1.0.XXXX.0
Copyright (C) Microsoft Corp. 1998-2001

minimal permission set:
<PermissionSet class="System.Security.PermissionSet"
                version="1">
   <IPermission class="System.Security.Permissions.FileIOPermission"
                version="1"
                Unrestricted="true"/>
</PermissionSet>
optional permission set:
<PermissionSet class="System.Security.PermissionSet"
                version="1"
                Unrestricted="true"/>
refused permission set:
  Not specified
```

User Identity

User identity is a common means of controlling access to a business application or limiting the options available within that application. The *System.Security.Principal* namespace contains classes that help make such role-based security determinations. These classes are highly extensible. They allow host code to provide its own user identity and role information, or they allow it to expose the user account and group information provided by Windows. For more complete details regarding how to extend the role-based security system, consult the .NET Framework SDK Developer's Guide.

If you simply need to check the user's Windows user name and group memberships from a client application, here is how. The *WindowsIdentity* class represents an authenticated Windows user, and the *WindowsPrincipal* class that encapsulates the *WindowsIdentity* contains information about the user's role memberships. These objects representing the current user are accessible using either a static property of the *Thread* object or a static method of the *WindowsIdentity* object. We'll look at examples of both shortly.

Accessing the current principal from the *Thread* object is the standard approach, and it works for all types of principal objects. But because this method returns an *IPrincipal*, it must be cast as a *WindowsPrincipal* before it can be used as one. Notice that before the current principal is accessed, a call to *SetPrincipalPolicy* is made. This is noteworthy because without this call the principal returned would be a *GenericPrincipal* containing no user information. Because the call to *SetPrincipalPolicy* requires the *ControlPrincipal Security-Permission* (one not normally given out to less-than-fully-trusted code), this prevents semitrusted code (such as that running off the Internet) from gaining access to a user's account name.

```
' Get the Current User's Security Policy
AppDomain.CurrentDomain.SetPrincipalPolicy( _
    PrincipalPolicy.WindowsPrincipal)
Dim user As WindowsPrincipal = _
    CType(System.Threading.Thread.CurrentPrincipal, WindowsPrincipal)
Dim ident As WindowsIdentity = user.Identity
```

Checking for a Windows identity is a very common case, so this identity is easily accessible by using the static *GetCurrent* method of the *WindowsIdentity* class, as shown in the following example. Please note, however, that this method requires the same level of permission as the one above.

```
Dim ident As WindowsIdentity = WindowsIdentity.GetCurrent()
Dim user As New WindowsPrincipal(ident)
```

Once a *WindowsPrincipal* object is retrieved, a user's group membership can be determined using the *IsInRole* method. If the goal of checking role group membership is to deny access to an application (as opposed to customizing the user experience), an even simpler approach is to use the *Principal-Permission* to demand the required role.

Scripting Security

The .NET Framework SDK ships with some tools you can use to script user, machine, and enterprise security policies.

Scripting Security Policy Changes

The CLR ships with an advanced security policy system that allows for three policy levels: the enterprise policy, the machine policy, and the user policy. Each policy level consists of a tree of code groups. Each code group consists of a membership condition (which might be based on URL of origin or publisher certificate, for example) and an associated permission set. Code is granted the permission set associated with a code group if it meets the respective membership condition. By changing code groups in the user, machine, or enterprise policy, administrators can determine what permissions are granted to assemblies.

If you need to script policy changes, you can use the Code Access Security Policy (Caspol.exe) command-line tool to create batch files containing policy change commands.

Note   For all standard administrative tasks, it is highly recommended that you use the Common Language Runtime Configuration (Mscorcfg.msc) tool. For more information on the policy system, see the security documentation in the Frameworks SDK.

The Code Access Security Policy (Caspol.exe) Utility

The Framework SDK comes with the Caspol command-line policy administration tool, which you can use to create batch files for scripting security policy changes. Type **caspol -?** at the command line to see the available options.

Scripting Against Named Code Groups

The CLR's default policy gives each code group a unique name. If code groups have not been deleted or renamed, you can uniquely script changes against these code groups. The most common code group names for scripting are listed in Table 9-3.

Table 9-3
Common Code Group Names for Scripting

Name	Description
All_Code	The root code group in every policy level
My_Computer_Zone	The code group that applies to code on local computer
Internet_Zone Code	The code group that applies to code from the Internet
LocalIntranet_Zone	The code group that applies to code from the intranet

To see a complete list of code groups and their names in all policy levels, you can use the following caspol command:

```
caspol -all -listgroups
```

To change a code group's permission set, include a command of the following form in your batch script:

```
caspol PolicyLevel -chggroup Name of code group PermissionSetName
```

To add a new code group, include a command of the following form in your batch script:

```
caspol PolicyLevel -addgroup <Name of Parent code group>
 MembershipCondition PermissionSetName CodeGroupFlags
```

To reset policy to the default state at a policy level, include a command of the following form in your batch script:

```
caspol PolicyLevel -reset
```

The following caspol batch script resets policy to the default on all policy levels and grants full trust to intranet applications. Because the granted permissions to code are calculated as the intersection between policy levels and (in default policy) both enterprise and user policy levels are set to full trust, you need to change only the machine policy level in order to guarantee that intranet applications receive full trust. In our example, the following script guarantees that intranet applications will run with full trust (while code from other places of origin will run with the permissions given it by default policy):

```
caspol -all -reset
caspol -machine -chggroup LocalIntranet_Zone FullTrust
```

The first line in the following script of caspol commands shows how to set policy so code from the Internet will not receive any permissions from machine policy. The second command shows how to add a code group for granting full trust to code signed by the publisher that signed Myexe.exe. Note that the new code group is hung off the root of the machine policy.

```
caspol -machine -chggroup Internet_Zone Nothing
caspol -machine -addgroup All_Code -pub -file Myexe.exe FullTrust
```

Authentication and Authorization

Next, we'll look at .NET and operating system interaction in the areas of authentication and authorization.

Windows Identity in Server Applications

When you use ASP.NET Windows authentication, ASP.NET attaches a *WindowsPrincipal* object to the current request. This object is used for URL authorization. The application can also use it programmatically to determine whether a requesting identity is in a given role.

```
If User.IsInRole("Administrators") Then
    DisplayPrivilegedContent()
End If
```

The *WindowsPrincipal* class determines the roles of the user's NT group membership. ASP.NET applications that want to determine their own roles can do so by handling the *WindowsAuthentication_OnAuthenticate* event in their Global.asax file and attaching their own class that implements *System.Security.Principal.IPrincipal* to the request, as shown in the following example:

```
' Create a class that implements IPrincipal
Public Class MyPrincipal : Implements IPrincipal
  ' Implement application-defined role mappings
End Class

' In a Global.asax file
Public Sub WindowsAuthentication_OnAuthenticate(Source As Object, _
   e As WindowsAuthenticationEventArgs)
   ' Attach a new application-defined class that implements IPrincipal to
   ' the request.
   ' Note that since IIS has already performed authentication, the provided
   ' identity is used.
   e.User = New MyPrincipal(e.Identity)
End Sub
```

Forms-Based Authentication

Forms-based authentication is an ASP.NET authentication service that enables applications to provide their own logon user interface and do their own credential verification. ASP.NET authenticates users, redirecting unauthenticated users to the logon page and performing all the necessary cookie management. This sort of authentication is used by many Web sites.

An application must be configured to use forms-based authentication; you set *<authentication>* to *Forms* and deny access to anonymous users. The following example shows how this can be done in the Web.config file for the desired application:

```
<configuration>
  <system.web>
    <authentication mode="Forms"/>
    <authorization>
        <deny users="?" />
    </authorization>
  </system.web>
</configuration>
```

Administrators use forms-based authentication to configure the name of the cookie to use, the protection type, the URL to use for the logon page, the length of time the cookie will be in effect, and the path to use for the issued cookie. Table 9-4 shows the valid attributes for the *<Forms>* element, which is a subelement of the *<authentication>* element shown in the following example:

```
<authentication mode="Forms">
    <forms name=".ASPXCOOKIEDEMO" loginUrl="login.aspx" protection=
        "all" timeout="30" path="/">
        <!-- protection="[All|None|Encryption|Validation]" -->
    </forms>
</authentication>
```

Table 9-4
Security-Related Forms Attributes

Attribute	Description
loginUrl	The URL of a page to which unauthenticated users are redirected. It usually contains the login interface or at least a message informing the user that she isn't authorized to use the form. This page can be on the same computer or a remote one. If it is on a remote computer, both computers must use the same value for the *decryptionkey* attribute.
Name	The name of the HTTP cookie to use for authentication purposes. If more than one application wants to use forms-based authentication services on a single computer, the applications should each configure a unique cookie value. To avoid causing dependencies in URLs, ASP.NET uses "/" as the *Path* value when setting authentication cookies so the cookies will be sent back to every application on the site.
timeout	An integer value that specifies the amount of time, minutes, after which the cookie will expire. The default value is 30. This attribute is a sliding value, expiring n minutes from the time the last request was received. To avoid adversely affecting performance and to avoid multiple browser warnings for those who have cookies warnings turned on, the cookie is updated if the time is more than half elapsed. (This means a loss of possible precision in some cases.)

Table 9-4
Security-Related Forms Attributes

Attribute	Description
Path	The path to use for the issued cookie. The default value is "/" to avoid difficulties with mismatched case in paths because browsers are case-sensitive when returning cookies. Applications in a shared-server environment should use the default path to maintain private cookies. (Alternatively, they can specify the path at run time using the APIs to issue cookies.)
Protection	The method used to protect cookie data. Valid values are:
	All: Uses both data validation and encryption to protect the cookie. The configured data validation algorithm is based on the element. Triple DES is used for encryption, if available and if the key is long enough (48 bytes). *All* is the default (and recommended) value.
	None: Use for sites that use cookies only for personalization and have weaker security requirements. Both encryption and validation can be disabled. You should use caution if you use cookies without encryption (because the cookie can be shared between sites that issue cookies to the client—potentially infringing on the client's privacy), but this setting provides the best performance of any method of personalization using the .NET Framework.
	Encryption: Encrypts the cookie using TripleDES or DES but doesn't perform data validation on the cookie.
	Validation: Does not encrypt the contents of the cookie but validates that the cookie data has not been altered in transit. To create the cookie, the validation key is concatenated in a buffer with the cookie data and a MAC is computed and appended to the outgoing cookie.

After the application has been configured, you need to provide a logon page. The following example shows a simple logon page. When the sample is run, it requests the Default.aspx page. Unauthenticated requests are redirected to the logon page (Login.aspx), which presents a simple form that prompts for an e-mail address and a password. (Use *Username* and *Password* as the credentials.)

After validating the credentials, the application calls the following:

```
FormsAuthentication.RedirectFromLoginPage(UserEmail.Value, _
    PersistCookie.Checked)
```

This redirects the user back to the originally requested URL. Applications that do not want to perform the redirection can call *FormsAuthentication.GetAuth-Cookie* to retrieve the cookie value or *FormsAuthentication.SetAuthCookie* to attach a properly encrypted cookie to the outgoing response. These techniques can be useful for applications that provide a logon user interface embedded in the containing page or that want to have more control over where users are redirected. Authentication cookies can be temporary or permanent (persistent). Temporary cookies last only for the duration of the current browser session. When the browser is closed, the cookie is lost. Permanent cookies are saved by the browser and are sent back across browser sessions unless explicitly deleted by the user.

The authentication cookie used by forms authentication consists of one version of the *System.Web.Security.FormsAuthenticationTicket* class. The information includes the username (but not the password), the version of forms authentication used, the date the cookie was issued, and a field for optional application-specific data.

Application code can revoke or remove authentication cookies using the *FormsAuthentication.SignOut* method, which removes the authentication cookie regardless of whether it is temporary or permanent.

It's also possible to supply forms-based authentication services with a list of valid credentials using configuration, as shown in the following example:

```
<authentication>
    <credentials passwordFormat="SHA1" >
        <user name="Mary" password="GASDFSA9823598ASDBAD"/>
        <user name="John" password="ZASDFADSFASD23483142"/>
    </credentials>
</authentication>
```

The application can then call *FormsAuthentication.Authenticate*, supplying the username and password, and ASP.NET will verify the credentials. Credentials can be stored in cleartext or as SHA1 or MD5 hashes, according to the value of the *passwordFormat* attribute. The possible values are listed in Table 9-5.

Table 9-5
Values of the *passwordFormat* Attribute

Value	Description
Clear	Passwords are stored in cleartext.
SHA1	Passwords are stored as SHA1 digests.
MD5	Passwords are stored as MD5 digests.

Authorizing Users and Roles

ASP.NET is used to control client access to URL resources. It is configurable for the HTTP method used to make the request (*GET* or *POST*) and can be configured to allow or deny access to groups of users or roles. To illustrate ASP.NET in action, consider an example in which you want to grant access to the user John and to the Admins role. All other users are denied access. The following example shows part of the XML code that needs to be included in Web.config:

```
<authorization>
    <allow users="john@microsoft.com" />
    <allow roles="Admins" />
    <deny users="*" />
</authorization>
```

Permissible elements for authorization directives are *allow* or *deny*. Each *allow* or *deny* element must contain a *users* or a *roles* attribute. You can specify multiple users or roles in a single element by providing a comma-separated list.

```
<allow users="John,Mary" />
```

You can indicate the HTTP method by using the *Verb* attribute:

```
<allow VERB="POST" users="John,Mary" />
<deny VERB="POST" users="*" />
<allow VERB="GET" users="*" />
```

This example lets Mary and John *POST* to the protected resources, while allowing everyone else only to use *GET*.

Two special (reserved) usernames are similar to the Everyone and Anonymous accounts in Windows:

```
*: All users
?: Anonymous (unauthenticated) users
```

These special usernames are commonly used by applications that use forms-based authentication to deny access to unauthenticated users, as shown in the following example:

```
<authorization>
    <deny users="?" />
</authorization>
```

URL authorization is computed hierarchically, and the rules used to determine access are as follows:

- Rules relevant to the URL are collected from across the hierarchy, and a merged list of rules is constructed.

- The most recent rules are placed at the head of the list. This means that configuration in the current directory is at the head of the list, followed by configuration in the immediate parent, and so on, up to the top-level file for the computer.

- Rules are checked until a match is found. If the match is allowable, access is granted. If not, access is disallowed.

This means applications that are not interested in inheriting their configuration should explicitly configure all of the possibilities relevant to them.

The default top-level Web.config file for a given computer allows access to all users. Unless an application is configured to the contrary (and assuming that a user is authenticated and passes the file authorization ACL check), access is granted.

When roles are checked, URL authorization effectively marches down the list of configured roles and does something that looks like the following pseudocode:

```
If User.IsInRole("ConfiguredRole") Then
  ApplyRule()
End If
```

What this means for your application is that you use your own class that implements *System.Security.Principal.IPrincipal* to provide your own role-mapping semantics (as explained earlier).

Conclusion

As you've seen in this chapter, Visual Basic .NET implements its security infrastructure via the key components in the .NET Framework model. However, it doesn't eliminate the need for careful design and development of an application with due attention to security. When you use Visual Basic .NET to implement custom permission objects, authorization mechanisms, or any security relevant functionality, you must be familiar with the .NET Framework's architecture. Good practices in security deployment and administration—strong account management policies, patch management, lockdown operation, and so forth—are still important. The most secure applications will take advantage of the best of security in Windows and .NET because they offer different perspectives. Using the STRIDE model to develop application threat models can give you further guidance about which platform to use in which situations.

A frequently heard phrase among Microsoft security developers is "security job = job security." Given that applications have evolved from simple, static data-manipulation channels into complex, dynamic, translation-oriented pillars of commerce, this statement is probably not too far from the truth.

Part III

Performance and Debugging

10

Essential Debugging Techniques

The techniques used to debug Microsoft Visual Basic .NET are varied and can be quite complex. In addition to the simple concept of a debugger, the .NET Framework also provides a set of tools that you can leverage to diagnose and instrument your applications. The essence of debugging is to discover the root cause of a failure. In certain situations, this can be a simple process and debuggers can be extremely helpful tools. But debuggers are not always appropriate. When they are not the answer, you need to do other things to diagnose the problems. That's what this chapter is all about.

I'll first give you an overview of the common Windows debuggers. Then we'll look at what you can do within your own applications to leverage the .NET Framework to simplify not only debugging but also diagnosing general application problems and failures. This is of critical importance when you either don't have debuggers available or the debuggers alone are not helpful in tracking down problems.

Debuggers

Debuggers are truly the developer's bread and butter. Without these critical tools, it would be challenging to diagnose most runtime problems. We all know how difficult it can be to spot even minor errors in code. Without the benefit of runtime debugging, the challenge of development would be much harder than it is now. Thankfully, we don't have to worry about this possibility because there are more than enough debuggers to go around. In fact, the choices can be somewhat daunting.

To simplify our discussion, I'll lump debuggers into two categories: the Visual Studio .NET debugger and everything else.

Note You might ask, why talk about other debuggers? Isn't the Visual Basic .NET debugger good enough? It's true that the Visual Basic .NET debugger is very capable and full-featured, but it has some limitations. In addition, you must install Visual Basic .NET to get it. This is not usually feasible on a production server or typical client workstation. In these cases, the other tools can give you a lightweight way to diagnose problems regardless of where the application is.

The Visual Studio .NET Debugger

The Visual Studio .NET debugger, shown in Figure 10-1, is an extremely powerful and full-featured debugger and yet one of the easiest to use. You've likely used it many times. After all, when you build and run an application (by hitting F5), you're already using the Visual Studio .NET debugger. This is the debugger that Visual Basic developers most commonly use—certainly through all of your development and some runtime testing.

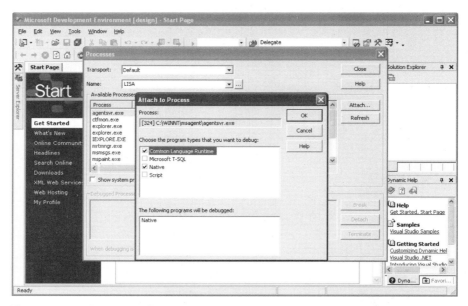

Figure 10-1 The Visual Studio .NET debugger with process dialog boxes open.

The Visual Studio .NET debugger is designed to work well with simple projects and also provides a bevy of advanced features that can address a wide variety of needs. Here are some of these advanced features:

- **Remote debugging**   This allows you to launch and debug a program stored on a remote machine. On the remote machine, you must install the Remote Debugging Components from Visual Studio .NET. You do not, however, need to install the complete Visual Studio .NET—just a small subset. There are some additional requirements that you need to be aware of. First, you need to select the DCOM protocol to debug Visual Basic .NET applications. In addition, the user context the debugger is running in must be a member of the Debugger user group on the remote machine. For more information, see "Remote Debug Setup" in the Visual Studio .NET help documentation.

- **Native code debugging**   In addition to supporting your Visual Basic .NET managed code, the Visual Studio .NET IDE can also step into native code (if you have the symbols and source code). This can be extremely helpful in debugging interop scenarios.

- **Multiple-process debugging**   You can use the same instance of the IDE to attach to many difference processes, local or remote. (But you must have access permissions.)

You can, of course, avoid all of these features if you don't need them. But it's nice to have the flexibility.

Other Debuggers

Debuggers can generally be classified into those that support managed code and those that don't. Table 10-1 compares some of the debuggers. All of the "classical" native debuggers, such as the Windows Debugger (WinDbg), don't understand managed code or managed stack traces. Another major distinction between debuggers is the user interface: some are console-based, and others are GUI-based. Their raw functionality might not very different, but they often use dramatically different syntax and commands. The console-based category of debuggers generally requires a better low-level understanding of debugging in general.

Table 10-1
Debuggers and Supported Environments

Debugger	Type	Managed	Native
Visual Studio .NET	GUI	✓	✓
CorDbg	Console	✓	
DbgClr	GUI	✓	
CDB	Console		✓
NTSD	Console		✓
WinDbg	Console/GUI		✓

Why turn to any of these debuggers? Remember that you do not always have the luxury of installing the Visual Basic .NET IDE on every machine your application is running on. All of the debuggers listed in the table are relatively lightweight and can be easily removed. This makes them extremely useful when you're working with production servers and client machines because you're unlikely to want or be able to install the full Visual Basic .NET IDE.

If you're interested only in debugging managed code, CorDbg and DbgClr are great choices. Both of these debuggers are available with the .NET Framework SDK. You can install the SDK with Visual Basic .NET, but the SDK is also available in standalone form.

The native debuggers are designed—surprise—to debug only native applications. All of these debuggers can be considered very sophisticated and hence rather obtuse and nonintuitive. But they are not without their uses. You should at least know they are available. All of the native debuggers I'll discuss here can be found in one easy place. By installing the Debugging Tools for Windows toolkit, you get three debuggers: CDB, NTSD, and WinDbg. You can go to the Debugging Tools for Windows page at *http://www.microsoft.com/ddk/debugging/* to get not only this toolkit but additional information on how to get symbols to help you with your debugging efforts.

The Microsoft CLR Debugger

The Microsoft Common Language Runtime (CLR) Debugger (DbgClr.exe) is a managed GUI debugger. If you're most comfortable with a GUI system instead of a console-based application, the CLR Debugger is a great choice. Even if you aren't familiar with debugging managed applications, this debugger can be a great tool to help you learn the ropes and are comfortable enough to move to another debugger.

The CLR Debugger is actually a subset of the Visual Studio .NET Debugger, so the interface should look somewhat familiar—see Figure 10-2—but it is more lightweight and doesn't require installation of Visual Studio .NET (quite an advantage). It is a very capable managed debugger and is easy to use. If you're already comfortable with the Visual Studio .NET debugger, you'll be immediately comfortable with this tool.

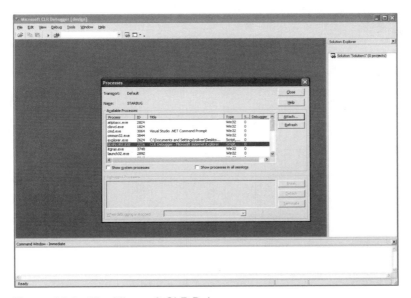

Figure 10-2   The Microsoft CLR Debugger.

Unfortunately, this debugger is not without its limitations. Because it is only a subset of the Visual Studio .NET Debugger, it does not support all of the parent debugger's features. For example, it does not support remote debugging or native code debugging, and the Disassembly and Register windows aren't very useful.

The CorDbg Debugger

CorDbg is a console-based managed debugging tool. (See Figure 10-3.) I love using this debugger, especially for performance and stress debugging. The simple interface, combined with a great set of debugging features, makes it an invaluable tool. CorDbg is by far the lowest-level managed debugger and is extremely lightweight (hence its usefulness in performance and stress scenarios). However, it also has certain limitations—it can't be used to perform remote debugging, for example.

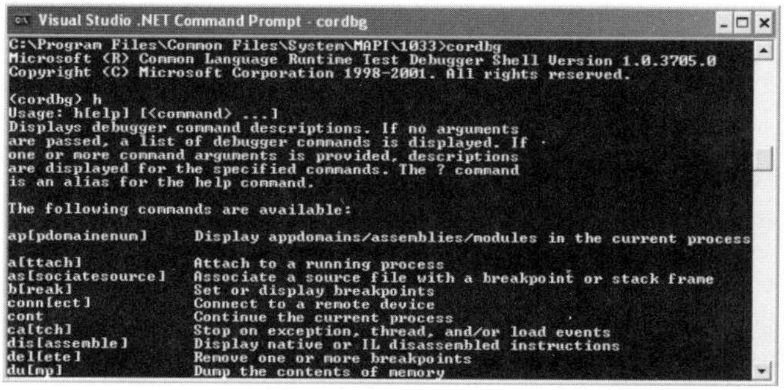

Figure 10-3 The CorDbg command-line debugger.

CorDbg is so named because it is an application that implements the *ICorDebug* set of debugging interfaces. If you have the .NET Framework SDK installed, you'll discover a wealth of low-level debugging samples and information. Microsoft even ships the source code for this tool so you can learn how the runtime debug API can be used. Unfortunately, the examples are in Visual C++ and are well beyond the scope of this text.

The Microsoft Console Debugger and Microsoft NT Symbolic Debugger

The Microsoft Console Debugger (CDB) and Microsoft NT Symbolic Debugger (NTSD) are both console-based and are meant for user-mode debugging. NTSD, shown in Figure 10-4, is virtually identical to CDB. The only difference is that it spawns a new window for the debugger instead of using the current console window. These debuggers are very lightweight and are very useful in debugging live applications or crashed dumps.

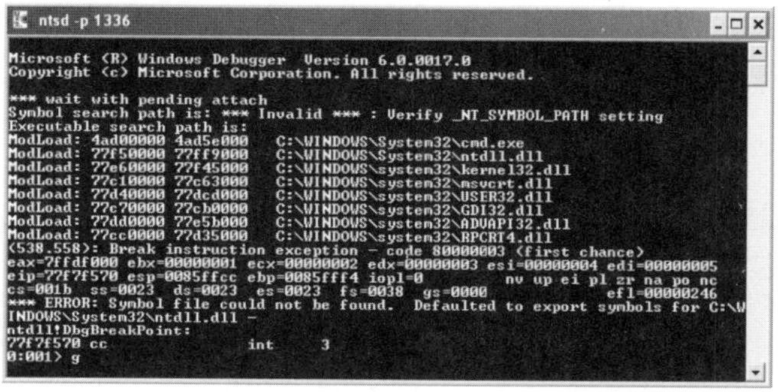

Figure 10-4 The NT Symbolic Debugger.

NTSD and CDB are not for casual debugging. Many of the commands and operations are fairly esoteric and hard to understand. I certainly would not recommend starting with these debuggers until you master the WinDbg debugger.

The Windows Debugger

The Microsoft Windows Debugger (WinDbg), shown in Figure 10-5, is a GUI-based debugger built on the foundation of the CDB and NTSD console debuggers. It is quite powerful and can be used to view source code, breakpoints, call stack, and so forth. Thanks to its GUI interface, more of the debugging features are more accessible to the casual user than with CDB or NTSD. This debugger's help system, although not always complete, makes the debugger much easier to use.

Figure 10-5   The Windows Debugger in action.

Although WinDbg is a GUI-based debugger, you can also use it from the command line. This is more of an advanced feature, so you should first attain a degree of comfort with the commands and options available through the WinDbg GUI.

Better Debugging with the .NET Diagnostic Tools

I mentioned earlier that debuggers are not always helpful in diagnosing problems. This might seem counterintuitive—after all, debuggers are all about diagnosing problems in your code. But at times debugging is reminiscent of a principle of quantum mechanics: you cannot observe a system without affecting the outcome. A example that comes to mind is threading. It is not unusual for timing to be a critical factor in a software failure (known as a *race condition*). By attaching the debugger, you can slow the system down, and while you might avert the problem, you won't learn where and why the failure is occurring. You might be left scratching your head and asking, "Why does this work only when the debugger is attached?"

This is where many of the classes in the *System.Diagnostics* namespace come in handy. This namespace contains a bunch of utility classes that provide a whole host of features you can use to instrument an application (by adding debugging hooks, posting events to the event log, creating performance counters, and outputting status information) and debug its runtime behavior. The three features I'll focus on are communicating with a debugger, using the event logs, and using the *Trace* and *Debug* statements.

The *Debugger* Class

The *Debugger* class enables your application to communicate with an attached debugger. This can be useful when you have complex debugging conditions that you are having difficulty otherwise re-creating. Imagine a situation in which an exception has been generated by an application under stress. To re-create the problem, you might have to apply a large amount of stress (for example, simulate a large number of simultaneous clients) while also attaching a debugger to wait for the error. The problem is that applications tend to throw exceptions quite frequently. If the type of exception you're interested in is quite frequently thrown, locating the actual failure point can be like looking for a needle in a haystack.

This is where the *Debugger* class can help out. Using the various shared members of this class, you can programmatically cause an attached debugger to break at a specific line of code, launch a new debugger, and send messages to the attached debugger. Table 10-2 describes the shared properties and methods of the *Debugger* class.

Table 10-2
Shared Members of the Debugger Class

Name	Member Type	Description
IsAttached	Property	Indicates whether a debugger is attached to the current process.
Break	*Method*	Signals the currently attached debugger that it should break into the code at the current line. If no debugger is attached, this has no effect.
IsLogging	*Method*	Indicates whether logging is currently enabled by the attached debugger.
Launch	*Method*	Causes a debugger to be launched and attached to the current process.
Log	*Method*	Logs information to the attached debugger.

All of the public members of the *Debugger* class are shared. This makes the features extremely easy to use, as shown in the following example:

```
' Break into an attached debugger.
If Debugger.IsAttached Then Debugger.Break()

' Send a message to an attached debugger.
Debugger.Log("Hi There!")
```

Easy, right? The features of the *Debugger* class are easy to access, but they have a myriad of uses that are limited only by your imagination.

Event Logs

Windows event logging provides a centralized mechanism for applications to report important events. The Windows event-logging service stores events from various sources into a single event collection (known as an *event log*). Event logs are commonly used by Windows services applications for the precise reason that they do not present a user interface. The event log provides a single location where a system administrator can check the status of a machine and all of the services running on a device. The contents of the available event logs can be viewed using the Event Viewer, which is shown in Figure 10-6.

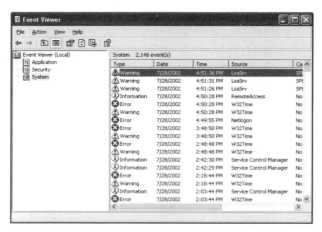

Figure 10-6   The Event Viewer.

The Windows Event Log supports several important features. First, it supports logging different kinds of events: *Info*, *Warning*, *Success*, *Failure*, and *Error* events. This gives applications some degree of flexibility in what kind of status information they can report. It also lets a user or system administrator easily determine what, if any, failures are occurring. Second, the Event Log supports multiple logs. This enables an application to post its events to a specific log that is most appropriate. (The standard logs are Application, Security, and System).

The ability to work with event logs of all stripes is provided by the all-important *EventLog* class in the *System.Diagnostics* namespace. This class is used to create, manage, monitor, delete, and post to event logs. It enables flexible management of all types of logs. These logs can reside on the local system or on any system the current user has access to. The most typical use, however, is for accessing event logs on the local system.

Note   Every system has three standard event logs: Application, Security, and System. Only two of these can be written to by an application: Application and System. The Security log can be written to only by the operating system.

Creating New Event Log Entries

Creating new entries in an event log is simple. The *EventLog* class sports the *WriteEntry* method for just this purpose. Using this method (or one of its many overloads), you can easily write entries to the event log of your choice (except the Security log). There are, in fact, 10 overloads of the *WriteEntry* method. Five of these methods are *Shared*, allowing you to easily write an information to the Application log much like in the following example:

```
EventLog.WriteEntry("MyApplicationName", "This is a test")
```

You can think of this as an easy way to "one-off" a entry to an event log. The only caveat is that you must first register your own event source (essentially your application's name) and the log associated with that source. Alternatively, you can create an instance of the *EventLog* class, providing the name of the log you want to write to. Then you can call one of the five *WriteEntry* instance members and write the entry to the log of your choice. In the following sample, I again write an information entry to the Application log:

```
Dim evtLog As New EventLog("Application")
evtLog.Source = "My Application"
evtLog.WriteEntry("This is an event message")
evtLog.Dispose()
```

The previous two samples touched only lightly on posting an event to a log. There is much additional information you can specify, including information on the type of event, an event ID, an event category, and binary data about the event. The other overloads of the *WriteEntry* methods give you this capability.

Before we move on, we should discuss the benefits of the shared methods versus the instance methods of the *WriteEntry* method of the *EventLog* class. From a performance perspective, if you expect to make calls to an event log in an application that has strict performance requirements (an application that can't afford to spend any more time than is necessary to post an event), you should create an instance of the *EventLog* class and call one of the nonshared *WriteEntry* methods. When you call the shared *WriteEntry* methods, you are implicitly creating a new *EventLog* instance each time you write a new log entry.

Shared methods still have a use, however. If you're likely to report an event only when an error or exception occurs, it might be easiest to use the *Shared* methods—you won't have to write the *EventLog* initialization code.

Creating Event Logs

The two major concepts related to the event log system are sources and logs. An event source is really just an application name. A source is a way of identifying the application that created an event. You can create and delete your own logs, and you can also define your own sources. When you create, or register, a new event source, you specify the log that the source is associated with. The following example creates a new event source called *MySource* and associates it with the *Application* event log:

```
EventLog.CreateEventSource("MySource", "Application")
```

Of course, this is nothing spectacular. The default behavior of the *EventLog.WriteEntry* method is to post all entries to the Application log. So this is really just duplicative. It gets interesting if I specify a different log name:

```
EventLog.CreateEventSource("MySource", "MyLog")
```

What happens here? The system not only registers my new source with the log named MyLog, but it also creates that log if it doesn't already exist. This is a simple, one-step way to register a new event source and create a custom event log. From now on, once I post events using the *MySource* identifier, all of the events will be written to the MyLog event log. Great! But there's a problem. What if the event source already exists? Registering an event source twice will cause an exception, so you need to be able to tell if the source already exists. The *EventLog.SourceExists* methods allow you to find out. Your code to register an event source would now look more like the following:

```
If Not EventLog.SourceExists("MySource") Then
    EventLog.CreateEventSource("MySource", "MyLog")
End If
```

Then there's the converse problem: how to unregister a source and delete a log. Deregistering a source is easy using the *EventLog.DeleteEventSource* shared method. Another shared method, *EventLog.Delete*, allows you to delete custom logs. The following example demonstrates how both of these methods work:

```
If EventLog.SourceExists("MySource") Then
    EventLog.DeleteEventSource("MySource")
End If
If EventLog.Exists("MyLog") Then
    EventLog.Delete("MyLog")
End If
```

This is not the only way to create your own sources and event logs. Instead of using a runtime programmatic means of creating and deleting your logs, you can handle these tasks at install time using the *EventLogInstaller* class.

The *EventLogInstaller* class   Like the other installer classes we looked at in Chapter 7 and Chapter 8, the *EventLogInstaller* class makes it easy to install and uninstall event logs and sources. It provides a unified way to set up all of your application's install/uninstall issues.

The mechanics for creating your own event log installer should be familiar:

1.   Create an installer class derived from *EventLogInstaller*.

2.   Mark this class with the *RunInstaller* attribute.

3.   Set the inherited *Source* and *Log* properties of the class in the constructor.

That's it. Thanks to the magic of the installer utility (InstallUtil.exe), this minimal amount of code handles both the install and uninstall of your event logs. The following sample demonstrates this:

```
Imports System.Diagnostics
Imports System.ComponentModel

<RunInstaller(True)> _
Public Class MyEventLogInstaller
    Inherits EventLogInstaller

    Public Sub New()
        MyBase.New()

        Me.Source = "EventLogSample"
        Me.Log = "MyEventLog"
    End Sub
End Class
```

If I compile this code into an assembly and run the InstallUtil.exe application against it, a new event log, such as the one shown in Figure 10-7, will be created, as expected. That's pretty easy, and it neatly solves our install and uninstall issues. If this approach works for you, I highly recommend it.

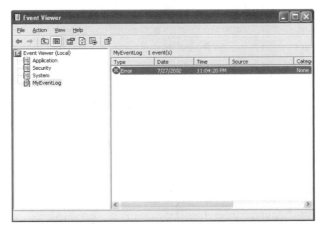

Figure 10-7   The result of the *MyEventLogInstaller* class.

Monitoring an Event Log

Not only does the *EventLog* class allow you to create new logs and post events, but it also allows you to monitor the activity of any log. *EventLog* allows you to capture events as they are written to a log as well as access all of the current event entries in a log. Before we talk about how to do this, let's spend a little time talking about the *EventLogEntry* class, a subject I have avoided until now.

The *EventLogEntry* class   The *EventLogEntry* object represents a single event entry in an event log. When I called the *EventLog.WriteEntry* method earlier, I implicitly created these objects. The *EventLogEntry* class supports an array of properties that describe all of the information about a specific entry in an event log. Table 10-3 lists the properties of the *EventLogEntry* class.

Table 10-3
Properties of the *EventLogEntry* Class

Property	Description
Category	Retrieves text related to the *CategoryNumber* for this event log entry
CategoryNumber	The category number of this event log entry
Data	The binary data associated with the entry
EntryType	The event type of this entry
EventID	The application-specific event identifier of this event entry
Index	The index of this event entry in the event log
MachineName	The name of the computer where this entry was created

Table 10-3
Properties of the *EventLogEntry* Class

Property	Description
Message	The message contained within this entry
Source	The name of the application that created this event
TimeGenerated	The time when this entry was created
TimeWritten	The time when this entry was written to the log
UserName	The name of the user who's responsible for this event

You cannot directly create new entries of the *EventLogEntry* class. Only the system can do that. You can cause instances of the class to be generated by calling one of the *EventLog.WriteEntry* methods, but you can never alter the contents of any of the properties. This is quite purposeful. The entries in an event log are intended to be immutable. All you can do is inspect the individual properties.

Accessing the Event Log Entries

Accessing the entries of a log is simple. When you create an instance of the *EventLog* class, you can specify the log the object points to. When you do this, the *Entries* property, a collection of *EventLogEntry* objects, is populated. You can iterate this collection and look at each entries and process them however you want. Simple.

In addition to just reading the contents of a log, the *EventLog* class supports the *EntryWritten* event, which you can use to monitor entries as they are posted to the log. Furthermore, you can turn the monitoring for an event log on and off using the *EnableRaisingEvents* property of *EventLog*. The following sample demonstrates how you might do this:

```
Dim evtLog As New EventLog("Application")
evtLog.EnableRaisingEvents = True
AddHandler evtLog.EntryWritten, AddressOf EventMethod

...

Public Sub EventMethod(ByVal sender As Object, _
                       ByVal e As EntryWrittenEventArgs )
   Dim entry As EventLogEntry = e.Entry
   Console.WriteLine(entry.Message)
End Sub
```

By default, the *EventLog* class does not raise the *EntryWritten* event, so you must explicitly enable it by setting the *EnableRaisingEvents* to *True*. You can just as easily disable this event by setting the *EnableRaisingEvents* property to *False*. From this sample you can also see how the *EventLogEntry* class is passed to the handler for the *EntryWritten* event. The *EventLogEntry* object is easily accessible, and you can access all of the information about that particular event.

The ability to monitor event log postings can have many uses. For example, you can create an application to monitor a set of services on a machine (or set of machines). By checking the *Source* and *EntryType* parameters, you can easily determine if there are problems with the applications you're monitoring (as long as they post to the event log).

The EventLog Sample Application

I created the EventLog Sample application, shown in Figure 10-8, to demonstrate a number of event logging concepts. This sample includes supporting an *EventLogInstaller*, writing entries to a log, and monitoring the entries posted to that log.

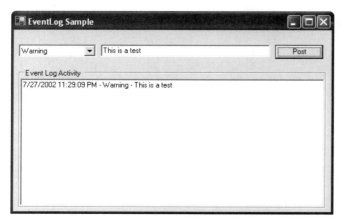

Figure 10-8   The EventLog Sample application.

Let's start at the top. First, I create an *EventLogInstaller* to create my event log. I set my source to the name of the application (*"EventLogSample"*) and I call my new log *"MyEventLog"*. Here's the code:

```
Imports System.Diagnostics
Imports System.ComponentModel

<RunInstaller(True)> _
Public Class MyEventLogInstaller
    Inherits EventLogInstaller
```

```
Public Sub New()
    MyBase.New()

    Me.Source = "EventLogSample"
    Me.Log = "MyEventLog"
End Sub
End Class
```

When the application is compiled, I must run the InstallUtil.exe application to set up the event log; otherwise, the application will, by design, fail when calling the form's *Load* event. You typically won't run into problems until you create the *EventLog* object or call one of the *Shared WriteEntry* methods, but I wanted to make sure the sample handled this cleanly—you'll know right off the bat if you haven't run the installer. Let's take a look at the code in this form:

```
Public Class Form1
    Inherits System.Windows.Forms.Form

#Region " Windows Form Designer generated code "

    Dim WithEvents evtLog As EventLog

    Private Sub Form1_Load(ByVal sender As System.Object, _
                          ByVal e As System.EventArgs) Handles MyBase.Load

        ' Create the source and event log
        If Not EventLog.SourceExists("EventLogSample") Then
            MsgBox("Run InstallUtil.exe on this application " & _
                "to install the event logs")
            Me.Close()
            Return
        End If

        ' Create a new instance of the EventLog class and attach to the
        ' MyEventLog log
        evtLog = New EventLog("MyEventLog")
        evtLog.Source = "EventLogSample"

        ' Assign our event log instance to the newly created log
        evtLog.EnableRaisingEvents = True

        ' Initialize the Form's ComboBox
        LogType.Items.AddRange(New Object() {EventLogEntryType.Error, _
                                            EventLogEntryType.Information, _
                                            EventLogEntryType.FailureAudit, _
                                            EventLogEntryType.SuccessAudit, _
                                            EventLogEntryType.Warning})

    End Sub
```

```
Private Sub Form1_Closing(ByVal sender As Object, _
                  ByVal e As System.ComponentModel.CancelEventArgs) _
                  Handles MyBase.Closing
    If Not evtLog Is Nothing Then
       evtLog.Dispose()
    End If
End Sub

Private Sub PostButton_Click(ByVal sender As System.Object, _
                  ByVal e As System.EventArgs _
                  ) Handles PostButton.Click

    If LogType.SelectedItem Is Nothing Then
       MsgBox("Please specify an event type...")
       Return
    End If

    evtLog.WriteEntry(Message.Text, LogType.SelectedItem)
End Sub

Private Sub evtLog_EntryWritten(ByVal sender As Object, _
                  ByVal e As EntryWrittenEventArgs _
                  ) Handles evtLog.EntryWritten

    Dim evt As EventLogEntry = e.Entry
    Dim s As String = String.Format("{0} - {1} - {2}", _
                          evt.TimeGenerated, _
                          evt.EntryType, evt.Message)

    EventLogActivity.AppendText(s & vbCrLf)
    End Sub
End Class
```

You can see that the form's *Load* event handles a number of tasks. It not only creates an instance of *EventLog* and populates the *Log* and *Source* properties, but it also enables the *EntryWritten* event. The *Form1_Load* method's final task is to populate the form's *ComboBox* with the values of the *EntryType* enumeration. This allows the user to select from the available event entry types when posting a new event.

All of the real action takes place in the *PostButton_Click* and *evtLog_EntryWritten* methods. In *PostButton_Click*, I used the *EventLog.WriteEntry* method to post a new event to the application's even log. I used an overload of the *WriteEntry* method so I could specify not only the message but also the event type. The *evtLog_EntryWritten* method is fired after every call to *PostButton_Click*. I captured some of the information about the event and appended it to the form's text field so you can see how the event is processed in the application. For additional verification, you can use the Event Viewer application to see where the events end up.

The *Trace* and *Debug* Classes

The *Trace* and *Debug* classes are closely related. Both enable the developer to post messages about the progress of an application (typically to an attached debugger). But these classes do serve different purposes. The *Debug* class is intended for use with debug builds of an assembly and the *Trace* class is for instrumenting your application.

Both classes are based on a more generic form of output. While the *Debugger* class allows direct communication to a debugger, the *Debug* and *Trace* classes care little about who is receiving the output. The general idea is that the *Debug* and *Trace* classes send their output to a collection of *Listener* objects. What these *Listener* objects do with the information is completely up to them. Neither of the classes really cares what, if anything, is done with the information provided. Developers therefore gain a lot of flexibility, including the ability to create custom *Listener* objects to deal with the output of the *Debug* and *Trace* classes.

Using *Debug* and *Trace*

The *Debug* and *Trace* classes sport exactly the same set of methods and properties (although, strangely, they don't share a common interface). All of the members of these classes are shared. This means that any modification to the output settings are global for the process. Table 10-4 lists all of the members supported by both classes. The purpose of the *Write* and *WriteLine* methods is fairly intuitive, but other methods are more involved. For instance, some of the methods (*Assert* and *WriteIf*) conditionally output messages, and others (*Indent* and *Unindent*) modify the output.

Table 10-4
Shared Members of the *Debug* and *Trace* Classes

Member	Type	Description
Assert	*Method*	Checks for a condition. If the condition is false, it writes information to the trace listeners in the *Listeners* collection.
Close	*Method*	Flushes the output buffer and then closes the *Listener* objects. This disables further output until new *Listener* objects are created.
Fail	*Method*	Displays an error message.
Flush	*Method*	Flushes the output buffer and causes buffered data to be written to the *Listener* objects.
Indent	*Method*	Increments the current *IndentLevel*.
Unindent	*Method*	Decrements the current *IndentLevel*.
Write	*Method*	Writes information about the trace to the trace listeners in the *Listeners* collection.
WriteIf	*Method*	Writes information about the trace to the trace listeners in the *Listeners* collection if a specified condition is true. (This condition is passed as a parameter to this method.)
WriteLine	*Method*	Writes information about the trace to the trace listeners in the *Listeners* collection.
WriteLineIf	*Method*	Writes information about the trace to the trace listeners in the *Listeners* collection if a specified condition is true. (This condition is passed as a parameter to this method.)
AutoFlush	*Property*	Gets or sets whether *Flush* should be called on the Listener objects after every write.
IndentLevel	*Property*	Gets or sets the indent level.
IndentSize	*Property*	Gets or sets the number of spaces in an indent.
Listeners	*Property*	Gets the collection of listeners that is monitoring the trace output.

All of these properties, with the exception of the *Listeners* collection, have to do with controlling the output of the *Debug* or *Trace* statements. The *Listeners* collection contains all of the registered listener objects. As I mentioned before, these objects are the recipients of the *Debug* and *Trace* statements' output.

The following example shows how easy these classes are to use:

```
' The ol' standard WriteLine method
Debug.WriteLine("This is a Debug test")
Trace.WriteLine("This is a Trace test")

' Playing with the Assert statements
Debug.Assert( False, "This always prints")
Trace.Assert( True, "This never prints")

Debug.Fail("This is a failure message")
Trace.Fail("This is another failure message")

' Demonstrating how indenting works
Debug.Indent()
Debug.WriteLine("This is indented")
Trace.WriteLine("This is not indented")
Debug.Unindent()
Debug.WriteLine("This is not indented")
```

So you get the point: the *Debug* and *Trace* classes are equally easy to use. If you know how to use one, you know how to use the other—they work exactly the same. The only difference is in the message's intended purpose.

Enabling and Disabling *Debug* and *Trace*

If the *Debug* and *Trace* classes are so similar, why have both? The main difference between these classes is in their purpose rather than their functionality. The *Debug* class should be used only to generate statements that are specifically related to debugging a project. You don't have to do it this way, but it is the recommended approach. The *Trace* class is intended to be included with deployed applications—it lets you trace the execution of a code path within an application. *Debug* statements should never make it into deployed applications. You can clarify the distinction between the two classes by asking yourself whether this statement should be included in our deployed application. If not, it should probably be a *Debug* statement instead of a *Trace* statement.

Using compile-time switches, you can include or omit the *Debug* and *Trace* statements. On the Build Configuration property page for your Visual Basic .NET project (Figure 10-9), you can control whether *Debug* and *Trace* statements are included in a build. By default, a debug build includes both *Debug* and *Trace* statements. A retail build is configured, by default, to include only the *Trace* statements.

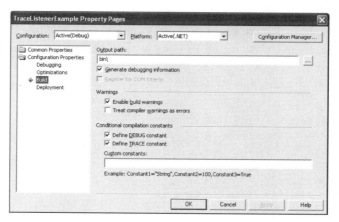

Figure 10-9 The Build Configuration property page.

Note that when you deselect one of these options—say, Debug—any calls to that class are completely omitted from the compiled application. This allows you to speed up your application's performance by omitting these statements and without having to manually remove or comment them out. When you think about it, this is a powerful feature. It allows you to be prolific with your debugging statements when you're developing an application and, with the flick of a compiler switch, generate an application completely free of these statements. Pretty darn cool.

TraceListener Objects

I've already mentioned *Listener* objects in passing. If you look at the Visual Studio .NET documentation, you'll see that the *Listeners* collections of both the *Debug* and *Trace* classes are of type *TraceListenerCollection*. A trace listener is a generic class that monitors an application's trace and debug output. All classes that implement this functionality derive from the *TraceListener* class. Contrary to what the name suggests, the *TraceListener* class is used to monitor output from both the *Debug* and *Trace* statements. It's pretty much source-agnostic.

Here's something else that is not intuitively obvious: the two apparently distinct *Listener* collections of *Trace* and *Debug* are in fact one and the same. The same collection is exposed on two different objects. This means that adding a *TraceListener* to the *Trace.Listeners* collection has the same effect as adding it to the *Debug.Listeners* collection. If you were to add a *TraceListener* to both collections, you would end up with duplicated output because you'd really be adding the same object to a collection twice.

Predefined *TraceListener* classes   The .NET Framework comes with a set of predefined *TraceListener* classes. The most commonly used listener is the *DefaultTraceListener* because it is—surprise—the default. When your application starts up, an instance of the *DefaultTraceListener* class is automatically created and added to the application's *TraceListeners* collection. The *DefaultTraceListener* class is designed to give the maximum flexibility for your debug and trace output. All program output through the tracing statements is passed to both the OutputDebugString API and the *VisualBasic Log* method. This ensures a default behavior that allows your application's debug output to be easily monitored.

In addition to the *DefaultTraceListener*, there are two additional predefined *TraceListener* objects: *EventLogTraceListener* and *TextWriterTraceListener*. Both provide additional functionality above and beyond the *DefaultTraceListener* class. The *EventLogTraceListener* can be used to send all trace and debug output to the event log. This frees the developer from having to attach a debugger just to see what is going on in an application. The following code demonstrates the use of the *EventLogTraceListener* class and how to add it to your application's *Listeners* collection.

```
Dim etl1 As New EventLogTraceListener()
Dim etl2 As New EventLogTraceListener("MyApplication")
Dim etl3 As New EventLogTraceListener(New EventLog("Application"))

' Two different ways to add the listeners
Debug.Listeners.Add(etl1)
Trace.Listeners.AddRange(New TraceListener() {etl2, etl3})
```

The *TextWriterTraceListener* also enables you to redirect your application's trace and debug output to a number of locations, including the console, a file, or a specific *TextWriterStream*. The following example demonstrates several ways to create a *TextWriterTraceListener* and add it to your application's *Listeners* collection:

```
Dim tws1 As New TextWriterTraceListener("myLog.log")
Dim tws2 As New TextWriterTraceListener(Console.Out)
Dim tws3 As New TextWriterTraceListener(New StreamWriter("myLog2.log"))

' Two different ways to add the listeners
Debug.Listeners.Add(tws1)
Trace.Listeners.AddRange(New TraceListener() {tws2, tws3})
```

One final piece of information about the built-in trace listeners. I mentioned that the *DefaultTraceListener* is created and added to both the *Debug.Listeners* collection and the *Trace.Listeners* collection. You can add as many additional listeners you please, but you might want to remove the default listener if it doesn't suit your purposes (to save on overhead). How do you do this? Easy. It's just in a collection. You can quickly handle this in a number of ways. You can clear the *Listeners* collection if you know that there won't be anything else in there you want to keep. Alternatively, you can pass a new instance of the *DefaultTraceListener* class to the *Listeners.Remove* method:

```
' Quick and dirty way to clear the collection
Debug.Listeners.Clear()


' Removing only the DefaultTraceListener from the collection
Trace.Listeners.Remove(new DefaultTraceListener())
```

Another way to customize your application's *Listeners* collection is through the application's configuration file. The following example demonstrates how this works. You can add and remove listeners without recompiling the application.

```
<configuration>
<system.diagnostics>
   <trace>
      <listeners>
         <remove type="System.Diagnostics.DefaultTraceListener,System"/>
         <add name="myEventListener"
            type="System.Diagnostics.EventLogTraceListener,System"
            initializeData="Application"
            />
         <add name="myTextListener"
            type="System.Diagnostics.TextWriterTraceListener,System"
            initializeData="c:\myListener.log"
            />
      </listeners>
   </trace>
</system.diagnostics>
</configuration>
```

Any modifications to this configuration file must be made before an application starts (or restarts) to take effect. You can even add custom *TraceListener* classes (our next subject).

Creating a custom *TraceListener*   Creating your own *TraceListener* is not that difficult. In the simplest case, you can create a class that inherits from *TraceListener*. The only thing you're required to do is to override two base class methods: *Write* and *WriteLine*. The following example *TraceListener* raises a custom event whenever a call to *Write* or *WriteLine* is made:

```
Imports System.Diagnostics

Public Class Tracer
   Inherits TraceListener

   Public Sub New()
      MyBase.New()

      Trace.Listeners.Add(Me)
   End Sub

   Public Delegate Sub TraceHandler(ByVal s As String)
   Public Event TraceEvent As TraceHandler

   Public Overloads Overrides Sub Write(ByVal s As String)
      RaiseEvent TraceEvent(s)
   End Sub

   Public Overloads Overrides Sub WriteLine(ByVal s As String)
      RaiseEvent TraceEvent(s)
   End Sub
End Class
```

You can take this sample even further. For example, there are a host of methods of the *TraceListener* class (including *Close*, *Fail*, and *Flush*) that you can overload to provide the exact behaviors you're looking for.

Controlling *Debug* and *Trace* Output

You've seen two ways to customize the *Debug* and *Trace* output of an application. The first approach uses the compile-time flags to selectively enable or disable debug and trace output. The second approach modifies the application's *TraceListener* collection and develops custom *TraceListener* classes. But all of these approaches use brute force. Next, I want to demonstrate how you can fine-tune your *Debug* and *Trace* output using your application's configuration file and the *Switch* classes. The *Switch* classes provide you with a runtime mechanism for controlling *Trace* and *Debug* output. They give you control of your debug output through the configuration files. Instead of disabling your *Trace* and *Debug* output outright, you can control various levels of output.

A switch provides a mechanism for controlling tracing and debugging output at run time. Switch-based classes can read the configuration information from the application's configuration file, giving an application the flexibility to alter the amount of information, if any, generated by its tracing and debugging statements. Two switch classes are of immediate interest to us: *BooleanSwitch* and *TraceSwitch*.

The *BooleanSwitch* class The *BooleanSwitch* class is pretty simple. It provide a basic on/off behavior for displaying output. All you need to do is create a new instance of the *BooleanSwitch* class and pass it the name of the switch. (This is looked up in the application's configuration file.) Then your code only needs to check its *Enabled* property. The following code demonstrates how you can do this:

```
Dim bs As New BooleanSwitch("mySwitch", "My Switch Description")
If bs.Enabled Then
   Console.WriteLine("The switch is enabled")
End If
```

Of course, if you do nothing else, the *Console.WriteLine* statement will never execute. You must enable the switch somehow. This is easily done in the configuration file, as shown here:

```
<configuration>
   <system.diagnostics>
      <switches>
         <add name="mySwitch" value="1" />
      </switches>
   </system.diagnostics>
</configuration>
```

When I specify the switch in the above XML, I have to provide a value. (Otherwise, it will always be false.) If I specify a value of 0 (or omit the value attribute) the *BooleanSwitch* will not be enabled. If I specify a value of 1 (or any other nonzero integer) the specified *BooleanSwitch* will be enabled. Pretty easy.

The *TraceSwitch* class The *TraceSwitch* class is, as you might expect, somewhat more sophisticated than the *Boolean* switch. This class is really designed to provide a much more tightly controlled set of output options. Using the *Trace-Switch*, you can specify what kind of output you're interested in. Five trace levels are supported. Table 10-5 lists these levels as well as the corresponding value that you can use in the application's configuration file to set this switch.

Table 10-5
Trace-Level Values

Level	Value	Description
Off	*0*	Disables output of *Trace* and *Debug* messages
Error	*1*	Outputs only error messages
Warning	*2*	Outputs only warnings and error messages

Table 10-5
Trace-Level Values

Level	Value	Description
Info	*3*	Outputs informational, warning, and error messages
Verbose	*4*	Outputs all *Trace* and *Debug* messages

The *TraceSwitch* class supports a number of properties that allow you to work with the various configuration settings. The *Level* property reports the current value of the specified *TraceSwitch* instance. Four other properties provide a simpler approach to determining the currently allowed tracing level: *TraceError*, *TraceInfo*, *TraceVerbose*, and *TraceWarning*. To see how you can work with these properties, take a look at this example:

```
Dim ts As New TraceSwitch("myTraceSwitch", "A Trace Switch")

Console.WriteLine("The trace switch level: {0}", ts.Level)
If ts.TraceError Then Console.WriteLine("Trace level allows errors")
If ts.TraceWarning Then Console.WriteLine("Trace level allows warnings")
If ts.TraceInfo Then Console.WriteLine("Trace level allows information")
If ts.TraceVerbose Then Console.WriteLine("Trace level is verbose")
```

Of course, you still need to specify the switch in the configuration file. The following example does just that. Using the value *1* from Table 10-5, this example enables the *myTraceSwitch* switch with an *Error* trace level.

```
<configuration>
   <system.diagnostics>
      <switches>
         <add name="myTraceSwitch" value="1" />
      </switches>
   </system.diagnostics>
</configuration>
```

I have included a sample console application among the book's sample files called SwitchExamples that allows you to play with both types of switches and the configuration file and quickly see the results.

The *Switch* classes   The last remaining question is how and when to use the *Switch* classes. Certainly, it is not highly desirable to litter your code with all sorts of *If* statements unless it is absolutely necessary. I would advocate creating a custom *TraceListener* and implement the *TraceSwitch* or *BooleanSwitch* in that class. That way, if you disable tracing, your application won't end up with *If* trace statements all over the place.

Conclusion

There is a lot more to performance testing and debugging than I could possibly cover in a single chapter, but the technologies and techniques identified here should serve as an excellent starting point for your own applications. Going forward you'll want to look more closely at all the classes provided by the *System.Diagnostics* namespace. One of the topics I haven't covered but well worth investigating is the ability to create custom performance counters. Regardless, you should be able to make a start at instrumenting your own applications and making the whole process of error handling more predictable and manageable. Build off of the material in this chapter and add debugging and error handling features to your own applications.

11

Common Performance Issues

In the previous chapter, I discussed methodologies for finding functional issues with your applications. In this chapter, we'll look at the some of the most common and significant causes of performance problems. Resolving performance issues in any application is not an easy task. You can think of this chapter as a "cheat sheet" for the most common issues.

I'll cover a wide variety of topics, but this chapter will by no means be comprehensive. There are, after all, a virtually infinite number of ways to shoot yourself in the foot. My focus will be on the most common issues that developers need to worry about. But I'll also discuss some issues that are good to be aware of just for the sake of good programming practice. Whether you're investigating performance or resource problems in an existing application or designing a new product, the material in this chapter should provide an essential reference.

In this chapter, you'll see a number of examples of compiled Microsoft intermediate language (MSIL) code because most of the performance problems I'll discuss are the result of bad programming practices or mistaken assumptions. Microsoft Visual Basic has always had a reputation for making development easier, but of course this often means that the compiler inserts a lot of code under the covers to implement those language features. I'll try to show you the implications of those features so you'll know what to avoid and so you can have another tool for analyzing your code.

> **Note** You don't have to understand MSIL in order to understand this chapter. I'll try to explain as much as necessary for the examples provided, and the material can serve as a starting point for your own investigations. However, it's important that you have at least a basic understanding of what the Visual Basic .NET compiler produces. This can help you to make better decisions.

Visual Basic .NET Performance vs. Visual C# .NET Performance

A lot of people have had questions about the performance of Visual Basic .NET versus that of Microsoft Visual C# .NET. Their concern has had mostly to do with Visual Basic's former reputation as slow and inefficient (at least compared to Visual C++). Because C# is based on the C++ syntax, the assumption has been carried over into the .NET world that, all things being equal, C# is faster than Visual Basic.

This is not the case. You can always prove it to yourself with your own tests, but directly equivalent code will perform the same and the compilers will generate nearly identical MSIL. You can run into problems, however, when you use some of the convenient but inefficient features of Visual Basic .NET (or any of the backward-compatibility features). But the performance of the language you develop with ultimately has comparatively little to do with the performance of your application. The greatest impact on performance comes from choices that individual developers make that are unrelated to the specific development language. Bad decisions or wrong assumptions will quickly sink any ship. Don't blame the language.

String Concatenation

It can be surprising how much negative impact string concatenation can have on your application's performance. String concatenation has always been the bane of the Visual Basic programmer. Previous versions of Visual Basic provided no alternatives to the & operator, which is slow. The reasons for this were fairly straightforward. Take the following example:

```
Dim s As String
s = "Select FName, LName From Authors Where LName Like '%" & name & "%'"
```

You might not know it, but Visual Basic cannot combine two strings per se. What it does is create a new string object that contains the combined source strings' values. Using the *&* results in a new string being created each time you use it (unless it is used in a *Const* statement, in which case it is evaluated at compile time). The above example causes the creation of three strings just to assign one to the variable *s*. This leads to unnecessary—or at least unwanted—memory allocation to build just one string. And it gets much worse as you add more to the string.

Desperate developers have had to resort to creating custom COM components to do string concatenation efficiently. Others have just lived with the problem or have never been aware of it in the first place. Visual Basic .NET finally has an answer to the problem, thanks to the .NET Framework: *StringBuilder*.

Note   String concatenation using the *&* operator does not work much differently in Visual Basic .NET compared to earlier versions of Visual Basic. It is still inherently inefficient, but that doesn't mean you should never use it. It is still useful and relatively lightweight for minimal string concatenation. However, when performance is key and you have to do a lot of string concatenation, you need to look at alternatives.

StringBuilder Makes the Grade

The *System.Text.StringBuilder* class finally gives Visual Basic developers the tools they need to do efficient string manipulation operations. *StringBuilder* provides a buffer-oriented mechanism to manipulate string information. String concatenation is not its only use, but that's the most common one. The following example shows how to use *StringBuilder* to perform a concatenation task equivalent to the previous example:

```
Dim s As String
Dim sb As New StringBuilder()
sb.Append("Select FName, LName From Authors Where LName Like '%")
sb.Append(name)
sb.Append("%'")
s = sb.ToString()
```

It's amusing to think that this example, which uses more code than the first example, actually runs faster and is more efficient (if you ignore the cost of creating the *StringBuilder* object). This demonstrates the cardinal rule of performance: less code does not always run faster.

Note   *StringBuilder* doesn't manipulate a string per se. Strings are immutable. *StringBuilder* is just a wrapper for a buffer of characters that you can manipulate in interesting ways. When you call the *ToString* method of *StringBuilder*, that's when a true string object is created.

You can tune the performance of *StringBuilder* by specifying its initial buffer size. When you create a default instance of a *StringBuilder* (when you use the constructor without arguments), *StringBuilder* allocates a default buffer of 16 characters. If, however, you know that you'll be creating a very large string (or if you at least know the ballpark size), you can specify the initial capacity of the buffer. This allows *StringBuilder* to avoid most or all additional memory allocation as strings are appended to it. Don't take this as an argument for always creating large buffers. For most operations, you probably needn't worry, but it is always useful to know that you can tweak things if you need to.

Note   Don't assume that *StringBuilder* is always more efficient than the *&* operator. When you have a very simple string that requires minimal use of *&*, *StringBuilder* is not really appropriate. Remember that you have to create a new instance of the *StringBuilder* class, and that's not free. In order for you to realize a performance gain, the equivalent concatenation operation must be slower than the combined work of creating a *StringBuilder*, doing the necessary work, and then converting the result to a string (using *ToString*).

Format Strings

The string formatting mechanism provided by the .NET Framework is extremely powerful. In fact, you've already seen it used countless times in this book with the *Console.WriteLine* method. It offers an exciting addition to Visual Basic's capabilities: very fine control over how strings are built and how different types and values are represented in strings. This mechanism is extremely flexible and enables you to generate sophisticated customized string output very easily. The simplest form looks like the following example:

```
Console.WriteLine("This is a {0}", "test" )
Console.WriteLine("This is {0} {1}", "another", "test" )
```

The *WriteLine* method supports using a string input, with an argument list. You can see how easy it is to have values inserted into the string. This is a very easy-to-read way to build strings. Format strings are used in many ways through the .NET Framework's type system, but here we're interested only in the *String.Format* method and the *StringBuilder.AppendFormat* method. The following example demonstrates the use of both:

```
Dim sb As New StringBuilder()
sb.AppendFormat( _
   "Select FName, LName From Authors Where LName Like '%{0}%'", name)

Dim s As String = String.Format( _
   "Select FName, LName From Authors Where LName Like '%{0}%'", name)
```

I have to admit that I really like the format methods and use them often. When performance is not critical, this approach can be an effective and readable way to deal with strings. You can safely assume that the rules for string concatenation apply to format strings as well. In other words, for small concatenation operations, using the *String.Format* method is probably more efficient than using the *StringBuilder.AppendFormat* method. When you start increasing the number of concatenation operations, however, *StringBuilder* becomes the clear winner. We'll look at this more closely in the next section.

Note Things get even more interesting when you look at how to format numbers and how you can manipulate the string output. Unfortunately, I can't even attempt to do justice to this topic here. If you're interested in how to do more with format strings, search the Visual Studio .NET Help documentation for "Formatting Overview" using the "Visual Basic and Related" filter and select the Search In Titles Only check box.

String Performance by the Numbers

So far, I've shown you four ways to create strings and essentially told you which methods are preferable and when. But don't take my word for it. For the sake of demonstrating the performance advantages and disadvantages of the different forms of string concatenation, I created four methods: *StringContact*, *StringFormat*, *StringBuilder*, and *StringBuilderFormat*. Here's what they look like:

```
Sub StringConcat()
    Dim i As Integer
    Dim s As String
    For i = 0 To MAX_LOOP
        s = "Insert Into Authors (au_lname, au_fname, phone, " _
                & "address, city, state, zip, contract) Values ( "
        s &= "'" & lName & "',"
        s &= "'" & fName & "',"
        s &= "'" & phone & "',"
        s &= "'" & address & "',"
        s &= "'" & city & "',"
        s &= "'" & state & "',"
        s &= "'" & zip & "',"
        s &= contract.ToString() & " )"
    Next
End Sub


Private sb as New StringBuilder()

Sub StringBuilderConcat()
    Dim s As String
    Dim i As Integer

    For i = 0 To MAX_LOOP
        sb.Append("Insert Into Authors (au_lname, au_fname, phone, " _
                & "address, city, state, zip, contract) Values ( "
        sb.Append("'")
        sb.Append(lName)
        sb.Append("', '")
        sb.Append(fName)
        sb.Append("', '")
        sb.Append(phone)
        sb.Append("', '")
        sb.Append(address)
        sb.Append("', '")
        sb.Append(city)
        sb.Append("', '")
        sb.Append(state)
        sb.Append("', '")
```

```
            sb.Append(zip)
            sb.Append("',")
            sb.Append(contract)
            sb.Append(" )")
            s = sb.ToString()
            sb.Length = 0
        Next
    End Sub

    Sub StringBuilderFormat()
        Dim s As String
        Dim i As Integer
        For i = 0 To MAX_LOOP
            sb.Append("Insert Into Authors (au_lname, au_fname, phone, " _
                    & "address, city, state, zip, contract) Values ( "
            sb.AppendFormat("'{0}', '{1}', ", lName, fName)
            sb.AppendFormat("'{0}', '{1}', ", phone, address)
            sb.AppendFormat("'{0}', '{1}', ", city, state)
            sb.AppendFormat("'{0}', {1} )", zip, contract)

            s = sb.ToString()
            sb.Length = 0
        Next
    End Sub

    Sub StringFormat()
        Dim i As Integer
        Dim s As String
        For i = 0 To MAX_LOOP
            s = "Insert Into Authors (au_lname, au_fname, phone, " _
                    & "address, city, state, zip, contract) Values ( "
            s &= String.Format("Values ( '{0}', '{1}', ", lName, fName)
            s &= String.Format("'{0}', '{1}', ", phone, address)
            s &= String.Format("'{0}', '{1}', ", city, state)
            s &= String.Format("'{0}', {1} )", zip, contract)
        Next
    End Sub
```

Using the test application StringConcatPerformance (which is included with this chapter's sample files), I put these methods through their paces. The results are as follows:

```
                  Normal    Format
Concat            680.98    1341.93   1.97 times slower than StringConcat
StringBuilder     410.59     911.31   2.22 times slower than StringBuilder
                    1.66x     1.47x
```

Let's discuss these results for a moment. Comparing string concatenation and *StringBuilder.Append*, you can see that it took about half the time to run the *StringBuilder* method. This is a significant difference. You can also see that the difference is only slightly less when you compare *String.Format* and *String-Builder.AppendFormat*. What might be surprising is how much slower in general the format methods are. In retrospect, this does make some sense. Using format strings requires parsing the input string and generating the specific variable formats, whereas the "Normal" methods require only combining strings—nothing more.

Note Your numbers will vary depending on your system. My machine isn't quite as fast as it used to be, but the relationships between the samples should remain roughly similar—unless, of course, work is done on future releases of the CLR to improve string performance (something I consider highly likely).

You should also note that *StringBuilder.AppendFormat* is only slightly slower than regular string concatenation. This is interesting because *String-Builder.AppendFormat* is far more flexible and easier to work with.

Note If you're using *StringBuilder*, I recommend a mix of calls to *Append* and *AppendFormat*. Calling *AppendFormat* with only a string and no arguments is a waste of resources.

Late Binding

In Chapter 2, I discussed late binding and why it is a bad programming practice. I also mentioned that along with problems related to functional and coding standards, late binding is also a performance killer. This has everything to do with how late binding works. Essentially, late binding requires runtime function lookups to execute every method and evaluate every property, or to resolve type information. This adds significant overhead. To help convince you of this, I built a late binding performance sample called LateBindingPerformance (which is among this chapter's samples files). The following code is an excerpt, which should give you an idea of what we're testing.

```vb
Public lbClass As Object
Public ebClass As Employee

Public Sub LateBoundTest()
    lbClass.Name = "Mr. Ted"
    lbClass.SSN = "123-45-6789"
    Dim age As Integer = Now.Subtract(lbClass.DateOfBirth).Days / 365.25
End Sub

Public Sub EarlyBoundTest()
    ebClass.Name = "Mr. Ted"
    ebClass.SSN = "123-45-6789"
    Dim age As Integer = _
        CInt(Now.Subtract(ebClass.DateOfBirth).Days / 365.25)
End Sub


Public Class Employee
    Private m_name As String
    Private m_ssn As String
    Private m_dob As Date

    Public Sub New(ByVal name As String, ByVal ssn As String, _
        ByVal dob As Date)
        MyBase.New()
        m_name = name
        m_ssn = ssn
        m_dob = dob
    End Sub

    Public Property Name() As String
        Get
            Return m_name
        End Get
        Set(ByVal Value As String)
            m_name = Value
        End Set
    End Property

    Public Property SSN() As String
        Get
            Return m_ssn
        End Get
        Set(ByVal Value As String)
            m_ssn = Value
        End Set
    End Property
```

```
Public Property DateOfBirth() As Date
   Get
      Return m_dob
   End Get
   Set(ByVal Value As Date)
      m_dob = Value
   End Set
End Property
```

```
End Class
```

What we're doing in the *LateBoundTest* and *EarlyBoundTest* methods is admittedly arbitrary, but it serves its purpose—accessing both early and late-bound methods and properties. The results demonstrate quite a difference. Check out the program output:

```
EarlyBound Time:    1001420
LateBound Time :  312342898

EarlyBinding example is ~312 times faster
```

It's important to understand that this does not tell the whole story. In the LateBindingPerformance sample, the properties we access do very little work. As a result, the overhead of calling a late-bound property or method is large compared to the execution time of that property or method. If the property or method were to do a lot of work, the amount of time added by the overhead of late binding would be minimal, if not insignificant, by comparison. Imagine that you call a method that takes a half-second to execute. The cost of calling a late-bound method is probably measured in hundreds of processor cycles. So making a late-bound call in this case wouldn't affect your performance in any noticeable way. (But remember that there are other reasons to avoid late binding. You should just consider it a generally bad idea.)

Designing Types

You might recall from Chapter 2 the distinction between value types and reference types. I said that value types demonstrate intrinsically better performance in accessing members than reference types do because value types are stack-based entities and reference types live in the heap.

Let's examine this further. I created a sample to illustrate this situation. I created two types, *PointStruct* and *PointClass*, that both serve to contain a pair of *x* and *y* coordinates. You can see from the following definition that they're exactly equivalent:

```
Structure PointStruct
    Public x, y As Double
    Public Sub New(ByVal xCoord As Double, ByVal yCoord As Double)
        x = xCoord
        y = yCoord
    End Sub
End Structure

Class PointClass
    Public x, y As Double
    Public Sub New(ByVal xCoord As Double, ByVal yCoord As Double)
        x = xCoord
        y = yCoord
    End Sub
End Class
```

What we'll do with these is simple. We'll create a large array of both types and insert random data. Then we'll iterate through the arrays of points, calculating the slope and distance between adjacent points and at the same time calculating the length of the overall line represented by the respective array (which we won't do anything with).

The ValueTypePerformance example (one of this chapter's samples files) demonstrates what the performance looks like for more intensive calculations—which is, after all, where the memory advantages of the value type become apparent. So even though the following might cause flashbacks to 10th-grade math class, it's a worthwhile example:

```
Module Module1
    Const ARRAY_SIZE As Integer = 10000

    Sub StructTest()
        Dim i As Integer
        Dim x, y As Double
        Dim rand As New Random()

        ' Initialize the Array
        Dim ps() As PointStruct = New PointStruct(ARRAY_SIZE) {}
        For i = 0 To ARRAY_SIZE
            x = rand.Next()
            y = rand.Next()
            ps(i) = New PointStruct(x, y)
        Next

        ' Calculate the slope and distance between each point
        Dim length As Double = 0
        Dim slope, distance As Double
        Dim dx, dy As Double
```

```
        For i = 1 To ARRAY_SIZE
            dx = (ps(i).x - ps(i - 1).x)
            dy = (ps(i).y - ps(i - 1).y)
            slope = dy / dx
            distance = Math.Sqrt(Math.Pow(dx, 2) + Math.Pow(dy, 2))

            length += distance
        Next
    End Sub

    Sub ClassTest()
        Dim i As Integer
        Dim x, y As Double
        Dim rand As New Random()
        Dim pc() As PointClass = New PointClass(ARRAY_SIZE) {}
        For i = 0 To ARRAY_SIZE
            x = rand.Next()
            y = rand.Next()
            pc(i) = New PointClass(x, y)
        Next

        ' Calculate the slope and distance between each point
        Dim length As Double = 0
        Dim slope, distance As Double
        Dim dx, dy As Double
        For i = 1 To ARRAY_SIZE
            dx = (pc(i).x - pc(i - 1).x)
            dy = (pc(i).y - pc(i - 1).y)
            slope = dy / dx
            distance = Math.Sqrt(Math.Pow(dx, 2) + Math.Pow(dy, 2))

            length += distance
        Next
    End Sub

    Sub Main()
        Dim i As Integer
        Dim sTime, cTime As TimeSpan
        Dim start, finish As Date

        start = Now()
        For i = 0 To 100
            StructTest()
        Next
        finish = Now()
        sTime = finish.Subtract(start)
```

```
    start = Now()
    For i = 0 To 100
        ClassTest()
    Next
    finish = Now()
    cTime = finish.Subtract(start)

    Console.WriteLine("StructTest {0,10} ticks", sTime.Ticks)
    Console.WriteLine("ClassTest  {0,10} ticks", cTime.Ticks)
    Console.WriteLine("          {0,10:0.00%}", _
                            sTime.Ticks / cTime.Ticks)

    Console.ReadLine()
  End Sub

End Module
```

From the following program output, you can see that the *StructTest* offers a performance advantage in this case. The performance difference is related solely to the additional overhead of accessing heap resident objects. Granted, the difference isn't earth-shattering, but a roughly 10 percent reduction in run-time is generally considered a successful attempt at performance optimization.

```
StructTest   17781132 ticks
ClassTest    19978800 ticks
             89.00%
```

Does this mean that you should always use structures and avoid classes whenever possible? Absolutely not. Each type has its own advantages. In this case, structures were the obvious choice. But when the performance advantages aren't as significant or are even negligible (which is most of the time), classes are usually the best route. Ultimately, you have to determine what makes the most sense for your application's design. If you need to create a type that contains only data and little, if any, logic, a structure might be the better approach. Bottom line: use your own discretion.

Caution   You can quickly kill the performance advantage of a structure and end up worse off if you do a lot of boxing and unboxing. (See the section titled "Type Magic: Boxing and Unboxing" in Chapter 2.)

Error Handling

Error handling is a fact of life for applications, but that doesn't mean it should slow you down. Here are a few tips for avoiding potential error-handling-related performance issues.

On Error Goto and *On Error Resume Next* vs. Exceptions

The *On Error* statement should be familiar to Visual Basic developers. After all, it was the only error-handling mechanism built into previous versions of Visual Basic. Visual Basic .NET does provide these error-handling constructs, but they're for backward compatibility only. Structured exception handling is now the order of the day. Even though it's not necessarily obvious, just adding *On Error* to a method will result in your code running more slowly, regardless of whether errors are actually occurring. To see why this is true, let's compare two methods:

```
Private Sub TryCatch_Simple()
   Try
      Console.Write("This ")
      Console.Write("is ")
      Console.Write("a ")
      Console.Write("good ")
      Console.WriteLine("test.")
   Catch ex As Exception
      Console.WriteLine("The command failed")
   End Try
End Sub

Private Sub OnError_Simple()
   On Error Resume Next
   Console.Write("This ")
   Console.Write("is ")
   Console.Write("a ")
   Console.Write("bad ")
   Console.WriteLine("test.")
End Sub
```

Someone comparing the two methods might think that the *OnError_Simple* method is more efficient merely because it appears to contain less code. This couldn't be further from the truth. The compiled code can be quite different. I'll leave the exercise of checking out the actual MSIL output to you, but I've grabbed some information that demonstrates, in part, what the problem is:

```
.method private static void  TryCatch_Simple() cil managed
{
  // Code size        77 (0x4d)
  ...
} // end of method Module1::TryCatch_Simple

.method private static void  OnError_Simple() cil managed
{
  // Code size        180 (0xb4)
  ...
} // end of method Module1::OnError_Simple
```

What should you make of these two MSIL examples? First, notice how much longer *OnError_Simple* is. At the top of each example, you'll see a comment that describes the code size of each method. The *OnError_Simple* method weighs in at 180 bytes, while the *TryCatch_Simple* method weighs in at 77 bytes (less than half). But of course, this doesn't tell the whole story. Remember, I said that less code does not always run faster, but here it definitely does. To help illustrate this, I created a sample application called OnErrorPerformance (one of this chapter's samples files) using both the *TryCatch_Simple* and *OnError_Simple* methods described above and two similar, but larger, methods (essentially duplicating the internal code several times). The numbers are interesting:

Test Name	Try Catch	On Error	Diff
Simple Test	1602192	2503425	64.0%
Simple Test	1602192	2303151	69.6%
Simple Test	1602192	2403288	66.7%
Simple Test	1502055	2403288	62.5%
Longer Test	3204384	12617262	25.4%
Longer Test	3204384	12717399	25.2%
Longer Test	3304521	12416988	26.6%
Longer Test	3204384	12517125	25.6%

You can see that using *On Error* is about 25 percent slower than using *Try Catch* for the "Simple Test". Not too bad, right? Well, as you can see, it gets worse. In fact, it gets much worse. The larger the method, the worse the effect on performance. The larger method tests demonstrate that admirably. The *OnError_Longer* method is almost four times slower than the *TryCatch_Longer* method. Wow.

Using the old Visual Basic style of error handling is terrible for performance. Incidentally, this was also true in Visual Basic 6.0. Essentially, *On Error* injects a lot of code into a method to perform its magic. This results in your method containing a placeholder for each physical line of code, similar to using a line label. The method is then enclosed in one *Try...Catch*, and when an exception occurs, the line to go to is determined by a switch clause and the last saved location. As you might expect, this results in a large amount of overhead for such a little statement. The reality is that this is one of the most inefficient forms of error handling you can use. (Of course, some industrious individual might prove us wrong—someone can always come up with a more inefficient solution.)

Burn this into your brain before you go on to the next section: exception handling good. *On Error* bad. Really bad.

Exception Handling Best Practices

I talked a lot about proper exception handling in Chapter 2, and I don't want to belabor the subject here. I will, however say this: exceptions should be exceptional. Exception handling is fairly expensive. Granted, when no exceptions are being thrown, there is little impact on performance. But if you throw exceptions regularly in your code, you'll likely experience significant performance degradation. Two rules should apply to exception handling:

- Never throw an exception unless something truly exceptional occurs.

- Never catch an exception if all you'll do is rethrow it.

    OK, everyone clear? Good. Let's move on.

Database Issues

Databases are critical to most applications these days. Problems with database access occur most frequently in a small number of areas. These problems are not always easy to track down, but they can have catastrophic effects on the performance of any application. For the most part, I'll focus on using the *SqlClient* namespace data classes, for two reasons. First, they provide performance counters that enable you to track the state of the data layer. Second, I'm talking about high-performance applications that are likely to be using an industrial-level database system such as Microsoft SQL Server anyway.

Database Connection Leaks and Connection Pooling

Connection pooling is a critical part of the data access infrastructure of modern applications. The general idea behind pooling is that establishing connections with a database is an expensive process, especially when that database will most likely exist on another system. Consider a Web application that deals with a high volume of incoming requests. It will likely talk to the one database or set of databases. Creating a new database connection for each incoming request is not especially efficient. A connection pool allows the application to reuse existing database connections that aren't in use but are still open. The application can therefore open a minimal number of database connections to satisfy a much larger set of incoming requests.

So how does this work? The connection pool mechanism comes into play when you call the *Open* method on a connection object. The *Open* logic first checks to see whether a connection pool exists for the specified connection string. If a connection pool doesn't already exist, a new connection will be created, opened, and inserted into a new connection pool. If a pool does exist, *Open* will look for an available open connection. If it finds one, *Open* will succeed. If no open connections are available but space is available in the pool, a new connection will be opened and added to the pool. On the other hand, if there are no available open connections and no empty slots in the pool, the *Open* method will wait up to 30 seconds for a chance at a connection in the pool. If one is not made available in that time, an *InvalidOperationException* will be generated. Figure 11-1 illustrates this process using the *SqlConnection* pooling system.

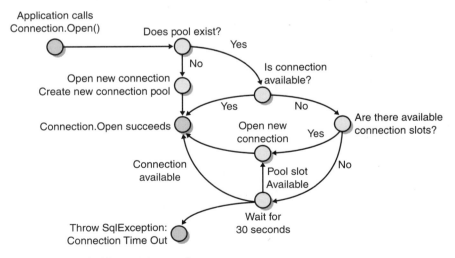

Figure 11-1   *SqlConnection* pooling.

That covers the process of opening connections, but you need to know three additional facts about *SqlConnection* pools:

- Pools are limited to a finite number of open connections. You can specify a custom pool size in your connection string (this applies to the *SqlConnection* but not the *OleDbConnection*), but it will always be finite and I don't recommend changing the default size unless absolutely necessary.

- Pools are based on connection strings. Different connection strings will generate separate connection pools, each with its own connection limit.

- Calling *Close* or *Dispose* on a *SqlConnection* object will return the open connection to the pool. If you don't call *Close* or *Dispose* on the connection, it will eventually be destroyed by the garbage collector and will not be returned to the connection pool. This will also cause what I call a "connection leak." (I'll get into that a little bit later on.)

Making the Most of Connection Pools

Three main rules will allow you to make the most of connection pooling in your applications:

- Always use the same connection string to talk to the same database. This will ensure that all of those connections end up in the same pool.

- Always call *Close* or *Dispose* on your *SqlConnection* object. This will ensure that the connection ends up back in the connection pool.

- Open your connections as late as possible and close them as soon as possible. This will increase connection churn and should help avoid timeouts with other threads that are waiting for available connections.

This is all well and good, but if you have a large application that's performing poorly, how can you tell whether the problem is related to pooling or to connection leaks? Read on.

Tracking Down Connection Leaks

Frankly, tracking down connection leaks can be a real pain. I spent days trying to find the cause of performance and scalability problems in a Web application that were actually caused by several connection leaks. The problem was that the application ran fine for a single user, but as additional users added stress, the application suddenly hit a wall. The worst part was that the application didn't really look like it was working all that hard, nor did the database. (In fact, processor use was next to nothing on both boxes.)

Symptoms of a potential connection leak   You should look out for four major symptoms when you test your application under various loads. If any of the following scenarios is true, you might have one or more connection leaks:

- Database connections continually increase under light application stress until the connection pool size limit is reached.

- Under a constant but heavier load, your application starts creating more and more connections, eventually hitting the pool size limit.

- Your application is throwing timeout exceptions from the connection's *Open* method.

- Your application runs fine for a single user but quickly croaks as more users are added.

- Your application is running slowly under stress and is exhibiting low processor usage.

Avoiding connection leaks   The simplest way to avoid connection leaks is to always close your connections. Easy, right? OK. Let's think through a scenario. You've gone through your application and have closed all of the connections explicitly. Great. But you notice that, under stress, your application still exhibits some connection leak behavior (albeit at a much slower rate). What have you done wrong? It turns out that closing a connection isn't always so simple. Look at the following example:

```
Dim conn As New SqlConnection(connectionString)
conn.Open()
DoStuff( conn )
conn.Close()
```

Is this a form of potential connection leak? You bet! The problem is in the *DoStuff* section. Let's say an exception is thrown—which is certainly not out of the question. Will *Close* be called? No. The reference to the connection object will be lost, and it will be up to the garbage collector to clean up, when it gets around to it. So this code can be deceiving. It seems to be doing all of the right things, but it doesn't handle itself well in an error situation. Some might say that you should just fix *DoStuff*, but that misses the point. Bad things always happen in applications. As developers, we all need to plan for success as well as failure. In this case, the exception might be thrown by invalid input (from a hacker, maybe). If that input is repeated, it might cause a denial of service attack because your application will eventually run out of available connections and stall.

The best way out of this situation is to use a *Try...Finally* block to ensure that your connections will always be closed, regardless of what happens. In this way, your code will behave as expected in the case of either success or failure. The following example demonstrates this:

```
Dim conn As New SqlConnection(connectionString)
Try
   conn.Open()
   DoStuff( conn )
Finally
   conn.Close()
End Try
```

Note that I don't open the connection in the *Try* block—because I don't care about the *Open* method failing. If it fails, no connection will be opened, so I don't need to close it. This doesn't mean that you can't nest *Try* blocks to deal with an exception. In that case, you might try something like the following:

```
Dim conn As New SqlConnection(connectionString)
Try
   conn.Open()
   Try
      DoStuff( conn )
   Finally
      conn.Close()
   End Try
Catch ex As Exception
   Debug.WriteLine( ex.ToString() )
End Try
```

Using a *DataReader* with a Stored Proc Whenever Possible

Microsoft ADO.NET provides many ways of getting data from a database to your application—too many ways. For the best performance, you should use only database stored procedures on the server and use a *DataReader* only in your application. The *DataReader* is the most efficient way to get data because it reads the incoming information "right off the wire." It is a forward-only data model but has minimal overhead. Essentially, the *DataReader* processes only the current record from the database connection. Each call to *Read* causes the *DataReader* to process only the next immediate row of data and throw away the previous row. You can't get much more efficient than that.

```
Dim conn As New SqlConnection(connString)
Dim cmd As New SqlCommand("MyStoredProc", conn )
Dim rdr As SqlDataReader
```

```
conn.Open()
Try
   rdr = cmd.ExecuteReader()
   While rdr.Read()
      Console.WriteLine( rdr(0) )
   End While
   rdr.Close()
Finally
   conn.Close()
End Try
```

The other data models in ADO.NET all require a lot more processing overhead. Of course, they're also more flexible. But for sheer performance, you can't beat a *DataReader*.

Using Ordinals Instead of Column Names

One of the most common performance mistakes made in database applications is using column names to access row column data. We've all created programs that have done this, at one time or another. (This is mostly a classic ADO bad practice, but ADO.NET makes it just as easy to do.) The following example should feel fairly familiar to most readers:

```
While dr.Read()
    sb.AppendFormat("CustomerID = '{0}' ", dr("CustomerID"))
    sb.AppendFormat("CompanyName = '{0}' ", dr("CompanyName"))
    sb.AppendFormat("ContactName = '{0}' ", dr("ContactName"))
    sb.AppendFormat("ContactTitle = '{0} '", dr("ContactTitle"))
    sb.AppendFormat("Address = '{0}' ", dr("Address"))
    sb.AppendFormat("City = '{0}' ", dr("City"))
    sb.AppendFormat("Region = '{0}' ", dr("Region"))
    sb.AppendFormat("PostalCode = '{0}' ", dr("PostalCode"))
    sb.AppendFormat("Country = '{0}' ", dr("Country"))
    sb.AppendFormat("Phone = '{0}' ", dr("Phone"))
    sb.AppendFormat("Fax = '{0}'{1}", dr("Fax"), vbCrLf)
End While
```

Using strings to access column data is a horribly bad idea. The most efficient and appropriate method is to use the actual column numbers (ordinals) to access the data. This is extremely efficient and is a huge time-saver. It frees ADO.NET from having to look up the column name every time. The following example demonstrates this:

```
While dr.Read()
    sb.AppendFormat("CustomerID = '{0}' ", dr(0))
    sb.AppendFormat("CompanyName = '{0}'", dr(1))
    sb.AppendFormat("ContactName = '{0}' ", dr(2))
```

```
    sb.AppendFormat("ContactTitle = '{0}' ", dr(3))
    sb.AppendFormat("Address = '{0}' ", dr(4))
    sb.AppendFormat("City = '{0}' ", dr(5))
    sb.AppendFormat("Region = '{0}' ", dr(6))
    sb.AppendFormat("PostalCode = '{0}' ", dr(7))
    sb.AppendFormat("Country = '{0}' ", dr(8))
    sb.AppendFormat("Phone = '{0}' ", dr(9))
    sb.AppendFormat("Fax = '{0}'{1}", dr(10), vbCrLf)
End While
```

The one major problem with the example is that you run into problems if someone changes the column ordering of the database query. If a column is added in the middle of the column collection or two columns are switched, bad things will happen. So intuitively this feels more fragile, albeit faster, than using the column names. Using column names at least affords you the flexibility of not knowing the exact column positions in advance. Thankfully, a happy medium is available: *IDataRecord.GetOrdinal*, which is implemented by both *SqlDataReader* and *OleDbDataReader*.

Essentially, the *IDataRecord.GetOrdinal* method allows you to perform an ordinal lookup for a column name. You can store the value of an ordinal in a variable once and then reuse it in a loop. This is advantageous because it allows for column position flexibility, while at the same time minimizing the use of column name lookups. So this really is the best of both worlds. The following example demonstrates this:

```
Dim CustomerID As Integer = dr.GetOrdinal("CustomerID")
Dim CompanyName As Integer = dr.GetOrdinal("CompanyName")
Dim ContactName As Integer = dr.GetOrdinal("ContactName")
Dim ContactTitle As Integer = dr.GetOrdinal("ContactTitle")
Dim Address As Integer = dr.GetOrdinal("Address")
Dim City As Integer = dr.GetOrdinal("City")
Dim Region As Integer = dr.GetOrdinal("Region")
Dim PostalCode As Integer = dr.GetOrdinal("PostalCode")
Dim Country As Integer = dr.GetOrdinal("Country")
Dim Phone As Integer = dr.GetOrdinal("Phone")
Dim Fax As Integer = dr.GetOrdinal("Fax")

While dr.Read()
    sb.AppendFormat("CustomerID = '{0}' ", dr(CustomerID))
    sb.AppendFormat("CompanyName = '{0}'", dr(CompanyName))
    sb.AppendFormat("ContactName = '{0} '", dr(ContactName))
    sb.AppendFormat("ContactTitle = '{0} '", dr(ContactTitle))
    sb.AppendFormat("Address = '{0}' ", dr(Address))
    sb.AppendFormat("City = '{0}' ", dr(City))
    sb.AppendFormat("Region = '{0}' ", dr(Region))
    sb.AppendFormat("PostalCode = '{0}' ", dr(PostalCode))
```

```
    sb.AppendFormat("Country = '{0}' ", dr(Country))
    sb.AppendFormat("Phone = '{0}' ", dr(Phone))
    sb.AppendFormat("Fax = '{0}'{1}", dr(Fax), vbCrLf)
End While
```

Yet again, we see a situation in which more code can actually be faster. The first example had less code but required more work at run time, whereas the last example minimized the actual amount of work done by paying a one-time, up-front penalty (looking up the column names) instead of paying for it each time through the loop.

Resource Management and *IDisposable*

Despite what some might think, resource management is still an important part of developing applications with Visual Basic .NET. You might assume that the garbage collector is supposed to do all of your cleanup and memory management for you, and for the most part that's true. The problem is that applications can have specific resource requirements that the garbage collector cannot anticipate. So even though the garbage collector can deal with most of the memory management aspects of your applications, in some situations you need to do some additional work.

The reason this can become an issue is the nondeterministic nature of garbage collection. There are no guarantees about when objects will be cleaned up—only that they'll be cleaned up eventually. This is a problem mainly when you mix very strict performance and scalability requirements with objects that allocate unmanaged system resources (file handles, GDI+ graphics devices, window handles, COM objects, and so forth). If you have an application or service that has to do a lot of work or deals with many simultaneous incoming requests, you might run out of system resources quickly if you don't dispose of them quickly. In other words, your application might get ahead of the garbage collection cleanup and exceed the available resource on the system before the garbage collector gets around to cleaning up the unused objects.

Obviously, this can be a real problem—not just the cleaning up, but identifying which objects need to be cleaned up immediately. The CLR solution to this problem is the *IDisposable* interface. *IDisposable* defines only one method: *IDisposable.Dispose*. The idea behind *IDisposable* is simple. If your object allocates unmanaged resources that persist for the lifetime of the object, you should implement *IDisposable*. This rule applies to your own code as well to the classes in the .NET Framework.

> **Note**   Nothing in Visual Basic .NET or the CLR forces you to clean up unmanaged resources in your own classes or to implement *IDisposable*. This is simply the recommended practice, and it ensures that other developers will know which classes require additional cleanup.

ASP.NET

I don't talk about ASP.NET much in this book, mainly because other books are dedicated to this topic and I want to provide content that's hard to find anywhere else. However, this is a perfectly good place to highlight some of the performance issues you might run into with ASP.NET. Let's face it: Web applications are playing an increasingly important role throughout the enterprise. And tracking down some of the performance issues—which are usually the fault of bad assumptions—can be a real pain.

ASP.NET Session State

Session state is probably one of the most misused technologies in ASP. It's one of those things that provides great convenience but causes most of the scalability and performance problems associated with Web applications. The situation is no different in ASP.NET. Session state has its advantages, but it's important to understand its limitations so you can avoid expensive mistakes. Here are three key guidelines:

- If you don't need it, don't use it.

- Don't store COM components in session state.

- Don't store objects with handles to fixed resources (such as database connections and local files) in session state.

STA COM Interop in ASP.NET

I mentioned in Chapter 4 that you can use the *AspCompat* page directive to play nice with COM components. You should follow certain rules to ensure that you don't shoot yourself in the foot, especially when you're dealing with single-threaded apartment (STA) COM components. COM interop always introduces some performance hit to your Visual Basic .NET applications, but there are special considerations for ASP.NET.

Fun with Construction

You should know by now that if you want to do COM interop with STA COM components in ASP.NET, you must enable the *AspCompat* page directive. But that doesn't tell the whole story. In fact, there's a really big catch. Even though the *AspCompat* directive ensures that your ASP.NET page *executes* on an STA thread, it does not ensure that it is *constructed* on an STA thread. This causes a huge problem when you instantiate COM objects in the constructor (either implicitly or explicitly)—it essentially creates a COM object on a multithreaded apartment (MTA) thread, not a STA thread. So the following is a really bad idea:

```
Imports MyLibrary

Public Class WebForm1
   Inherits System.Web.Page

   Dim cls As Class1
   Dim cls1 As New Class1() ' Implicit constructor call

   Public Sub New()
      MyBase.New()
      cls = New Class1() ' Explict constructor call
   End Sub

End Class
```

If you want to create a COM object, you should do so in the *Page_Load* event instead of the constructor. The *Page_Load* event is called after the page constructor and before the *Page_Render* event. If *AspCompat* is enabled, the *Page_Load* event is guaranteed to be executed on a STA thread. So you can consider the *Page_Load* event as a kind of proxy constructor. The previous example should look like the following instead:

```
Imports MyLibrary

Public Class WebForm1
   Inherits System.Web.Page

   Dim cls As Class1
   Dim cls1 As Class1

   Public Sub New()
      MyBase.New()
   End Sub

   Private Sub Page_Load(ByVal sender As System.Object, _
      ByVal e As System.EventArgs) Handles MyBase.Load
```

```
    ' This is the correct way to handle creating the COM objects
    cls = New Class1()
    cls1 = New Class1()
  End Sub

End Class
```

But, yet again, this doesn't tell the whole story. Creating ASP.NET pages in this way, using code-behind, makes it easy to control how your objects are created. But this is not the only way you can create pages. In fact, you don't have to use the code-behind model at all. Take a look at the following example, which is a self-contained ASPX page:

```
<@ Import Namespace="MyLibrary">

<SCRIPT LANGUAGE=VB RUNAT=SERVER>
    ' This is implicitly initialized during construction
    Dim cls1 As New Class1()
</SCRIPT>
<%
    ' This is initialized in the Page_Render method
    Dim cls2 As New Class1()
%>
```

You can see in the preceding example how easy it is to trip up and accidentally create a COM object in the page's constructor. You can still get around this using the *Page_Load* method:

```
<@ Import Namespace="MyLibrary">

<SCRIPT LANGUAGE=VB RUNAT=SERVER>
    Dim cls1 As Class1

    Private Sub Page_Load(ByVal sender As System.Object, _
        ByVal e As System.EventArgs) Handles MyBase.Load

        ' This is the correct way to handle creating the COM object
        cls1 = New Class1()
End Sub

</SCRIPT>
<%
    ' This is initialized in the Page_Render method
    Dim cls2 As New Class1()
%>
```

This all has to do with how the ASP.NET pages are built and then compiled. As you can see, it is possible to create a COM object in the constructor in three different ways—all of them bad.

COM, Session State, and the *Application* Object

What can I say here? Just don't do it. Don't use COM objects with session state or the *Application* object. COM does not mix with either. It's the surest way to toast your Web application's performance.

Loading the Right Runtime

It might surprise you to learn that two different runtimes are available to all .NET applications. The most commonly used version (and the default) is the workstation build of the runtime (which is contained in mscorwks.dll). The second version, which is optimized for server applications, is contained in mscorsvr.dll. These builds are designed to provide optimal performance for client applications and multiprocessor server applications. The server build of the runtime makes better use of multiple processors, enabling garbage collection to be done on all processors concurrently (in parallel).

Which runtime will your application use? All applications generated by Visual Basic .NET will use the workstation runtime, regardless of what system it is running on or what type of application (Windows Forms, Windows service, console application, and so forth). Only ASP.NET applications run under the server runtime (provided that the machine has four or more processors). Unfortunately, there is currently no way to tell Visual Basic .NET to use the server runtime instead of the default workstation runtime. The only way to tell it to use the server runtime is to host the CLR in your own wrapper. Unfortunately, this means you need to build a native Visual C++ skeleton application that does the work of hosting the CLR and launching your application with the setting you want.

CLR Hosting

Visual Basic .NET applications don't just "run" on a machine. First, the operating system has to look at the executable header. When you install the .NET runtime, the operating system learns to recognize managed applications. Then it invokes a default "wrapper" application that, among other things, creates an instance of the CLR (essentially "hosting" it) and instructs the CLR to run the application you attempted to run. This wrapper loads the workstation runtime and sets other default runtime properties.

There are distinct advantages to creating your own CLR host other than just loading the server version of the runtime. You can tweak various properties of the CLR, including the number of worker threads (as mentioned in Chapter 3) and completion threads. Among other things, you can:

- Specify the desired runtime version

- Optimize how assemblies are loaded

- Control the garbage collector behavior

More Info To really see what's possible when you use your own CLR host, you should consult the .NET Framework documentation. Look for the *CorBindToRuntimeEx* function as a starting point for your search.

The CLR is available via a set of COM interfaces, which means you can also host the CLR in a Visual Basic 6.0 application. But I don't recommend doing that. The most efficient way to host the CLR is with a native application. Hosting it in Visual Basic 6.0 would mean you'd be hosting a runtime within a runtime. That would be ugly, and your performance would probably be awful.

To help illustrate how to host the CLR with a native application, I built a sample application called SvrLoader (one of the sample files for this chapter) in Visual C++—it's the only C++ example in this entire book. It's pretty simple and does not support passing command-line parameters to the .NET executable, but you can add that at your leisure.

```cpp
// SvrLoader.cpp : Loads an application using the server runtime
//

#include "stdafx.h"
#include "mscoree.h"
#include "stdio.h"
#import "mscorlib.tlb" named_guids no_namespace raw_interfaces_only
no_implementation exclude("IID_IObjectHandle", "IObjectHandle")

const WCHAR APPLICATION_NAME[] = L"test.exe";
const DWORD MAX_WORKER_THREADS = 20;
const DWORD MAX_COMPLETION_THREADS = 30;

ICorRuntimeHost* Init()
{
    // Initialize COM
    HRESULT hrCOM = ::CoInitialize(NULL);
    if (FAILED(hrCOM))
```

```
    {
        printf("Unable to initialize COM.\n");
        return NULL;
    }

    LPWSTR pszFlavor = L"svr"; // use mscorsvr.dll

    // Pointer for the Runtime Interface
    ICorRuntimeHost* pCorHost = NULL;

    // We attempt to load the 'svr' Runtime here. If it is not available,
    // in the case of a workstation OS, then the 'wks' Runtime will be
    // loaded by default.
    HRESULT hr = CorBindToRuntimeEx(
                        NULL,
                        pszFlavor,
                        NULL,
                        CLSID_CorRuntimeHost,
                        IID_ICorRuntimeHost,
                        (void**)&pCorHost);

    if( FAILED(hr) )
    {
        printf("Unable to create the Hosting interface.\n");
        return NULL;
    }

    // Try to start the Runtime
    hr = pCorHost->Start();

    if( FAILED(hr) )
    {
        pCorHost->Release(); // Release the Runtime interface

        printf("Unable to instantiate COM+ Runtime.\n");
        return NULL;
    }
    return pCorHost;
}

void Shutdown( ICorRuntimeHost* pCorHost )
{
    if( pCorHost != NULL )
        pCorHost->Release();

    // Cleanup COM
    ::CoUninitialize();
}
```

```
BOOL SetMaxThreads()
{
   // set max threads
   ICorThreadpool *pTpool;
   HRESULT hr;
   hr = CoCreateInstance(CLSID_CorRuntimeHost,
                         NULL,
                         CLSCTX_INPROC_SERVER,
                         IID_ICorThreadpool,
                         (void**)&pTpool);
   if (FAILED(hr))
   {
      printf("Unable to acquire threadpool interface.\n");
      return FALSE;
   }

   hr = pTpool->CorSetMaxThreads(MAX_WORKER_THREADS,
                                 MAX_COMPLETION_THREADS);
   pTpool->Release();
   if( FAILED(hr) )
   {
      printf("Unable to set max threads for threadpool.\n");
      return FALSE;
   }
   return TRUE;
}

LONG ExecuteAssembly(ICorRuntimeHost* pCorHost)
{
   LONG retVal = 0;

   // get the default AppDomain
   IUnknown *pUnkAppDomain = NULL;
   HRESULT hr = pCorHost->GetDefaultDomain(&pUnkAppDomain);
   if( FAILED(hr) )
   {
      printf("Unable to acquire IUnknown interface for default domain.\n");
      return false;
   }

   // get the _AppDomain interface
   _AppDomain *pDomain = NULL;
   hr = pUnkAppDomain->QueryInterface(IID__AppDomain, (void**)&pDomain);
   if (FAILED(hr))
   {
      printf("Unable to acquire AppDomain interface.\n");
      pUnkAppDomain->Release();
      return 1;
   }
```

```
    // we no longer need pUnkAppDomain
    pUnkAppDomain->Release();

    // execute the specified assembly
    BSTR bstrAssemblyName = SysAllocString(APPLICATION_NAME);
    hr = pDomain->ExecuteAssembly_2(bstrAssemblyName, &retVal);
    pDomain->Release();

    // free assembly BSTR
    SysFreeString(bstrAssemblyName);

    if (FAILED(hr))
    {
        if (hr == 0x80070002)
        {
            printf("Unable to find managed assembly: %s", APPLICATION_NAME);
        }
        else
        {
            printf("Error executing assembly (hresult=0x%x).\n", hr);
        }
        return retVal;
    }
    return retVal;
}

//
int _tmain(int argc, _TCHAR* argv[])
{
    ICorRuntimeHost *pCorHost = NULL;
    pCorHost = Init();

    long retVal = 1;
    if( pCorHost != NULL )
    {
        if( SetMaxThreads() )
        {
            // Execute the assembly
            retVal = ExecuteAssembly( pCorHost );
        }
        // Stop the Runtime
        pCorHost->Stop();
    }
    // Clean up and exit
    Shutdown(pCorHost);

    return retVal;
}
```

You can enhance this code to your heart's content. For example, you can

- Create your own set of registry keys for your application's runtime hosting settings (which will allow you to tweak the application without rebuilding it)

- Allow passing command line arguments to the .NET application

If this is too much for you, don't worry about it. For most systems, the workstation runtime will always be loaded, regardless of which runtime is requested. Essentially, the workstation runtime will always outperform the server runtime on systems with one or two processors, so it won't let you choose otherwise. Loading the server runtime is most critical for server applications on systems with four or more processors. I've included this discussion simply for the sake of completeness. After all, this is a book about enterprise development.

Conclusion

This chapter is meant to serve as a hit list for performance issues. It's by no means comprehensive, but the discussion here should take care of the most common areas where developers can trip up. You can use this chapter as a reference as you build applications and also as a starting point for tracking down issues in existing applications.

Happy bug hunting.

More Info   The Visual Basic .NET documentation includes several valuable documents that discuss other performance issues.

12

The Art of
Performance Tuning

Building an application is one thing. Expecting it to perform flawlessly from the get-go is quite another. No applications I have developed or come across have demonstrated acceptable performance out of the gate. The complementary disciplines of *performance testing* and *performance tuning* must come into play. Performance testing is the process of generating reliable and consistent performance statistics for an application. Contrary to what you might think, performance testing is not about just getting simple performance statistics. It is about generating a performance profile for a wide range of user loads. Performance tuning is the process of using that information to divine the root cause of any performance deficiencies.

This chapter focuses on the performance issues you're likely to encounter with your applications and the process you need to go through to solve the problems. Unlike Chapter 11, which simply listed specific performance issues and recommendations, this chapter is all about locating the cause(s) of problems in your applications.

Performance Testing

Performance testing is a critical step in developing of any large-scale system. As applications are built, component upon component, performance problems abound because these components can interact in unintended ways. This might be surprising, given that you might have already functionally tested the system. Unfortunately, simple functional testing will not give you a complete picture of the interactions of components in your application. Only by performance-testing your application can you complete this picture. The additional stress on your application's infrastructure caused by performance testing will help you find most component interaction problems that would otherwise be missed in simple functional testing.

You can easily generate performance numbers for individual operations, and you can also look at the performance of individual methods in your application. You'll get raw performance numbers that you can use to optimize parts of an application. This information is valuable, but it doesn't tell the full story. It will not tell you how these components or methods interact when simultaneous calls are made. This is where stress testing comes into play.

A stress test simulates the activity of multiple simultaneous requests on a system. For example, if you want to test a Web application to determine the peak requests per second, you can do this only by simulating multiple clients all hitting the application at the same time. This will produce stress on your application and give you an indicator of the scalability of the system.

Tools of the Trade

Many tools are available for testing and analyzing an application, including built-in tools and third-party development tools. I'll introduce a number of useful and often critical tools for performance testing. Most are available on any Windows platform, but I'll occasionally mention third-party tools as well. I'll cover the following major sets of tools:

- Windows Task Manager
- Performance monitor
- Debuggers
- Profilers
- Performance and stress tools

Windows Task Manager

Windows Task Manager is a sort of one-stop shop for information about the health of your machine. It is also a great first-tier performance analysis tool. Windows Task Manager comes with every copy of Windows, it's always a click away, it doesn't interfere greatly with the system, and it provides a wealth of useful information in a compact and simple way.

You can bring up Windows Task Manager in three ways:

■   Press Ctrl+Shift+Esc

■   Right-click on the taskbar and choose Task Manager

■   Press Ctrl+Alt+Delete and click the Task Manager button

Figure 12-1 shows Windows Task Manager with the Performance tab selected. Quite a lot of information is available, including the CPU usage and memory statistics. The CPU usage information tells you quite a lot. The green lines on the graph indicate the amount of processor time actively being used. The red lines tell you how much of the processor's time is spent in the kernel (usually doing system tasks or I/O operations). If your system has more than one processor, you'll see a separate graph for each processor. This is handy for figuring out how well an application behaves on a multiprocessor system.

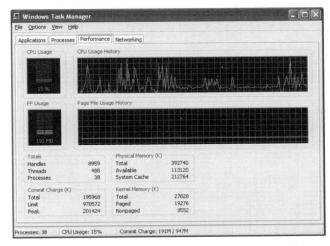

Figure 12-1   The Performance tab of Windows Task Manager.

The memory indicators can also help you understand how an application is using its memory. The graph shows a runtime history of the memory of the system (admittedly for a narrow window of time, but it's still quite handy).

Another useful feature comes in the form of the Networking tab, which is shown in Figure 12-2. This tab was added to Windows Task Manager in Windows XP. It offers a simple and concise view of how much of your network bandwidth is currently being consumed.

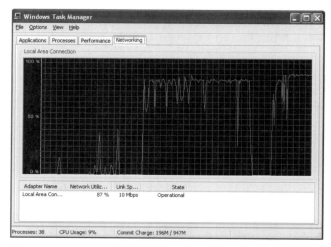

Figure 12-2   The Networking tab of Windows Task Manager.

I'll go into further detail about Windows Task Manager information later in the chapter.

Performance Monitor

Performance monitor is one of the most valuable monitoring tools available. The Performance monitor console, shown in Figure 12-3, allows you to view and log performance counters. You can use these counters to monitor the health of any machine on your network—you get information about the operating system, services, applications, network usage, and so forth.

The Performance monitor console is easily accessible. You can open it in three ways:

- Type **perfmon** at the command line or in the Run dialog box.

- From the Start menu, choose All Programs, Administrative Tools, and then click on the Performance icon.

- Open a saved Performance monitor MSC file.

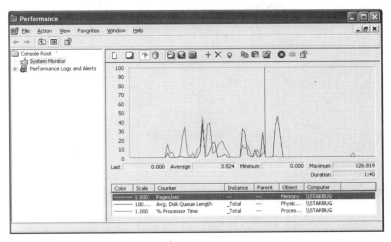

Figure 12-3   The Performance monitor.

The Performance monitor lets you do the following:

- Monitor many performance counters, both on the local machine and on other machines on your network, all within the same console

- Control the sampling rate for the counters you're monitoring.

- Adjust the display scale of any of the counters to make them easier to read.

- Set up performance counter logs. You can then sample a large series of data to disk over a period of time. You can analyze the results at your convenience. This is a more powerful option than just using the Performance monitor, which is limited to displaying only the latest 100 samples.

- Designate performance counter alerts. This allows you to monitor performance counters and cause some action to occur if any of your criteria are exceeded.

Every system comes with a number of performance counters already defined. Applications and services can also define their own counters, enabling anyone (with the appropriate permissions) to monitor various performance metrics of a system. Figure 12-4 shows the Add Counters dialog box from Performance monitor. You can select performance counters and also designate the name of the machine you want to monitor.

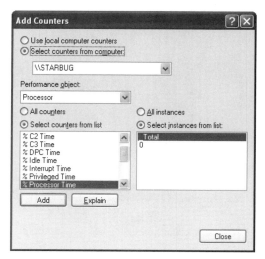

Figure 12-4   The Add Counters dialog box.

Popular performance counters include those for processor usage, memory, connections, throughput, response time, SQL Server, and ASP.NET. Appendix C and Appendix D describe many of the common built-in performance counters that you should be aware of.

Debuggers

Debuggers are designed to find functional problems with an application, but they can also serve other purposes. When you consider a debugger for performance testing, your first requirement should be that it be lightweight. My preference is to use a command-line debugger such as cordbg because it requires little overhead and tends to not interfere too severely with the running of the application. Attaching a debugger will change the performance characteristics of your application—usually slowing it down. Using a debugger that requires as few resources as possible (both memory and processor) will minimize the effect the debugger has on the system under test.

It might seem counterintuitive that attaching a debugger can occasionally result in a performance increase. How can this be? The answer is pretty simple: thread synchronization and shared resources. You might have a race condition in your application, and attaching the debugger will allow the system enough time to avoid the problem. For example, say your *WaitHandle.Wait* statements have too long a timeout. Shorting the timeout period might allow your application to avoid the race condition (or lengthen it).

> **Note**   Performance testing and tuning is an art. Strange things can happen when you apply familiar tools and techniques to performance analysis. Everything that happens is a potential clue, even if the result is counterintuitive.

Debuggers can tell you a lot of other things. If your application is throwing exceptions under stress, this can indicate that something is wrong. You can then catch one of the exceptions and discover where it's coming from in your code. However, in some situations exceptions are perfectly normal behavior—for example, the *ThreadAbortException* generated by the *Response.Redirect* method used in ASP.NET. A normal call to *Response.Redirect* will cause a *ThreadAbortException*. It turns out that this is the most efficient way to end the execution of an ASP.NET page, so it should not be considered an error. Unfortunately, this can be confusing to someone who is not used to seeing this.

A good debugger can also provide information about an application just by breaking into the code. Say your application is periodically hanging for 20 seconds and then resuming processing of requests. Using a debugger, you can break into the application during this down period and generate a list of the threads and their stack traces. This might provide some insight into where the application is getting stuck.

Profilers

Profilers allow you to see in-depth where the processing is spending time in your code. They locate the slowest or most time-consuming parts of your system and show you how often methods are called. Profiling tools are not a panacea, however. They will not tell you everything you need to know. When I start with an application that is not performing well, I typically go through the list of usual suspects (exceptions and database connection leaks) before I even think of bringing up the profiler.

You must also be deliberate about the use of your profiler. Depending on the features it supports, you might need to be sure that the numbers you're getting reflect what you think you're getting. I've seen situations in which the application startup time is so significant that it drowns out all other information, thereby skewing the profiling results. If you're aware of this possibility, however, you should be able to adjust your profiling strategy accordingly to omit bad or unhelpful data.

You can take advantage of the built-in .NET profiling features, but this is not for the faint-hearted. It requires a good knowledge of COM, stacks, and performance analysis. You must create a COM object that implements the *ICorProfilerCallback* COM interface, and then you must register the object with the common language runtime (CLR). If you're interested in pursuing this further, you can look at the two profiling samples included with the .NET Framework SDK. They can be found under the Program Files\Microsoft Visual Studio .NET\FrameworkSDK\Tool Developers Guide\Samples\profiler directory.

> **Note** If you're not in the mood to build your own profiling tool—and you're not alone on this, trust me—you can use a third-party tool to do the job. Look in stores that cater to developers, or search online for companies that develop .NET profiling tools.

Performance and Stress Tools

You have a lot of options when it comes to third-party performance and stress tools. You might be familiar with names such as Rational Software and other companies that provide testing suites. These tools vary in price rather dramatically—you'll need to find the best fit based on your budget.

These tools generally fall into two categories: user interface testing tools and Web testing tools. Microsoft does not provide a user interface testing tool. One popular choice is the Rational Visual Test tool, which also supports .NET Windows Forms.

Plenty of Web testing tools are available. Microsoft provides a free Web testing tool called the Web Application Stress Tool (WAS). You can use it to generate both performance and stress tests against a Web site. WAS suffers from some limitations, but these have been addressed in the Web testing tool provided with Visual Studio .NET Enterprise Edition, which is called Application Center Test (ACT). ACT provides a more feature-laden architecture that allows you to customize your tests and develop sophisticated testing that includes complex Web Forms and XML Web Services. Appendix B provides an overview of the ACT application.

> **Note** WAS is available through the Windows 2000 Internet Information Services Resource Kit. Alternatively, you can download it from the MSDN Web site at *http://webtool.rte.microsoft.com*.

Performance Test Planning

Planning your performance testing is extremely important. Going through a formal process helps you document the performance requirements for your application and sets general expectations. I suggest that you start with the following three steps:

1. Draw up a list of basic scenarios. These scenarios should be specific user operations that can be performed. (They might more appropriately be considered usage scenarios if your application does not have a user interface.) Show this list to the various people involved, and try to reach agreement on the nature of the scenarios. You can also get input on what other scenarios people might deem important. Organize this list based on the importance of these scenarios to the success of the product.

2. Build a testing framework to test and simulate various user loads on your application. You need a tool, custom or otherwise, that can give you accurate and consistent performance results. Ideally, you'll be able to use your simulation tool to implement your user scenarios so you can ultimately provide a constant level of stress on your application that accurately approximates real-world traffic.

3. Using your testing framework, get performance numbers for a single-user scenario as a benchmark. If your performance is acceptable for a single user, you'll have a reference to determine where your worst performance degradation occurs. These benchmark numbers will also allow you to compare different builds of an application. As the development team does more and more work, having a baseline to compare against will enable you to identify problems quickly. It will also allow you to validate fixes or optimizations in new builds.

You reduce the problem of testing a large system to a manageable size by breaking down all of the possible user actions into a set of well-defined and well-understood usage scenarios. This is a simple way to prioritize performance or scalability problems. If you simply walk through your classes and interfaces looking for performance issues, you're unlikely to improve the overall user experience. By focusing on specific user scenarios, you can directly affect the perceived performance of your system.

Furthermore, once you define these scenarios, you can break them down into suboperations. This process requires you to think through all of the parts of the application that are affected by your user scenarios. Once you have the set of low-level operations, you will have narrowed down where any performance problems can lie. You can use this as a checklist for your investigations.

Note   When you break down your scenarios, you'll typically identify common problem areas. If you're seeing similar performance degradation in these scenarios, common components are the likely source of the problem. On the other hand, if you have two scenarios with some common components but one has a performance problem and the other doesn't, it is quite likely that the problem does not reside in the common components.

Deciding on Acceptable Results

Generating performance numbers is all well and good, but you need a set of performance and scalability goals to compare them against. This is easier said than done. Anyone can tell you that more is always better. The more requests or users that a single system can handle, the lower the cost to the potential customer.

You first have to know what is unacceptable before you can tackle the problem. Consider the development of a Web-based online store. If the site must be able to handle, say, 1000 concurrent users and your application will support only 100 per server, you must put together a server farm of server boxes to handle the load. Because most server farms are designed to peak at about 80 percent usage (you always need a safety margin to handle the freak loads that happen from time to time), you'll need around 13 servers—an expensive proposition when a single server can run into the tens of thousands of dollars. If, on the other hand, you increase the application's ability to serve users by 20 percent, the company will need to buy only 11 machines (based on 120 peak users and each server running at 80 percent of capacity).

The value of supporting a higher user load is obvious, but where do you set the bar? I think it's reasonable for your design team to set some goals ahead of time—goals that are reasonable, conservative, and subject to modification. You ultimately cannot know what is possible until you have a working version of the application available to test. Then you can get real performance numbers and determine where your application needs to be. Granted, if you're lucky enough to have existing competitors or previous versions of your product, you can produce a reasonable set of performance goals. In all other cases, you'll have to wing it.

If your application is not meeting your performance objectives, you can spend the time to go through the necessary performance optimization steps, but you might reach a point at which further optimization is unlikely or unfeasible. It is not unreasonable to apply the 80-20 rule (also known as the Pareto principle, in which 20 percent of effort produces 80 percent of the results) to performance tuning. You should tune performance for your critical scenarios first. Then you should draw up a further list of items, in order of priority. Performance testing will not only give you a look at your application's performance (response times), but it will also provide insight into how well your application will scale as the user load increases.

Building a Performance Profile

I generally prefer to generate performance results under a wide variety of conditions. Figure 12-5 shows a scalability chart for simulated users vs. processors. You can see how you should expect an application's performance to increase as more processors are added to the system. This theoretical result is not universally true, but you should attempt to demonstrate your application's performance based on the processor, memory, or storage usage.

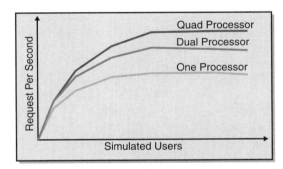

Figure 12-5   A theoretical scalability profile of a Web application.

Building such graphs helps you determine how your application is performing. An application should not generally exhibit erratic scaling behavior. You should target smooth scaling curves with a gentle performance degradation after the peak has been achieved.

Performance Tuning

Here's a cardinal rule of development: regardless of the amount of effort you put into the design and function testing, you'll always encounter surprises when it comes to performance. This is just a fact of life. No design is without its flaws, and performance problems are often due to mistaken assumptions made quite early in the development process.

Whenever I start a performance investigation, I do a "sanity check" to gauge potential problem areas. From there, I proceed to a more detailed investigation using various tools. If that doesn't get me what I need, I can go even further, using lower-level tools to debug and profile critical areas of the application. The general idea is to start at the top and work your way into more and more detailed checks. This allows you to avoid digging into the wrong places and wasting your time and energy on red herrings.

The Sanity Check

The sanity check is all about getting a feel for the application. This usually entails running the application under stress and seeing what effect this has on the system. In my experience, Windows Task Manager is usually sufficient for this. I look at processor usage, memory behavior, and network usage. All of these simple variables can give you insight into what's happening in the application.

Processor Usage

The processor usage profile gives you an indication of how the application is executing. The profile generated by an application under stress can be very telling. I break down this profile into several categories.

Pegged processor   In this situation, the processor is completely maxed out at 100 percent usage or close to 100 percent. This might or might not be a bad thing. It depends on what your user load is. If I were running a Web site and simulating 10 simultaneous users, I'd probably say this is a bad thing. However, if the load or tasks being accomplished are known to be computationally intensive (graphics rendering or something similar), this percentage could be unremarkable.

Single processor pegged (multiprocessor machine)   In a machine with more than one processor, Windows Task Manager will display the activity of all the active processors. If you get the impression from the data that your application is not fully utilizing the processors, you might see what looks like a high load that is constantly switching from one processor to another. In my experience, in this situation you'll notice that your processor usage will not greatly exceed what you'd expect from a single processor. (For example, on a two-processor system, the usage will not greatly exceed 50 percent, and on a four-processor system it will not greatly exceed 25 percent.) If you notice this pattern, you might want to look closely at how (if at all) your application implements threading.

Cyclic processor   If the processor usage profile is undulating, almost like a wave, the performance tests are probably not providing a sufficiently uniform stress load. However, this might also indicate a threading synchronization or shared resource issue in the application.

Erratic Processor   Abrupt transitions in the profile can indicate locked resources or shared resource issues such as a hot spot in a database. For example, SQL Server performs both page and row-locking features. If a single row is being updated, it is locked by the server; if multiple clients try to access that same record, you might experience a slowdown because of the locking behavior.

Stalled Processor   If hits are coming in but the machine doesn't seem to be doing anything, you might have a resource constraint or something might be blocking your threads. The most common culprit is a connection leak for your *SqlConnection* object pool—somewhere in the application code, the *Close* method is not being called. Or you might have a deadlock condition with your threads. If you have a shared resource that, for some reason, wasn't released (perhaps a thread terminated prematurely and didn't release a lock), you can easily cause your application to grind to a halt.

Memory Behavior

The behavior of an application's memory usage can indicate several things, but primarily resource usage—that is, is your application releasing resources properly, is it releasing resources too soon, and is there a possibility of reusing resources instead of constantly creating and disposing of them?

Stable memory usage   A stable memory size can be good or bad. If your application's memory commitment doesn't scale with increasing activity, your application might be starved for resources. (Perhaps you have a pool or several pools whose size needs to be increased.) On the other hand, the memory usage might be stable but excessive in size (hundreds of megabytes), which might point to inefficient resource usage (unnecessary allocation of large structures).

Undulating memory usage   If your memory usage keeps moving up and down, this might suggest an inefficient use of resources. An application might be constantly creating and disposing of objects that can be shared. Creating and destroying objects is expensive. Reusing objects rather than re-creating them can be a big performance and efficiency win. Consider whether the application makes appropriate use of object pooling.

Another possibility is that the application is performing unnecessary or large recursion operations. Recursion (a method invoking itself repeatedly) is a common programming practice that can enable simple and elegant solutions. But some problems might require too many function calls (or levels of recursion). Calling a method repeatedly takes up a fair bit of memory and time. If this is happening, you might need to go back and reimplement the offending code to use an iterative solution (loop structure) instead.

Ever-increasing memory usage   This trend means that some resources are not released explicitly. Remember that the runtime does not make any guarantees about garbage collection. If your application is allocating unmanaged memory through *PInvoke* or COM Interop that is not being released, you have a problem. Generally speaking, your application's memory should not continuously increase with a constant simulated user load. There is the inevitable shakeout period as the application is started up (where you'll see memory increasing as objects are allocated and pools are filled), the application should reach a point where everything stays more or less constant.

Network Usage

The network usage of the system is an important indicator of an application's performance. When you're testing a system, you can generally ignore any potential network issues because the environment is closely controlled.

Low   If you're not seeing a lot of network usage, your application might not be very chatty. On the other hand, if you'd expect to see more usage based on the user load, the problem might be due to resource sharing in the application itself.

High   Are you sending too much information across the wire? If your application uses Remoting or XML Web services, you might want to check to see what is being sent. Serialization of objects can lead to unintentionally sending an excessive amount of information.

That's All, Folks

Remember that any of these checks can be informative or not. Every application is different. Sometimes indicators that look suspect might just be part of your application's performance signature. You should not assume that there is a perfect profile for an application—there isn't. We all want applications that make the best use of the resources available, but sometimes the problem has less to do with the application than with the system it's running on. Also, results are often subject to interpretation, and investigations often proceed on hunches rather than solid data.

Attaching a Debugger

Now you have a qualitative feel for what an application is doing. But what you really need is something quantitative. In my experience, nothing says quantitative quite like a debugger. By attaching a debugger to a running process, you can quickly see if any unexpected exceptions are being generated. I usually start by running through each user scenario individually with the debugger attached. I try to pick up on any exceptions that shouldn't be happening. When the application is "clean" of any unwanted exceptions, I try running a set of user scenarios at a low-stress level. If you have major threading or resource sharing issues, they'll typically show up almost immediately when you apply any real stress to an application. Keeping the stress level low tends to keep things understandable without deluging the user with an avalanche of potentially duplicate exceptions.

Once you can reasonably say that the application is running fine at a low-stress level (I'd give it some time to make sure), it's time to ratchet things up. Increasing the stress level can help you discover any additional threading or resource sharing issues. Watch out for timeout exceptions, which can suggest that object requests waiting in queues are timing out before they can be processed. This is not uncommon with *SqlConnection* objects in the *Open* method, but you could also see timeout exceptions with your own pooled objects.

Performance Counters

Performance counters are the developer's best friend. You can access the same information in Windows Task Manager, but the Performance monitor console offers a greater wealth of information. You can monitor the size of your SQL connection pools, application response times, and so forth. You can also monitor any custom performance counters that your application makes available.

Monitoring the performance counters in conjunction with using the debugger can allow you to peek into your application when strange things appear to be happening. I already mentioned the example of a stalled application (breaking in and viewing the state of all of the application's threads). There are many other conditions where this is useful. Remember to see Appendix C and Appendix D for performance counters that might be of use to you.

Low-Level Analysis

Low-level performance analysis is usually my last resort—for several reasons, not least of which is that it's the most involved part of all performance tuning. When you get down to the low-level analysis, you're talking about using application profiling and trace and debug statements to track down performance issues. You might also use specialized custom performance counters provided by your application. And you might also need to use a low-level debugger such as WinDbg to view inactive threads.

Profiling is probably the one of the best low-level tools you can use. I've found it to be invaluable in finding hot spots in an application. If an application is not doing what you expect, you can use a profiling tool to find out a lot of information about an application—possibly more that you would ever want to know.

Conclusion

Performance analysis and tuning can be more art than science. The challenge is to tease out the information from your application that will give you insight into what the problems are. Believe me, it's not always easy. By using a well-defined and methodical process to track down issues, you can more easily divine their root causes. This process can include implementing your own set of performance counters to directly track your application's performance instead of relying completely on the built-in counters.

Appendix A

Using Visual Basic .NET in a Multideveloper Environment

The Microsoft Visual Studio .NET Integrated Development Environment (IDE) provides a whole new set of tools to facilitate team development. Theoretically, you don't need to purchase Visual Studio .NET just to do .NET development (you can use the command-line compilers that come with the Microsoft .NET Framework SDK instead), but Visual Studio provides a rich development environment that can dramatically increase your productivity and offers tools to help manage your project's complexity. Team development invites a whole cornucopia of management, coordination, and technical challenges. Visual Studio .NET can help. It is by far the most powerful development environment to come out of Microsoft, and its toolset is nothing to sniff at.

Architecture and Design Issues

It's not unheard of for developers to just jump in and write code—a sort of design-as-you-go approach. Such enthusiasm is laudable, but it rarely leads to applications that are maintainable or extensible. It's best to view the development process as only a small part of a much larger, system-level approach.

"Design" can mean many things in software development. When you write a function, you're effectively designing that function's implementation. At a higher level, someone had to design the function's interface (access level, name, parameters, and return values) as a part of the larger software system. Moving further out, someone had to sit down and draw up the system's functional and feature requirements. All of these tiers of design contribute to the overall success of any project. Failure to adequately design at any level will lead to problems that put the budget, schedule, and ultimate success of a project at risk.

More Info   I'll touch only briefly on the software development process, so you might want to consult *Code Complete* by Steve McConnell (Microsoft Press, 1993) for more information. This classic book details a process-oriented approach to software development.

Before you write even a single line of code, you should have an appropriate architecture and have as much of your design detailed as possible. The more time you spend in the design phase, the less time you'll spend fixing design-related bugs later. Keep in mind a fundamental truth of software development: bugs cost less to fix the sooner they're found.

Analyzing Business Requirements

Before you start on any project, you should clearly define the target market and what problem you're trying to solve. Understanding the customer problem is the key to success, not code. No matter how well the code is written or how efficient it is, it won't be of any use if it doesn't help solve the customer's business problem. Many a project has failed because the designers simply didn't understand what they were trying to achieve. You should design with extensibility in mind so the application can accommodate the customer's changing needs. A good market assessment, with help from folks in the field, can be critical to determining your application's business requirements.

Defining the Technical Architecture for a Project

The design process can be crudely broken down into two phases: logical design and physical design. Logical design is when you logically organize and segment your application into assemblies, namespaces, and classes. The process is about strictly enforcing architectural integrity. Physical design refers to how components of the application are physically separated. In this case, you must think in terms of implementing physically tiered architectures.

Visual Studio .NET Enterprise Architect

Visual Studio .NET does not provide anything to help you through the business requirements phase, but it has a plethora of tools to help you through the physical and logical design phases. It also offers tools to assist with other aspects of team development, including

■   Visio for Enterprise Architects (for Unified Modeling Language [UML] code modeling)

■   Enterprise templates (for defining project templates and development policies)

■   Microsoft Visual SourceSafe (for source control)

Most of the features described in following sections require the installation of Visual Studio .NET Enterprise Architect, Visual SourceSafe, and the Visio product that accompanies Visual Studio .NET. If you don't have these installed, it might be a little tough to follow along.

Note   If, when you install Visual SourceSafe, you select the Custom option, be sure to select the Enable SourceSafe Integration option.

Making the Most of Visual Studio .NET

Lest you get bored by repeatedly hearing about the "powerful tools" included with Visual Studio .NET Enterprise Architect, it's time you actually saw some of them.

Modeling Tools

Visual Studio .NET Enterprise Architect comes with Visio for Enterprise Architects, which allows you to do UML code modeling and helps you generate application architecture and functional models. Visio is a powerful tool, but it's not for the faint of heart. UML takes a significant investment of time just to learn, let alone master. Visual Studio tries to make this process easier and somewhat more natural, however.

When you design your application, it can be worthwhile to create skeleton code—to essentially define the object interfaces and hierarchy. If you take this route, you can translate your code into UML models that you can then enhance to your heart's content. This process is referred to as *reverse-engineering*. Figure A-1 shows how to use the Reverse Engineering command.

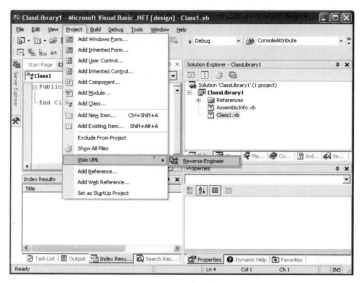

Figure A-1   The UML Reverse Engineer command.

Using Visual Studio in conjunction with Visio, you can reverse-engineer existing code into UML diagrams and generate new code in the language of your choice from UML diagrams. Check out the documentation that accompanies Visio to find out more about what you can do.

More Info   For more information about UML and resources to help you understand the process, check out the Rational Web site's UML Resource Center (*http://www.rational.com/uml/index.jsp*).

Enterprise Templates

Enterprise templates allow you to define project and architecture templates. Using templates, system architects can define the initial structure of a complex project. Creating templates is easy—you can do it from the New Project dialog box (shown in Figure A-2). Just select Enterprise Template Project in the list of templates. Figure A-2 also shows the default templates that are available right out of the box:

■   Visual Basic Simple Distributed Application

■   Visual Basic Distributed Application

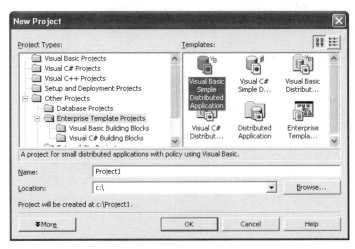

Figure A-2   Creating a new project based on an enterprise template.

Delving further, under the Visual Basic Building Blocks folder, you'll also find components for various types of systems, including the following project types:

- Business Facade
- Business Rules
- Data Access
- System
- ASP.NET Web Service
- WebUI
- WinUI

One difficulty that development teams face when they develop multitier applications is the sheer number of items (classes, assemblies, and references) that can be added to projects. Template Definition Language (TDL) provides a way to define a *policy* to enforce with enterprise templates. A policy can filter the items available to build each portion of the application, leaving out unneeded features (methods, properties, and so forth) that provide no advantage or might create significant problems.

Each template can be assigned a policy, and subtemplates can be assigned different policies. You can exclude objects, control the use of Visual Studio menu commands, and allow and disallow the addition of specific items to projects. The TDL files are formatted in XML and can be easily edited from Visual Studio .NET. The following is a excerpt from one of the default templates:

```
<ELEMENT>
    <ID>elementName</ID>
    <CONTEXT>
        <CTXTKEYWORD>HelpKeyword1</CTXTKEYWORD>
        <CTXTATTRIBUTE>
            <NAME>Product</NAME>
            <VALUE>VS</VALUE>
        </CTXTATTRIBUTE>
    </CONTEXT>
    <IDENTIFIERS>
        <IDENTIFIER>
            <TYPE>identifierType</TYPE>
            <IDENTIFIERDATA>
                <NAME>identifierName</NAME>
                <VALUE>identifierValue</VALUE>
            </IDENTIFIERDATA>
        </IDENTIFIER>
    </IDENTIFIERS>
    <PROTOTYPES>
        <PROTOTYPE>[VB]\VBProjects\WizardName.vsz</PROTOTYPE>
        <PROTOTYPE>[VB]\VBProjects\FileName.ext</PROTOTYPE>
    </PROTOTYPES>
    <CONSTRAINTS>
        <PROPERTYCONSTRAINTS>
            <PROPERTYCONSTRAINT>
                <NAME>propertyName</NAME>
                <READONLY>1</READONLY>
                <DEFAULT> defValue</DEFAULT>
                <MINVALUE>0</MINVALUE>
                <MAXVALUE> 9999</MAXVALUE>
            </PROPERTYCONSTRAINT>
        </PROPERTYCONSTRAINTS>
        <MENUCONSTRAINTS>
            <MENUCONSTRAINT>
                <ID>menuProject.AddUserControl</ID>
                <ENABLED> 0</ENABLED>
            </MENUCONSTRAINT>
        </MENUCONSTRAINTS>
        <TOOLBOXCONSTRAINTS>
            <TOOLBOXCONSTRAINT>
                <ID>tboxDataSQLConnection</ID>
                <ENABLED> 0</ENABLED>
            </TOOLBOXCONSTRAINT>
        </TOOLBOXCONSTRAINTS>
    </CONSTRAINTS>
    <ELEMENTSET>
        <DEFAULTACTION>EXCLUDE</DEFAULTACTION>
        <ORDER> INCLUDEEXCLUDE</ORDER>
```

```
<INCLUDE>elementName</INCLUDE>
<INCLUDE> categoryName</INCLUDE>
<EXCLUDE>elementExpression</EXCLUDE>
<CONSTRAINTS>
    <PROPERTYCONSTRAINTS>
        <PROPERTYCONSTRAINT>
            <NAME>propertyName</NAME>
            <READONLY> 1</READONLY>
            <DEFAULT>defValue</DEFAULT>
            <MINVALUE> 0</MINVALUE>
            <MAXVALUE>9999</MAXVALUE>
        </PROPERTYCONSTRAINT>
    </PROPERTYCONSTRAINTS>
    <MENUCONSTRAINTS>
        <MENUCONSTRAINT>
            <ID>menuProject.AddUserControl</ID>
            <ENABLED>0</ENABLED>
        </MENUCONSTRAINT>
    </MENUCONSTRAINTS>
    <TOOLBOXCONSTRAINTS>
        <TOOLBOXCONSTRAINT>
            <ID>tboxDataSQLConnection</ID>
            <ENABLED>0</ENABLED>
        </TOOLBOXCONSTRAINT>
    </TOOLBOXCONSTRAINTS>
</CONSTRAINTS>
<MEMBERCONSTRAINTS>
    <MEMBERCONSTRAINT>
        <ID>memberID</ID>
        <PROPERTYCONSTRAINTS>
            <PROPERTYCONSTRAINT>
                <NAME>propertyName</NAME>
                <READONLY>1</READONLY>
                <DEFAULT> defValue</DEFAULT>
                <MINVALUE>0</MINVALUE>
                <MAXVALUE> 9999</MAXVALUE>
            </PROPERTYCONSTRAINT>
        </PROPERTYCONSTRAINTS>
        <MENUCONSTRAINTS>
            <MENUCONSTRAINT>
                <ID>menuProject.AddUserControl</ID>
                <ENABLED> 0</ENABLED>
            </MENUCONSTRAINT>
        </MENUCONSTRAINTS>
    </MEMBERCONSTRAINT>
</MEMBERCONSTRAINTS>
    </ELEMENTSET>
</ELEMENT>
```

As you can see, interesting possibilities are available for controlling how developers can use the Visual Studio IDE. By limiting what can be used, you can ensure a greater degree of consistency within your projects.

More Info   The help files that accompany Visual Studio provide much more detail on how to use these policy files. The example here shows all of the available options, but typical entries might use only a subset of these features.

Visual SourceSafe and Source Control

Source control is important for any serious development project and is crucial in a multideveloper project. The ability to track file changes and reverse changes is a significant advantage as more people are added to projects. We all make mistakes from time to time, and the chances that mistakes will be made grows exponentially as more people become involved. Microsoft provides an integrated solution for source control called Visual SourceSafe.

You're probably familiar with Visual SourceSafe—it's been around for years. Visual SourceSafe has been an excellent single-developer solution and, with a little help, can work well in a multiple-developer situation. Visual Studio .NET provides higher-level integration with Visual SourceSafe than Visual Studio ever has in the past. A primary benefit of the unified IDE is that the source control mechanism is consistent across projects and solutions. There are three main issues that you need to worry about:

- Adding your projects to the source control repository

- Creating a project from the source control repository

- Exclusive checkouts that prevent simultaneous development

- Project organization

Adding a Project to the Source Control Repository

For simple projects, you don't need to do anything special to place a project under source control. You can right-click on the project or solution to place the entire solution under source control (as shown in Figure A-3). Any additional projects that you create or add to the solution will then be added to Visual SourceSafe as well.

Figure A-3   Adding a project to the source control repository.

You might have to get a little creative to best manage your Visual Source-Safe project hierarchy. Adding separate solutions to the source control repository can lead to frustrating attempts to maintain your project hierarchies. I've found that a good approach is to create a single solution that represents the entire development project. When you need to add a code project to the repository, open the solution file and add the project. This will ensure that the newly added project ends up as a subproject of the solution file and as a peer to the other existing projects.

You'll have to experiment a little with Visual SourceSafe to understand what I'm saying, but creating a single, master solution is generally a good strategy.

Creating a Project from the Source Control Repository

Creating a project from the source control repository is just as easy as adding a project. The File menu's Source Control submenu has a host of commands related to source control, including ones for opening a project or a solution from the source control repository (as shown in Figure A-4).

Figure A-4   Opening a solution from the source control repository.

You have several options when it comes to individual projects. You can open the entire solution stored in Visual SourceSafe, or you can be more selective. If you create additional projects that are not already in the source control repository, you can add projects to that solution (using the Add Project From Source Control option) on a project-by-project basis.

Exclusive Checkouts

Visual SourceSafe can be a fairly flexible source control system, but is not set up by default to handle multideveloper development very well. First, Visual SourceSafe defaults to allowing only exclusive file checkouts. This prevents other developers from making modifications to files if any one developer already has it checked out. Of course, there's a way around this problem. Your Visual SourceSafe administrator must open the database with the Administration tool and, in the SourceSafe Options dialog box (shown in Figure A-5), select the Allow Multiple Checkouts option.

Figure A-5   The Visual SourceSafe database administrator's
SourceSafe Options dialog box.

More than one developer can then check out the same file. If a file is checked in with conflicting changes, the developer checking in the overlapping code must merge his changes with the version in Visual SourceSafe. The merging tool, built into Visual SourceSafe, allows you to see where any conflicts in the code occur. This tool is automatically brought up when conflicting changes have been checked into the database. If you're already familiar with the interface provided by WinDiff (a Windows file comparison tool that is also included with the Visual Studio .NET installation but is not on by default), you'll be instantly comfortable with this tool. As a part of the check-in process, you must accept or reject certain changes. This allows you to merge the contents of two separate files and preserve the correct changes. You must do this with care because accepting or rejecting the wrong change can cause problems. Not to worry, though—you can always roll back any changes you might have made.

Managing Web Projects

Managing the development of Web projects (ASP.NET or Web services) can be challenging. There are three main ways that ASP.NET applications can use Visual Studio .NET:

- The complete application can be developed on the developers' local machines.

- Developers can use a common server but have different virtual roots for their pages.

- Developers can use a common Web server with same vroot.

The first method is the recommend approach because when a developer debugs a project on a Web server, the debugger locks the assemblies on that server. This presents a real problem when you have other active developers making changes or attempting to build their components. Local development with Visual SourceSafe makes the process more manageable. You simply have to be sure that you have the latest source code before you check in your changes (to reduce the possibility of introducing incompatible code into the system).

Managing Dependencies

Dependencies take many forms in Visual Basic .NET applications, and managing those dependencies can be a challenge. For the most part, dependencies take the form of references: project, assembly, and Web references. Wherever possible, you should use project references rather than file references. Project references help the Visual Studio .NET build system resolve project dependencies and build your application. They also help you avoid circular references and use the appropriate configuration settings (debug or retail) for all projects. When you use file references, the individual project files store the relative path to the assembly if the referenced assembly is from a local drive, and they store the complete path if the assembly is located on a network share.

Every assembly reference has a property called *Copy Local*. The default is *False* for components that exist in the Global Assembly Cache (GAC) and *true* for all other assemblies. For the most part, you shouldn't need to change these settings. When *Copy Local* is *True*, Visual Studio will automatically copy the referenced assemblies (and any assemblies it might depend on) to the project's bin folder. The advantage of this is that every time a project is built, Visual Studio will automatically check the date and time stamp for each referenced assembly and, if the assembly has been modified, copy it locally to the bin directory.

> **Warning**   You should never directly add a *Copy Local* reference to components that exist in the GAC. There should ever be only a single instance of an assembly registered in the GAC. Copying locally would produce applications that are not running with the latest version of those assemblies, potentially opening up your applications to security or performance problems.

If you have multiple solutions and have to use file references, you can store the assemblies in a UNC path (or you can use a common mapped drive). The advantage of picking up file references from a common build server is that your project will always have the latest assembly and the drive letter or UNC path will work from any development machine. The disadvantage is that you have no control over how and when you pick up the latest assembly, and that can break your application. Also, the build server must always be available, which prevents you from working off line. If using references from a build server is too problematic for your needs, you can periodically copy stable builds locally.

Database Dependencies

It is not uncommon for developers to use a development, or staging, database server. To make it easier to work within your own environment, you can take advantage of the app.config configuration file. A production app.config might declare a configuration file like this:

```
<configuration>
 <appSettings file="developer.config">
  <add key="databaseConnection"
     value="server=ProductionDatabase;Integrated Security=SSPI;database=
     myDatabase"/>
 </appSettings>
</configuration>
```

An alternative configuration file, developer.config, might contain the following database connection value:

```
<appSettings>
  <add key="databaseConnection"
     value="server=(local);Integrated Security=SSPI;database=
     myDatabase "/>
 </appSettings>
```

The code in your application to retrieve the configuration information might look like this:

```
Private Function getDatabaseConnectoin() As String
    Return ConfigurationSettings.AppSettings("databaseConnection")
End Function
```

COM Dependencies

As explained in Chapter 4, you should use primary Interop assemblies (PIAs) whenever possible. When it is not possible, you should manually generate an interop assembly using Visual Studio, by adding a COM reference to your project, or using the TlbImp utility, and then you should be sure that all developers are using the same version of the Interop assembly. Note that the COM type library for the component must exist on all developer machines; otherwise, there will be problems. Including the interop assemblies only on the developer machines is not sufficient—the COM component itself must be registered on each machine that the application is intended to run on.

Customizing the Start Page

Anyone who has launched Visual Studio .NET has seen the Start page (shown in Figure A-6). But did you know that you can customize it? In fact, you can replace it altogether. This can be helpful for managing your projects and aiding communication between team members. You can also use it to provide common documentation or reference materials.

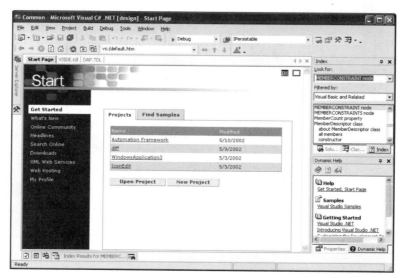

Figure A-6   The Visual Studio .NET Start page.

Making the change is simple. From the Tools menu, choose Options. In the Options dialog box, select the Web Browser option (as shown in Figure A-7). You can then alter both the Home page and the Search page.

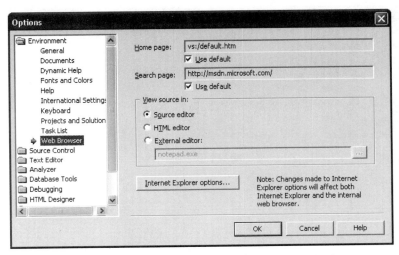

Figure A-7   The Web browser options in the Options dialog box.

Creating a custom page is absurdly simple. Creating a good one, on the other hand, is a little more challenging. (Seasoned Web developers will appreciate what I'm saying). To help demonstrate how easy the process is, I created my own simple, and ugly, Start page. I created a file called c:\Start.htm and tossed in the following HTML:

```
<HTML>
<HEAD>
<TITLE>TEST</TITLE>
</HEAD>
<BODY BGCOLOR="CYAN">
<H3>Hello</H3>
<IFRAME SRC="vs:/default.htm" WIDTH=500 HEIGHT=250></IFRAME>
</BODY>
</HTML>
```

I then went back to the Visual Studio Options dialog box and gave the Home page the same path as my new Start page. That's it. Now I have a really hideous Start page (as shown in Figure A-8).

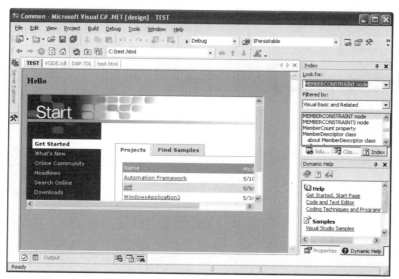

Figure A-8   An ugly custom Start page.

That pretty much wraps things up. You'll find as you delve deeper into the collaborative features provided by Visual Studio .NET that they give you rather sophisticated control over projects, policies, and design methodologies. Going forward, you should consider how you can leverage some or all of these features in your own projects. Bringing order out of chaos is well worth the effort!

Appendix B

Getting Started with Application Center Test

Application Center Test (ACT) is a powerful new tool that ships with Microsoft Visual Studio .NET Enterprise Edition (Developer and Architect). You use it to create and run performance tests against Web applications. Those of you who are familiar with the history of Microsoft performance tools might have encountered the Web Application Stress (WAS) tool. ACT is a follow-up product to WAS. The WAS tool was useful because it allowed a user to record a test scenario by simply navigating a Web site. This made it possible to create and run simple performance tests. But WAS tended to fall short when you needed more advanced testing behavior. ACT continues in the tradition of making test creation easy while adding significant new functionality that removes many of the limitations of WAS.

Note   ACT is not a standalone product. It ships with Microsoft Visual Studio Enterprise Edition (Developer and Architect) and cannot be obtained in any other way. This is in contrast to WAS, which was, and still is, available for free on the MSDN Web site.

The heart of ACT is the Active Test Script (ATS) Object Model. All recorded tests are translated into a set of Visual Basic Script (VBS) methods, which you can then customize to your heart's content. You can record scripts that will produce tests written in VBS, or you can create your own scripts from scratch in

VBS or JScript. The recording process does so much for you that you're unlikely to use JScript to develop your tests. (Why create more work for yourself?)

Because the ACT tests use a script engine, you gain a great deal of flexibility. ACT effectively lifts most functional limitations on the capabilities of your test scripts. You can, for example, create COM objects and additional utilities all from within ACT. This essentially enables you to develop tests that can serve a functional purpose as well as test for performance and stress. You can use ACT to test all sorts of Web applications, from straight HTML to ASP.NET and from Web Forms to Web services. As long as what you want to test talks HTTP, ACT can do the job.

This appendix introduces the ACT application and offers some common, helpful methods that you might want to use in your own ACT tests. The appendix concludes with a quick reference to the ACT Test Object Model.

An Overview of ACT

Once you install ACT with Visual Studio .NET, you can use it in two different ways. ACT is provided as a standalone application, under the Visual Studio .NET Programs folder, and you can also use it from within Visual Studio .NET. You can create an ACT project in Visual Studio .NET—you save it in the Application Center Test Projects folder, as shown in the New Project dialog box in Figure B-1—and you can add an existing ACT project to a Visual Studio .NET solution. It is really very flexible. For the most part, I'll focus on using ACT as a standalone application. You can figure out for yourself how to use it in Visual Studio .NET—there's not much to it.

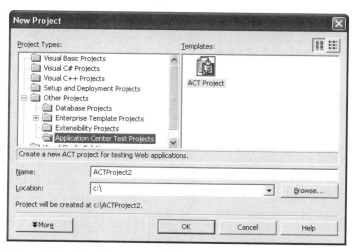

Figure B-1   Creating a new ACT project in Visual Studio .NET.

Using the Standalone Version of ACT

The standalone version of ACT offers by far the most flexibility. (See Figure B-2.) The interface is clean and uncluttered, and the application itself is designed using an Explorer metaphor. On the left is a tree view that displays the current project name, all tests contained within the project, and the results node. To the right is the content area.

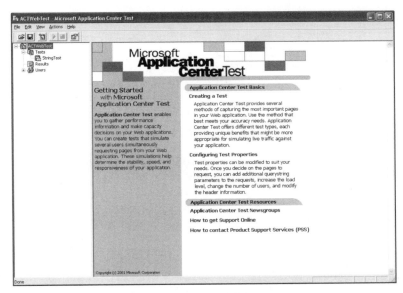

Figure B-2   The standalone version of ACT.

You can select nodes in the tree to view the results, test contents (essentially the script code), and test results. You can view the test properties by selecting a node and clicking the Properties toolbar button (or by right-clicking the node and choosing Properties from the shortcut menu). Figure B-3 shows some of the settings that you can manipulate through the Properties window. These are all common settings that you can probably figure out for yourself.

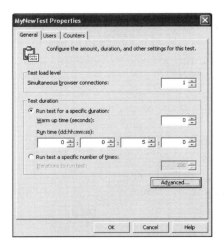

Figure B-3 The ACT Test Properties window.

To create a new test, you click the New Test toolbar button to start a wizard (shown in Figure B-4) that allows you to create a blank test or a recorded test. You'll generally want to select a recorded test because starting from scratch is usually too painful. Recording a test is simple. You'll be presented with a dialog box that has a Start Recording button. Clicking this button causes a blank Microsoft Internet Explorer browser window to appear. Type the URL for the site you want to test, and you're off. All you need to do is navigate to the areas of interest, play around with the pages as necessary (mainly to test the features you're interested in), and then close the browser. The recording dialog box will still be there waiting for you, but you'll notice that the text box containing the request details will have a bunch of entries in it. Click Stop Recording and continue with the wizard—the only thing left to do is name the test.

Figure B-4   The ACT New Test Wizard.

When you finish with the New Test Wizard, ACT will open your new test and display it in the content window (as shown in Figure B-5). You'll see the script code in the larger panel and a spot where you can provide descriptive information about your test (a notes field). This is the typical view you'll have when you view and edit tests from within ACT—it's a notepad-like editing experience.

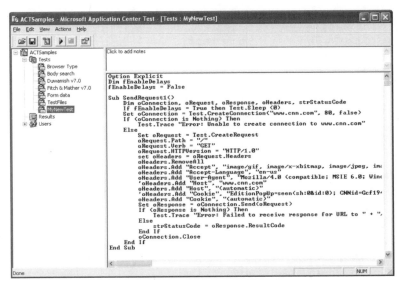

Figure B-5   What your new ACT test might look like.

> **Note** If you want a little more in the way of editing help, you can add the ACT project to a Visual Studio .NET solution. You can then edit the test file in the IDE, which has much more sophisticated editing features (but, alas, no IntelliSense).

After you create a new test, you might want to rerun it to make sure it really works. Select your new test in the tree view and click the Start toolbar button. You'll see the dialog box similar to the one shown in Figure B-6. If you don't see the graph, click the Show Details button. This particular graph is really impressive—it allows you to watch the performance of your site in real time. It's also fun to see what happens when you start making changes to your application while the test is running. (You can really make the requests-per-second (RPS) graph jump around.)

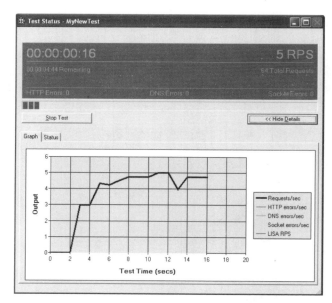

Figure B-6 The Test Status dialog box with a real-time graph.

Once the test has completed, you'll definitely want to check out the results. ACT makes this easy. Select the Results node in the tree to bring up the results viewer in the content window (as shown in Figure B-7). From here, you can look at all of the results from all of the tests run within your project. ACT provides a number of graphs and other ways to view the results (from an overall set of test statistics all the way down to the individual request level). ACT allows you to combine graphs across different reports for the same test. This is helpful when you're trying to gauge the effect of code changes to your application.

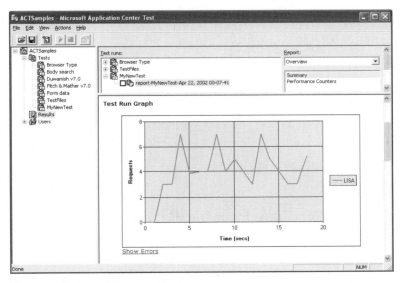

Figure B-7   The ACT Results view.

For more information, consult the documentation provided with ACT. There's a lot of good information there.

Useful Techniques for Customizing ACT Tests

The following sections offer a quick reference to a few common tasks that you'll most likely want to do in your ACT test once you've decided that you want to customize it. You can easily use these functions in your own tests.

Inserting Random Delay into Your Tests

Using random delays is an important part of performance testing. It allows the test to provide a more even loading of a site under test. Without adding delays, you'd generate many simultaneous, and possibly identical, requests. This would be an unrealistic way to stress a site and would increase the possibility of hitting a "hot spot" in your database, leading you to chase down performance "bugs" that are not very interesting. (Who cares if your application performs poorly if a single user generates the same 1000 requests simultaneously? It's just not realistic.)

Spreading out your requests provides a more realistic stimulus for your application. The following code sample demonstrates how you can implement a sub that produces a random delay in a test (within certain boundaries specified by the *MIN_DELAY* and *MAX_DELAY* constants).

```
Const MAX_DELAY = 500
Const MIN_DELAY = 0


Dim InitRand
Sub Delay()
   If InitRand Then
      Randomize()
      InitRand = false
   End If

   Test.Sleep ((MAX_DELAY - MIN_DELAY) * Rnd()) + MIN_DELAY
End Sub
```

Extracting ASP.NET *ViewState* from the *Response* Object

ViewState is an important component of ASP.NET *WebForm* objects. The *ViewState* is contained in the HTML of a Web page within a hidden form field with the name *__VIEWSTATE*. The following code shows you how to extract the *ViewState* from the *Response* object. You can then use this information when you create a post-back request to the *WebForm*.

```
Function GetViewState(oResponse)
   Dim Pos, PosStart, PosEnd

   If (oResponse Is Nothing) Then
      Test.Trace "The response was Nothing" & vbcrlf
   Else
      Pos = InStr(oResponse.Body, "__VIEWSTATE")
      If Pos > 0 Then
         PosStart = InStr(Pos, oResponse.Body, "value="""")
         PosStart = PosStart + Len ("value="""")
         PosEnd = InStr(PosStart, oResponse.Body, """")
         GetViewState = Mid(oResponse.Body, PosStart, PosEnd - PosStart)
      End If
   End If
End Sub
```

Appending ASP.NET *ViewState* to a Request

The following code sample shows you how to insert the *ViewState* into the contents of the *Request* object:

```
Sub SetViewState(oRequest, viewState)
   If (oRequest Is Nothing) Then
      Test.Trace "The request object was Nothing" & vbcrlf
   Else
      oRequest.Body = oRequest.Body & vbcrlf & _
                      "__VIEWSTATE=" & viewState & vbcrlf
   End If
End Sub
```

The ACT Test Object Model

Building your own tests from scratch would be a lot of work, for two simple reasons: the ACT test development environment does not support IDE niceties such as IntelliSense, which we all know and love, and Web tests can get really complicated. The best way to develop your own tests is to record your test scripts first and then customize them.

Of course, to do all of that, you need to become familiar with the ACT Test Object Model, which is depicted in Figure B-8. This isn't really all that difficult. The classes and relationships are well designed—you just need some time to get familiar with them. Believe me, the time spent on learning this will pay for itself in the end.

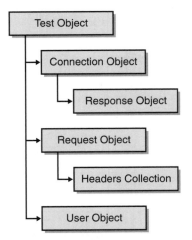

Figure B-8   The ACT Test Object Model.

Tables B-1 through B-4 provide a quick reference to the ACT Test Object Model objects shown in Figure B-8.

Table B-1
Methods and Property of the *Test* Object

Method	Description
CreateConnection	Creates a new connection to the server.
CreateRequest	Creates a new *Request* object that can be sent using the *Connection.Send* method.
GetCurrentUser	Gets the current user for the test.
GetGlobalIndex	Gets the value of a global index variable that is stored between iterations of the test.
GetGlobalVariable	Gets a previously assigned global variable or creates a new one if necessary.
GetNextUser	Gets the next user object for the test and makes it the active account.
IncrementGlobalIndex	Increments or decrements the value of a global index variable.
SendRequest	Sends a URL request to the server and returns the server response.
SetGlobalIndex	Sets the value of a global index variable that is stored between iterations of the test.
SetGlobalVariable	Sets a global variable that is stored between iterations of the test.
Sleep	Pauses the test for the specified number of milliseconds.
StopTest	Stops the current test.
Trace	Adds an entry to the ACTTrace.log file.

Property	Description
TraceLevel	Gets or sets the amount of detail stored in the ACTTrace.log file.

Table B-2
Properties of the *Request* Object

Property	Description
Body	Gets or sets the HTTP request body.
CodePage	Gets or sets the code page for the request body.
EncodeBody	Specifies whether ACT automatically URL-encodes the request body. The default value is *True*.
EncodeQueryAsUTF8	Specifies whether ACT automatically UTF-8-encodes the request's query string. The default value is *False*.
Headers	Gets the HTTP *Headers* collection object.
HTTPVersion	Gets or sets the HTTP version.
Path	Gets or sets the HTTP path.
ResponseBufferSize	Gets or sets the size of the buffer used to store the response body.
Verb	Gets or sets the HTTP method verb.

Table B-3
Properties and Methods of the *Connection* object

Property	Description
IsOpen	Checks whether the connection is open.
Port	Gets the port number used by the connection.
RedirectDepth	Gets or sets the number of HTTP header redirections that are followed.
Server	Gets the host name or IP address of the server the client is connected to.
UseSSL	Checks whether the HTTP connection between the client and the server is using the SSL protocol (that is, whether the protocol is HTTPS).

Method	Description
Close	Closes the connection if it is open. Does not return an error if the connection is already closed.
Send	Sends an HTTP request to the server.

Table B-4
Properties of the *Response* Object

Property	Description
Body	Gets the body of the HTTP response. Returns only the portion of the body stored in the response buffer.
BytesRecv	Gets the number of bytes the client received in the response.
BytesSent	Gets the number of bytes sent in the HTTP request.
CodePage	Gets or sets the code page used for setting the body of the HTTP response.
ContentLength	Gets the size, in bytes, of the response body.
Headers	Gets a collection of headers in the response.
HeaderSize	Gets the combined size, in bytes, of all the response headers.
HTTPVersion	Gets the HTTP version used by the server for this response.
Path	Gets the path that was requested.
Port	Gets the server port used for the request.
ResultCode	Gets the server's response status code.
Server	Gets the name of the server that sent the response.
TTFB	Gets the number of milliseconds that elapsed before the first byte of the response was received.
TTLB	Gets the number of milliseconds that elapsed before the last byte of the response was received.
UseSSL	Checks whether the server and client used an SSL connection for the request and response.

Appendix C

Common Language Runtime Performance Counters

If it weren't for performance counters, troubleshooting applications would be a whole lot more difficult. Not to say that performance counters always make it easy, but they can give you a solid indicator of the health of your application. This appendix is a reference to the common set of Microsoft .NET performance counters. All of the information here is available in the documentation that ships with Microsoft Visual Basic .NET, but not all of it is easy to find or convenient to access.

Figure C-1 shows the counters we're interested in.

Of the counters that appear in the figure, those listed after the figure are the managed or ASP.NET counters of interest.

Note You'll notice some duplication under the ASP.NET counters in Figure C-1 (the v1.0.3705.0 counters). Those are exact duplicates of the other two ASP.NET counters, with the exception that they are build-specific. This will enable you in the future to profile different versions of ASP.NET running on the same machine. For the time being, you can ignore them; the two groups listed here are functionally equivalent for now.

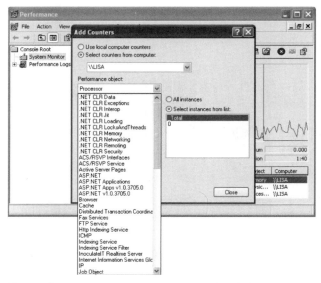

Figure C-1 A view of the .NET and ASP.NET performance counters.

.NET Performance Counters

- .NET CLR Data

- .NET CLR Exception

- .NET CLR Interop

- .NET CLR JIT

- .NET CLR Loading

- .NET CLR Lock and Thread

- .NET CLR Memory

- .NET CLR Networking

- .NET CLR Remoting

- .NET CLR Security

ASP.NET Performance Counters

- ASP.NET

- ASP.NET Application

.NET Performance Counters

The following sections describe the common .NET performance counters that you're likely to be interested in for observing your applications.

.NET CLR Data

The SQL Server .NET Data Provider adds several performance counters that enable you to fine-tune connection pooling characteristics, detect intermittent problems related to failed connection attempts, and detect problems related to timed-out requests to your SQL Server. Table C-1 describes the connection pooling counters in the .NET CLR Data category.

Table C-1
SQL Connection Pooling Counters

Counter	Description
SqlClient: Current # of pooled and non pooled connections	Current number of connections, pooled or not.
SqlClient: Current # pooled connections	Current number of connections in all pools associated with the process.
SqlClient: Current # connection pools	Current number of pools associated with the process.
SqlClient: Peak # pooled connections	The highest number of connections in all pools since the process started. (This counter is available only when associated with a specific process instance. The _Global instance will always return 0.
SqlClient: Total # failed connects	The total number of connection open attempts that have failed for any reason.

.NET CLR Exceptions

The Performance console's .NET CLR Exceptions category includes counters that provide information about the exceptions thrown by an application. Table C-2 describes these performance counters.

Table C-2
Counters Related to Exceptions

Counter	Description
# of Exceps Thrown	Displays the total number of exceptions thrown since the application started. This includes both .NET exceptions and unmanaged exceptions that are converted into .NET exceptions. For example, an *HRESULT* returned from unmanaged code is converted to an exception in managed code.
	This counter includes both handled and unhandled exceptions. Exceptions that are rethrown are counted again.
# of Exceps Thrown / Sec	Displays the number of exceptions thrown per second. This includes both .NET exceptions and unmanaged exceptions that are converted into .NET exceptions. For example, an *HRESULT* returned from unmanaged code is converted to an exception in managed code.
	This counter includes both handled and unhandled exceptions. It is not an average over time; it displays the difference between the values observed in the last two samples divided by the duration of the sample interval. This counter is an indicator of potential performance problems if a large number of exceptions (several hundred or more) are thrown.
# of Filters / Sec	Displays the number of .NET exception filters executed per second. An exception filter evaluates regardless of whether an exception is handled.
	This counter is not an average over time; it displays the difference between the values observed in the last two samples divided by the duration of the sample interval.
# of Finallys / Sec	Displays the number of *finally* blocks executed per second. A *finally* block is guaranteed to be executed regardless of how the try block was exited.
	This counter is not an average over time; it displays the difference between the values observed in the last two samples divided by the duration of the sample interval.
Throw to Catch Depth / Sec	Displays the number of stack frames traversed, from the frame that threw the exception to the frame that handled the exception, per second. This counter resets to zero when an exception handler is entered, so nested exceptions show the handler-to-handler stack depth.
	This counter is not an average over time; it displays the difference between the values observed in the last two samples divided by the duration of the sample interval.

.NET CLR Interop

The Performance console's .NET CLR Interop category includes counters that provide information about an application's interaction with COM components, COM+ services, and external type libraries. Table C-3 describes these performance counters.

Table C-3
.NET CLR Interop Performance Counters

Counter	Description
# of CCWs	Displays the current number of COM Callable Wrappers (CCWs). A CCW is a proxy for a managed object being referenced from an unmanaged COM client. This counter indicates the number of managed objects referenced by unmanaged COM code.
# of marshalling	Displays the total number of times arguments and return values have been marshaled from managed to unmanaged code, and vice-versa, since the application started. This counter is not incremented if the stubs are inlined. (Stubs are responsible for marshaling arguments and return values.) Stubs are usually inlined if the marshaling overhead is small.
# of Stubs	Displays the current number of stubs created by the common language runtime. Stubs are responsible for marshaling arguments and return values from managed to unmanaged code, and vice-versa, during a COM interop call or a Platform Invoke call.
# of TLB exports / sec	Reserved for future use.
# of TLB imports / sec	Reserved for future use.

.NET CLR JIT

The Performance console's .NET CLR JIT category includes counters that provide information about code that has been JIT-compiled. Table C-4 describes these performance counters.

Table C-4
.NET CLR JIT Performance Counters

Counter	Description
# of IL bytes JITted	Displays the total number of Microsoft intermediate language (MSIL) bytes compiled by the just-in-time (JIT) compiler since the application started. This counter is equivalent to the Total # of IL Bytes Jitted counter.
# of IL methods JITted	Displays the total number of methods JIT-compiled since the application started. This counter does not include pre-JIT-compiled methods.
% Time in Jit	Displays the percentage of elapsed time spent in JIT compilation since the last JIT compilation phase. This counter is updated at the end of every JIT compilation phase. A JIT compilation phase occurs when a method and its dependencies are compiled.
IL bytes Jitted / sec	Displays the number of MSIL bytes that are JIT-compiled per second. This counter is not an average over time; it displays the difference between the values observed in the last two samples divided by the duration of the sample interval.
Standard Jit Failures	Displays the peak number of methods the JIT compiler has failed to compile since the application started. This failure can occur if the MSIL cannot be verified or if there is an internal error in the JIT compiler.
Total # of IL Bytes Jitted	Displays the total MSIL bytes JIT-compiled since the application started. This counter is equivalent to the # of IL Bytes Jitted counter.

.NET CLR Loading

The Performance console's .NET CLR Loading category includes counters that provide information about assemblies, classes, and application domains that are loaded. Table C-5 describes these performance counters.

Table C-5
.NET CLR Loading Performance Counters

Counter	Description
% Time Loading	Reserved for future use.
Assembly Search Length	Reserved for future use.
Bytes in Loader Heap	Displays the current size, in bytes, of the memory committed by the class loader across all application domains. Committed memory is the physical space reserved in the disk paging file.
Current appdomains	Displays the current number of application domains loaded in this application.
Current Assemblies	Displays the current number of assemblies loaded across all application domains in the currently running application. If the assembly is loaded as domain-neutral from multiple application domains, this counter is incremented only once.
Current Classes Loaded	Displays the current number of classes loaded in all assemblies.
Rate of appdomains	Displays the number of application domains loaded per second. This counter is not an average over time; it displays the difference between the values observed in the last two samples divided by the duration of the sample interval.
Rate of appdomains unloaded	Displays the number of application domains unloaded per second. This counter is not an average over time; it displays the difference between the values observed in the last two samples divided by the duration of the sample interval.
Rate of Assemblies	Displays the number of assemblies loaded per second across all application domains. If the assembly is loaded as domain-neutral from multiple application domains, this counter is incremented only once.
	This counter is not an average over time; it displays the difference between the values observed in the last two samples divided by the duration of the sample interval.

Table C-5
.NET CLR Loading Performance Counters

Counter	Description
Rate of Classes Loaded	Displays the number of classes loaded per second in all assemblies. This counter is not an average over time; it displays the difference between the values observed in the last two samples divided by the duration of the sample interval.
Rate of Load Failures	Displays the number of classes that failed to load per second. Load failures can occur for many reasons, such as inadequate security or invalid format. For details, see the profiling services Help.
	This counter is not an average over time; it displays the difference between the values observed in the last two samples divided by the duration of the sample interval.
Total # of Load Failures	Displays the peak number of classes that have failed to load since the application started.
	Load failures can occur for many reasons, such as inadequate security or invalid format. For details, see the profiling services Help.
Total Appdomains	Displays the peak number of application domains loaded since the application started.
Total appdomains unloaded	Displays the total number of application domains unloaded since the application started. If an application domain is loaded and unloaded multiple times, this counter will increment each time the application domain is unloaded.
Total Assemblies	Displays the total number of assemblies loaded since the application started. If the assembly is loaded as domain-neutral from multiple application domains, this counter will be incremented only once.
Total Classes Loaded	Displays the cumulative number of classes loaded in all assemblies since the application started.

.NET CLR LocksAndThreads

The Performance console's .NET CLR LocksAndThreads category includes counters that provide information about managed locks and threads that an application uses. Table C-6 describes these performance counters.

Table C-6
.NET CLR LocksAndThreads Performance Counters

Counter	Description
# of current logical Threads	Displays the number of current managed thread objects in the application. This counter maintains the count of both running and stopped threads. This counter is not an average over time; it displays only the last observed value.
# of current physical Threads	Displays the number of native operating system threads created and owned by the common language runtime to act as underlying threads for managed thread objects. This counter's value does not include the threads used by the runtime in its internal operations; it is a subset of the threads in the operating system process.
# of current recognized threads	Displays the number of threads that are currently recognized by the runtime. These threads are associated with a corresponding managed thread object. The runtime does not create these threads, but they have run inside the runtime at least once. Only unique threads are tracked; threads with the same thread ID that reenter the runtime or are re-created after the thread exits are not counted twice.
# of total recognized Threads	Displays the total number of threads that have been recognized by the runtime since the application started. These threads are associated with a corresponding managed thread object. The runtime does not create these threads, but they have run inside the runtime at least once. Only unique threads are tracked; threads with the same thread ID that reenter the runtime or are re-created after the thread exits are not counted twice.
Contention Rate / Sec	Displays the rate at which threads in the runtime attempt to acquire a managed lock unsuccessfully.

**Table C-6
.NET CLR LocksAndThreads Performance Counters**

Counter	Description
Current Queue Length	Displays the total number of threads that are currently waiting to acquire a managed lock in the application. This counter is not an average over time; it displays the last observed value.
Queue Length / Sec	Displays the number of threads per second that are waiting to acquire a lock in the application. This counter is not an average over time; it displays the difference between the values observed in the last two samples divided by the duration of the sample interval.
Queue Length Peak	Displays the total number of threads that have waited to acquire a managed lock since the application started.
Rate of recognized threads / Sec	Displays the number of threads per second that have been recognized by the runtime. These threads are associated with a corresponding managed thread object. The runtime does not create these threads, but they have run inside the runtime at least once.
	Only unique threads are tracked; threads with the same thread ID that reenter the runtime or are re-created after the thread exits are not counted twice.
	This counter is not an average over time; it displays the difference between the values observed in the last two samples divided by the duration of the sample interval.
Total # of Contentions	Displays the total number of times that threads in the runtime have attempted to acquire a managed lock unsuccessfully.

.NET CLR Memory

The Performance console's .NET CLR Memory category includes counters that provide information about the garbage collector. Table C-7 describes these performance counters.

Table C-7
.NET CLR Memory Performance Counters

Counter	Description
# Bytes in all Heaps	Displays the sum of the Gen 0 Heap Size, Gen 1 Heap Size, Gen 2 Heap Size, and the Large Object Heap Size counters. This counter indicates the current memory allocated in bytes on the garbage collection heaps.
# GC Handles	Displays the number of garbage collection handles in use. Garbage collection handles are handles to resources external to the common language runtime and the managed environment.
# Gen 0 Collections	Displays the number of times the generation 0 objects (that is, the youngest, most recently allocated objects) are garbage-collected since the application started.
	Generation 0 garbage collection occurs when the available memory in generation 0 is not sufficient to satisfy an allocation request. This counter is incremented at the end of a generation 0 garbage collection. Higher-generation garbage collections include all lower-generation collections. This counter is explicitly incremented when a higher-generation (generation 1 or 2) garbage collection occurs.
	This counter displays the last observed value. The *_Global_* counter value is not accurate and should be ignored.
# Gen 1 Collections	Displays the number of times the generation 1 objects have been garbage-collected since the application started.
	The counter is incremented at the end of a generation 1 garbage collection. Higher-generation garbage collections include all lower-generation collections. This counter is also incremented when a higher-generation (generation 2) garbage collection occurs.
	This counter displays the last observed value. The *_Global_* counter value is not accurate and should be ignored.

Table C-7
.NET CLR Memory Performance Counters

Counter	Description
# Gen 2 Collections	Displays the number of times the generation 2 objects have been garbage-collected since the application started. The counter is incremented at the end of a generation 2 garbage collection (also called a full garbage collection). This counter displays the last observed value. The _Global_ counter value is not accurate and should be ignored.
# Induced GC	Displays the peak number of times garbage collection was performed because of an explicit call to *GC.Collect*. It is good practice to let the garbage collector tune the frequency of its collections.
# of Pinned Objects	Displays the number of pinned objects encountered in the last garbage collection. A pinned object is one that the garbage collector cannot move in memory. This counter tracks the pinned objects only in the heaps that are garbage-collected. For example, a generation 0 garbage collection causes enumeration of pinned objects only in the generation 0 heap.
# of Sink Blocks in use	Displays the current number of synchronization blocks in use. Synchronization blocks are per-object data structures allocated for storing synchronization information. Synchronization blocks hold weak references to managed objects and must be scanned by the garbage collector. Synchronization blocks are not limited to storing synchronization information; they can also store COM Interop metadata. This counter indicates performance problems with heavy use of synchronization primitives.
# Total committed Bytes	Displays the amount of virtual memory, in bytes, currently committed by the garbage collector. Committed memory is the physical memory for which space has been reserved in the disk paging file.
# Total reserved Bytes	Displays the amount of virtual memory, in bytes, currently reserved by the garbage collector. Reserved memory is the virtual memory space reserved for the application but no disk or main memory pages have been used.

Table C-7
.NET CLR Memory Performance Counters

Counter	Description
% Time in GC	Displays the percentage of elapsed time that was spent performing a garbage collection since the last garbage collection cycle. This counter usually indicates the work done by the garbage collector to collect and compact memory on behalf of the application. This counter is updated only at the end of every garbage collection. This counter is not an average; its value reflects the last observed value.
Allocated Bytes/Second	Displays the number of bytes per second allocated on the garbage collection heap. This counter is updated at the end of every garbage collection, not at each allocation. This counter is not an average over time; it displays the difference between the values observed in the last two samples divided by the duration of the sample interval.
Finalization Survivors	Displays the number of garbage-collected objects that have survived a collection because they are waiting to be finalized. If these objects hold references to other objects, those objects also survive but are not counted by this counter. The *Promoted Finalization-Memory from Gen 0* and *Promoted Finalization-Memory from Gen 1* counters represent all the memory that survived due to finalization.
	This counter is not cumulative; it is updated at the end of every garbage collection with the count of the survivors during that particular collection only. This counter indicates the extra overhead that the application might incur because of finalization.

Table C-7
.NET CLR Memory Performance Counters

Counter	Description
Gen 0 heap size	Displays the maximum bytes that can be allocated in generation 0; it does not indicate the current number of bytes allocated in generation 0.
	A generation 0 garbage collection occurs when the allocations since the last collection exceed this size. The generation 0 size is tuned by the garbage collector and can change during the execution of the application. At the end of a generation 0 collection, the size of the generation 0 heap is 0 bytes. This counter displays the size, in bytes, of allocations that invokes the next generation 0 garbage collection.
	This counter is updated at the end of a garbage collection, not at each allocation.
Gen 0 Promoted Rules/Sec	Displays the bytes per second that are promoted from generation 0 to generation 1. Memory is promoted when it survives a garbage collection. This counter is an indicator of relatively long-lived objects being created per second.
	This counter displays the difference between the values observed in the last two samples divided by the duration of the sample interval.
Gen 1 heap size	Displays the current number of bytes in generation 1; this counter does not display the maximum size of generation 1. Objects are not directly allocated in this generation; they are promoted from previous generation 0 garbage collections. This counter is updated at the end of a garbage collection, not at each allocation.
Gen 1 Promoted Bytes/Sec	Displays the bytes per second that are promoted from generation 1 to generation 2. Objects that are promoted only because they are waiting to be finalized are not included in this counter.
	An object is promoted when it survives a garbage collection. Nothing is promoted from generation 2 because it is the oldest generation. This counter is an indicator of very long-lived objects being created per second.
	This counter displays the difference between the values observed in the last two samples divided by the duration of the sample interval.

Table C-7
.NET CLR Memory Performance Counters

Counter	Description
Gen 2 heap size	Displays the current number of bytes in generation 2. Objects are not directly allocated in this generation; they are promoted from generation 1 during previous generation 1 garbage collections. This counter is updated at the end of a garbage collection, not at each allocation.
Large Object Heap size	Displays the current size, in bytes, of the Large Object Heap. Objects greater than 20 KB are treated as large objects by the garbage collector and are directly allocated in a special heap; they are not promoted through the generations. This counter is updated at the end of a garbage collection, not at each allocation.
Promoted Finalization-Memory from Gen 0	Displays the bytes of memory that are promoted from generation 0 to generation 1 only because they are waiting to be finalized. This counter is not cumulative; it displays the value observed at the end of the last garbage collection.
Promoted Finalization-Memory from Gen 1	Displays the bytes of memory that are promoted from generation 1 to generation 2 only because they are waiting to be finalized. This counter is not cumulative; it displays the value observed at the end of the last garbage collection. This counter is reset to 0 if the last garbage collection was a generation 0 collection only.
Promoted Memory from Gen 0	Displays the bytes of memory that survive garbage collection and are promoted from generation 0 to generation 1. Objects that are promoted only because they are waiting to be finalized are not included in this counter. This counter is not cumulative; it displays the value observed at the end of the last garbage collection.
Promoted Memory from Gen 1	Displays the bytes of memory that survive garbage collection and are promoted from generation 1 to generation 2. Objects that are promoted only because they are waiting to be finalized are not included in this counter. This counter is not cumulative; it displays the value observed at the end of the last garbage collection. This counter is reset to 0 if the last garbage collection was a generation 0 collection only.

.NET CLR Networking

The Performance console's .NET CLR Networking category includes counters that provide information about data that an application sends and receives over the network. Table C-8 describes these performance counters.

Table C-8
.NET CLR Networking Performance Counters

Counter	Description
Bytes Received	Displays the cumulative number of bytes received over all open socket connections since the process started. This number includes data and any protocol information that is not defined by TCP/IP.
Bytes Sent	Displays the cumulative number of bytes sent over all open socket connections since the process started. This number includes data and any protocol information that is not defined by TCP/IP.
Connections Established	Displays the cumulative number of socket connections established for this process since it started.
Datagrams Received	Displays the cumulative number of datagram packets received since the process started.
Datagrams Sent	Displays the cumulative number of datagram packets sent since the process started.

.NET CLR Remoting

The Performance console's .NET CLR Remoting category includes counters that provide information about the remoted objects that an application uses. Table C-9 describes these performance counters.

Table C-9
.NET CLR Remoting Performance Counters

Counter	Description
Channels	Displays the total number of remoting channels registered across all application domains since application started. Channels transport messages to and from remote objects.
Context Proxies	Displays the total number of remoting proxy objects in this process since it started. A proxy object acts as a representative of the remote objects and ensures that all calls made on the proxy are forwarded to the correct remote object.
Context Bound Classes Loaded	Displays the current number of context-bound classes that are loaded. Classes that can be bound to a context are called context-bound classes. Context-bound classes are marked with context attributes, which provide usage rules for synchronization, thread affinity, transactions, and so on.
Context-Bound Objects Alloc / sec	Displays the number of context-bound objects allocated per second. Classes that can be bound to a context are called context-bound objects. Context-bound classes are marked with context attributes, which provide usage rules for synchronization, thread affinity, transactions, and so on.
	This counter is not an average over time; it displays the difference between the values observed in the last two samples divided by the duration of the sample interval.
Contexts	Displays the current number of remoting contexts in the application. A context is a boundary containing a collection of objects with the same usage rules such as synchronization, thread affinity, transactions, and so on.

Table C-9
.NET CLR Remoting Performance Counters

Counter	Description
Remote Calls / sec	Displays the number of remote procedure calls invoked per second. A remote procedure call is a call on any object outside the caller's application domain. This counter is not an average over time; it displays the difference between the values observed in the last two samples divided by the duration of the sample interval.
Total Remote Calls	Displays the total number of remote procedure calls invoked since the application started. A remote procedure call is a call on any object outside the caller's application domain.

.NET CLR Security

The Performance console's .NET CLR Security category includes counters that provide information about the security checks that the common language runtime performs for an application. Table C-10 describes these performance counters.

Table C-10
.NET CLR Security Performance Counters

Counter	Description
# Link Time Checks	Displays the total number of link-time code access security checks since the application started. Link-time code access security checks are performed when a caller demands a particular permission at just-in-time (JIT) compile time. A link-time check is performed once per caller. This count is not indicative of serious performance issues; it is merely indicative of the security system activity.
% Time in RT checks	Displays the percentage of elapsed time spent performing runtime code access security checks since the last sample. This counter is updated at the end of a .NET Framework security check. It is not an average; it represents the last observed value.
% Time Sig Authenticating	Reserved for future use.

Table C-10
.NET CLR Security Performance Counters

Counter	Description
Stack Walk Depth	Displays the depth of the stack during that last runtime code access security check. Runtime code access security checks are performed by walking the stack. This counter is not an average; it displays only the last observed value.
Total Runtime Checks	Displays the total number of runtime code access security checks performed since the application started. Runtime code access security checks are performed when a caller demands a particular permission. The runtime check is made on every call by the caller and examines the current thread stack of the caller. When used with the Stack Walk Depth counter, this counter indicates the performance penalty that occurs for security checks.

Performance Counters for ASP.NET

ASP.NET supports two groups of performance counters: system and application. The former are exposed in *PerfMon* in the ASP.NET *System* performance counter object; the latter are exposed in the ASP.NET *Applications* performance object.

Note   There's a significant difference between the State Server *Sessions* counters found in the ASP.NET *System* performance object and the *Sessions* counters found in the ASP.NET *Applications* performance object. The former apply only on the server computer on which the state server is running. The latter apply only to user sessions that occur in process.

Table C-11 lists the ASP.NET system performance counters. These aggregate information for all ASP.NET applications on a Web server computer, or they apply generally to a system of ASP.NET servers running the same applications. These can include Web farms and Web gardens.

Table C-11
ASP.NET System Performance Counters

Counter	Description
Application Restarts	The number of times that an application has been restarted during the Web server's lifetime. Application restarts are incremented with each *Application_OnEnd* event. This value will be reset every time the Internet Information Services (IIS) host is restarted.
Application Running	The number of applications running on the server computer.
Requests Disconnected	The number of requests disconnected due to a communication failure.
Requests Queued	The number of requests waiting for service from the queue.
Requests Rejected	The total number of requests not executed because of insufficient server resources to process them. This counter represents the number of requests that return a 503 HTTP status code, indicating that the server is too busy.
Request Wait Time	The number of milliseconds that the most recent request waited for processing in the queue.
State Server Sessions Abandoned	The number of user sessions that have been explicitly abandoned. These are sessions that are ended by specific user actions, such as closing the browser or navigating to another site. This counter is available only on the computer where the state server service (*aspnet_state*) is running.
State Server Sessions Active	The number of currently active user sessions. This counter is available only on the computer where the state server service (*aspnet_state*) is running.
State Server Sessions Timed Out	The number of user sessions that have become inactive through user inaction. This counter is available only on the machine where the state server service (*aspnet_state*) is running.

Table C-11
ASP.NET System Performance Counters

Counter	Description
State Server Sessions Total	The number of sessions created during the lifetime of the process. This counter is the cumulative value of *State Server Sessions Active, State Server Sessions Abandoned,* and *State Server Sessions Timed Out.* This counter is available only on the computer where the state server service (*aspnet_state*) is running.
Worker Process Restarts	The number of times a worker process has been restarted on the server computer.
Worker Process Running	The number of worker processes running on the server computer.

ASP.NET Applications

ASP.NET supports the application performance counters listed in Table C-12, which you can use to monitor the performance of a single instance of an ASP.NET application. A unique instance appears for these counters, named __Total__, which aggregates counters for all applications on a Web server (similar to the global counters above). The __Total__ instance is always available. The counters will display zero when no applications are present on the server.

Table C-12
ASP.NET Performance Counters

Counter	Description
Anonymous Requests	The cumulative number of requests using anonymous authentication. This number is reset when IIS is restarted (either through an IIS reset or a rebooting of the machine).
Anonymous Requests/Sec	The number of requests per second using anonymous authentication.
Cache Total Entries	The total number of entries in the cache. This counter includes both internal use of the cache by the ASP.NET page framework and external use of the cache through exposed APIs.

Table C-12
ASP.NET Performance Counters

Counter	Description
Cache Total Hits	The total number of hits from the cache. This counter includes both internal use of the cache by the ASP.NET page framework and external use of the cache through exposed APIs.
Cache Total Misses	The number of failed cache requests per application. This counter includes both internal use of the cache by ASP.NET and external use of the cache through exposed APIs.
Cache Total Hit Ratio	The ratio of hits to misses for the cache. This counter includes both internal use of the cache by ASP.NET and external use of the cache through exposed APIs.
Cache Total Turnover Rate	The number of additions and removals to the total cache per second. It is useful in helping determine how effectively the cache is being used. If the turnover is large, then the cache is not being used efficiently.
Cache API Entries	The total number of entries in the application cache.
Cache API Hits	The total number of hits from the cache when it is accessed through only the external cache APIs. This counter does not track any use of the cache internally by ASP.NET.
Cache API Misses	The total number of failed requests to the cache when accessed through the external cache APIs. This counter does not track any use of the cache internally by ASP.NET.
Cache API Hit Ratio	The cache hit to miss ratio when accessed through the external Cache APIs. This counter does not track any use of the cache internally by ASP.NET.
Cache API Turnover Rate	The number of additions and removals to the cache per second, when used through the external APIs (excluding internal use by the ASP.NET page framework). It is useful in helping determine how effectively the cache is being used. If the turnover is large, then the cache is not being used effectively.

Table C-12
ASP.NET Performance Counters

Counter	Description
Compilations Total	The total number of compilations that have taken place during the lifetime of the current Web server process. This occurs when a file with an .aspx, .asmx, .ascx, or .ashx extension, or a code-behind source file, is dynamically compiled on the server.
	Note that this number will initially climb to a peak value as requests are made to all parts of an application. Once a compilation occurs, however, the resulting binary is saved to disk, where it is reused until its source file changes. This means that, even in the event of a process restart, the counter can remain at zero (inactive) until the application is modified or redeployed.
Debugging Requests	The number of requests that occur while debugging was enabled.
Errors During Preprocessing	The number of errors that occurred during parsing. Excludes compilation and run time errors.
Errors During Compilation	The number of errors that occur during dynamic compilation. Excludes parser and run time errors.
Errors During Execution	The total number of errors that occur during the execution of an HTTP request. Excludes parser and compilation errors.
Errors Unhandled During Execution	The total number of unhandled errors that occur during the execution of HTTP requests.
	Note that an unhandled error is any uncaught run-time exception that escapes user code on the page and enters the ASP.NET internal error-handling logic. Exceptions to this rule occur when:
	Custom errors are enabled, an error page is defined, or both.
	The Page_Error event is defined in user code and the error is either cleared (using the *HttpServerUtility.ClearError Method* method) or a redirect is performed.
Errors Unhandled During Execution/Sec	The number of unhandled exceptions per second that occur during the execution of HTTP requests.

Table C-12
ASP.NET Performance Counters

Counter	Description
Errors Total	The total number of errors that occur during the execution of HTTP requests. Includes any parser, compilation, or run time errors. This counter is the sum of the *Errors During Compilation, Preprocessing*, and *Request Execution* counters.
Errors Total/Sec	The number of errors per second that occur during the execution of HTTP requests. Includes any parser, compilation, or run time error.
Output Cache Entries	The total number of entries in the output cache.
Output Cache Hits	The total number of requests serviced from the output cache.
Output Cache Misses	The number of failed output-cache requests per application.
Output Cache Hit Ratio	The percentage of total requests serviced from the output cache.
Output Cache Turnover Rate	The number of additions and removals to the output cache per second. This is useful in helping determine how effectively the cache is being used. If the turnover is large, then the cache is not being used effectively.
Pipeline Instance Count	The number of active pipeline instances.
Request Bytes In Total	The total size, in bytes, of all requests.
Request Bytes Out Total	The total size, in bytes, of responses sent to a client. This does not include standard HTTP response headers.
Requests Executing	The number of requests currently executing.
Requests Failed	The total number of failed requests, including requests that timed out, requests that were not authorized (401), or requests not found (404 or 414). Note: the equivalent ASP counter would also increment on requests rejected, which cannot be done (because the rejection is done by IIS and not the process model).

Table C-12
ASP.NET Performance Counters

Counter	Description
Requests Not Found	The number of requests that failed because resources were not found (status code 404, 414).
Requests Not Authorized	The number of requests that failed due to no authorization (status code 401).
Requests Succeeded	The number of requests that executed successfully (status code 200).
Requests Timed Out	The number of requests that timed out.
Requests Total	The total number of requests since the service was started.
Requests/Sec	The number of requests executed per second.
Sessions Active	The number of sessions currently active. This is supported only with in-memory session state.
Sessions Abandoned	The number of sessions that have been explicitly abandoned. This is supported only with in-memory session state.
Sessions Timed Out	The number of sessions that timed out. This is supported only with in-memory session state.
Sessions Total	The number of sessions timed out. This is supported only with in-memory session state.
Transactions Aborted	The number of transactions aborted.
Transactions Committed	The number of transactions committed.
Transactions Pending	The number of transactions in progress.
Transactions Total	The total number of transactions since the service was started.
Transactions/Sec	The number of transactions started per second.

Appendix D

Performance Counter Quick Reference

This appendix covers a common set of performance counters that can be useful for various types of applications. You'll invariably use a combination of these to achieve your goals. Keep in mind that no single performance counter will give you a complete picture of your application. Many of these counters must be used in combination to give you a clear picture of what is actually happening. Also note that some problems can never be clarified by performance counters.

You can find definitions of all of these counters in Appendix C. This appendix highlights the subset of counters that are of interest to various types of applications. There is a definite overlap, but it is important to know where to start monitoring your applications. Remember that this list is by no means definitive—it's just a starting point for your own work.

More Info You can always create your own performance counters to help you debug your applications. See Chapter 12 for more information.

Common Performance Counters

Virtually any application will need the counters listed in Table D-1. They are not managed, and they apply to any part of your system that you're monitoring. You can consider this a set of general health indicators, but they can also be useful in performance and stress situations for tracking down leaks, poorly written code, and other development bogeymen.

Table D-1
Performance Counters

Category	Counter	Description
Processor	*% Processor Time*	Indicates how much work the machine is doing.
Memory	*% Committed Bytes In Use*	Indicates the memory resources being consumed.
Thread	*Context Switches/Sec*	Helps put the % Processor Time counter in perspective. A context switch happens when CPU execution switches from one thread to another. A high rate of context switching might indicate that the machine is spinning between threads without doing any real work. This might indicate performance problems related to COM Interop, a bad threading implementation, and so forth.
Process	*% Processor Time*	This counter allows you to single out specific processes and how much processor time they're consuming.
.NET CLR LocksAnd- Threads	*Total # of Contentions*	Are you overusing a shared resource? This counter will help you figure out if there is a problem with shared resources protected by a thread synchronization construct. For example, have you implemented a mutex instead of a *ReaderWriterLock?* This counter might indicate that your threading model needs work. Remember that there is always some contention in a system.
Process	*Private Bytes*	Helps determine whether there are memory leaks in your application.
Process	*Working Set*	

Application-Specific Counters

The following sections describe counters for profiling specific types of technologies.

ASP.NET and Web Services

ASP.NET and Web service applications are both served up by Microsoft Internet Information Services (IIS) and the ASP.NET ISAPI filter. They are both, after all, HTTP-based. As a result, you can treat a Web service like just another ASP.NET application. Granted, there might be other things you need to keep an eye out for, depending on the application, but this relationship should hold for most applications. Table D-2 lists the common application-specific ASP.NET performance counters.

Table D-2
Application-Specific ASP.NET Performance Counters

Category	Counter	Description
.NET CLR ASP.NET Applications	*Requests/Sec*	Indicates the current number of HTTP requests served per second by the ASP.NET worker process. This gives a general indication of how well your application is performing. Obviously more is always better, but this number is best used to produce relative measurements (such as when a feature addition affects the application's performance by increasing or decreasing the requests per second).
.NET CLR ASP.NET Applications	*Requests Executing*	Shows how many requests are being executed concurrently by your application. If this number always stays high while your RPS stays low and your request queue grows, you might have a threading problem. (Check your context switches and thread locks.) Are you accessing a common resource that permits only mutually exclusive access?
.NET CLR ASP.NET	*Requests Queued*	Are requests coming in too fast to be processed immediately? This counter will tell you. In a deployment situation, it will let you know that you need to add another machine to your farm to handle the incoming requests. In development, it might indicate that you're taking too long serving requests. Or, if there is processor time to spare, it might indicate that you need to tune ASP.NET to generate more threads to handle the incoming requests.

Table D-2
Application-Specific ASP.NET Performance Counters

Category	Counter	Description
.NET CLR ASP.NET Applications	*Request Execution Time*	Gives a definite indication of how long requests are taking.
.NET CLR ASP.NET	*Worker Process Restarts*	Worker process restarts are generally not desirable, but they are periodically used to help ASP.NET recover from a bad state. You can tune ASP.NET's restart behavior in the Machine.config file. However, a worker process restart might mean that your application consumed too much memory or failed so severely that forcing a restart was ASP.NET's only way out. A worker process restart will also cause you to lose your session state information (unless you're using the Session State service).

SQL Database Applications

Working with SQL applications can be challenging, mainly because your database will typically reside on a separate machine from your application's data layer. Therefore, the performance counters are divided into two sections, SQL Server and Data Layer, as described in Tables D-3 and D-4.

Table D-3
SQL Server Performance Counters

Category	Counter	Description
SQLServer:General Statistics	User Connections	This counter can give you a good idea of how efficiently your application is using connection pooling and whether you have any connection leaks.
SQLServer:Databases	*Transactions/sec*	If you use transactions, this can be a good measure of how active your application is.
SQLServer:SQL Statistics	*SQL Compilations/sec*	If this number is high (in the hundreds or thousands) and the machine is running low on processor time, you might want to consider moving your dynamic T-SQL statements into stored procedures. This will reduce the number of SQL compilations and reduce the overhead per request.

Table D-4
Data Layer Performance Counters

Category	Counter	Description
.NET CLR Data	SqlClient: Current # pooled connections	This will definitely help you understand how well your pool is being utilized. By evaluating the behavior of this counter under varying load conditions, you can determine whether you have connection leaks. Use this in conjunction with the SQL Server User Connections counter to get a good handle on the pool usage.
.NET CLR Data	*SqlClient: Total # failed connections*	If the connection pool is being exhausted by the number of incoming requests, you'll begin to see connection failures. This is another indicator you can use to adjust your pooling behavior.

Applications That Use Interop or Remoting

Tracking the amount of Interop marshaling done by an application is an extremely important metric, as is tracking the remoting calls. As you'll recall from our discussion of chatty vs. chunky calls in Chapter 4—see page 148—you can use either of the performance counters described in Table D-5 to get an indication of how chatty your application might be.

Table D-5
COM Interop and Remoting Performance Counters

Category	Counter	Description
.NET CLR Interop	# of marshalling	On an application-by-application basis, you can evaluate how frequently your application is marshaling to and from the COM world. The ideal is to keep the amount of marshaling to a minimum. Remember the idea of chunky method calls from Chapter 4. If you're doing a lot of marshaling, consider whether you're doing as much work as possible.
.NET CLR Remoting	*Remote calls/sec*	The ideal is to keep the number of remote calls to a minimum. Remember the idea of chunky method calls from Chapter 4. If you're doing a lot of remote calls, consider whether you're doing as much work as possible with each method invocation.

Index

Symbols

& (concatenation operator), 352

A

Abort( ) (Thread class), 86, 89
Aborted state (threads), 81, 85
AbortRequested state (threads), 81
AcceptTcpClient( ) (TcpListener class), 209
access control, code, 306–308
accessing native methods. *See* native methods
accounts for Windows services, 221
ACID rules for COM+ transactions, 273
ACT (Application Center Test), 390, 415–426
  customizing tests, 421
    Test Object Model, 423–426
  standalone version, 417
Activate( ) (ServicedComponent class), 264
activating COM+ components, 256
activation models, remoting, 173
Active Test Script (ATS) Object Model, 415
ActivityId property (ContextUtil class), 258
AddHandler statement, 45
AddRef( ) (IUnknown interface), 139
addressing, 206–208
administration message queues, 283
algorithms, cryptographic, 301
Alias option, Declare statement, 113
All_Code code group, 312
AllocHGlobal( ) (Marshal class), 132
allowing inheritance, 51
And (logical operator), 26
AndAlso (logical operator), 27
Anonymous account, 318
ANSI encoding, 112
apartment threading, object pooling and, 264
App.Config file, 192
AppendFormat( ) (StringBuilder class), 355

Application Center Test (ACT), 390, 415–426
  customizing tests, 421
    Test Object Model, 423–426
  standalone version, 417
application domains, 75
application performance counters (ASP.NET), 447
ApplicationActivation property
    (ServicedComponent class), 257
ApplicationException class, 67
ApplicationId property (ContextUtil class), 258
ApplicationId property (RemotingConfiguration
    class), 171
ApplicationInstanceId property (ContextUtil
    class), 258
ApplicationName property
    (RemotingConfiguration class), 171
applications. *See* enterprise applications
architecture development, 8–11
  inheritance logic and, 50
As argument (enumeration declarations), 39
ASP.NET, 162
  authentication and authorization, 313–319
  forms-based authentication, 314–317
  performance, 374–377
  performance counters, 445–451, 455
  security features, 299
assemblies, 138
AssemblyDelaySign class, 307
AssemblyInfo.vb file, 254
AssemblyKeyFile property (ServicedComponent
    class), 254
asymmetric ciphers, 301
asynchronous network communications,
    199–203, 207
  messaging, 280–295
    automatic queue installation, 294

asynchronous network communications,
continued
creating and working with queue, 284–294
message queues, 281–283
priorities, 281
socket-level programming, 214–218
ATM application (example), 289
atomic operations, 99
atomicity of COM+ transactions, 273
ATS (Active Test Script) Object Model, 415
Authenticate property (MessageQueue class), 285
Authenticate( ) (FormsAuthentication), 317
authentication, 168–169, 298, 313–317
message queues, 285
network communications, 194
authorization, 299, 313, 318–319
AutoCommit property (ServicedComponent
class), 277
AutoComplete( ) (ServicedComponent class), 278
AutoFlush property (Debug, Trace classes), 342
AutoLog property (ServiceBase class), 232
AutoResetEvent class (Threading namespace),
93, 95
auxiliary message queues, 282
availability requirements, collecting, 7

B

background processes. *See* Windows services
basic (blittable) types, 119
BasicThreading module (example), 76
BeginAccept( ) (Socket class), 214
BeginConnect( ) (Socket class), 214
BeginGetHostByName( ) (Dns class), 208
BeginGetResponse( ) (WebRequest class), 194,
199–203
BeginReceive( ) (MessageQueue class), 288
BeginReceive( ) (Socket class), 214
BeginResolve( ) (Dns class), 208
BeginSend( ) (Socket class), 214
BeginSendTo( ) (Socket class), 214
bidirectional communication, 170
binary serialization, 154
BinaryFormatter class, 155
binding, 24–26, 139, 358
blittable (basic) types, 119

Body property (Request, Response classes),
425–426
BooleanSwitch class, 348
Break( ) (Debugger class), 331
broadcasting messages with UDP, 210
buffer overrun detection, 305
ByRef parameter, 119
passing null to, 143
Byte type, 119
BytesRecv, BytesSent properties (Response class,
ACT), 426
ByVal parameter, 119

C

calling overhead (Web services), 167
CallingConvention property (DllImport attribute),
116–118
CanBePooled( ) (ServicedComponent class), 265,
269
CanHandlePowerEvent property (ServiceBase
class), 232
CanPauseAndContinue property (ServiceBase
class), 232
CanPauseAndContinue property
(ServiceController class), 224, 226
CanShutdown property (ServiceBase class), 232
CanShutdown property (ServiceController class),
226
CanStop property (ServiceBase class), 232
CanStop property (ServiceController class), 224,
226
Caspol.exe utility, 311–313
Catch statement, 63
Category property (EventLogEntry class), 336
CategoryNumber property (EventLogEntry class),
336
CDB (Microsoft Console Debugger), 328
CCWs (COM callable wrappers), 144
CharSet option (StructLayout attribute), 129
CharSet property (DllImport attribute), 116
ciphers, symmetric and asymmetric, 301
ciphertext, 301
classes, 34
creating instances of, 60
inheritance. *See* inheritance
shared constructors, 59

client authentication, 194
client-only applications, 9
Close( )
  Connection class (ACT), 425
  Debug, Trace classes, 342
  ServiceController class, 226, 227
CLR (common language runtime), 20
  CLR Debugger, 326
  CLR hosting, 377
  performance counters, 427–445
CoCreateInstance API (COM), 138
Code Access Security Policy (Caspol) utility,
    311–313
code groups, scripting against, 312
code security, 305–310
  access, 306–308
  permissions, 308–310
CodePage property (Request, Response classes),
    425–426
coding techniques, 15–18
Collect( ) (System.GC class), 70
column names vs. ordinals (databases), 371
COM (Component Object Model), 13, 108,
    137–147
  COM callable wrappers (CCWs), 144
  COM vs. .NET object models, 137–139
  dependencies, managing, 412
  interoperability (COM interop service), 108,
    137, 374
    performance considerations, 147
    performance counters, 457
  reference counting and garbage collection, 139,
    144
  threading models, 147
  using from Visual Basic .NET, 140–144
  using Visual Basic .NET from, 144–147
  Visual Basic .NET COM Class file, 145
COM+, 251–280
  activating components, 256
  component requirements, 253
  context, component, 258–260
  just-in-time (JIT) activation, 269–272
    creating components, 270
  object construction, 260–261

object pooling, 262–269
  creating poolable objects, 265–269
  JIT activation, combined with, 270
  object life cycle, 262
  requirements, 264
serviced components, creating, 253
transactions, 272–280
  creating components, 273
  rules for, 273
  SimpleTransaction application (example),
    274–280
common language runtime (CLR), 20
communications protocols, 188–192
CompareExchange( ) (Mutex), 99
component architecture, 10
concatenating strings, performance of, 352–358
concatenation operator (&), 352
Configure( ) (RemotingConfiguration class), 172
Connect( ) (UdpClient class), 210
connection pooling, 366–370
  performance counters, 429
ConnectionGroupName property (WebRequest
    class), 196
ConnectionLimit property (ServicePoint class),
    195
consistency of COM+ transaction data, 273
constants, 120
  enumerations for, 39
  naming conventions for, 18
Construct( ) (ServicedComponent), 260
ConstructionEnabled property
    (ServicedComponent), 260, 276
constructors, 60
  shared, 59
consuming XML Web services, 163
content security, 169, 170
ContentLength property (Response class, ACT),
    426
context of COM+ components, 258–260
ContextId property (ContextUtil class), 259
ContextUtil class, 258–260
Continue( ) (ServiceController class), 227
cookie management (authentication), 314–317
CookieContainer property (HttpWebRequest
    class), 204

Copy( ) (Marshal class), 132
Copy Local property, 410
CorDbg Debugger, 327, 328
counters, performance, 387, 397, 427–451
   CLR (common language runtime), 427–445
   quick reference guide, 453–457
Create( ) (WebRequest class), 193, 198
CreateConnection( ) (Test class, ACT), 424
CreateRequest( ) (Test class, ACT), 424
CreationTimeout property (object pools), 262
CredentialCache class, 194
Credentials class, 205
Credentials property (WebRequest class), 194
credentials, security, 170. *See also* authentication
critical sections, 100
cryptography, 301–305
C-style arrays, marshaling, 143
CurrentThread class (Thread class), 85
custom serialization, 158–161
customer requirements, collecting, 7
customizing Visual Basic .NET start page, 412
CustomSerialization program (example), 158
cyclic processor usage, 395

D
Data property (EventLogEntry class), 336
data validation, 302
database applications, performance counters for,
   456
database dependencies, 411
database-related performance, 366–373
DataReader class, 370
DCOM (Distributed Component Object Model),
   153
Deactivate( ) (ServicedComponent class), 264
DeactivateOnReturn property (ContextUtil class),
   259
dead letter queues, 283
debugging, 323–349. *See also* exception handling
   Debug class, 341–349
      enabling and disabling, 343
      output control, 347
   Debug statements, 249
   Debugger class, 330–331

debuggers, 323–329
   CorDbg Debugger, 327
   Microsoft CLR Debugger, 326
   Microsoft Console Debugger, 328
   Microsoft NT Symbolic Debugger, 328
   performance testing/tuning with, 388, 397
   Visual Studio .NET Debugger, 324
   Windows Debugger (WinDbg), 329
.NET Diagnostic tools, 330–349
   event logs, 331–341
   Trace and Debug classes, 341–349
   poolable object creation, 268
   Windows services, 247–249
Declare statement, 29–32, 110–113
   Alias option, 113
Decrement( ) (Mutex), 99
DefaultNonPersistentConnectionLimit property
   (ServicePointManager class), 196
DefaultPersistentConnectionLimit property
   (ServicePointManager class), 195
DefaultTraceListener class, 345
delayed signing, 307
delaying thread execution, 88
delays in performance tests, 421
delegates, 41–43. *See also* events
Delete( ) (EventLog class), 334
DeleteEventSource( ) (EventLog class), 334
Demand identity, 306
dependencies, managing, 410
DependentServices property (ServiceController
   class), 226
deployment, 8, 12
deserialization. *See* serialization
design process, 8–11
   inheritance logic and, 50
DestroyStructure( ) (Marshal class), 132
detecting buffer overruns, 305
development process, 6–12
   design and architecture, 8–11
      inheritance logic and, 50
   implementation and deployment, 11–12
   requirements collection, 7–8
Diagnostics namespace, 330
digital signatures, 303

DisableCommit( ) (ContextUtil class), 259
Disabled (transaction option), 274
DisplayName property (ServiceController class), 226
DisplayName property (ServiceInstaller class), 244
Dispose( ) (IDisposable interface), 70–71, 373
DisposeObject( ) (ServicedComponent class), 255
distributed environment, 6
distributed programming, 153
  marshaling data
    interfaces vs. classes, 175
    security, 177
    singletons, 176
  remoting, 170–183, 234–237
    activation models, 173
    channel classes, 173, 177
    marshaling data, 174–175
    performance counters, 442
  serialization, 154–161
    custom, 158–161
    formats for, 154–157
  Web services, 161–170
    consuming, 163
    performance and limitations, 166–168
    security, 168–170
DllImport attribute, 31–32, 110, 114–118
DNS (Domain Name Service), 206
Dns class, 207
Domain Name Service (DNS), 206
DownloadData( ), DownloadFile( ) (WebClient class), 204
DropMulticastGroup( ) (UdpClient class), 210
durability of COM+ transactions, 273

E

early binding, 24–26
EnableCommit( ) (ContextUtil class), 259
EnableRaisingEvents( ) (EventLog class), 337
encapsulation, 56, 78–81
EncodeBody property (Request class, ACT), 425
EncodeQueryAsUTFS property (Request class, ACT), 425
encoding strings, 112
encryption
  how cryptography works, 301–305

message content (remoting), 178
message queue contents, 285
object serialization with, 170
EncryptionRequired property (MessageQueue class), 285
EndAccept( ) (Socket class), 214
EndConnect( ) (Socket class), 214
EndGetHostByName( ) (Dns class), 208
EndGetResponse( ) (WebRequest class), 194, 199–203
EndReceive( ) (MessageQueue class), 288
EndReceive( ) (Socket class), 214
EndResolve( ) (Dns class), 208
EndSend( ) (Socket class), 214
EndSendTo( ) (Socket class), 214
enterprise applications, 251–295
  definition of, 4
  development process, 6–12
    design and architecture, 8–11
    implementation, 11–12
    requirements collection, 7–8
Enterprise Architect, 401
enterprise security, 305–320
  authentication and authorization, 313–319
  changing policies, 311
  code groups, 312
  code security, 305–310
  user identity, 310
enterprise services
  COM+, 251–280
    activating components, 256
    component requirements, 253
    context, component, 258–260
    just-in time (JIT) activation, 269–272
    object construction, 260–261
    object pooling, 262–269, 270
    serviced components, creating, 253
    SimpleTransaction application (example), 274–280
    transactions, 272–280
  messaging, 280–295
    automatic queue installation, 294
    creating and working with queue, 284–294
    message queues, 281–283
    priorities, 281
enterprise templates, 402

EntryPoint property (DllImport attribute), 116
EntryType property (EventLogEntry class), 336
EntryWritten event, 337
Enum class, 40
enumerations, 38–41, 121
erratic processor usage, 395
error handling, 364–366. *See also* debugging; exception handling
event logs, 228–229, 331–341
  accessing events, 337
  creating entries, 333
  creating logs, 334
  monitoring logs, 336
EventID property (EventLogEntry class), 336
EventLog application (example), 338
EventLog class, 228, 332
EventLog property (ServiceBase class), 232
EventLogEntry class, 336
EventLogInstaller class, 335
EventLogTraceListener class, 345
events, 41–45
  delegates, 41–43
  logging. *See* event logs
  shared, 56–59
ever-increasing memory usage, 396
Everyone account, 318
evidence-based security, 299–301
ExactSpelling property (DllImport attribute), 117
Exception class, 63
exception handling, 63–68, 364, 366
  COM error handling, 139
  performance counters, 429
Exchange( ) (Mutex), 99
exclusive source control checkouts, 408
ExecuteCommand( ) (ServiceController class), 227
execution, thread, 81–92
  control methods, 85–91
  execution time (time slices), 75
  thread states, 81–85
explicit programming, 15
ExtendedConsole (example), 134–136

F

Fail( ) (Debug, Trace classes), 342
fat-client applications, 9
FileWebRequestCreator class, 196
Finalize( ) (Object class), 69
Finally clause, 63
Flush( ) (Debug, Trace classes), 342
Format( ) (String class), 355
Format( ) (System.Enum class), 40
forms-based authentication, 314–317
FormsAuthenticationTicket class, 317
FreeBSTR( ) (Marshal class), 132
FreeHGlobal( ) (Marshal class), 133
FTP (File Transfer Protocol), 192, 196
FtpWebRequest class (example), 197
FtpWebResponse class (example), 197
functions
  ByRef, ByVal parameters, 119
  directly calling Win32 functions, 29–32
  predefined values, 120
  returning strings, 125
  strings, marshaling, 123–127
  structures, marshaling, 127–132

G

GAC (Global Assembly Cache), 256
garbage collection, 69–71, 139, 144, 373
  remoting singletons and, 176
generating random numbers, 302
GetAuthCookie( ) (FormsAuthentication class), 317
GetBytes( ) (RNGCryptoServiceProvider class), 302
GetCommandLine function, 126
GetCurrent( ) (WindowsIdentity class), 311
GetCurrentUser( ) (Test class, ACT), 424
GetDevices( ) (ServiceController class), 227
GetExceptionCode( ) (Marshal class), 133
GetExceptionPointers( ) (Marshal class), 133
GetGlobalIndex( ) (Test class, ACT), 424
GetGlobalVariable( ) (Test class, ACT), 424
GetHostByAddress( ) (Dns class), 207
GetHostByName( ) (Dns class), 207

GetHostName( ) (Dns class), 207
GetLastWin32Error( ) (Marshal class), 133
GetName( ) (System.Enum class), 40
GetNamedProperty( ) (ContextUtil class), 259
GetNames( ) (System.Enum class), 40
GetNextUser( ) (Test class, ACT), 424
GetOrdinal( ) (IDataRecord interface), 372
GetRegistered...Types( ) (RemotingConfiguration class), 172
GetResponse( ) (WebRequest class), 193, 198
GetResponseStream( ) (WebRequest class), 193, 198
GetServices( ) (ServiceController class), 227
GetType( ) (System.Object class), 40
GetUnderlyingType( ) (System.Enum class), 40
GetValues( ) (System.Enum class), 40
Global Assembly Cache (GAC), 256
global.asax file, 299
globally unique identifiers (GUIDs), 138
GlobalProxySelection class, 205
growing memory usage, 396
GUIDs (globally unique identifiers), 138

H

Handles keyword, 44
handling events. *See* event logs; events
handling exceptions. *See* exception handling
hardware, infrastructure requirements, 7
hash functions, 301
header, SOAP, 163–166
Headers property (Request, Response classes), 425–426
HeaderSize property (Response class, ACT), 426
heap overruns, 305
HRESULT value, 139, 142
HTTP (Hypertext Transfer Protocol), 188
HttpChannel class, 174, 177
HTTPS (secure HTTP), 169
HTTPVersion property (Request, Response classes), 425–426
HttpWebRequest class, 193
HttpWebResponse class, 193
Hypertext Transfer Protocol (HTTP), 188

I

IAsyncResult interface, 200
IClassFactory interface (COM), 138
ICorProfilerCallback interface, 390
identity permissions, 306
identity, user, 310
IDispatch interface (COM), 139
IDisposable interface, 70–71, 373
IIS (Internet Information Services), 168
ILDASM (MSIL Disassembler), 115
implementation inheritance, 50
implementation process, 11
implicit programming, 15
importing native methods. *See* native methods
In attribute, 120
increasing memory usage, 396
Increment( ) (Interlocked class), 268
Increment( ) (Mutex), 99
IncrementGlobalIndex( ) (Test class, ACT), 424
Indent( ) (Debug, Trace classes), 342
IndentLevel property (Debug, Trace classes), 342
IndentSize property (Debug, Trace classes), 342
Index property (EventLogEntry class), 336
infrastructure requirements, collecting, 7
inheritance, 13, 14, 49–61
    COM vs. .NET object models, 138
    controlling, 51
    encapsulation, 56, 78–81
    interface vs. implementation inheritance, 50
    polymorphism, 52–56
    shared members, 56–59
InheritanceDemand identity, 306
INI configuration files, accessing, 30
InitializeComponent( ) (ProjectInstaller class), 245
InitializeLifetimeService( ) (MarshalByRef class), 176
InnerException property (Exception class), 65
in-process (library) activation (COM+), 256
Installer class, 246
installing message queue automatically, 294
installing Windows services, 244–246
InstallUtil.exe utility, 244
Integer type, 119
integration, 6

interfaces, 36–38, 138
  inheritance, 50. *See also* inheritance
  remoting, 175
Interlocked class (Threading namespace), 93, 98
Internet_Zone code group, 312
interop assemblies, 140–144
Interrupt( ) (Thread class), 86, 91
IntPtr type, 119, 125
IP (Internet Protocol), 189
IPAddress class, 206
IPEndPoint class, 206
IPSec (Internet Protocol Security Extensions), 177
IsActivationAllowed( ) (RemotingConfiguration
    class), 172
IsAttached property (Debugger class), 331
IsCallerInRole( ) (ContextUtil class), 260
IsDefined( ) (System.Enum class), 40
IsInRole( ) (WindowsIdentity class), 311
IsInTransaction property (ContextUtil class), 259
IsLogging( ) (Debugger class), 331
isolation of COM+ transactions, 273
IsOpen property (Connection class, ACT), 425
IsRemotelyActivatedClientType( )
    (RemotingConfiguration class), 172
IsSecurityEnabled property (ContextUtil class),
    259
IsWellKnownClientType( )
    (RemotingConfiguration class), 172

J

JIT (just-in-time) activation, 269–272
  creating components, 270
  performance counters, 431
Join( ) (Thread class), 86, 90
JoinMulticastGroup( ) (UdpClient class), 210
journal message queues, 282
just-in-time (JIT) activation, 269–272
  creating components, 270
  performance counters, 431

K

KeepAlive property (HttpWebRequest class), 196

L

late binding, 24–26, 139, 358
LateBindingPerformance application (example),
    358
Launch( ) (Debugger class), 331
LayoutKind option (StructLayout attribute), 129
leaks, database connection, 366–370
library activation (COM+), 256
lifetime leases (remoting), 176
limitations of threads, 75, 83
limited-access public APIs, 301
LinkDemand identity, 306
Listeners property (Debug, Trace classes), 342
LocalIntranet_Zone code group, 312
LocalService account, 221
LocalSystem account, 221
Log( ) (Debugger class), 331
logging events, 331–341. *See also* events
  accessing events, 337
  creating entries, 333
  creating logs, 334
  monitoring logs, 336
logical operators, 26–29
loginUrl attribute (forms-based security), 315
Long type, 119
low-level performance analysis, 397

M

Machine.config file, 191
MachineName property (EventLogEntry class),
    336
MachineName property (ServiceController class),
    226
managed code, security for, 299
managed runtime environment, 107
ManualResetEvent class (Threading namespace),
    93, 95, 201
Marshal class, 126, 132–134
MarshalAs parameter attribute, 120, 128
MarshalByRef class, 174
marshaling, 118–134, 174–175
  callback functions, 134–136
  C-style and multidimensional arrays, 143

interfaces vs. classes, 175
performance counters, 457
security, 177
singletons, 176
strings, 123–127
structures, 127–132
    definition shortcuts, 130
MaxIdleTime property (ServicePoint class), 196
MaximumQueueSize property (MessageQueue
    class), 285
MaxPoolSize property (object pools), 262
Me keyword, 54
memory
    behavior tuning, 395
    buffer overrun detection, 305
    object pooling, 265
    performance counters, 436
    PInvoke and COM interop, 148
    statistics, obtaining, 385
    thread limitations, 75
Message class, 284
Message property (EventLogEntry class), 337
MessageBeep function, 120
MessageQueue class, 284
MessageQueueInstaller class, 294
MessageReceived( ) (MessageQueue class), 292
messaging, 280–295
    automatic queue installation, 294
    cryptography. *See* cryptography; encryption
    message queues, 281–283
        creating, 284–294
    priorities, 281
Messaging namespace, 283
methods
    naming conventions for, 17
    native. *See* native methods
    overriding (polymorphism), 52–56. *See also*
        inheritance
    shared, 56–59
Microsoft CLR Debugger, 326
Microsoft Console Debugger, 328
Microsoft NT Symbolic Debugger, 328
MinPoolSize property (object pools), 262
mixed-client applications, 10
modules, 34

Monitor class (Threading namespace), 93, 100
monitoring event logs, 336
mscorwks.dll and mscorsvr.dll, 377
MSIL (Microsoft intermediate language), 305
MSIL Disassembler (ILDASM), 115
MTA (multithreaded apartment) model, 147
MTAThread attribute, 147
multideveloper environment, working in,
        399–414
    business requirements, 400
    dependency management, 410
    Enterprise Architect, 401
    enterprise templates, 402
    modeling tools, 401
    source control, 406–409
    start page, customizing, 412
    technical architecture, project, 400
    Web project management, 409
multidimensional arrays, marshaling, 143
multiple process debugging, 325
multithreaded programming, 73–105
    basic concepts, 74–78
    creating threads, 76–78
    COM threading models, 147
    controlling thread execution, 81–92
        control methods, 85–91
        thread states, 81–85
    encapsulation, 78–81
    object pooling and, 264
    performance counters for managed locks and
        threads, 434
    pooling, 102–104
    race conditions, 92, 330
    referencing current thread, 85
    safe points, 86
    STA COM components, 374
    synchronization, 92–102
multitier application architecture, 10
MustOverride keyword, 53
Mutex class (Threading namespace), 93, 98
My_Computer_Zone code group, 312
MyBase keyword, 54
MyClass keyword, 54
MyTransactionVote property (ContextUtil class),
        259

N

Name attribute (forms-based security), 315
named code groups, scripting against, 312
namespaces, 45–49
naming conventions, Visual Basic .NET, 16, 38
native code debugging, 325
native methods, 107, 109–137
  accessing (importing)
    Declare statement, 110–113
    DllImport attribute, 114–118
  ByRef, ByVal parameters, 119
  callback functions, 134–136
  COM interop. *See* COM
  importing with DllImport, 31–32
  In, Out parameter attributes, 120
  MarshalAs parameter attribute, 120
  marshaling, 118–134
    Marshal class, 132–134
    strings, 123–127
    structures, 127–132
  naming conventions, 17
  overriding (polymorphism), 52–56
  performance and memory considerations, 147
  predefined values, 120
  security concerns, 109
  shared methods, 56–59
  strings as parameters, 124
.NET Diagnostic tools, 330–349
  event logs, 331–341
  Trace and Debug classes, 341–349
.NET Framework security features, 298–305
  authentication and authorization, 313–319
  buffer overrun detection, 305
  cryptography, 301–305
  evidence-based security, 299–301
  role-based security, 298–299
  web application security, 299
network architectures, 10, 186–188
network bandwidth, monitoring, 385
network communications, 185–218
  asynchronous operations, 199–203, 207
    socket-level programming, 214–218
  communications protocols, 188–192
  connection management, 194–196
  performance counters, 442

  socket programming, 206–218
    addressing, 206–208
    TcpClient, TcpListener, UdpClient classes, 208–212
    WebClient class, 203–205
    WebRequest, WebResponse classes, 191–203
      custom protocol handlers, 196
Network Time Protocol (NTP), 233
network usage, profiling, 396
NetworkCredentials class, 194
NetworkService account, 221
NetworkStream class, 214
New operator, 138
NonInheritable keyword, 62
NonSerialized attribute, 157
Nothing value, 69
NotSupported (transaction option), 274
NTP (Network Time Protocol), 233
NTSD (Microsoft NT Symbolic Debugger), 328
numbers, random, 302

O

object constructors, 59–60
object pooling, 262–269
  creating poolable objects, 265–269
  JIT activation, combined with, 270
  object life cycle, 262
  requirements, 264
Object type (System class), 33
ObjectConstruction application (example), 260
object-oriented programming (OOP), 45–63
  inheritance, 49–61. *See also* inheritance
  namespaces, 45–49
  singletons, 61–63
ObjectPooling application (example), 266
ObjectPooling property (ServicedComponent class), 264
ObjectSerialization program (example), 155
On Error statement, 63, 364
OnContinue( ) (ServiceBase class), 232
OnCustomCommand( ) (ServiceBase class), 233
OnErrorPerformance application (example), 365
OnPause( ) (ServiceBase class), 232
OnPowerEvent( ) (ServiceBase class), 232
OnShutdown( ) (ServiceBase class), 233

OnStart( ) (ServiceBase class), 230, 232
  debugging, 248
  remoting with (example), 234
OnStop( ) (ServiceBase class), 230, 232
OOP (object-oriented programming), 45–63
  inheritance, 49–61. *See also* inheritance
  namespaces, 45–49
  singletons, 61–63
OpenRead( ), OpenWrite( ) (WebClient class),
  204
operators, logical, 26–29
Option Explicit compilation option, 21
Option Strict compilation option, 21–26
Or (logical operator), 26
ordinals vs. column names (databases), 371
OrElse (logical operator), 27
Out attribute, 120
out-of-process (server) activation (COM+), 256
Overridable keyword, 53
overriding methods (polymorphism), 52–56. *See
  also* inheritance

P

Pack option (StructLayout attribute), 130
Parse( ) (System.Enum class), 41
PartitionId property (ContextUtil class), 259
Path attribute (forms-based security), 316
Path property (Request, Response classes),
  425–426
Pause( ) (ServiceController class), 227
pegged processor usage, 394
performance, 4, 5, 351–382
  ASP.NET, 374–377
  boxing and unboxing types, 33
  coding techniques, 15–18
  COM+ component activation, 256
  counters, 387, 397, 427–451
    ASP.NET, 445–451
    CLR (common language runtime), 427–445
    quick reference guide, 453–457
  database issues, 366–373
  debuggers for, 388, 397
  error and exception handling, 364–366
  exception handling, 66
  JIT activation, 270
  late binding, 24–26, 358

network connection management, 194–196
object pooling, 262, 264
PInvoke and COM interop, 147
reference counting and garbage collection, 139,
    144
requirements for, determining, 8
resource management, 69–71, 139, 144, 373
  buffer overrun detection, 305
  object pooling, 264
runtimes, 377–382
string concatenation, 352–358
testing, 383–393
  acceptable results, defining, 392
  Application Center Test (ACT), 390, 415–426
  planning, 391–393
  tools for, 384–390
thread limitations, 75
tuning, 383, 393–398
  low-level analysis, 397
type designing, 360–363
using System.GC.Collect( ), 70
Visual Basic .NET vs. Visual C# .NET, 352
Web services, 166
Performance Monitor (perfmon) utility, 386
Permissions namespace, 306
permissions, code, 308–310
PERMVIEW tool, 308, 310
PIAs (primary interop assemblies), 141
ping functionality (example), 214–218
PInvoke (platform invoke) service, 108, 109–137
  callback functions, 134–136
  marshaling, 118–134
  performance considerations, 147
planning performance tests, 391–393
platform functions, calling directly, 29–32
platform-specific string encoding, 112
pluggable communications protocols, 191
  custom protocol handlers, 196
policies for security, changing, 311
polymorphism, 52, 56
pooling, 262–269, 366–370
  creating poolable objects, 265–269
  JIT activation, combined with, 270
  object life cycle, 262
  performance counters, 429
  requirements, 264
  threads, 102–104

Port property (Connection class, ACT), 425
Port property (Response class, ACT), 426
post numbers, 209
power state changes, responding to, 232
predefined values, 120
PreserveSig property (DllImport attribute), 117
preventing inheritance, 51
primary interop assemblies (PIAs), 141
primitive types, 32
Principal namespace, 310
principals (authentication), 298
priorities, message, 281
private message queues, 282
processes, threads and, 74–76
ProcessId property (RemotingConfiguration class), 171
processor usage profile, 394
profiles, 389, 393
ProjectInstaller class, 244
properties, shared, 56–59
Protection attribute (forms-based security), 316
PtrToStringAnsi( ) (Marshal class), 133
PtrToStringAuto( ) (Marshal class), 126, 133
PtrToStringBSTR( ) (Marshal class), 133
PtrToStringUni( ) (Marshal class), 133
PtrToStructure( ) (Marshal class), 133
public APIs, limited access to, 301
public key cryptography, 301
public message queues, 282

Q
queue, message, 281–283
   automatic installation, 294
   creating and working with, 284–294
   cryptography. *See* cryptography; encryption
   message priorities, 281
queued components (COM+), 283

R
race conditions, 92, 330
RaiseEvent( ), 44
random delays in performance tests, 421
random number generation, 302
RCWs (runtime callable wrappers), 140–144
ReadByte( ) (Marshal class), 133

ReaderWriterLock class (Threading namespace), 93, 101
ReadInt16( ), ReadInt32( ), ReadInt64( ) (Marshal class), 133
ReadIntPtr( ) (Marshal class), 133
ReAllocHGlobal( ) (Marshal class), 133
Receive( ) (UdpClient class), 210
receiving messages asynchronously, 288
recoverability of messages, 282
RedirectDepth property (Connection class, ACT), 425
reference, marshaling types by, 174
reference counting, 139, 144
reference types
   boxing and unboxing, 33, 363
   unions with, 143
   value types vs., 32
reflection, 139
Refresh( ) (ServiceController class), 227
RegisterActivatedClientType( ) (RemotingConfiguration class), 172
RegisterActivatedServiceType( ) (RemotingConfiguration class), 172
registering COM+ components, 255
registering types. *See* remoting
RegisterPrefix( ) (WebRequest class), 192, 196, 198
RegisterWellKnownClientType( ) (RemotingConfiguration class), 172
RegisterWellKnownServiceType( ) (RemotingConfiguration class), 172
registry dependency, 13, 14
RegularExpressionValidator control, 302
Release( ) (IUnknown interface), 139
reliability, 4, 5
remote debugging, 325
remoting, 170–183, 234–237
   activation models, 173
   channel classes, 173, 177
   marshaling data, 174–175
   performance counters, 442, 457
Remoting program (example), 178
RemotingConfiguration class, 171–173, 235
Remove( ) (Listeners class), 346
RemoveHandler statement, 45
Request objects, appending ViewState to, 422

requesting code permissions, 308–310
RequestMinimum permission request, 308
RequestOptional permission request, 308
RequestRefuse permission request, 308
Required (transactions option), 274
requirements collection, 7–8
RequiresNew (transaction option), 274
requiring inheritance, 51
Resolve( ) (Dns class), 207
resolving DNS issues, 207
resource management, 69–71, 139, 144, 373. *See also* performance
    buffer overrun detection, 305
    object pooling, 264
resource protection, 301
response message queues, 282
Response objects, extracting ViewState from, 422
ResponseBufferSize property (Request class, ACT), 425
ResponseHeaders property (WebClient class), 204
ResultCode property (Response class, ACT), 426
Resume( ) (Thread class), 86, 89
reusing existing network connections, 196
reverse engineering, 402
RNGCryptoServiceProvider class, 302
role authorization, 318–319
role-based security, 298–299
Run( ) (ServiceBase class), 230
RunInstaller attribute (ProjectInstaller class), 244
Running state (threads), 81, 83, 86, 89
runtime callable wrappers (RCWs), 140–144
runtimes, which to use, 377–382

S
safe points, 86
sanity check (performance tuning), 394–396
scalability, 4, 5
SCM (Service Control Manager), 220, 244. *See also* Windows services
scripts for security, 311–312
Secure Sockets Layer (SSL), 169
security, 297–320
    authentication, 168–169, 298, 313–317
        message queues, 285
        network communications, 194
    authorization, 299, 318–319

cryptography, 301–305
    enterprise scenarios, 305–320
        authentication and authorization, 313–319
        changing policies, 311
        code groups, 312
        code security, 305–310
        user identity, 310
    features of .NET Framework, 298–305
        buffer overrun detection, 305
        cryptography, 301–305
        evidence-based security, 299–301
        role-based security, 298–299
        web application security, 299
    IPSec (Internet Protocol Security Extensions), 177
    marshaling, 177
    native methods, 109
    performance counters, 444
    scripts for, 311–312
    Web services, 168–170
Select( ) (Socket class), 213
selective serialization, 157
self-registering COM+ components, 255
Send( ) (Connection class, ACT), 425
Send( ) (UdpClient class), 210
SendRequest( ) (Test class, ACT), 424
Serializable attribute, 157–161
serialization, 154–161
    custom, 158–161
    formats for, 154–157
    selective, 157
SerializationInfo class, 158
server activation (COM+), 256
Server Explorer feature, 284
Server property (Connection class, ACT), 425
Server property (Response class, ACT), 426
server runtime, 377
server-based timer (System.Timers), 238
Service Control Manager (SCM), 220, 244. *See also* Windows services
Service Manager application (example), 225–227
ServiceBase class, debugging OnStart( ) method, 248
ServiceController class, 222–227
serviced components, 252–253
ServicedComponent class, 252
ServiceInstaller class, 244

ServiceName property (ServiceController class), 223, 226

ServiceName property (ServiceInstaller class), 244

ServicePoint class, 195

ServicePointManager class, 195

ServiceProcessInstaller class, 244

Services Management Console (SMC), 220

services. *See* Windows services

ServicesDependedOn property (ServiceController class), 226

ServicesDependedOn property (ServiceInstaller class), 244

ServiceType property (ServiceController class), 227

session state (ASP.NET), 374

SetAbort( ) (ContextUtil class), 260, 277

SetAuthCookie( ) (FormsAuthentication class), 317

SetCommit( ) (ContextUtil class), 277

SetComplete( ) (ContextUtil class), 260

SetGlobalIndex( ) (Test class, ACT), 424

SetGlobalVariable( ) (Test class, ACT), 424

SetLastError property (DllImport attribute), 117

SetPrincipalPolicy( ) (WindowsPrincipal class), 311

Shadows keyword, 53

Shared keyword, 56–59

Short type, 119

short-circuiting logical operators, 26–29

signatures, digital, 303

SignOut( ) (FormsAuthentication), 317

SimpleComponent application (example), 254

single processor usage, 394

single-tier applications, 9

singletons, 61–63

singletons, remoting, 176

Size option (StructLayout attribute), 130

SizeOf( ) (Marshal class), 127, 133

Sleep( ) (Test class, ACT), 424

Sleep( ) (Thread class), 86, 87

SMC (Services Management Console), 220

SOAP (Standard Object Application Protocol), 161

  header extensions, 163–166

  serialization, 154

  services, 253

SOAPFormatter class, 155

SoapHeader class, 164

SoapHeaderAttribute class, 164

Socket class, 212–218

  asynchronous operations, 214–218

socket programming, 206–218

  addressing, 206–208

  socket-level, 212

  TcpClient, TcpListener, UdpClient classes, 208–212

source control, 406–409

Source property (EventLog class), 229

Source property (EventLogEntry class), 337

SourceExists( ) (EventLog class), 334

spinning, 88

SpinWait( ) (Thread class), 86, 88

SQL database application performance counters, 456

SqlClient namespace, 366

SqlConnection class, 367

SSL (Secure Sockets Layer), 169

STA (single-threaded apartment) model, 147

stable memory usage, 395

stalled processor usage, 395

start page, Visual Basic .NET, 412

Start( ) (ServiceController class), 223, 227

Start( ) (Thread class), 86

StartType property (ServiceInstaller class), 244

state of poolable objects, 264

STAThread attribute, 147

Status property (ServiceController class), 227

Stop( ) (ServiceController class), 224, 227

Stopped state (threads), 81, 84

StopTest( ) (Test class, ACT), 424

StreamingContext structure, 158

StreamReader class, 193

stress testing, 384, 390

String type, 125

StringBuilder class, 123, 353–358

StringConcatPerformance application (example), 357

strings

  concatenation, performance of, 352–358

  encoding, 112

  marshaling, 123–127

    structures and, 127

StringToBSTR( ) (Marshal class), 134

StringToHGlobalAnsi( ) (Marshal class), 134

StringToHGlobalAuto( ) (Marshal class), 134
StringToHGlobalUni( ) (Marshal class), 134
strong name identity permissions, 307
strongly typed classes, 241
StructLayout attribute, 127, 129
structures, 35–37
    marshaling, 127–132
StructureToPtr( ) (Marshal class), 134
subscribing to events. *See* events
Supported (transaction option), 274
Suspend( ) (Thread class), 86, 89
Suspended state (threads), 81, 84, 89
SuspendRequested state (threads), 82
SvrLoader application (example), 378
Switch classes, 347–349
symmetric ciphers, 301
synchronizing machine times (example), 233–243
synchronizing threads, 92–102
synchronous network operations, 212
SyncLock statement, 101
system performance counters (ASP.NET), 445
System.Messaging namespace, 283
System.Net namespace. *See* network
    communications
SystemException class, 67

T

TCP (Transmission Control Protocol), 190
TcpChannel class, 173, 177
TcpClient class, 208–212
TcpListener class, 208–212
TDL (Template Definition Language), 403
team development, 4
technologies of Visual Basic .NET, 5
Template Definition Language (TDL), 403
templates, enterprise, 402
testing enterprise application, 11
testing performance, 383–393. *See also*
        performance
    planning, 391–393
    tools for, 384–390
TextWriterTraceListener class, 345
thin-client applications, 9
third-party performance and stress tools, 390
Thread class (Threading namespace), 76
ThreadAbortException (Thread class), 89

threading. *See* multithreaded programming
ThreadPool class, 103–104
ThreadStart( ) delegate, 76
ThreadState property (Thread class), 81
throwing exceptions, 65. *See also* exception
    handling
tiered application architectures, 10
time slices, 75
time synchronization service (example), 233–243
TimeGenerated property (EventLogEntry class),
    337
timeout attribute (forms-based security), 315
timers (.NET Framework), 238
TimeWritten property (EventLogEntry class), 337
Tlbimp.exe utility, 142
ToObject( ) (System.Enum class), 41
Trace class, 249, 341–349
    enabling and disabling, 343
    output control, 347
Trace statements, 249
Trace( ) (Test class, ACT), 424
TraceLevel property (Test class, ACT), 424
TraceListener class, 344–347
    custom, creating, 346
TraceSwitch class, 348
Transaction property (ContextUtil class), 259
Transaction property (ServicedComponent class),
    274
transactional message queues, 283
TransactionId property (ContextUtil class), 259
transactions, COM+, 272–280
    creating components, 273
    rules for, 273
    SimpleTransaction application (example),
        274–280
trust, code, 299
Try statement, 63
TTFB property (Response class, ACT), 426
TTLB property (Response class, ACT), 426
tuning performance, 383, 393–398. *See also*
        performance
type libraries, 138
types, 32–45
    basic (blittable) types, 119
    boxing and unboxing, 33, 363
    classes and modules, 34
    constants and predefined values, 120

types, *continued*
delegates and events, 41–45
designing, 360–363
enumerations, 38–41, 121
interfaces, 36–38
late binding, 24–26, 358
marshaling. *See* marshaling
registration. *See* remoting
strings, 123–127
structures, 35–37, 127–132
value vs. reference types, 32

U

UDP (User Datagram Protocol), 190, 210
UdpClient class, 208, 210–212
UIntPtr type, 119
undulating memory usage, 395
Unicode encoding, 112
Unindent( ) (Debug, Trace classes), 342
unions with reference types, 143
Unstarted state (threads), 82, 83
UploadData( ), UploadFile( ) (WebClient class), 204
UploadValue( ) (WebClient class), 204
URIs (uniform resource identifiers), 191
URL authorization, 299, 318–319
user accounts for Windows services, 221
user authentication, 168–169, 298, 313–317
message queues, 285
network communications, 194
user authorization, 299, 318–319
user identity, 310
user interface design, 9
user interface testing tools, 390
UserName property (EventLogEntry class), 337
UseSSL property (Connection class, ACT), 425
UseSSL property (Response class, ACT), 426

V

validating data, 302
value types
boxing and unboxing, 33, 363
reference types vs., 32
ValueTypePerformance application (example), 361

variables
naming conventions for, 17
shared, 56–59
Verb property (Request class, ACT), 425
ViewState component (WebForm), 422
Visio for Enterprise Architects, 401
Visual Basic .NET, 12–18, 19–72
coding techniques, 15–18
COM vs. .NET object models, 137–139
cryptography, 303
exception handling, 63–68
implementation technologies, 5
messaging, 283–284
multideveloper environment, working in, 399–414
business requirements, 400
dependency management, 410
Enterprise Architect, 401
enterprise templates, 402
modeling tools, 401
source control, 406–409
start page, customizing, 412
technical architecture, project, 400
Web project management, 409
OOP (object-oriented programming), 45–63
inheritance, 49–61
namespaces, 45–49
singletons, 61–63
performance, 352
resource management, 69–71
start page, customizing, 412
threading. *See* multithreaded programming
types, 32–45. *See also* types
boxing and unboxing, 33
classes and modules, 34
delegates and events, 41–45
enumerations, 38–41
interfaces, 36–38
structures, 35–37
using COM from, 140–144
using from COM, 144–147
Visual Basic 6 and Windows services, 219
Visual C# .NET performance, 352
Visual SourceSafe, 406–409
Visual Studio .NET Debugger, 324

W

wait handles, defined, 94
WaitAll( ) (WaitHandle class), 95
WaitAny( ) (WaitHandle class), 95
WaitCallback( ) delegate, 104
WaitForStatus( ) (ServiceController class), 224,
    227
WaitHandle class (Threading namespace), 94
WaitHandleTest application (example), 96
WaitOne( ) (WaitHandle class), 94
WaitSleepJoin state (threads), 82, 84, 87
WAS (Web Application Stress) utility, 390, 415
Web application security, 299
Web Application Stress (WAS) utility, 390, 415
Web project management, 409
Web references, 163
Web services, XML, 161–170
    consuming, 163
    performance and limitations, 166–168
    performance counters, 455
    security, 168–170
Web testing tools, 390
WebClient class, 203–205
WebMethod attribute, 162
WebProxy class, 205
WebRequest class, 191, 192–203
    asynchronous operations, 199–203
    custom protocol handlers, 196
    WebClient class vs., 203
WebResponse class, 191, 192–193
    custom protocol handlers, 196
    WebClient class vs., 203
WebService class, 162
Win32 functions, calling directly, 29–32
Windows Debugger (WinDbg), 329
Windows event logging, 228–229, 331–341. *See
    also* events
    accessing events, 337
    creating entries, 333
    creating logs, 334
    monitoring logs, 336
windows event logging, 229
Windows Forms timer, 238
Windows Management Instrumentation (WMI),
    240, 241

Windows services, 219–250
    debugging, 247–249
    event logging, 228–229
    installing, 244–246
    Service Control Manager (SCM), 220, 244
    Service Manager application (example),
        225–227
    ServiceController class, 222–227
    simple service example, 230–233
    time synchronization service (example),
        233–243
    Visual Basic 6 and, 219
Windows Task Manager, 384, 385
WindowsIdentity class, 310
WindowsPrincipal class, 299, 310, 313
WithEvents keyword, 44
WMI (Windows Management Instrumentation),
    240, 241
workstation runtime, 377
Write( ) (Debug, Trace classes), 341, 342
WriteByte( ) (Marshal class), 134
WriteEntry( ) (EventLog class), 229, 333–335
WriteIf( ) (Debug, Trace classes), 342
WriteInt16( ), WriteInt32( ), WriteInt64( ) (Marshal
    class), 134
WriteIntPtr( ) (Marshal class), 134
WriteLine( )
    Console class, 354
    Debug class, 341
    Trace class, 249, 341
WriteLineIf( ) (Debug, Trace classes), 342

X

XML Digital Signature specification (XMLDSIG),
    303
XML serialization, 154
XML Web services, 161–170
    consuming, 163
    performance and limitations, 166–168
    performance counters, 455
    security, 168–170

Robert Ian Oliver

Robert Ian Oliver coauthored *Upgrading Microsoft Visual Basic 6.0 to Microsoft Visual Basic .NET* (Microsoft Press, 2002). Currently a Program Manager in Microsoft's Trusted Platforms team, Ian was a member of the Visual Studio .NET Porting Lab team for over two-and-a-half years. During this period he worked with many real-world customer applications, porting them to the .NET platform and doing performance and architectural analysis. His previous experience varies widely, from being an independent Web consultant to working at the Intel Corporation as a component design engineer on the first Itanium server chipset. Ian has been involved in Web development as far back as 1995 and has designed and built many ecommerce applications over the years. Ian has a B.S. degree in Electrical Engineering from Seattle University.

Contributing Authors

Sarath Kumar Mallavarapu has more than seven years of experience in the software industry of which over four years are at Microsoft. He is currently an Escalation Engineer in critical problem resolution and helps resolve complex and technical customer issues with both the .NET Framework and Visual Studio .NET product suite. He has written numerous Microsoft Knowledge Base articles and has been involved with many MSDN white papers. Prior to his current position, Sarath involved in the Visual Studio .NET Joint Development Partners and Early Adopters projects. He also worked closely with the Visual Studio .NET Porting Lab team.

Devin Breshears is currently a developer on the MSN Home & Auto team. Prior to this he was a member of the Visual Studio Porting Lab team. Devin has extensive experience migrating WinDNA-based enterprise applications to Visual Studio .NET and the .NET Framework. He lives with his wife and three children on a small horse farm in Edgewood, Washington. When he is not working around his farm, you can find him golfing, fishing, or camping with his family.

Vishnu Patankar is a developer in the Windows Security team at Microsoft. He works on Security Policy and Security Management products and strategies for the Windows operating system. Prior to joining Microsoft, Vishnu worked at the Intel Corporation (analyzing symmetric multiprocessor [SMP] cache-coherence protocols and microarchitecture trade-offs) and Texas Instruments (simulating combinational logic for digital signal processors). Vishnu has an M.S. degree in Computer Engineering from Carnegie Mellon University (Pittsburgh) and an M.S. in Mathematics and a B.E. in Electronics Engineering from the Birla Institute of Technology and Science (Pilani).

Wood File

The unique characteristics of wood have made it a basic material for housing, furniture, tools, vehicles, and many other uses throughout history. Woodworking, in fact, was one of mankind's first skills. Down through the centuries, as people discovered that different woods have their own textures, hues, and fragrances, artisans developed hand and power tools to bring out the special qualities of each wood. Most hand tools used today have changed very little since the Middle Ages. One traditional hand tool is the **wood file**, which is used to smooth and shape wood before adding further refinements such as sanding and varnishing. Speaking of tradition, Visual Basic has long been the tool of choice for programmers who want to create smooth-running, well-shaped applications. The power and flexibility of the latest version, Visual Basic .NET, makes it a good tool for creating applications for the enterprise.[1]

At Microsoft Press, we use tools to illustrate our books for software developers and IT professionals. Tools very simply and powerfully symbolize human inventiveness. They're a metaphor for people extending their capabilities, precision, and reach. From simple calipers and pliers to digital micrometers and lasers, these stylized illustrations give each book a visual identity, and a personality to the series. With tools and knowledge, there's no limit to creativity and innovation. Our tagline says it all: *the tools you need to put technology to work.*

The manuscript for this book was prepared and galleyed using Microsoft Word. Pages were composed by Microsoft Press using Adobe FrameMaker+SGML for Microsoft Windows, with text in Garamond and display type in Helvetica Condensed. Composed pages were delivered to the printer as electronic prepress files.

Cover Designer:	Methodologie, Inc.
Interior Graphic Designer:	James D. Kramer
Principal Compositor:	Elizabeth Hansford
Electronic Artist:	Michael Kloepfer
Principal Copy Editor:	Ina Chang
Indexer:	Seth Maislin

1. *Microsoft® Encarta® Reference Library 2002. © 1993-2001 Microsoft Corporation. All rights reserved.

Create killer applications
using best practices for Visual Basic .NET!

Practical Standards for Microsoft® Visual Basic® .NET
U.S.A. $49.99
Canada $72.99
ISBN: 0-7356-1356-7

The same attributes that make Visual Basic .NET exceptionally productive and easy to use can also lead to unexpected problems, especially when you upgrade. Using standardized programming techniques can help you solve those problems so you can exploit all the power of rapid development—without creating hidden land mines in performance and maintainability. This book shows you proven practices to help you eliminate "voodoo variables," create interfaces that make users more productive, write self-documenting code, simplify code modifications, and more. Each chapter illustrates common pitfalls and practical solutions with code samples—many from real-world projects. Whether you're writing just a few lines of code or working with a team to build an enterprise application, you'll learn how to use practical standards to develop better, more reliable code for every process.

microsoft.com/mspress

Get a **Free**
e-mail newsletter, updates,
special offers, links to related books,
and more when you

register on line!

Register your Microsoft Press® title on our Web site and you'll get a FREE subscription to our e-mail newsletter, *Microsoft Press Book Connections.* You'll find out about newly released and upcoming books and learning tools, online events, software downloads, special offers and coupons for Microsoft Press customers, and information about major Microsoft® product releases. You can also read useful additional information about all the titles we publish, such as detailed book descriptions, tables of contents and indexes, sample chapters, links to related books and book series, author biographies, and reviews by other customers.

Registration is easy. Just visit this Web page and fill in your information:

http://www.microsoft.com/mspress/register

Microsoft®

Proof of Purchase

Use this page as proof of purchase if participating in a promotion or rebate offer on this title. Proof of purchase must be used in conjunction with other proof(s) of payment such as your dated sales receipt—see offer details.

Designing Enterprise Applications with Microsoft® Visual Basic® .NET
0-7356-1721-X

CUSTOMER NAME

Microsoft Press, PO Box 97017, Redmond, WA 98073-9830